Character Assassination throughout the Ages

Character Assassination throughout the Ages

Edited by
Martijn Icks and Eric Shiraev

palgrave
macmillan

CHARACTER ASSASSINATION THROUGHOUT THE AGES
Copyright © Martijn Icks and Eric Shiraev, 2014.

First published in 2014 by PALGRAVE MACMILLAN® in the United States—a division of St. Martin's Press LLC, 175 Fifth Avenue, New York, NY 10010.

Where this book is distributed in the UK, Europe and the rest of the world, this is by Palgrave Macmillan, a division of Macmillan Publishers Limited, registered in England, company number 785998, of Houndmills, Basingstoke, Hampshire RG21 6XS.

Palgrave Macmillan is the global academic imprint of the above companies and has companies and representatives throughout the world.

Palgrave® and Macmillan® are registered trademarks in the United States, the United Kingdom, Europe and other countries.

ISBN: 978-1-137-39786-7

Library of Congress Cataloging-in-Publication Data

    Character assassination throughout the ages / edited by Martijn Icks and Eric Shiraev.
      pages cm
    Includes bibliographical references and index.
    ISBN 978-1-137-39786-7 (hardcover : alk. paper)
     1. Libel and slander—History. 2. Politicians—Public opinion—History. 3. Heads of state—Public opinion—History. 4. Reputation—History. 5. Gossip—History. 6. Political ethics—History. I. Icks, Martijn, 1981– II. Shiraev, Eric, 1960–
BJ1535.S6C43 2014
177'.3—dc23

                              2014003021

A catalogue record of the book is available from the British Library.

Design by Amnet.

First edition: July 2014

10 9 8 7 6 5 4 3 2 1

Contents

List of Figures

List of Tables

Acknowledgments

In the summer of 2011, we organized a conference on character assassination throughout the ages at the University of Heidelberg, funded by the 7th Framework Program of the European Union. An international group of historians, political scientists, and political psychologists attended, presenting papers on such diverse topics as invective speech in the Roman Republic, Duke Louis of Orléans and Queen Isabeau of Bavaria as victims of Burgundian propaganda, and the use of the "mental disease" label to slander opponents in modern politics. This volume is the result of that stimulating event. It would not have seen the light of day without the contributions, assistance, and support of a great many people, all of whom we would like to thank for their efforts.

Most of the participants of the conference have written articles for this volume, so there is no need to list all of their names here; we trust that a simple yet heartfelt expression of gratitude will suffice. We thank Henning Börm, Charles Walton, Vincent Viaene, Christoph Jahr, Sergei Tsytsarev, and Andreas Umland for delivering their excellent presentations during the conference, as well as their contributions to the many animated debates we have had. We also owe a debt of thanks to Alicia Hooper and Alexandra Eppinger, without whose tireless assistance the conference would not have run nearly as smoothly as it did.

During our preparations for the conference and this volume, many colleagues proved willing to exchange ideas, offer suggestions, point out facts, and provide us with food for thought. In particular, Anthony Barrett, Christian Witschel, Sebastian Schmidt-Hofner, Johannes Wienand, Marco Mattheis, George Marcus, Vladislav Zubok, David Levy, Alexandra Tyson, Alicia Hooper, Christian Michel, and Alex Farrington deserve to be mentioned here.

A particular word of appreciation is due to the administration, faculty, staff, and students at our academic institutions in Germany and the United States, where we have been consistently provided with an abundance of encouragement, assistance, and validation.

We also want to express our thanks to our editorial team at Palgrave Macmillan, whose good care has seen this volume to publication: Steven Kennedy, Isabella Yeager, Farideh Koohi-Kamali, Carol McGillivray, Jeff LaSala, and Sara Doskow. Last but not least, we would like to mention our friends and family, whose impact on this volume was mostly inspirational, but no less appreciated.

—Martijn Icks and Eric Shiraev

Introduction

Martijn Icks and Eric Shiraev

Throughout history, people have used the torch, the pitchfork, the bullet, the cannon, and (recently) the missile to damage, destroy, and kill. To protect themselves from attacks, people have built shields, armor, trenches, and fortresses, established military doctrines, and launched counterattacks. This book discusses attacks and defenses. Yet we have turned our attention to destructive power of a different kind: words and images. Across countries and time, people have used images and words to harm, devastate, and completely destroy other people's reputation, status, and character.

Bang, bang, bang! A newspaper headline launches a personal attack against yet another public figure. Never mind all his hard work. Never mind her accomplishments. Everything will be shattered in a fire of exaggerations, accusations, half-truths, name-calling, and cheap shots. *Drip, drip, drip.* The venom of words from the pen of a commentator trickles down and taints the reputation of a late ruler. A Roman emperor appears as a sadistic maniac. A Byzantine empress is portrayed as an incestuous monster. A top Communist leader is transformed into a cheater, renegade, and traitor. Attacking someone's name and reputation is about tickling a receptive audience's imagination. Under attack, which might be either furious or measured, a public official suddenly becomes a crook. A prominent scientist turns into a notorious womanizer. A female presidential candidate appears as an eerie witch. A flamboyant opposition leader or a king becomes a stupid drunkard. Need examples? Here are just two for starters.

On September 18, 1989, *Pravda*, the official paper of the Communist Party of the Soviet Union, published a translation of an article from the Italian daily *La Repubblica*. The piece contained embarrassing details about Boris Yeltsin, a member of the Soviet parliament at that time and a leader of the growing anti-Communist opposition. The publication alleged that Yeltsin, during his recent trip to the United States, had appeared drunk for his press conferences, had acted silly, and had been constantly incoherent and boorish. Other scandalous reports began to appear in the government press about Yeltsin's alleged flamboyant behavior, impulsivity, drunkenness, extramarital affairs, and rude outbursts. Yeltsin denied all the allusions and accusations. He argued that these fabrications were part of a massive and coordinated smear campaign launched by the Communist establishment to destroy his image: after all, the official press was in the hands of the Communist Party.

Figure I.1 A nineteenth-century pamphlet portraying the Dutch King William III as a beastly man.

Source: Rijksmuseum website. "Uit het leven van koning Gorilla" (From the Life of King Gorilla), Sicco Ernst Willem Roorda van Eysinga, K.A. Bos, 1897.

Labeling someone an out-of-control drunk in a publication is certainly not an invention of modern politics. In 1887, the Dutch King William III was targeted in the pamphlet *From the Life of King Gorilla*, which scorned his alcoholism and violent outbursts, his visits to brothels, and his rude, boorish behavior (Figure I.1). Although the pamphlet was published anonymously, its author was later revealed to be the Socialist Sicco Roorda van Eysinga, who advocated the abolition of the monarchy in the Netherlands. The slander was successful. The pamphlet sold tens of thousands of copies within weeks but also ignited an "Orange fury" by staunch monarchists (orange being the color associated with the royal house), who assaulted Socialists and attacked shops selling the pamphlet.

These two episodes happened about a hundred years apart and took place in different countries and different political cultures. Yet they probably reflect a common feature of the human psyche and behavior. In fact, in every corner of history we find people of all ranks, occupations, and persuasions attempting to damage or destroy the reputation of their opponents to win political battles, discredit unwelcome views, or settle personal scores. In the dying days of the Roman Republic, the future emperor Caesar Augustus and Mark Antony were engaged in a fierce war of words, painting each other as either a usurping social upstart or a debauched slave of "oriental" vices, respectively.[1] Protestant reformers in countless pamphlets viciously attacked the Renaissance popes, who were portrayed as decadent, corrupt, and in league with demonic forces.[2] Nineteenth-century politicians used newspapers to unleash their fury on their opponents. American president Abraham Lincoln was smeared as an "ape" and a "baboon," which were modest slurs when compared with the more vicious vulgarities and name-calling published at the time. Public figures and celebrities in the twentieth century and later have tasted the venom of personal accusations and vicious attacks delivered by means of various mass media, including radio broadcasts and TV ads. U.S. president Richard Nixon was painted as a paranoid schemer. British prime minister Tony Blair was pictured as a poodle, as Washington's pet. A U.S. vice presidential candidate, Sarah Palin, emerged as a slut. A picture of German chancellor Angela Merkel was photoshopped so that she appeared as a female Hitler, with the characteristic mustache.

In modern politics, as well as in historical times, character attacks abound. They have distorted and damaged the reputations of so many people. Yet what are character attack and character assassination? How do they work? When and why do character "assassins" deploy their fatal weapons of words and images? Why do many people give up and fall so easily when they are under attack? How do others resist and fight back? We will try to answer these and many other related questions.

On Character

The term *character* in American social sciences and psychology acquired its more or less distinct meaning approximately in the 1920s. Earlier in the century, professionals used the terms *character*, *personality*, and *temperament* almost interchangeably. Gradually, *temperament* was commonly associated with biological factors. *Personality* meant the totality of stable features of an individual. *Character* then referred to the moral aspects of an individual's behavior and experience.[3] Thus "good character" meant something compatible to proper behavior, honesty, industry, humility, or similar defining social markers. Although some of these standards differ from culture to culture, and may not even be agreed upon *within* a culture, they impose limitations on what one can and cannot do and say. As we will see in this book, figures occupying important positions in the public sphere—whether they are emperors, kings, presidents, generals, bishops, or scholars—have to ostensibly adhere to general moral and behavioral standards and expectations. It is important for these people to maintain a good reputation in the eyes of the general public, or at least those parts of it that are relevant to them. If they fail to do so, they might lose the necessary support and will not be able to keep their position in the long term. That these assumptions do not exclusively apply to democratically elected leaders becomes clear when we consider, for instance, the numerous Roman emperors who lost the respect of vital supporters and were killed in military revolts or court conspiracies.

On the Terms *Character Attacks* and *Character Assassination*

Character assassination is the deliberate destruction of an individual's reputation. Most notable targets or victims of character assassination are political leaders, officials, celebrities, scientists, athletes, and other public figures. "Character assassins" target the private lives, behavior, values, and identity of their victims. Biographical details are altered or fabricated. Intimate features are made public. Achievements are questioned. Good intentions are doubted. Using exaggerations, mockery, allegations, insinuations, and lies, the attackers try to damage the victim's moral standing in the eye of the public; also, they try to elicit a negative emotional response from the public toward the victim.

We distinguish between character attacks and character assassination. *Character attacks* are assaults aimed at a particular individual—as opposed to attacks aimed at certain groups, movements, or nationalities, such as happen in the construction of enemy images.[4] As a form of defamation, they are akin to the argumentum ad hominem, a rhetorical strategy that concerns the undermining of an opponent's credibility.[5] Contrary to the ad hominem, however, character attacks do not have to take place in the context of a debate. They include spoken remarks, written statements, jokes, name-callings, cartoons, and many other forms of verbal and nonverbal expression. Character attacks can target a person's allegiance, trustworthiness, aspirations, family background, ethnicity, sexual behavior, and any other behavioral and character-related features. The attackers hope to influence the way in which a certain person is perceived. If they succeed in destroying their victim's reputation, we speak of successful attacks and *character assassination*. However, attacks can also fail. They may even cause a backlash against the attacker, as we shall see in the book.

The term *character assassination* seems to have come into use, in political-communication studies in the United States around the mid-twentieth century.[6] A book titled *Character Assassination* by the sociologist and labor organizer Jerome Davis was published in 1950.[7] It was mostly autobiographical. Although he made interesting observations about human fear, ignorance, and envy as catalysts of rumors and lies, his book was mostly concerned with self-defense against personal attacks. In the 1960s, television, radio, and daily papers brought an exciting element of spectatorship to the political process, including campaigning and voting. Character attacks and defenses against them increasingly often became part of political candidates' electoral strategies. At the same time, the social sciences and psychology provided important insights into the basic mechanisms of persuasion in politics, including emotions and perceptions.[8] Researchers began to focus on specific cases of character assassination within particular periods and political systems.[9] In the United States, as well as in other countries, the literature on "negative campaigning" has provided interesting materials on smear tactics in local and national elections.[10]

The Complexities of Character Attacks

Because character assassination concerns the destruction of a person's *reputation*, it can be applied as a weapon against the dead as well as the living. Several possible motives to denigrate the dead exist. A new regime can justify its violent takeover by assassinating the character of the previous leader. ("The evil tyrant had to be removed!") Likewise, dictators can justify the execution of dissidents and former comrades by brandishing them as "traitors" and "revisionists," as Mao did in China. In these cases, character assassination follows upon and legitimizes actual assassination. Attacking the character of a dead ruler can also be a veiled attack against a current ruler, or a public figure who is descended from him or can for some other reason be associated with him—for instance because there are parallels in their behavior or policy. This strategy is particularly useful in cultures that do not guarantee freedom of speech. Denigrating the dead also occurs when the victim is perceived as an important symbol of a particular religion, movement, or ideology.

Overall, we hold that the following aspects are crucial in defining character attacks and character assassination.

Intentionality

Character attacks can only be counted as such if the attacker is deliberately attempting to damage the victim's reputation. If the damage is accidental (for instance caused by a thoughtless remark), this does not constitute character attack. To give an example, U.S. president Dwight Eisenhower at the very end of his presidency unwittingly smeared his vice president, Richard Nixon, who was running for president against John F. Kennedy. In the summer of 1960, a reporter asked Eisenhower, "Can you think of a major contribution that Nixon has made to your administration?" Eisenhower said, "If you give me a week, I might think of one." Kennedy used this quote to attack Nixon. It should be stressed that the attackers seldom acknowledge their aims and methods publicly, preferring to frame them as legitimate criticisms. However, there is some historical evidence, and sufficient anecdotal evidence, that character assassins often brag about their intentions and methods within their in-groups. (This anecdotal evidence was brought to us by one of the contributors to this volume, who has been engaged as a consultant in political campaigning in Washington DC.)

Public Nature

Since character attacks are concerned with reputation, they are by definition public in nature. Their victims are figures with a high public profile, such as politicians, religious leaders, leading academics, or celebrities. This public aspect distinguishes character attacks from interpersonal insults, which can occur in a private context and primarily aim to hurt the victim's feelings and self-esteem. It appears that there are no "secret" character assassinations, although sometimes the mere threat to go public with some potentially damaging information may suffice to get rid of a rival, who may resign, for example, or drop out of a political campaign.

Perception

In our view, it does not matter whether the allegations used by character attackers are true or false, grossly exaggerated or mildly distorted. The victim's reputation is damaged when the audience sees it that way. This means that the audience becomes an inseparable element of character assassination. Studies in political psychology provide interesting materials about attackers' strategies in relation to audiences' beliefs, values, and expectations.[11] Cross-cultural psychology also supplies valuable facts about cultural norms affecting perceptions of moral and immoral behavior.[12]

We want to emphasize that these and other social, political, and psychological aspects of character assassination are changeable, fluid categories. Undoubtedly, they will need to be adapted and rethought once we learn more about this fascinating topic.

The International Society for the Study of Character Assassination

In July 2011, scholars from nine countries gathered at the University of Heidelberg, Germany, to debate "the art of smear and defamation in history and today." The group included historians, political scientists, and political psychologists. To our pleasant surprise, this interdisciplinary crowd has quickly established a common language to effectively communicate, support, challenge, ask questions, and search for answers. In that year we formed The International Society for the Study of Character Assassination and started our regular online reviews and discussions on Facebook.[13]

Although individuals and circumstances change in the course of history, we argue that phenomena referring to human behavior are revealing themselves simultaneously in at least two dimensions: universal and culture specific. There is a core of *central* features in human behavior that appear in most cultural and historic settings. At the same time, there are *peripheral* features (no less important though) bound to particular cultural, political, and historic contexts. In short, we believe that discrediting public figures through personal attacks is as old as human civilization. As this volume will show, the key methods of character assassination remain amazingly consistent. At the same time, people constantly refine and enhance their character attacks. The speed and scope of attacks have grown tremendously, especially in the last 50 years. Due to the rise of modern democracies, mass media, and social networks, character attacks now reach a global audience in minutes.

Second, we also believe that a multidisciplinary approach to this topic will be fruitful. The defamation of public figures has been analyzed in individual cases from a variety of separate angles involving history, political science, and political psychology. However, very little attention has been paid to character assassination as a historical, international, and cross-cultural phenomenon. Nobody so far has examined character attacks across civilizations and cultures.[14] This book is a first humble attempt to look at character assassination from a multidisciplinary perspective.

Chapter Overviews

We have invited the contributors to this volume to reflect critically on the concept of character assassination and how it can be employed to examine personal attacks against individuals from many different angles and in a wide variety of cultural contexts.

Political psychologists have long been interested in character assassination. In the first chapter, Eric Shiraev reviews character attacks from the standpoint of political psychology and argues why this discipline is helpful for historians and political scientists studying character assassinations. The chapter describes the structure and dynamics of character attacks, their types, intentionality, timing, contents, methods, and effectiveness. It also presents attacks from the viewpoint of attackers and victims, and discusses why some attacks are effective while others are not.

After these conceptual remarks, we will dive into history (through four sections), traveling through antiquity, the medieval age, the early modern period, and recent history. Needless to say, one volume could never do justice to the myriad examples of character assassination provided by the various societies from the near and distant past. We have chosen to focus mostly on Western cultures, although we use several examples and cases from other parts of the world. Martina Klicperová-Baker, Eric Shiraev, and Zi Yang offer intriguing glimpses of defamation in Communist countries—Czechoslovakia and China. Most chapters refer to a specific time or episode in history. Other chapters provide a more general view, like the one written by Eric Shiraev and Jason Smart that deals with character attacks in U.S. presidential politics from George Washington to the present. This chapter also deals with specific types of character attacks, including cheap shots, ridiculing, name-calling, and fabrications.

Even with a primary focus on character assassination in Western cultures, the possibilities are endless, and rather than embarking on a hopeless quest in pursuit of historical "completeness"—whatever that might mean—we have decided to include a select number of cases from each of the four main periods mentioned above. Distribution through time has been one, but certainly not our only, criterion for selection. Thus, rather than attempting to give comprehensive coverage of the Middle Ages, we highlighted just several noteworthy aspects of the way defamation worked in medieval societies, such as the important role played by chroniclers and the employment of slander in the struggle for power between rival factions of nobility. In addition, each historic section aims to provide examples of concepts and ideas that can be applied to different time periods as well, such as the notion of "counterhistory" presented in the chapter by Kenneth Wolf.

In the section on ancient history, Henriette van der Blom takes us to the autumn days of the Roman Republic, a society in which character attacks were a prominent and accepted part of political life. The fact that political office was the prerogative of a relatively small group of senators, who often knew each other personally, did not deter opponents from smearing each other relentlessly. Van der Blom examines the defamation of one of the main political players of the Late Republic, the famous orator Cicero. Most of the attacks against this target—launched, for instance, during debates in the Senate—were of a specific nature, relating to a particular situation, and were not repeated on other occasions. Nevertheless, some recurring themes did develop in the defamation of Cicero, such as his relatively humble origins and the immodesty with which he boasted of his achievements.

Jan Meister focuses on Suetonius, the second-century biographer who wrote the lives of a dozen Roman emperors. Evidently, the freedom of speech that the Roman elite had enjoyed in Cicero's day was severely limited in imperial times, especially where the person of the emperor was concerned. However, senators and knights found ways to slander their rulers in secret, circulating pamphlets and spreading nasty gossip. (Intriguingly, the Latin word *fama* can mean both "reputation" and "rumor.") Many such tales concerned the sex lives of Roman emperors—a topic closely entwined with notions of manliness and power. As Meister argues, Suetonius appears to have been more interested in the reputation than in the actual deeds of his subjects. Recording numerous stories about the emperors' sex lives in his writings, he perpetuated these stories for centuries to come, thus helping to establish the bad name of many Roman rulers.

The topic of posthumous character assassination takes center stage in the chapter by Martijn Icks, who draws attention to the concept of "memory sanctions." In the Roman Empire, where "memory space" was a limited and precious commodity, members of the elite, including emperors, set great store by being remembered—and being remembered positively, as *exempla* of virtue and honor. Historians and biographers played a key role in the creation and preservation of public memory. If a deceased ruler had not lived and reigned by their standards, they could deliberately cast him in a negative light, modeling him as a "bad" emperor in their works. One suitable vehicle to achieve this was the description of a candidate's investiture with imperial authority, which could be used to highlight his (alleged) egoism, immorality, and lust for power.

Kenneth Wolf starts off our medieval section with a chapter on attacks against the Prophet Muhammad in eighth- and ninth-century Spain. Living as *dhimmis* under Muslim rule, Spanish Christians were keen to preserve their religious identity yet also had to come to terms with the fact that they were living in a predominantly Islamic society. Wolf analyzes two Christian "counterhistories" of Muhammad, which were produced during this period. While both seek to undermine the legitimacy of Islam by distorting the story of the Prophet, preserving some details and changing others, the extent to which they vilify Muhammad differs markedly: in one version, he is a diabolically inspired false prophet, whereas in the other, he is merely a misguided man. This seems to reflect the different degrees of willingness of Christian groups to live peacefully alongside their Muslim countrymen.

The next two chapters take us to the end of the Middle Ages. Tracy Adams focuses on the negative campaigns against Louis, Duke of Orléans, and the French queen, Isabeau of Bavaria, both of whom came under attack by the Dukes of Burgundy. With King Charles VI mentally incapacitated, Duke Philip of Burgundy and his son, Jean sans Peur, contested Louis's position as the rightful regent of France, accusing him of mismanagement, poisoning the king, and having an affair with the queen. These attempts at character assassination even continued after Jean sans Peur had had Louis murdered. However, Adams warns us about the difficulties of distinguishing between *reports* of character attacks and the actual degree of *success* that they achieved, which is hard to establish. She argues that later historians have been too fast in assuming that Louis of Orléans and Isabeau of Bavaria must indeed have suffered bad reputations during their lifetimes. Moreover, many scholars have been lax in questioning the negative images of Louis and Isabeau as found in the sources, taking most of the Burgundian attacks against their character at face value.

Rather than focusing on one or two victims of defamation, Gilles Lecuppre analyzes the emergence of a new theme in late-medieval slander campaigns: youth. In a time when kingly power was steadily growing, resistance against royal authority was also on the rise. Youthful monarchs were among the primary targets of character attacks, since their coming of age upset the balance of power—which might be transferred to a new generation or social group—while their immaturity was by definition morally suspect. The main perpetrators of these attacks tended to be clerics and monks, who played a key part in political and cultural life, as well as nobles who wanted to maintain or expand their influence. Examining five cases from the ruling families of England, Scotland, and France, Lecuppre remarks how the classical notion of the "tyrant" as a man who is only interested in the fulfillment of his own desires was connected with medical theories conceiving of youths as intermediate creatures possessing a hazardous mix of masculine ("hot") and feminine ("wet") characteristics. This opened the door for accusing young monarchs of a whole range of tyrannical vices, including irrationality, sensuality, and gullibility.

Our third section concerns the early modern age, when the invention of printing (ca. 1450) changed the game of character assassination. From then on, pamphlets, cartoons, and other means of defamation could be spread ever more easily to ever wider audiences. Bobbi Dykema looks at the first man who exploited these possibilities to launch a grand-scale defamation campaign: Martin Luther, whose attacks against the Roman Catholic Church paved the way for Protestantism. Arguing that spiritual and secular power should be strictly separated, Luther and his associate, the famous woodcutter Cranach the Elder, publish numerous pamphlets deriding the corruption of the clergy and, particularly, the pope. Whereas some of their early attacks were aimed at individual Church leaders, such as Popes Julius II and Leo X, they soon started to target the papacy in general, associating it with the figure of the Antichrist. Personal defamation thus gave way to a rejection of the Catholic Church as an institution.

Mette Harder takes us to the time of the French Revolution, a period in which character assassination not only destroyed people's reputations, but very often their actual lives, as well. Both during the Terror (1793–94) and the subsequent Thermidorian Reaction (1794–95), massive political purges took place among the revolutionaries. The rigid political climate of the time, combined with the general public's deep distrust of politicians, turned slander into a favorite tool to get rid of political rivals, generating a genuine hotbed of character attacks. Even people against whom there was little actual evidence of misconduct were frequently condemned and executed. In this culture of character assassination gone haywire, revolutionaries struggled to harmonize opposing ideals: democratic dialogue and a free press, on the one hand, versus protection against calumny and slander, on the other.

The Batavian Republic—as the Netherlands were called between 1795 and 1806—is the stage for Edwina Hagen's chapter on the defamation of Rutger Jan Schimmelpenninck. As grand pensionary of the newly formed Dutch republic, Schimmelpenninck's position depended largely on the goodwill of the Napoleonic government. Although the executive took great care to build up his good character, advertising himself as a sensitive family man, he only managed to stay in power for 13 months. Schimmelpenninck's rivals in Dutch politics persistently undermined his authority by harping on the quasi-royal pomp with which he surrounded himself, calling him a traitor to Republicanism and exploiting his developing blindness to hint at failing statesmanship. To make matters worse, an English author made allegations about his scandalous private life, wrecking the image of the wholesome family man. Napoleon's decision to remove the grand pensionary from power in 1806 underlines how a successful defamation campaign can be waged by turning a politician's carefully built-up personality cult against him.

Finally, our modern section starts off with a chapter by Jason Smart and Eric Shiraev, who reviewed many examples of character attacks in U.S. presidential politics over the past two and a half centuries. Focusing mainly on presidential campaigns of the past 50 years, the chapter presents and discusses three types of character attacks. *Cheap shots* typically allude to a victim's individual features, including, but not limited to, his or her credibility, competence, honesty, and so forth. *Falsifications* are lies, which by the time they are used in an attack are often difficult to distinguish from facts. *Direct attacks* involve strong accusations about a person's character flaws and tend to be based on facts. These types certainly overlap, yet they are often distinctly different because of the methods involved in their planning and execution. The chapter also discusses why and when certain character attacks become effective.

Eric Shiraev and Zi Yang bring to attention one of the least researched cases about the earliest case of initial political purges in China, just several years after the 1949 revolution that brought to power Mao Zedong and the Communist Party. Two prominent and relatively young party officials, Gao Gang and Rao Shushi, suddenly found themselves under a coordinated attack from the leadership. Along with ideological rhetoric thrown at them, they were accused of numerous "classical" character flaws, including infidelity, plagiarism, selfishness, and arrogance, to name a few. As members of the party, they were also attacked for character features incompatible with Communist norms. The chapter also discusses self-criticism, a popular method of self-incrimination widely used by the authorities to destroy a person's reputation and life.

The chapter by Martina Klicperová-Baker examines the case of playwright and former president of the Czech Republic, Václav Havel, and the attempts by the Communist government of Czechoslovakia to destroy his reputation and stop his human rights campaign in the 1970s and 1980s. The official press publicly attacked him for many alleged moral ills and transgressions. Moreover, many intellectuals were compelled to endorse the ongoing character assassination of Havel. This fact brings to light an intriguing discussion about an inner psychological "bargain" that some individuals accept to justify lies and falsifications against other people.

Of course, every chapter has brought to light many new questions. We know that women and men often face different types of attacks, yet we do not know enough to confidently describe these differences. And do character attacks occur only when the allegations in them are false? Does frank criticism of a person's behavior constitute a character attack? How do we distinguish honest criticism of a policy from a character assassination? Who could judge the difference? Can one commit character assassination if one has no malevolent intentions against the victim? Moreover, where should we draw the line between character assassination and humor? Are comedians the biggest character assassins?

This book is a collection of essays showing when and how character attacks have been launched and with what effect they have played out in the lives of individuals living in different historic epochs and countries. Our goals were modest. We did not attempt to create a unifying theory and methodology to examine character assassination. Maybe this will be our next task. Our project continues. Visit our "Character Assassination" page on Facebook.

Martijn Icks and Eric Shiraev
Düsseldorf, Germany—Washington, DC,
United States

Notes

1. Scott 1933; Johnson 1976. The latter work deals mostly with the posthumous defamation of Antony's character.
2. Edwards 1983; Edwards 1994; Scribner 1994; Pettegree 2005.
3. For discussion of terminology and its evolution, see Danziger 1997, pp. 124–32.
4. Much has been written on enemy images; see, for instance, Keen 1988; Benz 1996; Fiebig-von Hase and Lehmkuhl 1997; Satjukow and Gries 2004. Although we distinguish between the construction of enemy images and character attacks, enemy images can be, and often are, employed in the defamation of individuals—for instance when left-wing American politicians were brandished as Communists during the McCarthy era in the late 1940s.
5. Walton 1985; Walton 2007, pp. 161–97.
6. Although the term *character assassination* originated in the United States, we believe it is not necessarily U.S.-centric. German has a word for it as well, *Rufmord*, as does Dutch, *karaktermoord*. The Russian language has a variety of terms translated as "reputation attacks," and our Russian-speaking students had no problem finding equivalents for "character assassination" in Russian.
7. Davis 1950.
8. For a review, see Graber 2009; Shiraev and Sobel 2006.
9. Some notable examples include Flower 2006; Cameron 1970; Okerlund 2005; Scribner 1994; Darnton 2010; Halfin 2007.
10. See Sigelman and Shiraev 2002 for a review.
11. See Sigelmen and Kugler 2003.
12. See Shiraev and Levy, pp. 249–51.
13. The ISSCA website can be found at http://characterattack.wordpress.com.
14. Such diachronic, cross-cultural studies do exist for several related phenomena, such as propaganda and insults. See, for instance, Taylor 2003; Jowett and O'Donnell 2012; Neu 2008; Conley 2010.

Bibliography

Benz, W. 1996. *Feindbild und Vorurteil. Beiträge über Ausgrenzung und Verfolgung.* Munich: Deutscher Taschenbuch Verlag.

Cameron, A. 1970. *Claudian: Poetry and Propaganda at the Court of Honorius.* Oxford: Clarendon Press.

Conley, T. 2010. *Toward a Rhetoric of Insult.* Chicago: University of Chicago Press.

Danziger, K. 1997. *Naming the Mind: How Psychology Found Its Language.* London: Sage.

Darnton, R. 2010. *The Devil in the Holy Water, or The Art of Slander from Louis XIV to Napoleon*. Philadelphia: University of Pennsylvania Press.

Davis, J. 1950. *Character Assassination*. New York: The Philosophical Library.

Edwards Jr., M. U. 1983. *Luther's Last Battles: Politics and Polemics, 1531–1546*. Ithaca, NY: Cornell University Press.

Edwards Jr., M. U. 1994. *Printing, Propaganda, and Martin Luther*. Berkeley: University of California Press.

Fiebig-von Hase, R., and U. Lehmkuhl, eds. 1997. *Enemy Images in American History*. Providence: Berghahn.

Flower, H. I. 2006. *The Art of Forgetting: Disgrace and Oblivion in Roman Political Culture*. Chapel Hill: University of North Carolina Press.

Halfin, Y. 2007. *Intimate Enemies: Demonizing the Bolshevik Opposition, 1918–1928*. Pittsburgh: University of Pittsburgh Press.

Johnson, J. R. 1976. *Augustan Propaganda: The Battle of Actium, Mark Antony's Will, the* Fasti Capitolini Consulares, *and Early Imperial Historiography*. PhD diss., University of California.

Graber, Doris. 2009. *Mass Media and American Politics*. Washington, DC: CQ Press.

Jowett, G., and V. O'Donnell. 2012. *Propaganda and Persuasion*, 5th ed. Los Angeles: Sage.

Keen, S. 1988. *Faces of the Enemy: Reflections of the Hostile Imagination*. San Francisco: Harper.

Neu, J. 2008. *Sticks and Stones: The Philosophy of Insults*. Oxford: Oxford University Press.

Okerlund, A. 2005. *Elizabeth Wydeville: The Slandered Queen*. Stroud, UK: Tempus.

Pettegree, A. 2005. *Reformation and the Culture of Persuasion*. Cambridge: Cambridge University Press.

Satjukow, S., and R. Gries, eds. 2004. *Unsere Feinde. Konstruktionen des Anderen im Sozialismus*. Leipzig: Leipziger Universitäts-Verlag.

Scott, K. 1933. "The Political Propaganda of 44–30 BC." *Memoirs of the American Academy in Rome* 11: 7–49.

Scribner, R. W. 1994. *For the Sake of Simple Folk: Popular Propaganda for the German Reformation*, 2nd ed. Oxford: Clarendon Press.

Shiraev, E., and D. Levy. 2013. *Cross-Cultural Psychology*. Boston: Pearson.

Shiraev, E., and R. Sobel. 2006. *People and Their Opinions*. New York: Longman.

Sigelman, L., and M. Kugler. 2003. "Why Is Research on the Effects of Negative Campaigning So Inconclusive? Understanding Citizens' Perceptions of Negativity." *The Journal of Politics* 65 (1): 142–60.

Sigelman, L., and E. Shiraev. 2002. "The Rational Attacker in Russia? Negative Campaigning in Russian Presidential Elections." *The Journal of Politics* 64 (1): 45–62.

Taylor, P. M. 2003. *Munitions of the Mind: A History of Propaganda from the Ancient World to the Present Era*, 3rd ed. Manchester: Manchester University Press.

Walton, D. N. 1985. *Arguer's Position: A Pragmatic Study of Ad Hominem Attack, Criticism, Refutation, and Fallacy*. Westport, CT: Greenwood Press.

Walton, D. N. 2007. *Media Argumentation: Dialectic, Persuasion, and Rhetoric*. Cambridge: Cambridge University Press.

I

Character Assassination: How Political Psychologists Can Assist Historians

Eric Shiraev

Political psychology can provide a useful framework for studying charac-ter assassination for at least two reasons. First, as a discipline, political psychology examines the complex interaction between the world of poli-tics, on the one hand, and people's experience and behavior, on the other. Because most character assassination cases involve individuals in the context of politics, political psychology can suggest empirical methods to study such cases. Second, it provides theories to explain them. Since the inception of this scholarly discipline in the 1960s, political psychologists have felt comfortable assisting historians, sociologists, and political scientists. Political psycholo-gists borrow research methods and explanatory models from the behavioral and cognitive sciences, design their own research methods, and use them to study specific cases. Public figures, for obvious reasons, are unavailable for direct experimentation. Many of their actions, however, are on display and available for empirical analysis. Political psychologists learn from historians and then attempt to explain historical facts.

Conditions of Attacks

Why does an individual attack another person's character? First, for the sake of argument, we assume that the attacker's actions are mostly rational and pursue a reasonable goal. Of course, individuals may turn to personal attacks spontaneously, under the influence of strong emotions, such as anger, or in self-defense. Such attacks are usually brief. Do we not all from time to time call some people bad names when we feel frustrated and later regret this? In other cases, a person's motivation to attack reflects the attacker's desire to harm the reputation of the victim (see the book's introduction, where the key terms are defined). This reputation is judged in the court of public opinion. In other words, the attack should be public. The attack should diminish, shatter, or even destroy the victim's chances to succeed in a political campaign, a business endeavor, or a career. In the United States, public opinion has tended to view more negatively those political candidates who were accused of sexual or financial misconduct, lying, or hiding certain embarrassing biographical facts. Such candidates usually spend considerable energy and resources defending themselves against such attacks even if the accusations are grossly inaccurate or untrue.[1] During the 2008 presidential campaign and later, opponents of President Barack Obama repeatedly hinted that he was a Muslim and was hiding this fact. John McCain, his opponent, during the same campaign was accused of fathering an illegitimate child with a black woman some years ago. These allegations were untrue (Obama is Christian, and McCain had legally adopted a girl from Bangladesh), but the attacks caught the eyes of many. Uncertainty and prejudice become favorable conditions for attacks. For example, it was not very helpful to Obama that even in 2012, according to polls, 44 percent of Americans said they could not identify his religion.[2]

It must be noted, however, that a victim of character attacks is not necessarily an innocent individual falling under a barrage of lies. Some attacks may be completely untrue while others are based on facts. Former Russian president Boris Yeltsin, whose case was introduced in the introduction to this book, had a long history of placing himself in embarrassing situations. What is important is that these blunders were later exaggerated and used to attack him. Opponents of U.S. president Bill Clinton repeatedly called him a liar or "liar-in-chief" in the late 1990s, in the aftermath of his infamous sex scandal involving a female White House intern. Clinton tried to cover up this incident and publicly stated that he "did not have sexual relations" with the intern. Although he later apologized for his misleading statement, the "liar" label stuck and was repeated in numerous character attacks, as we will see later in chapter 11.

Who then becomes a victim of character assassination? What are the typical conditions under which a person's character is attacked?

Public Competition

One potential victim is a person who is engaged in a political or other type of competition requiring people's support or approval. An electoral campaign, a pageant, or any competitive selection procedure can provide favorable conditions for character attacks. Character assassination is the ultimate goal of the attacker because it eliminates a victim's chances of success. U.S. Senator George Allen of Virginia, during his reelection campaign in 2006, committed a verbal blunder when he during his speech jokingly called a person in the audience who was of Indian descent "macaca" (similar to the French word "macaque"). Allen then acknowledged his mistake and apologized. His opponents, however, immediately labeled him a racist and repeatedly stated that his gaffe was a reflection of Allen's deep-seated prejudice against minorities. It is difficult to measure the effectiveness of character attacks, but in Allen's case they coincided with his substantial drop in the polls in a very tight race and his subsequent defeat in the election two months later.[3]

Social Status

The victim of an attack is sometimes an individual who, though not competing for any office at the time, has already achieved high social status, an important and powerful social position, or an esteemed reputation (for example, a government post or an elevated place in the social hierarchy). Certainly, one needs a socially approved "character" before it can be attacked, damaged, or assassinated. For instance, accusations of being a Nazi sympathizer were launched against Pope Benedict XVI during his tenure. The attackers used the pope's biography to exaggerate the fact that in his youth he had to join the Hitler Youth. However, the attackers failed to mention that almost every boy in Germany at the time was forced to join this organization. American comedian Bill Maher in 2008 and actress Susan Sarandon in 2011 called the pope a "Nazi" as they were lashing out at the Catholic Church.[4]

Professional Accomplishments

A victim of character assassination is often someone who is successful in a certain field such as business, science, or an artistic arena. If one is socially or professionally successful or productive, this is a condition for character attacks. Such attacks usually have little to do with the victims' scientific or artistic input, but rather with their missteps in private life or other liabilities. Sigmund Freud was frequently accused during his life of being a "pervert" and "sex maniac." Freud, in his works published in the nineteenth and early twentieth centuries, emphasized the role of human sexuality in psychological disorders as well as everyday life. Sex was a delicate subject in the relatively conservative upper-class social atmosphere in Europe at that time. Freud's scientific interest in human sexuality served as a suitable excuse for his opponents to launch persistent character attacks against the psychiatrist.[5]

Affiliation

The victim may represent a powerful ideology, theory, or social or political cause, party, or movement. In these cases, the attackers attempt to weaken and trivialize the ideas for which the victim stands or stood. Another goal is to diminish future support and the number of followers. Some critics of Communism have long emphasized that Vladimir Lenin, the most prominent leader of the Russian Communist revolution, had contracted syphilis in his youth, which hastened his death in 1924.[6] Although the accuracy of these accusations is almost impossible to establish, this is rather unimportant in this case. Diehard Communists expectedly reject any associations of Lenin's name with sexually transmitted diseases. Anticommunists, on the other hand, may welcome such character attacks.

Before we further discuss the reasons behind character attacks, we should consider their different types.

Types of Attacks

Character attacks and character assassinations differ in terms of the scope of their targets (individual and collective), timing ("live" or postmortem attacks), and momentum (planned or spontaneous).

Scope: Individual and Summative Character Attacks

Most examples of character attacks refer to individuals as victims. Are there summative character attacks to smear a group of individuals? As mentioned in the introduction, such attacks are common during international conflicts.[7] Summative character attacks can also be designed to advance the attacker's domestic political goals. In the Soviet Union in the 1930s, China in the 1950s, and Vietnam in the 1950s, the ruling authorities conducted massive attacks against so-called rich peasants. Government newspapers routinely published stories about individual rich peasants, portraying them as greedy, mean, arrogant, and uncaring. By attacking an individual's character, the authorities were attacking a large group. In doing so, the Communist leaders were setting up the conditions for the most significant collectivization reforms in history, which placed most peasants in collective farms. Although there could be an interesting discussion about whether a group can have its own "character," this book is concerned with individual attacks.

Time: Live and Postmortem Attacks

Character attacks may target either living individuals or the deceased. For example, the lives of many twentieth-century leaders, including Joseph Stalin in Russia, Winston Churchill in the United Kingdom, U.S. presidents Franklin Roosevelt, John Kennedy, Ronald Reagan, and Richard Nixon, and Mohandas Gandhi in India, are constantly scrutinized today to uncover new and potentially embarrassing facts to deliberately exaggerate these leaders' faults or missteps. What is the point of attacking the deceased? We can certainly assume that a 'live' attack (that is taking place now) can seriously damage another person's reputation. But what can we assume about a post-mortem attack? Such attacks, as we will see in this book, can discredit someone's cause, a fallen dynasty, a political party, an idea, a theory, or an ideology that these individuals represented or stood for. Targeting a dead leader's character can be an effective method of attacking this person's supporters today.

Momentum: Planned or Spontaneous (Drive-By)

Although character attacks tend to be premeditated, attackers do not always take significant time to contemplate and execute. Like in real life, attacks can be very much spontaneous and opportunistic. We call them "drive-by" attacks, which is analogous to an infamous method of gang violence. A quick and timely character attack may be effective because the victim often does not have enough time or resources for self-defense. In one case, three professors, right after a heated scientific discussion, accused their colleague of being a plagiarist and profiteer. These accusations were posted online. As a result, the victim was forced to resign, even though the accusations were later rescinded due to a lack of evidence.[8] Other character attacks can become a prolonged campaign. From the early 1960s, Alexander Solzhenitsyn, the famous Russian writer and dissident, saw a massive campaign of lies and distortions organized by the Communist Party of the Soviet Union. Archival documents reveal how the authorities orchestrated this campaign.[9] In several media reports, he was portrayed as a Jew (an apparent offense against his Christian views), a traitor, a Nazi collaborator, a prison snitch, and even a paid agent of Western intelligence. Parts of his letters to his former wife were published without his consent and deliberately misquoted. In these attacks, Solzhenitsyn appeared as a selfish, histrionic individual obsessed with his fame and looks. He was accused of being a sadist who was attempting to destroy the reputation of the Soviet Union and Socialism.

Why do character attacks take place? Why do exaggerations, slander, and lies become effective in damaging someone's reputation? Why are some people incapable of detecting and unwilling to detect deception and fabrications in character attacks? Would it be more effective for the attackers to refrain from character assassination and use reason and fair criticisms instead?

Why They Choose Character Assassination: The Attacker's Side

Several models explain the reasons behind character attacks and their effectiveness. The first model tries to explain why certain individuals attack, while the latter two present more nuanced accounts of who is likely to attack whom and under what circumstances. Here follow nontechnical summaries of these models.[10]

Sway the Undecided

Political scientist William Riker (1996) applied game theory (mathematical principles to study the behavior of rational individuals) to political campaigning, especially to negative campaigning. He wanted to know why the Federalists (supporters of the American Constitution) and the Antifederalists (opponents of it), two key political groups in the United States in the eighteenth century, attacked one another over ratifying the Constitution. The differences between the groups were ideological and personal. Both sides, Riker assumed, consisted of rational actors who believed the voting public could make rational decisions as well. Both sides found it next to impossible to change the minds of those who had already made their choices. Therefore, both sides concentrated on trying to sway a proportion of undecided voters. The best way to do this was to use a scare tactic: try to convince the undecided that if the other side wins, something terrible will happen to all. Although Riker did not study character attacks, per se, he proposed a testable model or hypothesis for future studies: a character attack might not change the minds of the victim's supporters but could influence the attitudes and behavior of the undecided.

Political scientists Michael Davis and Michael Ferrantino (1996) suggested a model according to which politicians increase their chances of being elected by making exaggerated claims about the benefits that everyone will receive if these politicians win. On the other hand, they would decrease their opponents' electoral chances if they exaggerate the bad consequences of their opponents' victory. Character assassination in this case could be an effective way to excite, alarm, or scare some voters and sway them into a desirable course of action, such as voting or not voting (Figure 1.1). Candidates run little risk of being caught in a lie if they attack: if candidate A wins and candidate B loses, voters can use A's subsequent performance in office to test the candidate's positive campaign pledges; winning also renders untestable A's negative claims about what a horrible person B would have been if elected. This model explains why winners can get away with slandering their opponents: very often the opponents cannot reply to the slander. That is why attacking late public figures and associating them with an incumbent can be effective. As Martijn Icks points out in this book, "Since it was a risky business to antagonize living emperors, critics usually aimed their arrows at those rulers who were safely dead."

Create Uncertainty

For Stergios Skaperdas and Bernard Grofman (1995), attacks can be very effective during electoral races. A lot depends on the composition of a competition's field. In the two-candidate variant of the model, which is typical in the United States, the initial distribution of support for each candidate is known, as is the proportion of undecided voters. When X and Y wage equally positive

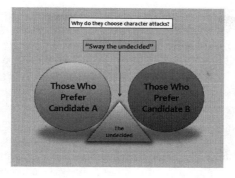

Figure 1.1   The "sway the undecided model" to explain character attacks.

campaigns, they are likely to split the undecided vote evenly. In this situation, X and Y encounter a problem of diminishing returns: the more positive their campaigns remain, the less extra support each wins from the shrinking pool of previously undecided voters. Alternatively, if X fiercely attacks Y, this could move some of Y's current supporters into the undecided column. Character attacks thus determine the support to be subtracted from each candidate, with lost voters joining the ranks of the undecided or uncommitted. The extent to which X or Y engages in attacks hinges on their relative standing in the political "horse race." Able to win without converting those who support the opposition, the front-runner engages in "more positive, and less negative, campaigning than his opponent."[11] On the other hand, if the competition is relatively tight, the front-runner will be motivated to try to convert the rival's supporters. In the three-candidate variant of the model, typical in other countries or during U.S. primaries, when several candidates from the same party compete for nomination, the best strategy is to attack the stronger opponent. Because no candidate will attack the weaker rival, attacks are directed either against the front-runner or from the front-runner.[12]

The primary elections in the United States in 2008 and the Republican Party primaries in 2012 showed that the leading candidates (Senator John McCain and Democratic Senator Barack Obama, after February 2008 when he took the lead in the primaries; Governor Mitt Romney from the onset of the primaries in 2012) were under intense personal attacks from their opponents in their own political camp! Such attacks might have appeared as self-destructive (and some of them probably were because they undermined the party's unity), but they were probably driven by the desire to create uncertainty among the voters and increase the attacker's own chances to get noticed.

Prevent Defections

For the "create uncertainty" model, whether and whom a candidate attacks should depend primarily on who is ahead and by how much. According to the Gideon Doron and Uri On model, where individuals stand in terms of ideology and political values also matters. Whereas favorable self-presentation is intended to strengthen the loyalty of X's supporters, the purpose of character attacks against opponents is to secure your supporters by leading them to see other, rival candidates or individuals as a threat. Attacking requires careful targeting: you have to attack those who may eventually "entice" and "steal" your own supporters. The selective attack, in this case, has two functions: it can make the other person unattractive to potential deserters from your "camp," and it can affect floating voters of other parties or candidates to come to your support. In simple terms, "one shakes the closest tree with the most apples so that they will fall next to him."[13] That is, the resources that X applies to attacking Y are determined not only by the current level of support for each individual, but also by the ideological gap between the candidates. The greater the distance between X and Y, the less likely it becomes that an attack by X can persuade those who had been leaning toward Y to vote for X instead. Of course, even if Y is X's nearest ideological neighbor, X will have little to gain from attacking Y if Y is unpopular. Thus, each side concentrates its attacks on the greatest rival within its own "political market" rather than attacking the rival who stands highest in the polls.[14] One study showed, for instance, that in U.S. senatorial elections in the past, attacking was generally more effective for the challenger than the incumbent.[15]

These formal models should make better sense if they are tested in various electoral situations. Several studies gathered empirical materials involving electoral advertisement and political speeches.[16] However, because the perceptions of character attacks are highly contextual and vary widely from person to person, researchers cannot rely solely on advertisement- and media content–based measures of negativity in attacks. Some scholars, therefore, turned to the measurement and interpretation of various effects of character attacks.[17] For example, the way in which the public perceives a character attack depends on whether the candidate has the same gender as the person evaluating the candidate. As an illustration, one study found that men tended to perceive a female candidate who attacked her opponents less favorably than another female candidate who did not, but this was not a factor when the attacker was male.[18]

In addition to explaining why character attacks take place, political psychologists also analyze the mechanisms and effects of character attacks. Although their studies have not systematically examined specific cases of character assassination, this research has provided valuable information about why and when personal attacks become effective.

What Character Assassination Achieves: The Witness' Side

When a media commentator launches an emotional character attack against a politician, we do not assume that every person in the audience takes this attack on its merits and believes every word of it. Only some individuals, as witnesses of a character attack, become susceptible to its message. How many and why? Several models explain why certain people are persuaded by character attacks while others are not.

The Update Processing Model

This model suggests that opinions and inclinations to act are formed at the time of exposure to a particular piece of information (such as a negative political ad about a candidate) and that people integrate the evaluative implications of this information by continuously updating their comprehensive evaluative tally. When it is necessary to express an opinion about this candidate, such a "summary tally" is immediately retrieved from memory.[19] But what type of information is retrieved?

Experimental research shows that people have a tendency to fit their immediate perceptions of reality into a mold that is heavily influenced by their old preferences. In other words, most people are predisposed to have certain opinions about particular issues and seldom change them. A character attack is unlikely to be effective, for example, against well-liked individuals because of the psychological resistance that most people display when their preferences are suddenly challenged. Such people's resistance to new information is explained by *cognitive balance* and *cognitive dissonance* theories founded on experimental laboratory studies.[20] This research demonstrates that people are highly selective in what information they choose to believe, preferring to accept the information that is most congruent with their existing attitudes or expectations, such as their actual voting record or support of a certain candidate in the past.[21] Such studies also demonstrate that people may accept an outrageous lie spread against another person if this acceptance may bring potential benefits. The chapter by Martina Klicperová-Baker in this book provides a fine illustration of cognitive dissonance theory.

In sum, according to this model, long-term commitments of individuals play a very important role in their reactions to character assassination attempts made by other people. More politically sophisticated individuals will be less likely to rely on some new unchecked information in forming their political preferences. Political sophistication entails the ability to link opinions about specific issues to one another and to organize them through broader, more abstract concepts.[22] To generalize, an educated and committed person is more likely to reject a character attack against a favorably viewed candidate than a less educated and uncommitted individual is.

The Ad-Hoc Processing Model

This model is also based on experimental research yet challenges the conclusions of the previous model. According to this model, individuals are constantly involved in *ad-hoc* ("for this") cognitive processing, which means that their opinions are constructed mostly at the time when their judgment is expected. In other words, judgments about social and political issues, especially if there is little or no prior knowledge about them, are probably formed immediately, "on the spot."[23] Studies provide a few examples of this.

For instance, a person's behavioral responses to certain words are faster when those words are primed by some related and emotionally charged labels.[24] This means that specific words and names attached to specific images can automatically activate emotional associations. The individual in such cases makes judgments based largely on feelings, not on logic.[25] Studies also show that people evaluate public figures and political candidates based on a relatively small number of personal characteristics. The first is integrity. The second is competence. And the third is personal characteristics, involving appearance, likability, charm, charisma, and warmth.[26] According to this model, people tend to quickly attribute these traits to individuals under evaluation, and by doing this, they make important judgments about them. Character attacks, for example, often provide such emotional background to people's evaluations.

The Hybrid Processing Model

This model attempts to merge the previous two models by suggesting that people form their responses to character attacks by using one of two types of information processing: either "update" or "ad-hoc." At least two factors explain why one is chosen over the other.

The first factor is *knowledge*. Less knowledgeable individuals rely more heavily on cognitively simpler (less abstract) and more accessible cues. Character attacks fall into this category. Less sophisticated individuals are likely to choose candidates on the basis of party, ideology, or ethnicity (directly, rather than incorporating issue positions). They are more likely to be influenced by considerations that are immediately accessible from memory and influenced by emotions.[27] People with more interest in and knowledge about politics are habitually involved in update processing and less influenced by immediate concerns.[28] In short, more knowledgeable individuals are less susceptible to character attacks against the people about whom they are to make their decisions.

The second factor is *interest*. Critical information can be conceptualized in terms of its relevance to an observer's interests and experience. Strong support of a public figure may filter all the negative facts, including character attacks against this individual. Nevertheless, ambivalence (the coexistence in one person of contradictory emotions or attitudes, such as sympathy and dislike) toward a candidate or an issue complicates our attempts to understand character assassination and its effectiveness.

The Anxiety Processing Model

Experimental research in cognitive psychology (the field examining how individuals process information) shows that people use two key systems in the limbic region of the brain: the disposition and surveillance systems.[29] The limbic area is generally associated with emotions and motivation and also tightly connected with the brain centers responsible for thinking and decision making.

For usual, recurring events, individuals commonly rely on the disposition system. People use their learned repertoires, common reactions, and standard evaluations to accomplish their everyday tasks. For example, many of us leave our apartments and houses, drive our cars, take public transportation, teach classes, go shopping, and so forth without making serious mental efforts because we perform these tasks routinely. In a similar way, many of us have electoral preferences that we exercise almost automatically: we vote routinely for political parties and not for the candidates on the ballot. Many voters are not involved in political discussions at the workplace and do not pay serious attention to political advertisements, including character attacks against political candidates.

However, when novel and unsettling circumstances emerge, the surveillance system is activated. Individuals then have to adjust by setting out on a new course, one that better meets the unexpected demands of an unusual situation. These people need new strategies by departing from the familiar and allowing them to sense danger and novelty in the environment.[30] Anxiety, or an emotional state of uncertainty and tension, can shift people from one mode of judgment to another, and back.

When anxiety levels are low, the automatic disposition system allows people to rely on existing opinions and stick to their habits because a low anxiety state signals that the environment is recognizable, safe, and predictable. In contrast, when anxiety is elevated—signaling that the environment is uncertain and threatening—a person seeks new cognitive strategies and responses. In such situations, it would likely be potentially dangerous to rely carelessly on familiar actions and not pay attention to new information. Thus the surveillance system is launched to take into consideration the new information. Reason and emotion influence each other in this process. In sum, when conditions are unpredictable, anxiety often plays an essential role in determining whether an individual shows greater reliance on "old" or "new" judgments and decisions. Character attacks in this situation may become effective. Sensational, disturbing, and ferocious, they may activate our surveillance system and thus affect our previous opinions and behavioral responses.

To summarize, the models explaining why and how character attacks work suggest the following: character attacks are effective because they take public support away from the victims by discouraging the victims' supporters and encouraging their opponents. Historic examples and experimental studies provide some factual validation for that statement. People launching character attacks reasonably expect to be successful if they have enough people susceptible to the content of these attacks. Most character assassins try to create an imaginary link between their victims' alleged inappropriate behavior, on the one hand, and their seemingly good reputation, on the other. If a character attack is effective, such a link is established, thus creating an unpleasant emotional state in the witnesses.

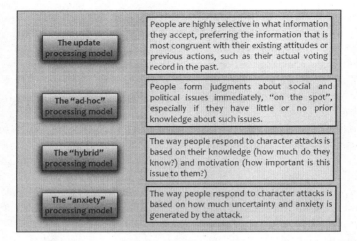

Figure 1.2   Various models of character attacks from witnesses' side: A summary.

Nevertheless, it remains a challenge to determine who might be most suscep-tible to the observed character attacks, when, under what circumstances, and to what degree. Studying the contents and methods of character assassination in history and today may provide some answers to these questions. See Figure 1.2.

Contents and Methods of Character Assassination

What specific methods have been used and how effective were they?

Anonymous Lies

This is a favorite weapon of attackers. Every chapter in this book contains historic examples describing such lies used in the character assassinations of kings, queens, emperors, Communist leaders, presidents, and private individuals. George Washington was accused of expressing regrets for starting the Revolution. Testimonies appeared suggesting Hillary Clinton was a lesbian. The anonymity of today's social networks and blogs makes lying particularly easy.

Misquoting

A common and surreptitious form of character assassination, misquoting is about taking a phrase or sentence out of context. Deliberate misquoting often pursues the goal of attacking someone's reputation. Francis Bacon, the seventeenth-century English philosopher and statesman, was a frequent victim of character attacks. His opponents deliberately misquoted his philo-sophical writings. As one of his contemporary biographer writes, "Scorn for the philosopher and scorn for the man are often overtly linked."[31] Doctoring of images is another effective form of distortion. It is based on emotionally compelling, but ultimately untrue, visual information.

Erasing from Memory and Silencing

Erasing from memory involves a systematic deleting of information from printed and other sources. Silencing (in the context of character assassination) is preventing a living person from defending his or her character, which has been attacked. As a result of erasing and silencing, an individual disappears from people's collective memory. The same fate followed the name and image of Nikolay Yezhov, head of Soviet security until his execution in 1940.* His name and image disappeared from official posters and documents. In the Internet age, however, silencing and erasing has become less effective than in the past.

Vandalism

George Washington's portrait was defaced in 1781 at the statehouse in Philadelphia when somebody broke into the building at night. Symbols representing a famed individual frequently become targets of violent acts by other people, who may be motivated by jealousy, prejudice, or a calculated plan. Pictures of well-known individuals or public officials are frequently defaced to embolden some individuals or make others angry. However, vandalism may backfire and hurt the reputation of the attackers if their identity is revealed.

Name-Calling

This method of attack does not usually require providing factual proof. This is a form of demonization, or portraying somebody simply as evil or bad. For example, in science, the "charlatan" label is often used to attack famous researchers. The term *charlatan* was used in attacks against Franz A. Mesmer, promoter of magnetism; Charles Darwin, founder of evolutionary theory; psychologist William James; psychiatrist Vladimir Bekhterev; inventor Thomas Edison; and many others. In politics, typical name-calling labels include "Communist," "Fascist," "Nazi," "capitalist," "imperialist," "terrorist," "traitor," "hypocrite," and others.

Accusations of Deviance

The personal life of politicians, researchers, and other public figures has repeatedly been an area of character attacks. With the growing influence of public opinion, having a "moral core" (regardless of how it is defined) became a desirable standard. A deviation from this standard could be an excuse for character attacks from opponents. Short-term character assassination attempts are frequently based on alleged inappropriate acts, such as having an extramarital affair. Long-term character attacks require allegations about a person's persistent pattern of "deviant" behavior. *Deviance* is defined differently in different times and cultures.

---

*See the companion website for the pictures related to Yezhov.

Which theories and models explain character assassination better than others? We shall compare several models by discussing character attacks using labels such as "mental illness" or "psychological problems" against their victims.

Using "Mental Illness" Accusations to Test Character Assassination Models

Spreading allegations that imply or overtly assert that a person has a mental illness is a common method of character assassination. Historically, a strong stigma has been attached to mental illness, which was commonly associated with insanity, instability, and irrationality. A random web search easily reveals psychiatric labels attached to the names of world leaders. Joseph Stalin appears as a "maniac," "sadist," "paranoid," and "delusional." Mohammad Mosaddeqh, prime minister of Iran in 1952–53, was frequently called a "drug addict" and "emotionally unstable." Critics of the late Libyan leader Muammar Kaddafi labeled him "paranoid," "unstable," and "delusional." Similar tags were applied to Saddam Hussein of Iraq. Dr. Chee Soon Juan, secretary general of the oppositional Singapore Democratic Party was repeatedly called a "psychopath."

It is not surprising that top leaders are among the most conveniently positioned individuals for character attacks. Accusations of alcoholism—true or exaggerated—have destroyed reputations. Boris Yeltsin, of Russia; movie producer and actor Mel Gibson; U.S. presidents Gerald Ford and George W. Bush; the late U.S. Senators Edward Kennedy, John Tower, and Bob Packwood, to name a few, were attacked as "alcoholics." Richard Nixon's name has been linked to the labels "paranoia," "paranoid schizophrenic," and "paranoid personality." The name of Ronald Reagan is inseparable from multiple references to "Alzheimer's dementia." Bill Clinton was labeled a "sex addict." (The chapter on U.S. presidential politics will discuss accusations of mental issues in character attacks further.)

Alleging the existence of mental illness in political opponents was a tactic used by Communist officials. Some dissidents in the former Soviet Union[32] and China[33] in the 1970s and 1980s were deliberately and wrongly diagnosed with a mental illness based on orders from government officials. The harsh clinical diagnosis was also used as a legal ground for placing the dissidents in secured mental facilities. One of the most convenient labels was "sluggish schizophrenia" with "delusion of reformation"—an unusual but serious diagnosis.[34]

Why should attacks accusing an individual of having mental problems work? It appears that labeling somebody "mentally ill" allows these individuals to be portrayed as mentally incapable, diminishes the significance of their political beliefs, and sets public opinion against them. However, the "sway the undecided" model seems problematic in this context. According to this model, voters cannot judge the truth or falsity of an attack until the campaign is over. That is why a character attack can be successful: some voters become confused and no longer support their initial choice. It also follows from this assumption that candidates have no incentive to be truthful and, unencumbered by such constraints, are free to attack one another relentlessly. Calling somebody "mentally ill," therefore, may be effective in theory. However, in today's elections, voters do not wait months in order to judge the validity of such attacks. They can almost immediately check on the web to determine whether the attacks are accurate.

As has been noted, labeling political dissidents as "mentally ill" was part of the policies by the Communist governments in the Soviet Union and China to discredit the political opposition and, most importantly, receive support from ordinary people. In fact, sociological observations conducted in the Soviet Union in the 1960s and 1970s show that most people believed in the government's alleged facts about political dissents being mentally ill.[35] In light of these facts, the "prevent defections" model makes sense. Instead of risking a public discussion about human rights and political freedoms, the Communist governments found an easy explanation of why political opposition had appeared in the first place: some people were mentally ill! The "anxiety processing" model also appears plausible here. Most ordinary people in China and the Soviet Union did not activate their anxieties about the lack of political freedoms in their countries: those people who had been arrested and detained were mentally ill, and thus they deserved mandatory isolation until they were medicated and "cured." The character assassination of dissidents helped the government, in some way, in keeping many people satisfied with the official explanations.

The "update processing" model might also help in understanding how people react to information about a political leader's alleged mental illness or a serious psychological problem. People who are aware of politics are unlikely to change their opinion about a politician or his or her reputation, and are likely to dismiss the "mental illness" allegations. On the other hand, this person's opponents are likely to consider such allegations important. For example, the fact that John McCain, the Republican presidential candidate in 2008, was imprisoned during the Vietnam War and was tortured in a Vietnamese prison led some critics to suggest that McCain must have developed and suffered from post-traumatic stress disorder. If this was the case, then the symptoms of this illness could have been detrimental to his job as president. His opponents attributed to McCain uncontrollable outbursts of anger, a tendency toward depression, and overall emotional instability.

Sensational statements about the mental health of top officials instantly attract public attention. For example, a study has alleged (without providing any serious support) that about 50 percent of U.S. presidents have suffered from some kind of mental illness.[36] The "ad-hoc processing" model might be used here to explain how people would react to these reports. Most knowledgeable people, who know what a professional diagnostic method involves, are very unlikely to believe that half of all American presidents have suffered from debilitating mental problems. However, a significant proportion of people still may easily believe in an outrageous theory or a blatant accusation. Such individuals can sway a close vote. It seems like most character assassination attempts can influence the opinions of a certain proportion of the population, which is exactly what character assassins are counting on. In fact, the "sway the undecided" and "create uncertainty" models claim that character assassination is effective exactly because there will always be people who can perceive allegations as facts or unquestionable truth, and then vote or act in a desirable—for the character attacker's—direction.

Conclusion

Political psychology tries to explain why and how character attacks become effective. Some individuals are eager to believe character attacks, especially if the attacks target a person with whom these individuals disagree or whom they dislike or abhor to begin with. All in all, the targets (victims) of character attacks—kings, queens, prime ministers, or presidents—are especially vulnerable when they are hated as individuals or rejected as public figures. Despite psychological resistance embedded in human cognition, some people, under some conditions and to a certain degree, may respond to character assassination attempts against other individuals they previously liked, had no opinion of, or did not know at all. Political psychology explains how this happens: to adjust to a rapidly changing social environment, we often pay more attention to the most recent news and facts. Most sensational, disturbing, and ferocious attacks can automatically activate our brain's surveillance system and challenge our prior opinions and behavioral habits. That is why vicious character attacks can be effective. Character attacks can backfire when the popularity of the person under attack is high and the attackers are equally disliked. This assumption, however, requires further research and discussion.

Notes

1. See Branan 2011 and Schultz and Pancer 1997.
2. See Gallup Polls online at http://www.gallup.com/poll/155315/many-americans-cant-name-obamas-religion.aspx.
3. Allen ran again for a Senate seat in 2012, and the 2008 incident reemerged as an issue in his opponent's campaign against him.
4. See http://bit.ly/180G0UV and http://huff.to/v6ysBC for details.
5. Gay 1998, 126–27.
6. See Chivers at http://nyti.ms/SrJ01O.
7. Keen 1991.
8. This story was conveyed to us in 2012, and the person behind it has asked us not to reveal his name.
9. Koenker and Bachman 1997, 289–91. The KGB, the Soviet state security agency, was involved in numerous character assassination campaigns. For example, on February 17, 1976, KGB officials asked the Central Committee of the Communist Party to commission an article in the popular satirical magazine Krokodil.

This article was supposed to attack and mock Andrei Sakharov, a prominent scientist, writer, dissident, and human-rights activist. See more at http://psi.ece.jhu.edu/~kaplan/IRUSS/BUK/GBARC/buk.html.

10. For a more detailed assessment of various models of character attacks, see the works of Lee Sigelman and his colleagues on negative campaigning in the United States and a few other countries (Sigelman and Shiraev 2002).
11. Skaperdas and Grofman 1995, 52.
12. Skaperdas and Grofman 1995, 50.
13. Doron and On 1983, 221.
14. Doron and On 1983, 221.
15. Lau and Pomper 2002.
16. See, for example, Lau et al. 1999; Sigelman and Shiraev 2002.
17. Sigelman and Kugler 2003.
18. Schultz and Pancer 1997.
19. Lodge and Steenbergen 1995.
20. These studies, especially by Fritz Heider and Leon Festinger, are considered classic, pioneering studies in experimental social psychology in the middle of the twentieth century.
21. Dolan and Holbrook 2001.
22. McGraw 2003.
23. Zaller and Feldman 1992.
24. Bargh 1997.
25. Morris et al. 2003.
26. Pancer et al. 1999.
27. McGraw 2003.
28. McGraw et al. 1990.
29. Marcus et al. 2005.
30. LeDoux 2000.
31. Matthews 1996, 407.
32. Bloch and Reddaway 1977.
33. Munro 2000.
34. Shiraev 2010, 13.
35. Shlapentokh 1986.
36. Davidson et al. 2006.

Bibliography

Bargh, J. A. 1997. "The Automaticity of Everyday Life." In R. S. Wyer Jr., ed., *The Automaticity of Everyday Life: Advances in Social Cognition*, vol. 10, 1–61. Mahwah, NJ: Erlbaum.

Berg, A. S. 2013. *Wilson*. New York: Penguin.

Bloch, S., and P. Reddaway. 1977. *Psychiatric Terror: How Soviet Psychiatry Is Used to Suppress Dissent*. New York: Basic Books.

Branan, N. 2011. "Why Smear Campaigning Works." *Scientific American*, January 14. http://www.scientificamerican.com/article.cfm?id=why-smear-campaigns-work.

Chernyaev, A. 2000. *My Six Years with Gorbachev*. University Park: Pennsylvania State University Press.

Chivers, C. 2004. "A Retrospective Diagnosis Says Lenin Had Syphilis." *The New York Times*, June 22. *http://nyti.ms/SrJ01O*.

Davidson, J. R., K. M. Connor, and M. Swartz. 2006. "Mental Illness in U.S. Presidents between 1776 and 1974: A Review of Biographical Sources." *The Journal of Nervous and Mental Disease* 194 (1): 47–51.

Davis, J. 1950. *Character Assassination*. New York: Philosophical Library.

Davis, M., and M. Ferrantino. 1996. "Towards a Positive Theory of Political Rhetoric: Why Do Politicians Lie?" *Public Choice* 88: 1–13.

DeFrank, T. 2007. *Write It When I Am Gone*. New York: Putnam Adult.

Dolan, K., and T. Holbrook. 2001. "Knowing versus Caring: The role of Affect and Cognition in Political Perceptions." *Political Psychology* 22 (1): 27–44.

Doron, G., and U. On. 1983. "A Rational Choice Model of Campaign Strategy." In Asher Arian, ed., *The Elections in Israel, 1981*, 213–231 Tel Aviv: Ramot Publishing.

Ford, W. C., J. Randolph, and J. Vadrill. 2012. *The Spurious Letters Attributed to Washington*. New York: Ulan Press.

Frank, J. 2007. *Bush on the Couch: Inside the Mind of the President*. New York: Harper.

Fraser, S. 1993. *Labor Will Rule: Sidney Hillman and the Rise of American Labor*. Ithaca, NY: Cornell University Press.

Gallup Polls. 2012. Survey of June 22. http://www.gallup.com/poll/155315/Many-Americans-Cant-Name-Obamas-Religion.aspx.

Heilemann, J. 2007. "The Loneliest President." *New York Magazine*, January 28. http://nymag.com/news/politics/Bush/26997/.

Gay, P. 1998. *Freud: A Life for Our Time*. New York: W. W. Norton

Keen, S. 1991. *Faces of the Enemy*. New York: Harpercollins

Kinder, D. 1986. "Presidential Character Revisited." In R. R. Lau and D. O. Sears, eds., *Political Cognition*, 233–55. Hillsdale, NJ: Erlbaum.

Koenker, D., and R. Bachman, eds. 1997. *Revelation from the Russian Archives*. Washington, DC: Library of Congress.

Lau, R., and G. Pomper. 2002. "Effectiveness of Negative Campaigning in US Senate Elections." *American Journal of Politics* 46 (1): 47–66.

Lau, R., L. Sigelman, and I. Rovner. 1999. "The Effects of Negative Political Campaigns: A Meta-analytic Reassessment." *Journal of Politics* 69 (4): 1176–1209.

LeDoux, J. 2000. "Emotion Circuits in the Brain." In *Annual Reviews Neuroscience*, vol. 23, 155–84. Palo Alto, CA: Annual Reviews.

Lengel, E. 2011. "Inventing George Washington." *The New York Times*, March 21. http://nyti.ms/ItOQ1v.

Levy, P. 2006. *The Madness of George W. Bush: A Reflection of Our Collective Psychosis*. New York: Authorhouse.

Lodge, M., and M. Steenbergen. 1995. "The Responsive Voter: Campaign Information and the Dynamics of Candidate Evaluation." *American Political Science Review* 89: 309–26.

Marcus, G., J. Sullivan, E. Theiss-Morse, and D. Stevens. 2005. "The Emotional Foundation of Political Cognition: The Impact of Extrinsic Anxiety on the Formation of Political Tolerance Judgments." *Political Psychology* 26 (6): 949–63.

Mathews, N. 1996. *Francis Bacon: The History of a Character Assassination*. New Haven, CT: Yale University Press.

McGraw, K., E. Hasecke, and K. Conger. 2003. "Ambivalence, Uncertainty, and Processes of Candidate Evaluation." *Political Psychology* 24 (3): 421–48.

Morris, J., N. Squires, C. Taber, and M. Lodge. 2003. "Activation of Political Attitudes: A Psychophysiological Examination of the Hot Cognition Hypothesis Source." *Political Psychology* 24 (4): 727–45. "Special Issue: Neuroscientific Contributions to Political Psychology."

Munro, R. 2000. "Judicial Psychiatry in China and Its Political Abuses." *Columbia Journal of Asian Law* 14: 1–125.

Pierce, P. 1993. "Political Sophistication and the Use of Candidate Traits in Candidate Evaluation." *Political Psychology* 14 (1): 21–35.

Pancer, S. M., S. Brown, and C. Barr. 1999. "Forming Impressions of Political Leaders: A Cross-National Comparison." *Political Psychology* 20 (2): 345–68.

Riker, W. 1996. *The Strategy of Rhetoric: Campaigning for the American Constitution.* New Haven, CT: Yale University Press.

Schultz, C., and S. M. Pancer. 1997. "Character Attacks and Their Effects on Perceptions of Male and Female Political Candidates." *Political Psychology* 18 (1): 93–102.

Shiraev, E. 2010. *A History of Psychology: A Global Perspective.* Thousand Oaks, CA: Sage.

Shiraev, E., and R. Sobel. 2006. *People and Their Opinions.* New York: Longman.

Shlapentokh, V. 1986. *Soviet Public Opinion and Ideology.* New York: Praeger.

Sigelman, L., and M. Kugler. 2003. "Why Is Research on the Effects of Negative Campaigning So Inconclusive? Understanding Citizens' Perceptions of Negativity." *The Journal of Politics* 65 (1): 142–60.

Sigelman, L., and E. Shiraev. 2002. "The Rational Attacker in Russia? Negative Campaigning in Russian Presidential Elections." *The Journal of Politics* 64 (1): 45–62.

Simonton, D. 2006. "Presidential IQ Openness, Intellectual Brilliance, and Leadership: Estimates and Correlations for 42 U.S. Chief Executives." *Political Psychology* 27 (4): 511–26.

Skaperdas, S., and B. Grofman. 1995. "Modeling Negative Campaigning." *American Political Science Review* 89: 49–61.

Zaller, J. R., and S. Feldman. 1992. "A Simple Theory of the Survey Response: Answering Questions versus Revealing Preferences." *American Journal of Political Science* 36: 579–616.

Ancient Rome

2

Character Attack and Invective Speech in the Roman Republic: Cicero as Target

Henriette van der Blom

Introduction

The greatest orator of ancient Rome, Marcus Tullius Cicero (106–43 BC), was a master of political invective and character assassination. Through denigration and denunciation, Cicero forced his fellow senator Catiline to flee Rome, provoked his senatorial colleague Clodius to the point where he sent Cicero himself into exile, and, finally, enraged the consul and military commander Mark Antony to such a degree that he ordered Cicero's murder. These were extreme outcomes of political oratory in ancient Rome, where invective formed an ingrained and accepted part of political life and daily political encounters. Nevertheless, these instances are indicative of the role played by oratory in making or breaking political careers and lives in the Roman Republic.

Cicero's invective encounters, briefly outlined above, neatly track the highs and lows of his public career. Growing up in Arpinum and thus outside the senatorial elite in Rome, Cicero nevertheless managed to create a public career for himself. He used his excellent oratorical talent and skills to become a famous and sought-after advocate in the courts, and he used this position as a springboard for his political career. Becoming elected to all the major magistracies, his career reached its climax in 63 BC, when he as consul crushed Catiline's conspiracy against the state. However, this deed was to become his ruin, leading to his exile from Rome in 58–57 BC; although recalled in triumphant style by the Senate and the people of Rome, he had to wait for more than a decade to attain the same level of influence that he had enjoyed in 63 BC. It was not until 44 BC, as a response to Caesar's murder and Mark Antony's attempts to take control of the state, that Cicero launched into his famous Philippic speeches against Antony. These speeches would—briefly—allow him the same political power as he had enjoyed in 63 BC, but their acerbic attacks on Antony's actions and character also led directly to Cicero's murder in 43 BC.

*   *   *

Cicero's verbal attacks have become famous for their elaborate use of rhetorical effects and explicit terms to heap abuse on his political opponents. His speeches have been studied by ancient and modern scholars as catalogues of invective motifs, examples of how far Roman politicians could go in defaming a political opponent and illustrations of the contexts of invective speeches in Roman republican politics and courts of law.

Here, however, Cicero and invective shall be explored from the opposite angle—namely, Cicero at the receiving end of verbal abuse. Cicero was ridiculed for being a newcomer in Roman politics, accused of tyranny in his actions as consul, blamed for corruption, reproached for unreliability in his political stance, rebuked for having divorced his longstanding wife for a rich teenage bride, and, finally and most consistently, scorned for his continued self-praise. The evidence of this criticism and slander is abundant and scattered across a range of sources; consequently, a full survey shall not be attempted here. Rather, a selection of examples typical of Roman invective speech shall be discussed in order to present attempts at character attacks within a Roman republican cultural and political context: the ways in which others used invective against Cicero, which categories for abuse were employed, how Cicero reacted to such criticism, and the impact of the attacks on Cicero's career and public standing. This analysis shall allow us to assess Cicero as a victim of character assassination.

Invective in Roman Republican Politics

Invective in modern English means "a violent attack in words," whether in speech or writing,[1] and it is personal and aimed at harming another person's reputation.[2] Invective is not character assassination, but it is related in that somebody aiming at destroying the reputation of another person, a character assassin,[3] can use the personal attacks characteristic of invective as one of several methods to achieve this end. In Roman republican politics, invective speech was seen as a perfectly acceptable style in exchanges between politicians bringing forward a complaint.[4] Although it could be incredibly offensive and destroy relationships, a politician at the receiving end did not necessarily suffer politically, and the abuse did not automatically lead to permanent and self-perpetuating enmity.[5] The orator could not be prosecuted for libel. Instead, the check on the orator was his need to protect his own reputation, as an obviously outlandish or outrageous allegation would bounce back and tarnish his own credibility. Cicero abused his senatorial colleagues and others many times during his career, and we have a handful of invective speeches in the strictest sense of the definition. Cicero's most famous attempts at character assassination include his speeches against the corrupt provincial governor Verres; the conspirator Catiline; his political archenemy, Clodius; two fellow senators, Piso and Vatinius; and his final political enemy, Mark Antony.[6] These attempts included outright invective speeches and also speeches delivered or circulated with a different focus, which nevertheless included deriding remarks, aimed at undermining the reputation of his political opponent.

In order to come closer to show how a Roman politician could and would employ invective speech, two rhetorical handbooks in Latin from the Ciceronian period provide useful perspective. In the anonymous *Rhetorica ad Herennium*, the author lists possible categories for abuse—namely, "external circumstances," which include descent, education, wealth, influence, titles of recognition, citizenship, and friendship; "physical attributes," such as agility, strength, looks, and health; and finally "character."[7] This list is mirrored in Cicero's early rhetorical work *De inventione*[8] and employed in his speeches. The contrast to modern court proceedings lies especially in the focus on the opponent's character. Character attack was a perfectly acceptable, highly effective, and therefore widespread element in Roman republican courts of law, where many trials were politically motivated.

A passage from one of Cicero's invective speeches illustrates just how far a politician could go. Cicero's speech against his fellow senator Piso was delivered in the Senate in 55 BC:[9]

> Do you not already see, monster, do you not already realize why men complain about your brow? No one complains that some Syrian from a band of newly acquired slaves is elected consul. We were not even deceived by that servile complexion of yours, or your hairy cheeks, or your decaying teeth; rather, your eyes, eyebrows, forehead, indeed your entire appearance, which is a kind of silent expression of the mind, this is what drove men into deception, this is what deceived, tricked and betrayed those who did not know you.[10]

Cicero then goes on to slander Piso's descent, his political career, his looks, and, most of all, his depraved and deceitful character.[11] Cicero's speech against Piso is one of the few proper invective speeches from antiquity we still have. The speech formed part of an exchange of speeches that took place over several years, initiated by Cicero, who was enraged at Piso's lack of support when Cicero was forced into exile during Piso's tenure as consul. Although Cicero dragged Piso's name through the mud, neither Piso's career nor Cicero's seem to have suffered directly from this abusive exchange. It was part of the very personal, competitive, and confrontational nature of Roman politics and would have been seen as a personal issue between Cicero and Piso.

Cicero under Attack

It is no surprise that Cicero himself, the prize orator of invective, had to endure similarly harsh and insulting assaults on his person. We have good information about the criticism leveled at Cicero by his contemporaries. Yet, we have no full speeches by any orator but Cicero from the republican period and, subsequently, no full invective speech against Cicero. Nor do we know for certain that the criticism of Cicero was expressed as part of such invective speeches proper. The fragmentary nature of this evidence sometimes makes it difficult to determine the context of the criticism. What we can see is that in some instances the criticism was expressed in verbal exchanges in the Senate or as part of speeches delivered in the Senate, the popular assemblies, and in the law courts, where the main content may not have been Cicero's person, but rather a political issue or a legal case. We can also imagine that some of these snide remarks came in other types of public speech, for example, in simple gossip circulated to harm Cicero.

Cicero was criticized for a number of things, but they all fall under the categories that the rhetorical handbooks listed for possible inclusion in an invective speech. In this sense, the criticism, although not expressed in a formal invective speech, drew on the themes and style often associated with invective.[12] Cicero was scorned for his humble ancestry, his political conduct as consul, for being a coward and turncoat, and for actions in private life. Although the extant sources do not record any attempt at censuring his looks and physical condition (a further category listed in the handbooks), he may well have suffered scorn because of his weak stomach, which discouraged him from participating in all-night parties and other such social events.

A sample of the kinds of rude remarks Cicero suffered is contained in a letter from Cicero to his close friend Atticus (summer of 61 BC). Here, Cicero describes developments in political life and his own involvement therein. At this point, Cicero had already been a consul, the top post in Roman politics, and had just been involved as a witness in the trial against his fellow senator Clodius, who was prosecuted for sacrilege. Cicero destroyed Clodius's alibi, but mass bribery secured acquittal nevertheless. In the wake of this trial, Cicero and Clodius clashed at a Senate meeting, and Cicero cites their exchange of words in this letter:

> Our little Beauty [Clodius] gets on his feet and accuses me of having been at Baiae—not true, but anyhow, "Well," I reply, "is that like saying I intruded on the Mysteries?" "What business has an Arpinum man with the waters?" "Tell that to your counsel," I retorted; "he was keen enough to get certain of them that belonged to an Arpinum man" (you know Marius' place of course). "How long," cried he, "are we going to put up with this king [*rex*]?" "You talk about kings," I answered, "when Rex didn't have a word to say about you?" (he had hoped to have the squandering of Rex's money). "So you've bought a house," said he. I rejoined, "One might think he was saying that I had bought a jury." "They didn't credit you on oath." "On the contrary 25 jurymen gave *me* credit and 31 gave

you none—they got their money in advance!" The roars of applause were too much for him and he collapsed into silence.[13]

Clodius's remarks (underlined in the quoted text) can be categorized under three separate attempts at attacking Cicero's person: Cicero's status as a new man in Roman politics, his alleged tyrannical behavior as consul, and his suspected immoral receipt of money for purchasing a house considered above his social status; these attacks shall be analyzed within each separate category.[14]

A New Man

In Cicero's paraphrase,[15] Clodius accuses Cicero of having been to the fashionable and notorious seaside resort of Baiae, south of Rome, where the Roman upper class could indulge in luxuries and less respectable activities, but Clodius also implies that Cicero, as a newcomer in the social and political upper class, should not feel entitled to mingle with the longstanding members of the upper class. Cicero came from the town of Arpinum, not Rome as would any man descended from a family with senatorial ancestors. He therefore counted as a "new man," a *homo novus*, in Roman political life, which occasioned sneers such as Clodius's and some disadvantage in elections, as his name would not be recognized by the electorate.[16]

Cicero had to endure such remarks about his humble background from others too. During his canvass for the consulship, the rival candidates Catiline and Antonius Hybrida engaged in such smears as a means to destroy Cicero's chances of election.[17] Catiline is known to have called Cicero an *inquilinus civis*—a lodger in a house belonging to others, referring to Cicero's background in Arpinum. The term was unjust because the town had enjoyed Roman citizenship for more than a century, but it reflects the arrogance shown by some senatorial families toward newcomers. Catiline's allegation appears to have been his response to Cicero's speech in the Senate (the *In toga candida*), in which Cicero made serious allegations of Catiline's immoral and murderous character; Catiline's retort illustrates exactly how such slanderous claims could fly about in the run-up to elections or over contentious political issues and how a formal speech in the Senate and formal responses could contain such invective elements. Each politician tried to denigrate his opponent by attacking the weak spots in his public profile. In Cicero's case, this was clearly his status as a "new man." Cicero's election to the consulship, together with Antonius Hybrida, shows that these belittling remarks, and indeed his status as newcomer, were not the only factors to influence elections. However, Catiline and Antonius would not have employed such remarks unless they expected them to have an impact with the audience and electorate.[18] The fact that Cicero continued to return to this issue of his humble background (*novitas*) in the following decade suggests that his successful election did not eradicate his background as a new man and that the snide remarks continued, also from Clodius.[19] In this context, Clodius's remark described in the letter is a variation on a well-known invective theme thrown at Cicero.

Rex/tyrannus

To go back to the letter and Cicero's description of his exchange with Clodius, Clodius's next point is more serious—namely, his equation of Cicero with a king.[20] This accusation went back to Cicero's handling of the Catilinarian conspiracy as consul a couple of years earlier. In the autumn of 63 BC, Cicero disclosed and fought down a conspiracy against the state led by his fellow senator Catiline, his former rival in the consular elections and the one calling Cicero an *inquilinus civis*. As part of his actions, Cicero ordered the execution of five captured coconspirators without a preceding trial to test their guilt. Although the conspirators had admitted their guilt and the Senate had recommended execution, Cicero's action was strongly criticized immediately afterward, and he was equated with a tyrant or a king, which amounted to the same in Roman republican culture.[21] The term "king," *rex*, reminded the Romans of the last king of Rome, who had been expelled for his tyrannical behavior, and any reference to kingly behavior was derogatory. A few months after the first allegation of kingship and Cicero's attempt at closing down the issue, the prosecutor of P. Cornelius Sulla, who was accused of being a Catilinarian conspirator and was defended by Cicero, called Cicero a *rex peregrinus*, a king of foreign origin.[22] This was a combination of the slander of Cicero's ancestry, being "foreign" and not from Rome, and of his alleged tyrannical behavior.[23] Related to this criticism was the accusation of cruelty, *crudelitas*, which meant the maltreatment of somebody who did not deserve this treatment or whose suffering went beyond his social status,[24] and referred also to the execution of the Catilinarian conspirators without trial.[25]

The context of this allegation was not the Senate, where Clodius had attacked Cicero, but the court, and Cicero was not the defendant, but the defendant's advocate. The trial of Sulla and Cicero's defense of Sulla could be said to be a special case because Cicero's heavy involvement in the issue of the Catilinarian conspiracy before the prosecution was launched naturally implicated a discussion of his role and, especially, his decision to defend a suspected conspirator. For us, it may seem inappropriate to involve the person of the advocate in the trial, but it was perfectly normal in Roman republican legal practice. An advocate was expected to throw his authority and status behind his client, and Cicero had won several cases by referring to his own authority (*auctoritas*) as surety for his client's credibility.[26] In the end, Sulla was acquitted, but the allegation of kingship and tyranny stuck to Cicero. Clodius's accusation of Cicero's kingly behavior in the exchange quoted formed part of his sustained attack on Cicero's handling of the Catilinarian affair, an attack that we can trace in Cicero's letters and speeches.[27]

Immoral Loan and Preposterous House-Owner

Clodius's third attempt at putting Cicero in a bad light was a reference to Cicero's recent purchase of a house on the slope between the Palatine Hill and the Forum Romanum in Rome. The criticism was aimed at Cicero's acceptance of a large loan to enable him to buy a house that would emphasize his new status as an ex-consul and prominent senator living next to the political center of the Forum.[28] The loan was provided by Sulla, whom Cicero had defended on charges of complicity in the Catilinarian conspiracy, as mentioned above. We have already seen how Cicero's decision to defend Sulla was criticized and occasioned a return to the allegation of kingship. We should also note that in the Republic, it was illegal for an advocate to charge a fee for his legal services, but it was part of Roman culture to repay favors at a later date. The offer of a loan of money, most likely on favorable terms, was one way of rewarding a successful advocate. Therefore, the loan itself was not necessarily offensive, but the circumstances surrounding it were. What seems to have caused the censure of Cicero in this case was, first of all, that the purchase of the house happened too soon after Cicero's defense of Sulla, so that it was seen as too crude and too closely linked. Secondly, Cicero had already been criticized for taking on the defense, and so his material gain from the case, although indirect, was a further thorn in the side of his political opponents. Finally, the prestigious location of the house and the prominence of its former owners made Cicero's wish to reside there appear pretentious and overambitious for a man of his humble background.[29] These three aspects in combination seem implicit in Clodius's remark.

Indeed, Cicero had to endure similar sneers from some of his senatorial colleagues about owning a countryside villa in Tusculum, which had previously belonged to the prominent consular Catulus.[30] As the allegation of kingship had been combined with references to his origin from Arpinum, so was the criticism of stepping up on the housing ladder also joined with scorn at his nonsenatorial background. This criticism also goes back to Clodius's remark on Cicero the social climber at the seaside resort of Baiae.[31] Years later, Cicero defended himself indirectly in his work *On Duties* (44 BC), where he wrote that a man who has reached the highest political offices must have a house that allows him to fulfill that prominence. His example of Cn. Octavius (consul in 165 BC), a new man and purchaser of a house on the Palatine like Cicero, is used to emphasize the need for a splendid house to receive guests and clients and to signal his status in society.[32] This fits with what the Greek biographer Plutarch reports as Cicero's justification—namely, that he purchased the house on the Palatine in order that those who came to pay their court to him should not have the trouble of a long walk.[33]

Cicero's report of the exchange in the Senate finishes with his final witty response to Clodius, which makes their audience laugh and Clodius give up on his slanderous abuse. Although Cicero may have won this exchange in the Senate, Clodius's points for slander of Cicero were neither new, nor would they go away, but instead stabbed at the heart of Cicero's political position as a "new man" in politics and the consul responsible for the execution of the Catilinarian conspirators two years earlier. Two years later, Clodius managed to have Cicero exiled exactly on the grounds of the illegality of the executions by referring to the alleged "kingship" or "tyranny" of Cicero, and so Clodius's invective against Cicero had very serious personal, political, and economic implications for the latter. Only a change in the political situation made it possible for Cicero to return from his exile, but he kept justifying his actions as consul—a sign of continued criticism. Indeed, the antagonism of Clodius continued until Clodius's death in 52 BC.[34] The war involving verbal abuse and the threat of character assassination did not stop.

Self-Praise and Poetry

While Cicero's wit and eloquence were recognized in antiquity,[35] he was also accused of being long-winded and boastful, especially about his consulship.[36] His speeches do preserve long passages of self-praise,[37] but it was his poetic expressions of praise that caused most consternation.[38] In his poem "On His Consulship," Cicero praised and sought to justify his actions as a consul, including the execution of the Catilinarian conspirators. The few lines still extant are preserved precisely because they gave rise to ridicule. Cicero's arch-enemy, Clodius, criticized Cicero's boasting and mocked Cicero for calling himself "Jupiter" and "the brother of Minerva," elements that probably came from Cicero's work.[39] Cicero's response was to accuse Clodius of sleeping with his sister: incest was a typical element in invective, which also Cicero suffered, as we shall see below.[40] The Piso whom Cicero defamed so systematically, as we saw above, argued that it was Cicero's poetic self-praise above all that angered people. Piso seems to have quoted the offensive verses "Let arms yield to the toga / and laurels to laudation" (*cedant arma togae / concedat laurea laudi*), which praised and elevated Cicero's actions as consul as more important than the contemporary military victories of Pompey the Great.[41] It has been argued that it was not just the self-praise of the poem that annoyed people, but the fact that he had taken the innovative step of writing it in the poetic genre to make his actions seem even more heroic.[42] Indeed, there is no evidence that his parallel self-praise in the speeches resulted in similarly hostile remarks.[43] A decade later, Mark Antony too derided the poem and Cicero's preposterous claims.[44] It is probably no coincidence that Cicero's work *On Duties*, which was written exactly when Antony ridiculed Cicero's poem, contains an attempt at justifying and legitimizing the self-praise.[45] The criticism continued after Cicero's death and into the next centuries, although a few authors were positive.[46] The most famous line comes from Seneca: "How many times does he curse that very consulship of his, which he had lauded not without cause, but without end [*non sine causa sed sine fine*]!"[47]

Cicero and Antony

As mentioned in the beginning of this chapter, Cicero attempted an all-out character assassination of Mark Antony, the consul of 44 BC and immediate heir to the murdered Caesar's power, and this is played out in Cicero's famous Philippic speeches.[48] However, Antony could not and would not let Cicero's attacks stand unanswered, and in some of Cicero's speeches, we see Antony's responses reflected, albeit through the distorting lens of Ciceronian bias— Cicero only took up the criticism that he could answer convincingly, and he is likely to have manipulated Antony's words to fit his own agenda.[49] But the overall picture is clear—namely, that Antony complained that Cicero had abused and harmed their political relationship, that Antony criticized Cicero's political actions severely, and, finally, that he attacked Cicero's person.[50] All of this could be said to fall under the categories for invectives listed in the rhetorical handbooks. A more dangerous accusation was Antony's allegation that Cicero had instigated the murders of both Clodius and Caesar.[51] While the murder of Clodius eight years previously (52 BC) had little political relevance in 44 BC, the murder of Caesar just six months previously was still extremely controversial: was the murder justified, and who was to take over the power and in what form? Although Cicero did not participate in the actual killing, he had reminded the conspirators of ancestral examples of tyrannicides and afterward praised the deed;[52] it was neither rhetorically nor politically impossible for Antony to argue that Cicero provided some of the inspiration for the conspirators. It was a serious allegation that Cicero had to counter; it could not just be warded off as a malicious and ludicrous diatribe, hence his reply to Antony. This is the kind of accusation that could have serious political and personal implications, and it shows the power of proper invective—namely, by exaggerating a perceived truth in a convincing way to damage the reputation of the person abused.

Cicero's most sustained reply to Antony's allegations was presented in his second Philippic speech. Although he never delivered this speech, it circulated in written form after Antony had left Rome. In this speech, Cicero's rhetorical strategy is to counter what was probably a selection of Antony's allegations with a combination of logical arguments, impassioned outbursts, and, most important here, with full-blown invective. Take a look at Cicero's response to Antony's criticism of Cicero's consulship: "Well then, in order to let you see what kind of consul he professes himself to be, he reproached me with *my* consulship . . . Who was ever heard abusing my consulship except yourself and Publius Clodius, whose fate awaits you, as it awaited Gaius Curio, since you have that in your house which proved fatal to them both?"[53] We know, of course, from our examination above that Cicero suffered strong and continuous criticism because of his consular actions, and his audience knew this too. Cicero's false claim that only Antony and Clodius had ever criticized his consulship serves merely as a rhetorical way of moving on to the comparison he wants to make between Antony and Clodius: that their criticisms of Cicero's consulship reveal their wicked character, which is proven in their choice of wife ("that in your house"), Fulvia, who was the wife of Clodius, then Curio, and presently Antony. What links Clodius and Antony to each other, Cicero argues, is their criticism of his consulship and the dangerous woman whose mere presence as wife will lead to a violent death, as proven in the cases of Clodius and Curio. Cicero's response to Antony's attacks was an even stronger counterattack.

Marriages and Military

Then again, Antony seems also to have criticized Cicero's private life in his replies to Cicero's Philippic speeches. The biographer Plutarch writes that Antony had censured Cicero for casting out the wife with whom he had grown old and that he made witty remarks about Cicero's housewifely habits and incompetence in business or military service.[54] Cicero had indeed divorced his wife Terentia after more than 20 years of marriage and two children, and this action was seen as disgraceful,[55] especially as shortly after he married the rich teenage girl Publilia, of whom he was heir in trust and whose property he looked after.[56] Again, Plutarch informs us that Terentia, the ex-wife, asserted that Cicero wanted Publilia for her youthful beauty—in other words, a trophy wife to the senior statesman—but also that Cicero's loyal freedman Tiro wrote that Cicero needed Publilia's money to pay off his debts.[57] Apparently, it was better to say that you married for money than for sex. Cicero's and Antony's attacks on each other's private lives were entirely in the vein of invective. What is remarkable, however, is Antony's readiness to enter into an oratorical contest with Rome's greatest orator, which says less about Antony's oratorical skills and more about the crucial importance of oratory in Roman politics: Antony simply had to respond to Cicero's allegations in order to keep his political reputation afloat, and his use of invective elements was to be expected and accepted.

Antony's other deriding comment about Cicero's incompetence in military matters easily played on Cicero's lack of interest in army life and military career. Although he did his military service as required, Cicero hardly referred to it afterward, and he avoided taking up a military command after his consulship.[58] He was sent out to the province of Cilicia as provincial governor against his wishes, and he was impatient to get back to Rome.[59] On the other hand, he liked to compare his political victories with military victories, referring to the odious poem about his consulship,[60] and was eager to reap military glory when the possibility arose in Cilicia.[61] His publicly advertised but unsuccessful attempt at receiving a triumph for his military activities in Cilicia would have made Antony's remark sting, especially since Antony himself was well-known for his military prowess.

Cicero continued his abuse of Antony over the following months and immortalized it in his Philippic speeches. The lasting damage to Antony's reputation and public image can be traced in the contemporary literature, its reception, and as late as the presentation of Antony as the rough and cavalier brute in the modern television series *Rome*.

Cowardice and Unreliability

A more serious criticism of Cicero's character was the accusation of cowardice and unreliability leveled against him. A prominent senator, Metellus Celer, wrote to Cicero in early 62 BC: "I did not think to find your own disposition so changeable [*mobile*] towards me and mine."[62] Celer responded to the news that Cicero had argued strongly against Celer's brother, Metellus Nepos, who himself had launched a verbal attack on Cicero. Celer seems not to have heard the full story, and Cicero responded politely but firmly that the accusation of untrustworthiness was unfair.[63] It is hard to trace further direct evidence of such a charge in contemporary sources, but some modern scholars have ana-lyzed Cicero's actions as cowardly or drawn on later sources to support such a view; especially, the speech put into the mouth of Cicero's political oppo-nent Fufius Calenus in the work of the third-century-AD historian Cassius Dio presents such an image of Cicero as a turncoat.[64] Dio may have built his constructed speech on criticism current in Cicero's day. For example, Antony could have hurled this type of censure at Cicero in his responses to Cicero's Philippic speeches, but if he did so, Cicero carefully avoided making men-tion of it in his replies. We know, however, that the contemporary historian Asinius Pollio was said to have been alone in his view of Cicero's cowardice.[65]

We also have a later source, which was attributed to the contemporary his-torian Sallust but is now commonly believed to be an anonymous rhetorical exercise of the Augustan age—that is, decades later.[66] This work is an exercise in invective aimed at Cicero, and it uses all the categories for abuse listed in the handbooks in a very explicit manner. One of the accusations is indeed that Cicero was untrustworthy in his public actions and alliances: "But on the contrary this man is totally unreliable [*levissimus*], deferential with his ene-mies, abusive to his friends, one moment he supports one side, then the next the other, loyal to nobody, a thoroughly undependable [*levissimus*] senator, a patron for a fee."[67] Being *levis*—"lightweight" and here "unreliable"—was a common accusation between political rivals,[68] but Cicero is, in fact, exoner-ated of this fault by the imperial writer Valerius Maximus.[69] The accusation of being a patron for a fee refers to Cicero acting as Sulla's advocate (patron) and his acceptance of the loan from Sulla, although this was never a fee as such. The pseudo-Sallustian invective here plays upon some themes of criticism current in Cicero's day and, most likely, blows such themes out of proportion in order to make a rhetorical point.

One indication of how these accusations are exaggerated is the allegation of incest between Cicero and his daughter Tullia.[70] This allegation should be seen as the almost mechanical use of a standard invective topic, as there is no hint of incest in any other sources. Moreover, Cicero's fatherly love is so well illustrated in his letters that such an allegation is entirely unbelievable. We should not forget that the pseudo-Sallustian work against Cicero was written to exercise the style of invective a long time after Cicero's death. At most, this source gives us an indication of how the abuse of Cicero was remembered and recorded decades later.[71] The pseudo-Sallustian invective picks up on most of the themes we have seen in the contemporary evidence (and even adds a few more): Cicero's self-praise in his poetry and speeches, his background as a new man in Roman politics, his purchase of a house on the Palatine, and his execution of the Catilinarian conspirators.[72] Let us end with one of the many colorful passages in this exercise in invective: "I implore you, Cicero, having acted and having achieved what you wanted: it is enough that the people have suffered. Will you burden our ears with your hatred; will you harass us with revolting words: 'Let arms yield to the toga and laurels to the tongue'? [*Cedant arma togae, concedat laurea linguae?*]"[73] Note the change from Cicero's original line "let laurels yield to laudation" (*concedat laurea laudi*) to "let laurels yield to the tongue" (*concedat laurea linguae*)—that is, Cicero's incessant self-praise in his public oratory.

Conclusion

We have seen a range of abuses thrown at Cicero, which censure his background, his political actions, and his self-promotion in words and deeds as out of proportion and criticize his actions in private life. A characteristic of these various invective topics hurled at Cicero is that most of them related to a specific situation and were used in this situation only, indicating how the immediate relevance of these invective remarks played a major part. On the other hand, a couple of these topics developed into themes by which Cicero would be censured for longer periods. The sneer at his status as a new man was most relevant around his election to the consulship, but his references to issues of humble birth (*novitas*) in the following decade suggest that he still had to endure the sneer when he was a consular and senior statesman. The disapproval of his purchase of the house on the Palatine and the loan he acquired was most significant just around the purchase because of the political overtones in relation to the trial of Cicero's client and creditor, Sulla. Yet Clodius's confiscation and elimination of Cicero's house a couple of years later and the subsequent return and rebuilding at state expense in the 50s BC contributed to the attention to Cicero's grand house and to the debate about the appropriateness of Cicero owning such a property. Indeed, Cicero still defended his purchase indirectly in his work *On Duties*, written almost two decades after his initial purchase. But the themes that had the longest life were that of kingship/tyranny—the issue of Cicero's handling of the Catilinarian conspirators—and, through his incessant self-justification, the condemnation of his self-praise. For the rest of his life, Cicero experienced attacks on both fronts and answered them with further self-justification and self-praise in an endless circle of praise and blame.

Cicero's constant justification of his consular actions and the continual criticism of his actions illustrate a characteristic pointed out by modern scholars: that we cannot brush aside common and repeated allegations as simply themes of invective without any relation to reality. The speaker or author must have thought such allegations effective for their purpose, personal or political; otherwise it made no sense to go on repeating them.[74] This is perfectly clear in the case of the censure of Cicero's consular actions and should also be considered for the other themes employed against him. Evidently, many of Cicero's colleagues of senatorial pedigree thought his status as a new man made him less worthy of political office and the associated status expressed through presence in the circles of the prominent senatorial families and in the fashionable quarters of the city. The same goes for the disapproval and ridicule of his self-congratulatory speeches and literary works. But what scholarship has also pointed out is that the *absence* of standard themes is much more telling.[75] If we compare a list of the standard themes enumerated in Cicero's invective speeches against others[76] with the themes launched at Cicero in our, admittedly, very limited source material, it is noteworthy that Cicero is never criticized for his physical appearance (body or dress), there is no hint of any gluttony or excess, and he is not censured for being unworthy of his family. Moreover, it is only in the pseudo-Sallustian invective that he is accused of sexual misconduct. This suggests that these themes were not helpful or plausible in the immediate contexts in which the other themes were applied and, since possibly never employed against Cicero, maybe even irrelevant in Cicero's case overall.

It is striking how Cicero in general reacted to the criticism by defending himself at great length. It seems that he only rarely responded to censure by keeping silent.[77] His great talent for oratory and writing, and his position as a new man underdog (at least in the eyes of the arrogant senatorial families), meant that his most common reaction was a public response. He had no family luster, military glory, or financial sheen to boost his public position, and so he had to rely on his words and to employ them often to keep his public position in as high a regard as possible. When responding, Cicero used both harsh invective and sharp witticisms to disarm his opponents, a habit that underlines his widely recognized skill in emotional appeal to the audience (*pathos*) and his famous wit. He could also use logical argument (*logos*) and bolster his arguments with his consular authority (*ethos*), but his main weapon against invective was a counterattack using emotional rhetoric and witty retorts.

Being a new man who reached the consulship meant that Cicero was open for attack—such was the nature of the highly competitive and confrontational Roman political life. Others suffered invectives too, not least the objects of Cicero's censure, and others endured exile and death. The evidence of invective and the political consequences of invective are abundant enough for the Ciceronian period to conclude that Cicero's case was not unique. Indeed, it would be difficult to imagine a high-ranking politician not suffering any abuse in the constant battle for accruing status (*dignitas*), authority (*auctoritas*), and a credible public persona in politics. While invective did not necessarily lead to exile or death, it remained a potent political weapon to sideline opponents and force through agendas. Any use of full-scale invective was an attempt to tarnish the reputation and standing of the opponent and, in its ultimate form, an attempt at character assassination.

Most of the criticism Cicero suffered was politically motivated: some wanted to put him out of action and leave space for another politician, others wanted to put him in his proper place as a newcomer not worthy of high office and great political influence, and others again simply disagreed with his political views and used personal attacks as a medium to stop his policies. The most dramatic attempts at character assassination, however, were more personally motivated: Clodius and Cicero were never reconciled, and their enmity appears to have gone deeper than simply politics; while Mark Antony decided to engage in an oratorical competition with Cicero about who could make the other lose face in public.

*   *   *

Cicero cannot be said to have suffered a full character assassination, but throughout his career, especially from the time when he was candidate to the consulship (64 BC) onward, he had to endure repeated attacks on his person and his actions that affected his standing and led to his exile. But it was his own attempt at employing character assassination, on Mark Antony in his Philippic speeches, that led Antony to order Cicero's murder in 43 BC. After Cicero's death, Antony and his wife Fulvia received his severed head and hand(s). Fulvia is said to have pierced the tongue and hand(s), before the severed members were put on public display. She did this as a final revenge over Cicero's invective oratory and writing.[78] That Cicero's portrait of Antony lived on in the following decades, and even today, is testament to his talent for invective and the fact that his character assassination of Antony reached far beyond his death.[79]

Notes

1. See the *Oxford English Dictionary* online.
2. Powell 2007, 2.
3. See the *Oxford English Dictionary* online.
4. *Rhetorica ad Herennium* 1.8 suggests that a speaker make his audience sympathetic to him by arousing hatred, unpopularity, and contempt in the audience toward the opponent by presenting him in a negative way.
5. See Powell 2007, 3, on the possibility of reconciliation between the opponents at a later date; Powell 2007 and Arena 2007 present good overviews of invective speech and its place in Roman political oratory.
6. Some modern scholars, such as Powell (2007, 2), would argue that Cicero's speeches against Catiline (Cicero, *In Catilinam* 1–4) are not strictly invectives, which is true, but when looking at all the speeches in which Cicero criticizes Catiline, also after Catiline's death, it is clear that at some junctures Cicero really did try to destroy Catiline's reputation. (For a similar argument regarding Cicero's speeches against Verres, see Arena 2007, 150). Craig (2002, 200–203) conveniently collects a list of the invective topics (with some references) that Cicero used against Clodius. Steel 2007 discusses Cicero's invectives of Clodius.
7. *Rhetorica ad Herennium* 3.10–15.
8. Cicero, *De inventione* 2.177–78. For the relationship between these two works, see Corbeill 2002a, 31–34.
9. For discussion of the speech, see Nisbet 1961 and Koster 1980, 210–89; and for the precursors to Cicero's criticism of Piso, see Koster 1980, 120–29; for further references to Cicero's use of Piso's physical appearance, see Gildenhard 2011, 21n5. For further scholarship on the *In Pisonem*, see the bibliographical list in May 2002, 595, to which could be added Dugan 2005, 21–74.
10. Cicero, *In Pisonem* 1, trans. Watts 1931 (amended).

11. Griffin 2001, 88–92.

12. Powell (2007, 17–18) argues that we cannot speak of a "genre" of invective based on the evidence available, and Arena (2007, 150) reminds us that "in ancient rhetorical treatises invective does not appear as a genus in itself."

13. Cicero, *Ad Atticum* 1.16.10 (SB 16), trans. Shackleton Bailey 1965.

14. The final remark about the jury's distrust in Cicero's witness statement will not be discussed here, as it did not hit home because of Cicero's witty rejoinder.

15. Cicero's record of Clodius's words seems, to a large extent, to reflect the abusive themes expressed by Clodius at the meeting because the same exchange of words is recorded in the fragments of a speech that was composed and circulated without Cicero's consent, on the basis of Cicero's speech in the Senate and the subsequent exchange with Clodius (Cicero, *In Clodium et Curionem* fr. 19). For discussion of this "speech," see Crawford 1994, 227–63.

16. Van der Blom 2010.

17. Asconius 93–94C; see also Asconius 91C; Scholia Bobiensia 80St.; Sallust, *Bellum Catilinae* 31.7, 35.5; Appian, *Bellum civile* 2.2. Ramsey (2007, 149) argues that Sallust has misplaced Catiline's hostile remark (*inquilinus*) to 63 BC, while Appian rightly places it during the election campaign of 64 BC, where Asconius provides evidence of such sneer. According to Cicero (Asconius 86C), Q. Mucius Orestinus, too, had alleged that Cicero was not worthy of the consulship (*me esse dignum consulatu negabas*).

18. See also Cicero, *De haruspicum responso* 17. The invective attributed to Sallust also revels in such denouncements of Cicero as a new man (Pseudo-Sallust, *Invectio in Ciceronem* 1.4.7). Although modern scholars think this invective a rhetorical exercise of the Augustan period and not a genuine work of Sallust, even Quintilian was misled (Quintilian, *Institutiones* 9.3.89). Juvenal also reuses the sneer at Cicero's background as *municipalis eques* (Juvenal 8.236–44). See Zielinski 1912, 280–88, for further discussion.

19. See the exchange between Clodius and Cicero recounted in Cicero, *Ad Atticum* 2.1.5 (SB 20) from June 60 BC, where Clodius's remarks hint at Cicero's limited ability in acting the part of patron to a community. See also Cicero, *Ad familiares* 3.7.4–5, with Hall 2009, 149–50, for similar arrogance toward Cicero as a new man by Clodius's brother.

20. Note how Clodius's remark—"How long," cried he, "are we going to put up with this king?" (*"quosque" inquit "hunc regem feremus"*)—must be a mocking reference to the beginning of Cicero's first speech against Catiline: "How long will you, Catilina, abuse our patience?" (*Quo usque tandem abutere, Catilina, patientia nostra?*) Cf. Tatum (1999, 278n127), who also notes this parallel.

21. A charge apparently initiated by tribunes Q. Metellus Nepos and L. Calpurnius Bestia in early 62 (Cicero, *Ad familiares* 5.2.7–8 [SB 2]; *Pro Sestio* 11; Aulus Gellius 18.7.7; Cassius Dio 37.42). Plutarch (*Cicero* 23.2) reports a proposal to recall Pompey to "put down arbitrary power of Cicero" (Κικέρωνος δυναστείαν), which also suggests tyranny. Cicero responded to Metellus Nepos's allegations in a speech called *Contra contionem Q. Metelli* by Quintilian (*Institutiones* 9.3.50); see Crawford 1994, 215–26, for fragments and discussion of this speech.

22. Cicero, *Pro Sulla* 22; see 21–25 for the whole passage, with Berry 1996, 180–84, for discussion. This is picked up by Plutarch, *Cicero* 26.4, 6. Lintott (2008, 151) remarks about the prosecutor Torquatus that "Torquatus is perhaps the first orator to oppose Cicero who can be seen to have got under his skin." In other words, this accusation hit Cicero's weak spot, also emotionally.

23. Cicero later referred to and even joked about these allegations (Cicero, *In Vatinium* 23, 29 [*tyrannos*]; *Ad familiares* 7.24.1 [SB 260] [*rex*]).

24. Lintott 1999, 46–7. For further discussion of the allegation of *crudelitas* against Cicero, see van der Blom 2013.

25. Cicero, *Pro Sulla* 93; *De domo sua* 75; *Ad familiares* 5.2.6–8 (SB 2). Cicero himself generally used *crudelis* as a standard epithet for political despotism (Cicero, *In Verrem* 2.1.82, 2.4.73, 2.5.143; *In Catilinam* 2.14; *De domo sua* 94; *Philippicae* 13.18; *De re publica* 1.44; *Ad familiares* 12.12.2 [SB 387]; *Ad Atticum* 9.10.3).

26. Powell and Paterson 2004, 15–16.

27. Cicero, *Ad Atticum* 1.14.5 (SB 14) (Clodius accuses Cicero of having "fully informed myself"—a reference to Cicero's underhanded way of acquiring intelligence about the conspiracy), 2.4.3 (SB 24), 2.5.3 (SB 25), 2.7.2–3 (SB 27), 2.9.1, 3 (SB 29), 2.12.1–2 (SB 30) (Cicero refers to Clodius's actions as tyranny, in a response to Clodius's accusations of tyranny on Cicero's side), 2.19.2 (SB 39), 2.22.1–2 (SB 42); Cicero, *De domo sua* 7 (Cicero as an enemy to the Capitol—*hostis Capitolinus*); 10.75 ("cruel tyrant"—*crudelis tyrannus*); *De haruspicum response* 17; *Pro Sestio* 109, with discussion in Tatum 1999, 158.

28. As Cicero himself described it (Cicero, *De domo sua* 100): "in full view of almost the whole city." See Cicero, *Ad Atticum* 1.13.6 (SB 13) about Cicero's concern to have a house reflecting his new status, and Allen, 1944; Tatum, 1999, pp.160–1 on the house and the social implications.

29. Aulus Gellius 12.12.2–4, with Berry 1996, 30–32, 39–42, on the details of the loan and purchase and the criticism of Cicero's wish to keep his interest in the house secret. On the loan, see Cicero, *Ad familiares* 5.6.2 (SB 4), with Rawson 1975, 92–93, who thought Cicero foolish in accepting the loan. The remainder of the money apparently came through a loan from C. Antonius (Cicero, *Ad familiares* 5.5.2–3 [SB 5]; *Ad Atticum* 1.12.1–2 [SB 12], 1.13.6 [SB 13], 1.14.7 [SB 14]). Cicero bought the house, which had previously been owned by M. Livius Drusus, from Crassus (tribune of the plebs in 91 BC) (Velleius Paterculus 2.14.3).

30. Cicero, *Ad Atticum* 4.5.2 (SB 80) June 56 BC: "Certain gentlemen who object to my owning a villa which once belonged to Catulus without recollecting that I bought it from Vettius, and say in the same breath that I ought not to have built my house and that I ought to sell it." See also the comment in Shackleton Bailey, 1965–70.

31. See also the discussion in Lafon 2001, 188–204, where all nine of Cicero's properties are listed and the sneer of the *nobiles* is discussed.

32. Cicero, *De officiis* 1.138–40, with Brunt 1982, 12–13.

33. Plutarch, *Cicero* 8.6. This may be a Plutarchan topos for "new men," as the same motivation in similar wording is repeated in the Life of Marius (Plutarch, *Marius* 32.1–2).

34. See, for example, the clash depicted in Cicero's speech *De domo sua*.

35. Juvenal 10.115 compares Cicero and Athen's greatest orator, Demosthenes. There were at least three collections of Cicero's sayings in circulation during his lifetime: Cicero, *Ad familiares* 7.32 (SB 113); 15.21.2 (SB 207); Quintilian, *Institutiones* 6.3.5; Macrobius, *Saturnalia* 2.1.12. For discussion see Rabbie 2007. Cicero himself refers to his reputation for being witty (Cicero, *Ad familiares* 9.16.4 [SB 190]) but also admits that some of his jokes were better than others (Cicero, *Pro Plancio* 35, with Scholia Bobiensia 85–91 St). See Balsdon 1965, 190–93, for some of Cicero's jokes.

36. Plutarch, *Cicero* 6.5, 24.1–3; Cassius Dio 37.38.2, 38.12.7; Quintilian, *Institutiones* 11.1.18; see Allen 1954 for the political and cultural context of Cicero's boasting.

37. See, for example, Cicero, *In Pisonem* 3–7; *Pro Flacco* 102; *Philippicae* 2.11–12. See Cicero, *De provinciis consularibus* for an attempt to justify his boasting.
38. Aside from the *De consulatu suo* ("On his consulship") in three books, he also wrote a sketch in Greek (Cicero, *Ad Atticum* 1.19.10 [SB 19], 20.6 [SB 20], 2.1.1–2 [SB 21]) and considered writing one in Latin too (Cicero, *Ad Atticum* 1.19.10 [SB 19]; *Ad familiares* 5.12.8 [SB 22]).
39. Steel (2005, 68) has argued that Cicero's comparison is likely to stem from his *De consulatu suo*—"On his consulship."
40. Cicero, *De domo sua* 92; Pseudo-Sallust, *Invectio in Ciceronem* 2; cf. §7 too. On Clodius's alleged incest, see Tatum 1999, 41–42. Clodius's supporters answered this allegation by shouting choruses about Pompey's alleged homosexual preferences (Cicero, *Ad Quintum fratrem* 2.3.2; Plutarch, *Pompey* 48.7). For discussion of this tactic, see Benner 1987, 84–85; Nippel 1995, 76; Lintott 1999, 10; Morstein-Marx 2004, 134–35.
41. Cicero, *In Pisonem* 72–74. The translation of the verses is that of Griffin and Atkins 1991.
42. Steel 2005, 68–69. See also Allen (1954, 135), who argues that Cicero's poems suffered a combination of literary criticism and criticism of vanity.
43. Cicero, *In Catilinam* 4.21.
44. Cicero, *Philippicae* 2.20, with Ramsey 2003, ad loc.
45. Cicero, *De officiis* 1.77.
46. Juv. 10.122–26; Quintilian, *Institutiones* 11.1.23–24. See Kurczyk 2006, 85–92, 115–18, for the background, criticism, and interpretation of these passages, and Ewbank 1933, 27–29, for a collection of further instances of criticism in the first and second centuries AD. For positive remarks, see Cicero, *Ad familiares* 13.13.1 (SB 280); Plinius Maior, *Naturalis historia* 7.117.
47. Seneca Minor, *De brevitate vitae* 5.1. As a final point on Cicero's long-windedness, note the remark of Cato in a letter to Cicero, explaining that he has written at some length to Cicero, contrary to his usual habit (Cicero, *Ad familiares* 15.5.3 [SB 111]). This could be read as a rebuke of Cicero's long-windedness; indeed, Cicero's response to Cato is unusually short for Cicero but in fact of roughly the same length as Cato's proclaimed "lengthy" letter.
48. There is abundant literature on Cicero's Philippics and the invective style applied. A concise summary of Ciceronian invective is Manuwald 2007, 1.105–9, with references to further scholarship.
49. Frisch (1946, 133–35) has attempted a reconstruction.
50. Political relationship (*amicitia*) violated (Cicero, *Philippicae* 2.3, 2.5–6); Cicero's political actions, especially his consulship (Cicero, *Philippicae* 2.11–12, 2.15–16, 2.17–18, 2.21–25, 28); Cicero's person, including vanity (Cicero, *Philippicae* 2.20, 2.30, 2.37–39, 2.40).
51. Cicero, *Philippicae* 2.21–25, 2.28.
52. Balsdon (1965, 198–99) puts Cicero's encouragement into the context of other such remarks throughout his career.
53. Cicero, *Philippicae* 2.11, trans. Shackleton Bailey, revised by Ramsey and Manuwald (2009).
54. Plutarch, *Cicero* 41.4. "Housewifely habits" (οἰκουρίαν): it seems likely that such criticisms would have been included in Antony's speech from September 19, 44 BC, responding to Cicero, *Philippicae* 1, although certainty is impossible.
55. Treggiari 2007, 129. The speech put into Fufius Calenus's mouth in Dio 46.18.3 focuses on the fact that Terentia had borne Cicero two children. On this speech, see Koster 1980, 200–10.

56. He may have been her tutor and she his ward, but the precise legal arrangements are unclear. For discussion see Treggiari 2007, 134.
57. Plutarch, *Cicero* 41.3.
58. Cicero, *Ad Atticum* 2.1.3 (SB 21); *In Pisonem* 5.
59. Cicero, *Ad familiares* 3.2.1 (SB 65), 15.12.2 (SB 102) (sent out to Cilicia against own wishes); *Ad Atticum* 5.1.1 (SB 94), 5.2.3 (SB 95), 5.9.2 (SB 102), 5.11.1, 5.11. 4 (SB 104), 5.17.5 (SB 110), 5.18.1 (SB 111), 5.20.7 (SB 113); *Ad familiares* 2.7.4 (SB 107), 2.8.3 (SB 80), 2.10.4 (SB 86), 3.8.9 (SB 70), 15.9.2 (SB 101), 15.13.3 (SB 109), 15.14.5 (SB 106) (impatience).
60. Cicero, *In Catilinam* 1.27–29, 4.21–23; *De officiis* 1.77–78. Cf. May 1988, 56–58, for a similar analysis of Cicero's self-representation as an *imperator togatus* ("a civil general"); Nicolet 1960, 245–52; Martin 1980, 850–58; Steel 2001, 166–73; van der Blom 2010, 297–300.
61. Cicero, *Ad Atticum* 5.20.3 (SB 113); *Ad familiares* 2.10.3 (SB 86), with van der Blom 2010, 239–40; and his efforts to argue for a full triumph, Cicero, *Ad familiares* 8.11.1–2 (SB 91), 15.5.1 (SB 111), 15.6 (SB 112).
62. Cicero, *Ad familiares* 5.1.2 (SB 1), trans. Shackleton Bailey 2002.
63. Cicero, *Ad familiares* 5.2 (SB 2).
64. Dio 46.1–28; see also 38.18–29, where Dio puts another speech that criticizes Cicero for being a turncoat into the mouth of a philosopher (Philiscus). Of modern scholars, Balsdon (1965, 196–98) gives a balanced view after his introductory remark that "Cicero was maligned as a coward," although he gives no references to who might have maligned Cicero at the time. On Cicero's justification of staying alive in the civil war when Cato the Younger committed suicide (Cicero, *De officiis* 1.112) and its relation to philosophy, see Griffin and Atkins 1991, 44. I would not consider Cicero's depressive streak (seen during his exile in 58–57 BC and his wait for Caesar's pardon in Brundisium in 48–47 BC, displayed in his letters at the time) as necessarily cowardly.
65. Seneca Maior, *Suasoriae* 6.14–15, 6.24–25.
66. Novokhatko 2009, 111–29. See also the discussion of the invective themes aimed at Cicero in the work of Koster 1980, 177–89.
67. Pseudo-Sallust, *Invectio in Ciceronem* 5, cf. §7, trans. Novokhatko, 2009.
68. Ernout 1962, 55; Opelt 1965, 164. For example, Marius was accused of being changeable: Liv. *Per.* 69, probably picking up on contemporary sources.
69. Valerius Maximus 4.2.4 on Cicero's initial verbal attacks on Gabinius and Vatinius and later defences of them when prosecuted: "this without incurring the charge of levity [*levitas*], rather with some credit [*laus*]," although it must be remembered that Cicero's decision to defend both was occasioned by his dependability of Pompey's and Caesar's goodwill—that is, political necessity rather than genuine change of heart.
70. Pseudo-Sallust, *Invectio in Ciceronem* 2.
71. Mitchell (1991, 67n8) takes it a bit further by arguing that the invective pieces in Cassius Dio 46.1–28 "provide the fullest illustration of the range and character of the accusations to which Cicero was exposed as a result of the executions."
72. Cicero's self-praise in his poetry and speeches (Pseudo-Sallust, *Invectio in Ciceronem* 1, 5, 6, 7); his background as a new man in Roman politics (§1, 4, 7); his purchase of a house on the Palatine (§2, 3); and his execution of the Catilinarian conspirators (§ 3, 5).
73. Pseudo-Sallust, *Invectio in Ciceronem* 6, trans. Novokhatko 2009 (amended in the citation of Cicero's poetry).

74. Powell 2007, 17.
75. Powell 2007, 17–18, with reference to Craig 2004.
76. Corbeill 2002b and Craig 2004, 190–92.
77. One example is his abstention from responding to the pamphlet written by Piso Caesoninus in 53 BC, an abstention that he felt he had to justify to his brother (Cicero, *Ad Quintum fratrem* 3.1.11 [Sept. 54 BC], with Griffin 2001, 94).
78. Plutarch, *Cicero* 48.4–49.1; Mark Antony 20.2; Butler 2002, 1–2, with more sources.
79. I should like to thank the organizers of the colloquium on character assassination for the kind invitation, the Carlsberg Foundation (Denmark) for funding the research that led to this chapter, Miriam Griffin for a good brainstorming session, and Kathryn Tempest for thinking with me.

Bibliography

Allen, W. 1944. "Cicero's House and *libertas*." *Transactions of the American Philological Association* 75: 1–9.

Allen, W. 1954. "Cicero's Conceit." *Transactions of the American Philological Association* 85: 121–44.

Arena, V. 2007. "Roman Oratorical Invective." In W. Dominik and J. Hall, eds., *A Companion to Roman Rhetoric*, 149–60. Malden, MA: Wiley-Blackwell.

Balsdon, J. P. V. D. 1965. "Cicero the Man." In T. A. Dorey, ed., *Cicero*, 171–214. London: Routledge and Kegan Paul.

Benner, H. 1987. *Die Politik des P. Clodius Pulcher.* Stuttgart: Steiner.

Berry, D. H. 1996. *Cicero. Pro P. Sulla Oratio.* Cambridge: Cambridge University Press.

Blom, H. van der. 2010. *Cicero's Role Models: The Political Strategy of a Newcomer.* Oxford: Oxford University Press.

Blom, H. van der. 2013. "Fragmentary Speeches: The Oratory and Political Career of Piso Caesoninus." In C. Steel and H. van der Blom, eds., *Community and Communication: Oratory and Politics in the Roman Republic*, 299–314. Oxford: Oxford University Press.

Brunt, P. A. 1982. *Nobilitas* and *novitas. Journal of Roman Studies* 72: 1–17.

Butler, S. 2002. *The Hand of Cicero.* London: Routledge.

Corbeill, A. 2002a. "Rhetorical Education in Cicero's Youth." In J. M. May, ed., *Brill's Companion to Cicero: Oratory and* Rhetoric, 23–48. Leiden: Brill.

Corbeill, A. 2002b. "Ciceronian Invective." In J. M. May, ed., *Brill's Companion to Cicero: Oratory and* Rhetoric, 197–217. Leiden: Brill.

Craig, C. 2004. "Audience Expectations, Invective, and Proof." In J. G. F. Powell and J. J. Paterson, eds., *Cicero the* Advocate, 187–213. Oxford: Oxford University Press.

Craig, C. 2007. "Self-Restraint, Invective, and Credibility in Cicero's *First Catilinarian Oration*." *American Journal of Philology* 128: 335–39.

Crawford, J. W. 1994. *M. Tullius Cicero: The Fragmentary Speeches.* Atlanta: Scholars Press.

Dugan, J. 2001. "How to Make (and Break) a Cicero: *Epideixis*, Textuality, and Self-Fashioning in the *Pro Archia* and *In Pisonem*." *Classical Antiquity* 20: 35–77.

Dugan, J. 2005. *Making a New Man: Ciceronian Self-Fashioning in the Rhetorical Works.* Oxford: Oxford University Press.

Epstein, D. F. 1987. *Personal Enmity in Roman Politics, 218–43 BC.* London: Croom Helm.

Ernout, A. 1962. *Pseudo-Salluste. Lettres a César invectives.* Paris: Belles Lettres.

Ewbank, W. W. 1933. *The Poems of Cicero.* London: University of London Press.

Frisch, H. 1946. *Cicero's Fight for the Republic.* Copenhagen: Gyldendal.

Griffin, M. 2001. "Piso, Cicero and Their Audience." In C. Avray-Assayas and D. Delattre, eds., *Cicéron et Philodème. La polémique en philosophie*, 85–99. Paris: Rue d'Ulm.

Griffin, M. T., and E. M. Atkins. 1991. *Cicero: On Duties.* Cambridge: Cambridge University Press.

Hall, J. 2009. *Politeness and Politics in Cicero's Letters.* Oxford: Oxford University Press.

Hickson-Hahn, F. 1998. "What's So Funny? Laughter and Incest in Invective Humor." *Syllecta Classica* 9: 1–36.

Koster, S. 1980. *Die Invektive in der griechischen und römischen Literatur.* Meisenheim am Glan: Hain.

Kurczyk, S. 2006. *Cicero und die Inszenierung der eigenen Vergangenheit. Autobiographisches Schreiben in der späten Römischen Republik.* Cologne: Böhlau.

Lafon, X. 2001. *Villa Maritima. Recherches sur les villas littorales de l'Italie Romaine (IIIe siècle av. J.-C. / IIIe siècle ap. J.-C.* Rome: Ecole française de Rome.

Lintott, A. 1999. *Violence in Republican Rome*, 2nd ed. Oxford: Oxford University Press.

Lintott, A. 2008. *Cicero as Evidence: A Historian's Companion.* Oxford: Oxford University Press.

Manuwald, G. 2007. *Cicero,* Philippics 3–9, 2 vols. Berlin: De Gruyter.

Martin, P. M. 1980. Cicéron *princeps. Latomus,* 39, 850–78.

May, J. M. 1988. *Trials of Character: The Eloquence of Ciceronian Ethos.* Chapel Hill: University of North Carolina Press.

May, J. M., ed. 2002. *Brill's Companion to Cicero: Oratory and Rhetoric.* Leiden: Brill.

Mitchell, T. 1991. *Cicero the Senior Statesman.* New Haven, CT: Yale University Press.

Morstein-Marx, 2004. *Mass Oratory and Political Power in the Late Roman Republic.* Cambridge: Cambridge University Press.

Nicolet, C. 1960. "*Consul togatus.* Remarques sur le vocabulaire politique de Cicéron et de Tite-Live." *Revue des Études Latines* 38: 236–63.

Nippel, W. 1995. *Public Order in Ancient Rome.* Cambridge: Cambridge University Press.

Nisbet, R. G. M. 1961. *M. Tvlli Ciceronis oratio in Pisonem.* Oxford: Oxford University Press.

Novokhatko, A. A. 2009. *The Invectives of Sallust and Cicero: Critical Edition with Introduction, Translation, and Commentary.* Berlin: De Gruyter.

Opelt, I. 1965. *Die lateinischen Schimpfwörter und verwandte sprachliche Erscheinungen. Eine Typologie.* Heidelberg: Ilona.

Pina Polo, F. 2010. "*Frigidus rumor*: The Creation of a (Negative) Public Image in Rome." In A. J. Turner, J. H. Kim On Chong-Gossard, and F. J. Vervaet, eds., *Private and Public Lies: The Discourse of Despotism and Deceit in the Ancient World*, 75–90. Leiden: Brill.

Powell, J. G. F. 2007. "Invective and the Orator: Ciceronian Theory and Practice." In J. Booth, ed., *Cicero on the Attack: Invective and Subversion in the Orations and Beyond*, 1–24. Swansea: Classical Press of Wales.

Powell, J. G. F., and J. J. Paterson. 2004. "Introduction." In J. G. F. Powell and J. J. Paterson, eds., *Cicero the Advocate*, 1–57. Oxford: Oxford University Press.

Rabbie, E. 2007. "Wit and Humor in Roman Rhetoric." In W. Dominik and J. Hall, eds., *A Companion to Roman Rhetoric*, 207–17. Malden, MA: Wiley Blackwell.

Ramsey, J. T. 2003. *Cicero: Philippics I–II.* Cambridge: Cambridge University Press.

Ramsey, J. T. 2007. *Sallust's* Bellum Catilinae. 2nd ed. Oxford: Oxford University Press.

Rawson, E. 1975. *Cicero: A Portrait*. London: Allen Lane.

Renda, C. 2002. "*Pisonis supercilium*: tratti e ritratti nellas *Pro Sestio* di Cicerone." *Bollettino di Studi Latini* 32: 395–405.

Riggsby, A. M. 1997. "Did the Romans Believe in Their Verdicts?" *Rhetorica* 15: 235–51.

Schindel, U. 1980. *Die Invektive gegen Cicero und die Theorie der Tadelrede*. Göttingen: Vandenhoeck & Ruprecht.

Schneider, W. C. 2000. "Vom Salz Ciceros. Zum politischen Witz, Schmäh und Sprachspiel bei Cicero." *Gymnasium* 107: 497–518.

Shackleton Bailey, D. R. 1965–70. *Cicero's Letters to Atticus I–VI + Indices*. Cambridge: Cambridge University Press.

Shackleton Bailey, D. R. 1999. *Cicero: Letters to Atticus I–IV*. Cambridge, MA: Harvard University Press.

Shackleton Bailey, D. R. 2001. *Cicero: Letters to Friends I–III*. Cambridge, MA: Harvard University Press.

Shackleton Bailey, D. R. 2002. *Cicero: Letters to Quintus and Brutus*. Cambridge, MA: Harvard University Press.

Shackleton Bailey, D. R. 2009. *Cicero: Philippics I–II*, revised by J. T. Ramsey and G. Manuwald. Cambridge, MA: Harvard University Press.

Steel, C. E. W. 2001. *Cicero, Rhetoric, and Empire*. Oxford: Oxford University Press.

Steel, C. 2005. *Reading Cicero*. London: Duckworth.

Steel, C. 2007. "Name and Shame? Invective against Clodius and Others in the Post-Exile Speeches." In J. Booth, ed., *Cicero on the Attack: Invective and Subversion in the Orations and Beyond*, 105–28. Swansea: Classical Press of Wales.

Sussman, L.A. 1998. "Antony the *meretrix audax*: Cicero's Novel Invective in *Philippic* 2.44–46." *Eranos* 96: 114–28.

Tatum, W.J. 1999. *The Patrician Tribune: Publius Clodius Pulcher*. Chapel Hill: University of North Carolina Press.

Treggiari, S. 2007. *Terentia, Tullia and Publilia: The Women of Cicero's Family*. London: Routledge.

Uría, J. 2006. "Personal Names and Invective in Cicero." In J. Booth and R. Maltby, eds., *What's in a Name? The Significance of Proper Names in Classical Latin Literature*, 13–31. Swansea: Classical Press of Wales.

Watts, N. H. 1931. *Cicero: The Speeches*. Cambridge, MA: Harvard University Press.

Zielinski, T. 1912. *Cicero im Wandel der Jahrhunderte*. Leipzig: Teubner.

3

Reports about the "Sex Life" of Early Roman Emperors: A Case of Character Assassination?

Jan Meister

Introduction[1]

The popular image of the early Roman emperors is marked by notions of unbridled sexuality and moral decadence. It is the work of the imperial biographer Suetonius more than any other that has given rise to this image. His biographies include reports about the sex lives of the emperors that leave absolutely nothing to the imagination: Augustus has his wife Livia procure young girls for him to deflower; Tiberius holds wild orgies in the seclusion of Capri; and Caligula indiscriminately rapes his sisters, respectable matrons, and Roman senators.[2] Evidence for the broad reception of these reports ranges from erotic engravings of the eighteenth century to the X-rated films of recent years.[3] Among scholars, by contrast, for a long time this "frivolous" subject received little attention.[4] Earlier scholars on Suetonius embarrassedly regarded the passages in question as merely further proof that Suetonius was a third-rate author interested in scandal and gossip from all kinds of unreliable sources.[5] Over the last decades, however, not only has Suetonius enjoyed a nuanced reassessment,[6] but also the discursive nature of sexuality itself has been the subject of extensive discussion.[7]

Building on these approaches, I argue in the following that Suetonius was not in fact interested in drawing individual sexual profiles.[8] This opinion, it will be shown, is anachronistic and distorts our perception of the way in which the Romans conceptualized sexual practices. Reports about the alleged sex lives of Roman emperors prove to be not ancient sexual profiles, but rather cases of character assassination.

Sexual Practices and Character Assassination

Suetonius was a Roman knight and a high-ranking official in the imperial administration during the early second century AD. As was quite common for a member of the Roman elite, he engaged in antiquarian studies and enjoyed some fame as a scholar.[9] Probably in the 120s he composed a total of 12 imperial biographies, from Julius Caesar to Domitian. An idiosyncrasy of these *Lives* is that they are arranged not chronologically, but topically. Suetonius thus reports together the wars that an emperor waged, the buildings that he built, the games that he gave, and so on. For historians who would like to reconstruct the chronology of the events it is an annoying practice.[10] If one asks, however, in what categories Suetonius thought and by what criteria he arranged and systematized the individual reports and events, the organization of the *Lives* according to topic proves to be a windfall. Even a cursory glance reveals that our modern notion of a "sex life" is not found as such in Suetonius: the marriages of the emperors, to modern thinking definitely part of one's sexual life, are generally listed together with the rest of the emperor's family affairs—namely, the way the emperor interacts with his children and how he manages the household. In most of the *Lives*, however, separate topics are concerned with the *libidines* and the *pudicitia* of the emperor. The latter—usually translated as "chastity"—is a key concept for the Roman understanding of sexuality.[11] The meaning of the word varies according to its context, but for free Roman men *pudicitia* in most cases denotes personal bodily integrity, which is lost if a man is sexually penetrated by others. If someone violates the *pudicitia* of another person, he accordingly commits a wrong that is denoted by the term *stuprum*. The motivation for doing so is usually an overactive sex drive—the *libidines* that serve as a second key word in Suetonius's topics alongside *pudicitia*. The biographer is thus interested in two things: on the one hand, in emperors who sacrifice their own *pudicitia* (i.e., let themselves be penetrated sexually by others) and, on the other, in emperors who violate the *pudicitia* of others in a socially unacceptable way.

Suetonius's arrangement of topics is not the only thing that departs from modern ideas of sexual life: on close inspection, it appears in many cases that Suetonius gives no verdict whether an emperor was *pudicus* or *impudicus*.[12] Already Wolf Steidle, in his important 1951 monograph on Suetonius, demonstrated that Suetonius does not merely repeat gossip, but rather shows interest in the *fama*—that is, in the reputation—of his protagonists.[13] *Fama* was decisive for public figures, and *infamia* (i.e., an evil reputation) could even have legal consequences. Stories about the sex life of a person furnished the most material for *infamia*. It is therefore unsurprising that sexual innuendos were not the exception but rather the rule for ancient character assassination.[14] An anonymous handbook of rhetoric from the first century BC explains how one should attack the character of one's opponent in court: at the top of the list is to insinuate that he surrenders his own *pudicitia* and violates that of others.[15]

Republican speeches and imperial satires and epigrams permit us to reconstruct what such attacks would have looked like in practice. We can identify three parameters that determined the way in which sexual practices were conceptualized and utilized in the context of invective. First of all, the Romans did not think in the modern categories of homo- or heterosexuality, but rather distinguished between active and passive roles. A man who performed actively—that is, penetrated another—was considered masculine, while the passive role was viewed as feminine. This implies that sexuality was thought of as a hierarchical relationship: the penetrator wields power and forces the penetrated person into a subordinate, "powerless" role.

This hierarchy of sexual practices naturally led to the necessity—and this is the second point—of respecting the social hierarchy when choosing sexual partners. That means, in concrete terms, a man could not penetrate everyone indiscriminately but had to take each partner's status into account. Free Roman men or boys were taboo: to penetrate such persons—completely independent of the question whether with or without their consent—was considered *stuprum*.[16] This is related to modern prohibitions against homosexuality only in a limited sense. The same act with a slave, as long as the slave played the passive part, posed no problem to the Romans. Adultery or the seduction of free girls was likewise considered *stuprum*. Just like freeborn men, such women also possessed *pudicitia* that could be threatened by extramarital sex.[17] Quintilian sketches a fictional court case that illustrates this: A rich man rapes the daughter of his poor host; he wrongly believed the girl was a slave because his host had claimed she was. Without realizing it, then, the rich man committed *stuprum*. The poor man attempts to force the rich man to marry his daughter in order to "heal" the delict, but the rich man alleges that he was misled with the claim that she was a slave precisely for that reason.[18] The court accordingly is not interested in the act of rape, but rather in the status of the parties involved.

A third point was also central to the ancient conceptualization of sexuality; Eckhardt Meyer-Zwiffelhoffer has described it as "ascetic behavior" (*asketische Haltung*).[19] What is meant is the ideal of (male) control of the appetites. The real man is distinguished by the ability to dominate his *libido*. Even though plausible lines of continuity to later ideals of chastity may be drawn here, in republican time this concept concerned the subordination of sexual desire to *ratio* rather than sexual abstinence. In one anecdote, for example, the puritanical Cato the Elder praised a young man for visiting a brothel, since this allowed him to satisfy his sexual appetite in a controlled manner.[20] The ideal was not so much chaste asceticism as a rational control of the appetites.

The conception of sexuality as a hierarchical relationship of active and passive roles, the status-determined *pudicitia* of potential sexual partners, and the ideal of masculine control of the appetites set the stage for invective: to allege sexual misconduct against one's opponent meant to accuse him of taking the passive role and surrendering his *pudicitia*, of violating the *pudicitia* of others without regard for their social status, and of not being in control of his appetites but instead dominated by them.[21]

The frequency of such allegations in Roman invective ultimately coalesced in a stereotypical character type: the effeminate *vir mollis*, who is also called *cinaedus* or *effeminatus*.[22] This "soft man" is distinguished by his inability to control himself; instead he gives in to his appetites and exhibits pronounced sexual vigor, whereby he may take both active and passive roles. The sexual practices of such men are merely one among many characteristics: "soft men" have a peculiar, mincing gait and mannered gestures; they dress their hair in stylish locks, which they drench in perfumed oil; they are clean shaven and even have their body hair depilated—all measures, according to the internal logic of this image, that serve to enhance their sex appeal. An invective normally attempts to establish the existence of one of these stereotypes in an adversary in order to associate all the other traits of a *vir mollis* with him. A fragment of a speech from the second century BC begins by rebuking the target for his perfumed locks, then refers to his shaved eyebrows, and ends with the conviction that there can be absolutely no doubt that such a man also indulged in passive sexual practices.[23] Similar allegations are found en masse in Republican speeches. If one leaves aside love poetry, one could even argue that sexual practices were a discursive subject primarily in the context of invectives.

Invectives against Caesar and Augustus

It is self-evident in Suetonius's *Lives* that he used such invectives as immediate sources. The report about the "sex life" of Julius Caesar begins with the statement that nothing had damaged Caesar's reputation for *pudicitia* more than his relationship with Nicomedes.[24] Nicomedes was a Bithynian king at whose court Caesar had stayed as a young man. This time at Nicomedes's court led to the rumor that Caesar had put his *pudicitia* at the king's disposal.[25] Suetonius offers a whole series of evidence, not of the alleged sex act, but rather of the damage to Caesar's reputation that resulted from the alleged liaison. It is above all the invectives of political rivals—for the most part prominent senators—that slander Caesar as "catamite," "queen," "stall of Nicomedes," or "Bithynian brothel."[26] The reproaches that Suetonius spreads correspond exactly to the stereotypical picture of the *vir mollis*: Caesar not only lets himself be penetrated passively, he also has overactive *libido*, which manifests in the numerous rumors about affairs with Roman matrons. Suetonius cites his sources of information here, too; unsurprisingly, it is the same people who had attacked Caesar because of Nicomedes.[27] Suetonius concludes the report with the statement, "So that no one should have any doubt that he had an evil reputation both for his *pudicitia* and for adultery, the elder Curio in one of his speeches calls him 'every woman's man and every man's woman.'"[28]

This quotation from a speech of the senator Curio shows us what Suetonius's real concern was: he does not intend to depict Caesar's sex life, but rather show what Caesar's reputation was. The invectives of Caesar's enemies, whose tendentious attitude Suetonius makes no effort to disguise, offer him an ideal source of information. His description of Caesar's marital sexuality remains utterly untouched by these allegations: Suetonius discusses Caesar's marriages in an entirely different context—namely, under the heading of his protagonist's career. Caesar's various marriages bring him money, friends, and a daughter, whom he uses to forge further marriage alliances.[29] These connections had nothing to do with the allegedly overactive *libido* of the dictator.

The *Life of Augustus* presents a similar picture. The future Augustus, according to Suetonius, had acquired a bad reputation already in his earliest youth.[30] The evidence of his *infamia* derives from Augustus's rivals during the civil war: Sextus Pompeius and Mark Antony. The latter alleged the entire stereotypical repertoire against Augustus: he supposedly prostituted himself to several persons, by means of which he even purchased his adoption by Caesar; he had his body hair removed with red-hot nutshells;[31] and he committed adultery with several women.[32] The opposition has its say as well: Augustus's friends argued that he committed adultery *non libidine, sed ratione*, not out of lust, but rather out of calculation, so as to learn something about his enemies' plans.[33] Even Suetonius thought this justification rather strange, and one might wonder just who the friends in question here actually were. It is nonetheless clear why Suetonius could see some justification in the claim: adultery is not denied as such, but the image of the lust-driven *vir mollis* is inverted by the suggestion that rational calculation was behind these sexual escapades, thus disarming the allegations at least in part.

It has long been recognized that such reports derive from campaigns of character assassination. Earlier research even described them as "propaganda" that Suetonius supposedly swallowed whole.[34] Yet a closer look at Suetonius's text shows us that the concept of "propaganda", which was coined for the comprehensive indoctrination of the public through modern mass media, is out of place here.[35] Suetonius makes no attempt to hide the polemical bias of his sources. He does not cite these texts because he believes them to be accurate per se, but rather because their mere existence serves as proof of the existence of *infamia*. This might seem trivial at first glance, but I consider it central: Suetonius's use of such sources permits us to assess to a certain extent how effective the Romans considered such invectives. In several passages, Cicero refers to the topical character of sexual allegations that seem scarcely believable on their own merits.[36] In order to be truly effective, an orator has to seize upon existing rumors of *infamia* and, building on them, attach all the remaining characteristics of the stereotypical *vir mollis*.[37] Whether modern propaganda in practice functions much differently is neither here nor there; what matters is that it presupposes a different conception of the power of media. The concept of propaganda assumes very powerful media that are able to influence the masses directly;[38] the Romans, however, appear to have regarded invective as a fairly weak form of media. Accordingly, Suetonius sees invectives such as that of the elder Curio not as the cause of a bad reputation, but primarily as a reflection of preexisting *fama* that otherwise has a life of its own.[39] It is the *fama* of his protagonists, carried along by its own momentum, in which Suetonius is interested; the putative "propaganda" of enemies serves as his evidence for the existence of this *fama*.

The peculiar momentum of *fama* is palpable in our sources. There is extensive evidence that the general public was actively interested in the reputation of prominent individuals and was absolutely capable of engaging in collective character assassination.[40] Caesar, for instance, is not only attacked by individual opponents, but even his own soldiers sang satirical songs about the sexual indiscretions of their general;[41] and the young Augustus was reproached as a *cinaedus* not only by Mark Antony, but also by the audience of a theater in Rome.[42] Such scenes illustrate not only simply that the sexual mores of Roman aristocrats were the object of political smear campaigns, but also that the general public took lively interest in such questions. That did not change even when Augustus no longer had any serious rivals after victory in the civil war. Suetonius obviously could no longer cite the invectives of political enemies for any of the following emperors; instead, he relies directly on anonymous rumors and insinuations, which now serve as his sources for the *infamia* of individual emperors.[43] This means, of course, that we encounter these rumors virtually as "raw material," and they no longer coalesce in stereotypical character portraits. At the same time, the new structures of the principate inspire new kinds of rumors. As a result, the sexual misconduct of later emperors appears far less stereotypical: while Caesar and Augustus exhibit all the traits of *molles viri*, from extravagant personal hygiene to active and passive sexual practices, reproaches against the later emperors often appear in isolation, which can give the false impression that Suetonius is actually trying to sketch individual sexual profiles.[44] Closer inspection reveals that even these apparently more personal reports are derived from the same paradigms as seemingly topical invectives.

Sexuality and Rumors in the Early Principate

This begins already with Augustus: after Suetonius has explained the *infamia* that the young Augustus had with respect to his *pudicitia*, he affirms that Augustus was able to refute this reputation by his chaste lifestyle. It is tempting to believe that, with the death of Mark Antony, merely the last rival perished who could keep this reputation alive, but that is too simple. Augustus was able to shrug off only the *infamia impudicitiae*; he could not leave behind the *libidines*. As evidence, Suetonius cites the strange story according to which Livia procured virgins for the aging Augustus to deflower.[45] The story is unparalleled, but it contains several disparaging barbs at once: Augustus is depicted as a lecherous old man who violates the *pudicitia* of young women, while Livia appears as his procuress. We can only speculate about the origin of this story. Certain structural elements, however, were present that favored such rumors: the increasing importance of the imperial house, which swiftly transformed into the real center of power and was inscrutable to outsiders, was the perfect breeding ground for all kinds of rumors. The fact that Augustus had transferred the cult of Vesta, which was tended by virgins, from the Forum to his private house might also potentially be the origin of the insinuations preserved by Suetonius, particularly since the cult was in the hands of the alleged procuress Livia.[46]

The lack of transparency in the imperial house presented other occasions for rumors that were well suited to compromise the reputation of the *princeps*. When Domitian brought the daughter of his deceased brother to the palace— nothing unusual per se—a sexual background was speculated. And when the young lady died, the reason was soon found: Domitian forced her to have an abortion so that their incest[47] would not be made public.[48] The fact that Domitian was overthrown certainly helped this rumor spread,[49] but the precondition for its publicity was the fact that it did not seem implausible per se to contemporaries: people apparently assumed that all kinds of things might have happened within the hidden confines of the imperial palace. Thus it did not seem at all absurd to Suetonius that Caligula had transformed his palace into a brothel and forced noble women and boys to prostitute themselves there, even if the parallel tradition in Cassius Dio implies that the victims were merely noble hostages.[50] The emperors themselves, of course, were not entirely blameless for the popularity of such rumors. Sexual misconduct was a reason often cited in order to remove troublesome women (and occasionally also men) from the center of power.[51] For the opinion that the imperial palace was the scene of obscure sexual intrigues, this only threw oil on the fire, and virtually from an official source.

The correlation of the lack of transparency at court and sexual insinuations is particularly clear in the case of Tiberius. In the second half of his reign, Tiberius retreated to Capri and lived there in relative isolation.[52] The ancient sources outdo themselves with wild speculation about imperial orgies.[53] Tiberius brought hordes of girls and male prostitutes,[54] according to Suetonius, to the island as his sexual playthings and invented entirely new sexual practices: so-called *spintriae*, a term that perhaps derived from the name of the anal sphincter and apparently denoted the "novel" sexual practices as well as the catamites who performed them.[55] The historian Tacitus knows of similar orgies, although he explicitly writes about freeborn boys; he explains that Tiberius was aroused especially by boys who possessed a long series of ancestor masks, in other words, who descended from the old republican nobility.[56] This reveals that the *spintriae* were not sex slaves but rather children and young men from senatorial families. This is confirmed by a remark of Suetonius about the later emperor Vitellius, who allegedly was one of Tiberius's catamites on Capri in his youth, which earned him the nickname "Spinter." His physical beauty supposedly helped advance his father's career in Rome.[57]

Thus in contrast to what Suetonius's report implies, the *spintriae* were not just any ordinary sex slaves, but rather the children of eminent senators. Their time on Capri moreover hardly served the *libido* of the emperor, but rather served pragmatic political purposes: on the one hand, it may well have been an honor if one's children were raised at the imperial court; on the other, as de facto hostages the children guaranteed the good behavior of their parents.[58] This situation apparently encouraged wild rumors to spread. It is not entirely clear, however, exactly whose reputation is damaged here. Tiberius of course is depicted as a tyrant who damages the *pudicitia* of others, but the story could also harm others: the prominence of the later emperor Vitellius might have inspired enemies to dredge up rumors about his youth as Tiberius's "Spinter," or it was possible to discredit his father by attributing his meteoric career to the prostitution of his son. A report in the *Life of Caligula* is interesting in this context: among the few good deeds of this emperor, Suetonius records Caligula's intention to throw Tiberius's *spintriae* into the sea; he relented only after desperate pleading and merely banished them from Rome.[59] If we follow the interpretation illustrated above, the "moral" action of Caligula appears in a very different light: Caligula accordingly seized on evil rumors probably circulating among the people as grounds for publicly inflicting *infamia* on his predecessor's noble hostages and let himself be supplicated by the aristocracy not to drown the alleged catamites in the sea. This would fit the later reign of this emperor, which was marked by harsh opposition to the Senate, perfectly.[60] It also shows how disparaging rumors could be instrumentalized by different persons for very different purposes.

The court was not only nontransparent; it also increasingly became a significant center of power. The new conditions of a de facto autocracy made imperial favor a much sought after commodity. Members of the imperial *domus*—freedmen, women, or lovers—could thus become the holders of significant political power for the simple reason that they had access to the emperor.[61] That irritated senators, since it meant that they had to cultivate persons who held a much lower social status than themselves. This balance of power simultaneously fed speculation about relationships between sex and power. That the career of Vitellius's father supposedly advanced because he let his son be sexually abused by Tiberius on Capri is just one example, like the allegation already mentioned that Augustus bought his adoption from Caesar by prostituting himself to him. Neither claim can be proven, but both make use of the allegation of lack of self-control prevalent in the invectives: it is in the nature of this reasoning to represent the political decisions of an unpopular ruler as dictated by his passions and simultaneously incriminate powerful persons around him of obtaining their prominence through sexual favors.

Powerful or particularly honored persons are thus often perceived as standing in a sexual relationship with the emperor:[62] the fact that Caligula showered prominence and honor on his sisters to an unusual extent (e.g., on coins) is well attested. The sources accordingly are quick to offer stories of an alleged incestuous relationship.[63] Under Vitellius, according to Suetonius, the freedman Asiaticus was particularly influential. Here too the reason is clear: Vitellius had been tied to this man by *mutua libido* (reciprocal lust) since his youth.[64] Likewise, Vitellius's predecessor Otho had been a close confidant of

Nero because, Suetonius reports, they had been bound to one another by a *consuetudo mutui stupri*—the habit of mutual sodomy.[65]

There are many examples of persons who allegedly secure their power with sexual relationships.[66] Characteristic of such allegations is that the sources are often divided with respect to the motivations of the individuals. The negative thrust of such stories accordingly shifts. The sources are unanimous, for example, that the praetorian prefect Macro supported Caligula's accession only because his wife was having an affair with him, but there is no consensus as to who in this ménage à trois was the driving force and who had the disreputable motives.[67] Different versions of the alleged sexual relationship between Agrippina and her son Nero also exist. Some claim that Nero—here quite the dissolute tyrant—was sexually attracted to his mother; others claim that Agrippina took the initiative in order to shore up her waning influence over her son.[68] Suetonius's version combines both: Nero was attracted to his mother, but he was dissuaded from incest because Agrippina's enemies pointed out that she would obtain too much power through this "token of favor" (*gratia*).[69] The story and its variations show two things: on the one hand, it was perfectly natural to explain power with sexual relationships; on the other, we again see that the same rumor could serve to discredit different persons—now Nero, now Agrippina, now both—according to received conceptual categories.

Yet not everything was insinuation and fiction: the concubines of the emperors, such as the freedwoman Acte under Nero, could achieve at least considerable wealth, which epigraphic sources also attest.[70] And some rumors were kindled by truly extravagantly staged imperial *libidines*. Relatively well attested is Nero's conduct with the freedman Sporus, whom he had castrated and married in a large ceremony during his tour of Greece.[71] It is explicitly stated that Nero wanted to make Sporus into an artificial woman and treated him like an empress.[72] That sounds more shocking than it really was: boy catamites were a widespread luxury good, and no one doubted that Nero was the active, penetrating partner. Despite the staged "wedding," Nero moreover maintained a marriage with an aristocratic Roman woman so that he did not violate social conventions in this respect either. In principle, Sporus seems to suit Nero's extravagant exhibition of luxury very well: writing about his Golden House (*domus aurea*), Tacitus says Nero had sought out architects who could create with art (*ars*) what nature (*natura*) could not accomplish.[73] Sporus, who was supposed to be transformed by art from a boy into a woman, appears to be an analogous case.[74] That the story must have some basis in fact is suggested by Sporus's later fate: he is not only Nero's sex object, but also one of his last companions at the hour of his death.[75] After Nero's demise, Sporus reappears in the company of the praetorian prefect Nymphidius Sabinus, who aspired to occupy the imperial throne;[76] then Otho, who likewise reigned briefly as emperor, took him in.[77] This pattern suggests that possession of Nero's artificial empress helped pretenders to underline their claim to the purple. This interpretation is supported not least by Otho's successor Vitellius, who did not regard Sporus as "empress" but intended to parade him before the people in a public spectacle (and thus demonstrate his control over him)—a demonstrative act of humiliation, which Sporus escaped by suicide.[78]

The reports about Nero's marriage to Sporus thus appear to have had a real basis, but they were not objectionable in Roman eyes per se. The same cannot be said of reports that Nero married a freedman named Pythagoras and consorted with him as a woman. This story is far less well attested. Only Tacitus and Cassius Dio know of Pythagoras.[79] Suetonius, in contrast, relates a story that largely corresponds to the episode recorded by Dio, but here Nero is married to a freedman named Doryphorus.[80] Tacitus and Cassius Dio know of such a freedman, not as Nero's husband, but rather as the powerful secretary *a libellis*, who fell victim to a plot in 62 and thus was already dead at the date of Nero's marriage to Sporus.[81] That Suetonius (in contrast to Dio and Tacitus) places Doryphorus in a sexual relationship with Nero is not surprising: it fits the pattern described above according to which imperial favor is frequently explained with sexual motives. It moreover requires little imagination to read an obscene phallic meaning in the Greek name Doryphorus ("spear bearer"). The fact that Doryphorus and Pythagoras appear interchangeable in analogous anecdotes undermines the credibility of the tradition. We should rather suppose that the spectacular, but not per se objectionable, marriage to Sporus inspired the construction of a disparaging equivalent, in which Nero had to be wed as a woman to a man—no matter who.

The extravagant marriage to Sporus, combined with the obscure configuration of power within the imperial *domus*, gave rise to rumors that take a far less obviously stereotypical form than the republican invectives but remain beholden to precisely the same patterns of thought in their disparaging purpose.

Protagonists, Rumors, and Character Assassination: Spread and Documentation of *infamia*

It is naturally difficult to infer character assassination from rumors. Rumors might permanently damage a person's reputation, but they have a momentum of their own that can scarcely be directed by individual players. It is no coincidence, though, that Suetonius records many such rumors about the sexual escapades of Roman emperors. The Roman aristocracy, of which Suetonius was a member, had a lively interest in drumming up such rumors. We hear of anonymous pamphlets and satires that circulated in senatorial circles and whose authors we should probably suspect were also members of the aristocracy.[82] In contrast to the republican period, it was not possible for an aristocrat to engage in open confrontation with the *princeps*, hurl insults directly to his face, and thus ridicule him in the presence of the public.[83]

Yet, in some cases, concrete individuals can be identified who attack a *princeps* in their own name. In the *Life of Caligula*, Suetonius mentions an aristocrat named Valerius Catullus who boasted that he had disgraced Caligula so often that his whole body grew faint.[84] That Caligula was still alive at this date is unlikely. We should rather suppose that a young noble was attempting to put his closeness to an overthrown emperor "in the right light." We meet another aristocrat in the *Life of Domitian*: a man of praetorian rank, by the name of Clodius Pollio, serves as evidence for Domitian's wild youth; he allegedly possessed and would display a letter from Domitian in which the latter promised him a night of pleasure.[85] The story can be assigned a specific date, since Pollio was a prominent figure at Nero's court: it thus falls into the Year of the Four Emperors, or the early Flavian period, a time marked by the latent tension between the two brothers Titus and Domitian.[86] The putative letter would fit this situation well; Pollio would thus be an adherent of Titus, attempting to damage Domitian's reputation with his slanders. Both cases follow an analogous pattern: both Pollio and Catullus appear to pursue political goals by means of character assassination, either against a toppled *princeps* or against the rival of an aspirant to the succession. Both, moreover, exploit their proximity to the target to describe themselves as "witnesses" of the alleged outrages, yet both significantly appear in the active, penetrating role. It would have fit the topos of the tyrant better if they had stylized themselves as victims of a tyrant's sexual aggression, but that was impossible without giving themselves the reputation of being *impudicus*.[87]

Aristocrats who took political action against potential claimants of the throne or toppled emperors are one source that probably contributed actively to rumors of imperial *infamia*; a further source is the allegations of the condemned, who had nothing left to lose. One famous case is Petronius: forced by Nero to commit suicide, he listed the sexual indiscretions of the emperor in his will in minute detail.[88] We are completely in the dark, of course, about whether such accusations had any greater effect beyond situational defamation. In this connection, the story of a matron named Mallonia, who was accused under Tiberius, is interesting. Before she took her own life, she reproached the emperor with his *obscenitas oris*.[89] That means she accused him of being a *cunnilingus*, the worst sexual insult that could be made to a man.[90] This case illustrates with some probability the effect that such accusations could have. Suetonius records that the crowd at the next Atellan farce wildly applauded at a dirty joke, the verse "The old goat licks the nanny goats' privates," thus attributing it to Tiberius.[91] We do not know whether Mallonia's allegation exploited existing rumors; but after the episode in the theater, a damaging rumor with wide effect had certainly grown out of the crude insinuation.

There were also different aristocratic persons who actively worked to bring rumors about the sexual misdeeds of the emperors into circulation and fan the flames of others. The uncommon situations in which a usurper challenged the emperor and the rivals attacked one another also functioned as rumor mills.[92] There also were abundant historians who willingly recorded and elaborated reports of the *infamia* of individual emperors for posterity.[93] That people gossip about their rulers is probably a universal phenomenon. What is special about the Roman case is the willingness of the elite to take up malicious gossip (mostly ignoring positive traditions)[94] and thus make it part of the history to be remembered. Even contemporaries were struck by the profound hatred of senatorial historiography for dead emperors. Thus Tacitus laments that the deeds of the emperors were falsified out of fear during in their lifetime and recorded with fresh hatred after their death.[95] His own portrait of Tiberius is obviously not exactly a model of impartial reporting, but such impartiality was probably no longer possible for a Roman aristocrat. The hatred of imperial historians noted by Tacitus did not consist in subjective antipathy but, rather, was to some extent a product of the system: since the principate was not openly a monarchy but pretended to continue the old Republic, the *princeps* was a constantly disruptive presence within this construct. The senators were nominally the masters of the world, and yet they had to court the favor of the *princeps* and his familiars in a way often felt to be humiliating. This almost inevitably led to discontent, particularly since very few emperors were up to the communicative challenges of their role. The sources reflect this malcontent. Yet aristocratic authors significantly did not call the system as such into question but, rather, personified the dysfunctional aspects caused by the system and interpreted these as character flaws of the individual emperors.[96]

Even the emperors themselves thought in terms of the old *res publica*, which made it easier for them to see, if not themselves, then probably their predecessors, as illegitimate tyrants in an egalitarian political order: to call to mind the *res publica* and label one's—ideally, overthrown—predecessor as a tyrant was not an uncommon procedure, to which senatorial authors were all too enthusiastically attached. It is hardly surprising that one would pass on rumors and elaborate them further, representing past emperors as tyrants who spared neither their own *pudicitia* nor that of others and whose political actions were driven by *libido*. Suetonius himself is part of this tradition: as he takes interest in the *fama* of his protagonists and spreads rumors, he simultaneously ensures that the usually damaging *fama* of the Caesars is passed down.

Conclusion: Suetonius, *Fama*, and Reality

It has been shown that the reports about the sexual escapades of the Caesars, preserved by Suetonius, have more to do with character assassination than with genuine sex lives. The concept of an individual sexual profile, such as one might expect in a modern biography, seems alien to Suetonius. Instead, he is interested in the *fama* of each emperor. In light of the importance attached to morality in Rome, this is hardly surprising. Most of the rumors preserved by Suetonius are harmful to the emperors' reputation, and the biographer makes some direct use of invectives or pamphlets: his reports about the sex lives of the emperors are in fact examples of character assassination. Yet Suetonius seems to be quite aware that a person's reputation need not always correspond to reality; in different passages he steps out of the role of "rumor collector" and states authoritatively how things really were.[97] Titus, for example, the ideal emperor himself, had a bad reputation before his accession but was able to turn it around for the better. That implies in turn that Titus himself was not bad, only his *fama* was.[98] The way in which Suetonius arrives at his conclusions, though, hardly inspires confidence: Suetonius "debunks" as rumor an alleged affair between Titus and his sister-in-law Domitia with the statement that Domitia disputed it but was such a debauched person that she would have boasted of the affair, if it had been real.[99]

Suetonius's somewhat helpless negotiation of the discrepancy between *fama* and reality shows that it was generally known in Rome that sexual misconduct could be the object of character assassination, yet no one apparently was capable of filtering the real core out of the mass of rumors and insinuations. Suetonius's authorial statements about how it really was seem to be guided largely by a preconceived opinion of the character of individuals. If his opinion, as with Titus, does not match a man's *fama*, then the latter must be malicious gossip; but on the other hand, Suetonius is prepared to believe even the most outrageous rumors about a tyrant such as Nero. Suetonius may also report rumors that he himself—as in the case of Titus—considers false. His interest here, though, is precisely not in reality but in the man's reputation as such. The question of how it really was is only important insofar as it shows whether the reputation was justified or not.[100] That might amaze the modern observer, but it shows that a person's reputation may ultimately be more important than what that person really did or did not do.

The Roman concept of *fama* is ambiguous. It can mean both "reputation" and "rumor." As Suetonius intends to document the reputation of his subjects, he simultaneously reports rumors that created that reputation in the first place. Seen in this light, Suetonius's *Lives* themselves are an example of character assassination: scarcely any other text has so profoundly reinforced the negative image of the early Roman emperors in European history than his reports about the supposed sex lives of the first twelve Caesars.

Notes

1. I am much indebted to John N. Dillon for providing the English translation.
2. Suetonius, *Augustus* 71.1; *Tiberius* 43–45; *Caligula* 24, 36.
3. Cf. Blanshard 2010, esp. 65–79.
4. In 1997 Alexander Demandt (1997, 12–21) still deemed it necessary to justify why the "private life" of the emperors is not per se a "frivolous subject" (*ein unseriöses Thema*).
5. Cf. for example Funaioli 1932. Meyer-Zwiffelhoffer (1995, 9–18) provides a good overview of the scholarship on Roman sexual practices prior to the 1990s.
6. The fundamental study is Wallace-Hadrill 1995; cf. Bradley 1991; Alföldy 1981.
7. Cf. Meyer-Zwiffelhoffer 1995; Hallet and Skinner 1997; Skinner 2005; Langlands 2006; Williams 2010. For Roman morals (not only concerning sexuality), see the fundamental study by Edwards 1993.
8. This was the common view well into the 1980s. Thus Baldwin (1983, 501–507) saw that Suetonius's focus on sexuality was unusual for an ancient biographer ("Outside of poetry, a man's sexual habits usually appear in Roman literature only

as the target for rhetorical or moralising obtrectation" [501]) but did not draw the obvious conclusion, that there is an interrelation between biography and invective (in this sense however, see Krenkel 1980) and instead stated that (501) "Suetonius is in obvious harmony with the biographical criteria of our own times. Whether that be compliment or insult is for the reader to say."

9. For Suetonius's life and work in the context of the second-century elite, see Wallace-Hadrill 1995, esp. 1–96.

10. Cf. Flach 1972.

11. Cf. Langlands 2006; Meyer-Zwiffelhoffer 1995, 197–210.

12. *Fama* and *infamia* are mentioned in connection with sexual practices in Suetonius, *Julius Caesar* 49–52; *Augustus* 68–71; *Tiberius* 44 (cf. 67.2); *Nero* 28.2 (here, however, in the sense of a specific "rumor"); *Titus* 7.1; *Domitian* 1.1, 22. In the other lives, too, Suetonius seldom poses as omniscient narrator, but rather tells what people say.

13. Steidle 1951, 58–60.

14. For the significance of *infamia*, see Richlin 1993, 555–61; for the term's legal connotations, see Greenidge 1894.

15. *Rhetorica ad Herennium* 4.52: *Suae pudicitiae proditor est, insidiator alienae.*

16. Cf. Williams 2010, 103–36.

17. The exact legal differentiation between adultery (*adulterium*) and *stuprum* is unclear; I follow the interpretation of Williams (2010, 130–36), who does not see a clear distinction between the two (at least not before the third or fourth century AD). Richlin (1993, 569–71), on the other hand, argues that the obscure *lex Scantinia* might be seen as a law banning homosexual relations between men and that *stuprum* is the term used to describe those relations—the source material, however, is too scarce to support such a narrow interpretation of *stuprum*.

18. Quintilian, *Declamationes minores* 301.

19. Meyer-Zwiffelhoffer 1995, 212ff.

20. Pseudo-Acro, *Sermones* 1.2.31f.

21. Female sexuality is a somewhat different case because the ideal of the inviolate body cannot be applied here. Matrimony, of course, did not in the least endanger a respectable woman's *pudicitia*, nor did frequent divorces and remarriages, which were a common practice among the elite (though there was the ideal of the *univira*, the woman who married only once in her life). Not unlike the masculine ideal of "ascetic behavior," women too were expected not to show too keen an appetite for intercourse (not even within matrimony), their main purpose being to beget legal children, not to experience sexual pleasure. Extramarital affairs, which were the result of passion, therefore made a woman lose her *pudicitia*. The notion of *pudicitia* thus depended more on a woman's inner bearing than on her inviolate body, as becomes clear when we consider the conceptualization of rape: the legendary rape victim Lucretia could actually become an ideal *exemplum* of Roman *pudicitia*. For a detailed discussion on the concept of *pudicitia* as a key to the conception of female sexuality, see Langlands 2006.

22. For the topos of *mollitia*, see Edwards 1993, 63–97; Meyer-Zwiffelhoffer 1995, 88–95, 134–53; Corbeill 1996, 128–73; Williams 2010, 137–76; for the ambiguity of the rhetorical figure of the *vir mollis*, see Meister 2009 and Meister 2012, 51–94.

23. Aulus Gellius 6.12.5 (*Oratorum Romanorum Fragmenta*[4], 127).

24. Suetonius, *Julius Caesar* 49.1: *Pudicitiae eius famam nihil quidem praeter Nicomedis contubernium laesit.*

25. For the historical background of the episode, see Osgood 2008.
26. Suetonius, *Julius Caesar* 49.1–2.
27. Suetonius, *Julius Caesar* 52.
28. Suetonius, *Julius Caesar* 52.3 (my translation): *at ne cui dubium omnino sit et impudicitiae et adulteriorum flagrasse infamia, Curio pater quadam eum oratione omnium mulierum virum et omnium virorum mulierem appellat.*
29. Cf. Suetonius, *Julius Caesar* 1.1, 6.2, 21—*fama* plays an important role here too (e.g., Caesar divorced Pompeia because a supposed affair with Clodius damaged her *fama*).
30. Suetonius, *Augustus* 68.
31. Suetonius, *Augustus* 68.
32. Suetonius, *Augustus* 69.
33. Suetonius, *Augustus* 69. The strategy is rather unusual. Thus Nicolaus of Damascus (V [12]) simply denies there being any truth in the rumors of Octavian's affairs; cf. Cicero, *Philippicae* 3.15. As J. N. Dillon pointed out to me, this unusual explanation does, however, hold some potential for placing the disgrace of adultery on Octavian's enemies: if he is learning of their plans by sleeping with their wives, they are not only weak opponents, but are not even real men who can control their wives.
34. For the belief this character assassination found in the sources, see Charlesworth 1933, esp. 177. See further Scott 1933 and more recently Pina Polo 2010, 87–90.
35. The problems of applying the modern term *propaganda* to ancient history are discussed by Weber and Zimmermann (2003) and, in that volume, especially by Eich (2003); for the modern concept of propaganda, see Bussemer 2008.
36. Cicero, *Pro Caelio* 6 and Cicero, *Pro Murena* 13 both defend a client by arguing that such accusations are common rhetorical stereotypes carrying little or no credibility; cf. Craig 2004; Meyer-Zwiffelhoffer 1995, 184–97.
37. The fundamental treatment is by Meyer-Zwiffelhoffer (1995, 184–97), who shows how invectives aim at linking an adversary's *fama* to well-known rhetorical stock figures (such as the adulterer, the *vir mollis*, or the *meretrix*).
38. This common view of "propaganda," dating back to the nineteenth century (and no longer used by up-to-date communication sciences), is discussed by Bussemer (2008, 63–250), who also discusses the "paradigms" of propaganda research closely linked to the supposed power of media (*Medienwirkung*) (51–62).
39. Vergil, *Aeneis* 4.173–94 is the *locus classicus* for the image of *fama* as a sinister creature with a life of its own.
40. Rumors in the city of Rome are discussed by Flaig (2003, esp. 358–63), who focuses on the collective character of the phenomenon that is beyond individual control. Further studies include Laurence 1994 and Pina Polo 2010, both of which, however, tend to overestimate the possibility of controlling and steering rumors, thus not giving sufficient credit to the collective dynamic of the phenomenon. Modern approaches to rumors are discussed by Kapferer (1995) and (in a critical fashion) by Froissart (2002).
41. Suetonius, *Julius Caesar* 49.4, 51; cf. Cassius Dio 43.20.
42. Suetonius, *Augustus* 68.
43. I take Suetonius to be an antiquarian who did not just "make up" the rumors he wrote about, although he certainly had no scruples using dubious sources and rearranging the material he found in ways that made sense to him in his own time. Kim On Chong-Gossard (2010), on the other hand, focuses primarily on Suetonius as an author of the second century AD and underestimates, in my

opinion, the antiquarian's dependence on his sources—sources that allow us, at least to a certain extent, to see how the Roman emperors' "sex lives" were a public issue in the first century AD.

44. The stereotype of the *vir mollis* would imply that the *mollitia* is visible in the "soft man's" body: Thus, Caesar's personal appearance is in harmony with his alleged *mollitia* (*Julius Caesar* 45 mentioning extravagant clothing, depilation, and a general vanity on Caesar's part). Likewise, the young Augustus is said to perform depilation and to use gestures considered typical for *cinaedi* (*Augustus* 68). In the later lives, however, only Otho (*Otho* 12.1) is portrayed as a stereotypical *vir mollis* whose *mollitia* is visible in his body; moreover, Suetonius only mentions this because Otho does not act the part but prefers to die like a man—an unexpected behavior, noted also by Tacitus, *Historiae* 1.22.1, 2.11.3, and Plutarch, *Galba* 24. Only Juvenal 2.99–109 portrays Otho as a "real" *vir mollis*. In the other lives, sexual practices appear isolated without the usual stylization to match the stereotype. Thus, Tiberius is active and has oral sex performed on him but guards his own *pudicitia*; Caligula plays an active and a passive role; Claudius is libidinous but interested only in women; Nero spares neither his own *pudicitia* nor that of others; Galba prefers mature men; Vespasian has several concubines; Titus has a bad *fama* that improves rapidly after he becomes emperor, and Domitian is said to have relinquished his *pudicitia* in his youth. The discussion of Domitian's passions later in the biography only mentions his extreme devotion to *libidines*—the actual reproaches, apart from the alleged incest with his niece, are, however, rather harmless in Roman terms. Those seemingly individual sexual profiles of the early emperors are discussed in Richlin 1993, 531f.

45. Suetonius, *Augustus* 71.

46. The Vesta cult in the emperor's *domus* is mentioned in the *fasti Caeretani* (*Corpus Inscriptionum Latinarum* I^2, 213) and the *fasti Praenestini* (*Corpus Inscriptionum Latinarum* I^2, 236); Cassius Dio 54.27.3 states that Augustus moved the official residence of the chief pontiff from the *regia* to his house on the Palatine; for a detailed discussion, see Koch 1958, 1757–59 and Kienast 1999, 236f, with an overview of recent scholarship. Whether Vesta had a temple on the Palatine is an issue of some discussion; the arguments against such a temple are presented by Fraschetti 1999. The relief base from Sorrento, perhaps depicting this temple, is discussed by Großmann 2008 (with further literature). For Livia's role in the cult, see Koch 1958, 1757. Aulus Gellius (1.12.11–17) describes the *captio* of vestal virgins performed by the chief pontiff (cf. Koch 1958, 1744–47), a ritual full of marriage metaphors; Augustus performing this ritual in his house, assisted by Livia, might have given rise to the story found in Suetonius.

47. The relationship between uncle and niece was generally considered to be incestuous and had long been illegal. In Domitian's time, however, the union would have been legally possible due to a law the emperor Claudius had enforced two generations earlier in order to marry his niece Agrippina (Suetonius, *Claudius* 26.3; Tacitus, *Annales* 12.5–7). The law still seems to have been in force in the second century (Gaius, *Institutiones* 1.62). However, neither were such unions common (Tacitus, *Annales* 12.7.2) nor were they considered morally unproblematic, as the slurs of Tacitus and Suetonius against Claudius's "incest" clearly show (Suetonius, *Claudius* 26.3; Tacitus, *Annales* 11.25.5, 12.8.1).

48. Suetonius, *Domitian* 22; cf. Plinius Minor, *Epistulae* 4.11.6; *Panegyricus* 63.7, 52.3; and Juvenal 2.29–33. Domitian's contemporary Martial (6.3) seems to know nothing of such accusations, unless he is to be seen as using irony or doublespeak

to secretly criticize the emperor (for this "art of safe criticism," see Ahl 1984; for a critical reassessment of humor in the political culture of imperial Rome, see now Meister 2014).

49. The postmortem character assassination of Domitian is discussed by Charles (2002) and Waters (1964).

50. Winterling 2011, 139–41; cf. Suetonius, *Caligula* 41; Cassius Dio 59.28.9. Tyrants forcing aristocratic women to prostitute themselves seems to be a topos: similar stories are told about Nero (cf. Tacitus, *Annales* 15.37.3; Cassius Dio 62.15.4–6; and, in a different context, Suetonius, *Nero* 27.3).

51. Examples in Suetonius include the two Julias banished under Augustus (*Augustus* 65), the sisters of Caligula (*Caligula* 24.3), Claudius's wife Messalina (*Claudius* 26.2), Nero's wife Octavia (*Nero* 35.2), and Domitian's wife Domitia, first banished because of an alleged affair with the actor Paris but then recalled due to the people's pleas (*Domitian* 3.1). Tacitus (*Annales* 5.3.2) states that Tiberius initiated the fall of his grandson Nero by accusing him of *impudicitia* in an official letter to the Senate. Furthermore, the moral legislation passed by several emperors (cf. Suetonius, *Augustus* 34.1; *Domitian* 8) kept reminding people that sexual morals were to be viewed as a public issue.

52. Absence from Rome generally leads to speculations about the absentee, who himself is unable to actively contradict those rumors; cf. Laurence 1994, 63f and Pina Polo 2010, 81, 90.

53. Suetonius, *Tiberius* 43–44; Tacitus, *Annales* 4.57, 6.1.

54. Suetonius speaks of *exoleti*—for the term, see Williams 2010, 9093.

55. Suetonius, *Tiberius* 43.1. Cf. Champlin 2011, with a thorough discussion and a new explanation of the term *spintriae*. A set of Julio-Claudian coins featuring obscene iconography is also known by the name *spintriae*; the name is, however, a modern appellation, and a connection between these coins and the rumors about Tiberius is (pace Buttrey 1973) highly unlikely.

56. Tacitus, *Annales* 6.1—according to Tacitus, the term *spintriae* was first applied in this context.

57. Suetonius, *Vitellius* 3.2. Cf. Murison (1987), who thinks this might be Flavian "propaganda."

58. A similar explanation is offered by Champlin 2011, 327–31.

59. Suetonius, *Caligula* 16.

60. Cf. Winterling 2011. The chronology causes some problems, for Suetonius seems to date the episode to the beginning of Caligula's reign; however, Suetonius's tendency to divide this emperor's reign into a "good" and a "bad" half and to assemble his deeds and misdeeds accordingly renders his supposed chronology highly suspect. Tiberius is treated in a similar fashion, and a comparison with Tacitus clearly shows the amount of chronological distortion thus caused (cf. Bringmann 1971 and Döpp 1972).

61. See Winterling 1999, esp. 161–94, for the imperial court and the significance of imperial favor, and Winterling 2001 (=Winterling 2009, 9–33), for the changes in society thus caused.

62. Cf. Kim On Chong-Gossard 2010.

63. Suetonius, *Caligula* 24, 36.1; Flavius Josephus, *Antiquitates Iudaicae* 19.204; Cassius Dio 59.3.6, 11.1, 22.6, 26.5. That Seneca fails to mention the incest is hardly a surprise: due to his close association with Caligula's sister Agrippina, such allegations would have been untactful.

64. Suetonius, *Vitellius* 12.

65. Suetonius, *Otho* 2.2.
66. Otho feigned to be in love with an old freedwoman of Nero in order to gain access to the emperor (Suetonius, *Otho* 2.2). The fact that Agrippina had the mighty freedman Pallas as an ally in Claudius's court probably led to the rumor of there being an affair between the two (Tacitus, *Annales* 14.2.2).
67 Philo, *Legatio ad Gaium* 39–40 (Marco's wife seduces Caligula and makes her unsuspecting husband support him); Suetonius, *Caligula* 12.2 (Caligula wants Marco's support and Marco's wife wants to become empress); Cassius Dio 58.28.4 (Marco makes his wife seduce Caligula in order to gain influence over him); Tacitus, *Annales* 4.45.3 (Marco makes his wife seduce Caligula; Caligula sees through the plan but plays along, seeing the arrangement as advantageous to himself because, according to Tacitus, he is even more deceitful than voluptuous). Cf. Winterling 2011, 48f.
68. Tacitus, *Annales* 14.2 relates the contrary opinions of the historians Cluvius (Agrippina takes the initiative) and Rusticus (Nero desires Agrippina); Tacitus himself believes Cluvius because his version is in accordance with the *fama*, and fits the character, of Agrippina. See also Cassius Dio 62.11.3–4.
69. Suetonius, *Nero* 28.2.
70. For Acte, see Stein 1899; see Mastino and Ruggeri 1995 for the epigraphic data.
71. Suetonius, *Nero* 28f; Cassius Dio 62.28, 63.12–13, 63.22.4; Dio Chrysostom 21.6–10; cf. Stein 1929. For recent scholarship see Champlin 2003, 145–50, who interprets the marriage to Sporus as spectacular performance, partly paying honor to the memory of the deceased Poppaea, partly as a theatrical joke—I largely agree with this, although the interpretation of Sporus as a "joke" cannot explain why the possession of Nero's artificial empress was an important feature for several of his would-be successors (see below). Recently a highly speculative (and rather absurd) theory has been proposed by Woods (2009), according to whom Nero had thought Sporus to be an illegitimate descendent of Tiberius and thus a potential rival, whom he neutralized by castrating and marrying him—Woods's (over)interpretation of the ancient sources, however, fails to convince.
72. Suetonius, *Nero* 28; Cassius Dio 63.12.3–13.2.
73. Tacitus, *Annales* 15.42.
74. Suetonius, *Nero* 28: *in muliebrem naturam transfigurare conatus*; Dio Chrysostom 21.7 knows of enormous sums Nero promised to the one who would be able to turn the boy into a woman.
75. Suetonius, *Nero* 48–49; Cassius Dio 63.27.3, 29.2.
76. Plutarch, *Galba* 9.3.
77. Cassius Dio 63(64).8.3.
78. Cassius Dio 64(65).10.1. The humiliating spectacle consisted in Sporus playing the role of Kore being raped by Hades. This is significant, for according to Suetonius (*Nero* 46.2), Sporus presented Nero with a ring depicting exactly this mythological scene shortly before the emperor's death. This recurring motive perhaps stems from an elaborate tale referring to the fate of the unlucky Sporus—Dio Chrysostom (21.9) seems to hint at something of that sort.
79. Tacitus, *Annales* 15.37.4; Cassius Dio 62.28.3, 63.13.2, 22.4. Champlin (2003, 165–71) sees these "marriages" mainly as theatrical performances, not all that unusual for the theater-emperor Nero; he tends, however, to take the sources at face value and does not view the offhand way in which Pythagoras can be replaced with Doryphorus as problematic.

80. Suetonius, *Nero* 29; cf. Cassius Dio 63.13.2: Both authors describe a bizarre scene, where Nero, dressed in an animal skin, "attacks" the genitals of his helpless victims. Suetonius adds that afterward Nero was himself "stabbed" by Doryphoros, while Dio speaks of Pythagoras.

81. Cassius Dio 61.5.4; Tacitus, *Annales* 14.65.

82. Suetonius, *Augustus* 55; *Nero* 39.

83. Pina Polo 2010, 77ff emphasizes the importance of public interaction and oratory in the formation of "public opinion" in Rome, and Corbeill 1996 shows how humor was used to ridicule and thus isolate one's adversary in front of a laughing public.

84. Suetonius, *Caligula* 36.1. This Catullus is most likely to be identified with Valerius Catullus pontifex, mentioned in *Corpus Inscriptionum Latinarum* XIV 2095; cf. Lunzer 1948 and Wiseman 2007, 59–64.

85. Suetonius, *Domitian* 1.1. The same passage also mentions the later emperor Nerva sodomizing the young Domitian; for a detailed discussion, see Charles 2006. The passage causes some problems because it might be seen to contain a slur against Nerva, founder of the dynasty still in power in Suetonius's own days. That need not be the case, however, for the story can be seen as an analogous case to Catullus raping Caligula, created after Domitian's murder and perhaps not so unfavorable to Nerva after all. Pollio is a different case, since he did not actually commit *stuprum* but just "documented" Domitian's willingness to sell his *pudicitia*. If Domitian was still alive at this time (but not yet emperor!), this line of action would make perfect sense, for it allows Pollio to slander Domitian without incriminating himself.

86. Pollio's prominent role at Nero's court is made clear by Suetonius, *Domitian* 1.1, mentioning a satirical poem on Pollio composed by the emperor himself. For the rivalry between Titus and Domitian, see Levick 1999, 188–92 and Plinius Minor, *Epistulae* 3.9. Character assassination against potential candidates to the throne probably was not untypical in cases of an unclear succession. Thus, under Tiberius we hear of a Sex. Vistilius, who, in the year 32, fell into disgrace for having composed a poem on Caligula's *impudicitia* (Tacitus, *Annales* 6.9.2).

87. Thus we lack "witnesses" testifying to having been passive victims of an emperor's sexual misconduct, even though that would have fit the topos of the aggressive tyrant penetrating the bodies of his subjects much better. But reports about tyrants sodomizing others are solely used to highlight the complete helplessness of the victim (e.g., Nero raping Britannicus before murdering him in Tacitus, *Annales* 13.17.2) or aim at defying everyone involved (e.g., the cases of Otho and Vitellius discussed above).

88. Tacitus, *Annales* 16.19.3.

89. Suetonius, *Tiberius* 45.

90. Cf. Williams, 2010, 218–24; for the hierarchy of sexual practices in general, see Meyer-Zwiffelhoffer 1995, 72–108, esp. 88–95.

91. Suetonius, *Tiberius* 4.

92. Thus Otho and Vitellius wrote letters in which they accused each other of having committed *stuprum* (Tacitus, *Historiae* 1.74.1), and Vindex held speeches attacking Nero because of his "marriages" to Sporus and Pythagoras (Cassius Dio 63.22). That these letters and speeches circulated in written form, as did invectives in republican times, is rather unlikely—Suetonius does not cite any written source, and the speech recorded by Dio is most likely a piece of rhetoric composed by the historian himself to fit the situation. The public, too, was different

from that of republican times: the prime addresses were either the rivals or the army, not the Roman *plebs*.

93. The change of medium is significant here: whereas "real" rumors circulated among the Roman *plebs* (cf. Flaig, 2003) and thus reflected some sort of "public opinion," aristocratic reports about rumors and *infamia* became a literary phenomenon circulating only within the writings of a small elite, which cannot be seen as representing the views of a broader public.

94. In a recent article, Edward Champlin argued that there seems to have been a popular tradition picturing Tiberius not as a "sex-monster," but as a "wise ruler"—a tradition completely ignored or distorted by senatorial sources; cf. Champlin 2008.

95. Tacitus, *Annales* 1.1.2: *Tiberii Gaique et Claudii ac Neronis res florentibus ipsis ob metum falsae, postquam occiderant recentibus odiis composita sunt.*

96. Cf. Fritz 1976.

97. Cf. Kim On Chong-Gossard 2010, 297f. These statements at times do show that sexual orientation, or even a sexual profile, was not completely alien to the ancient viewer (cf. Richlin 1993, 531ff); thus in three cases, sexual preferences of emperors are clearly described as individual traits: Suetonius, *Tiberius* 44.1–2 (Tiberius prefers oral sex), *Claudius* 33.2 (Claudius prefers women only), *Galba* 22 (Galba prefers grown-up men). The decisive point, however, is that individual sexual preferences, although not invisible to the ancients, do not constitute a discursive category in their own right.

98. Suetonius, *Titus* 7.1. Cf. *Titus* 1, where Suetonius writes of *vituperatio*, and 6.2, where he tries to offer a rational explanation for Titus's "cruelty" and speaks of an *adversus rumor*.

99. Suetonius, *Titus* 10.2.

100. Gascou (1984, 703–706) offers a discussion of Suetonius's treatment of rumors, remarking that the author's position remains obscure: he can refer to anonymous gossip in a distanced third-person mode and suddenly, at times even in the same sentence, switch into the role of an auctorial narrator presenting the same rumors as objective truth. Apparently, the truth behind rumors was not the main issue Suetonius was concerned with.

Bibliography

Ahl, F. 1984. "The Art of Safe Criticism in Greece and Rome." *American Journal of Philology* 105: 174–208.

Alföldy, G. 1980/81. Römisches Staats- und Gesellschaftsdenken bei Sueton. *Ancient Society* 11/12: 349–85.

Baldwin, B. 1983. *Suetonius*. Amsterdam: A. M. Hakkert.

Blanshard, A. J. L. 2010. *Sex: Vice and Love from Antiquity to Modernity*. Chichester, UK: Wiley-Blackwell.

Bradley, K. R. 1991. "The Imperial Ideal in Suetonius' 'Caesars.'" In *Aufstieg und Niedergang der römischen Welt* 2.33.5: 3701–32.

Bringmann, K. 1971. "Zur Tiberiusbiographie Suetons." *Rheinisches Museum* 114: 268–85.

Bussemer, T. 2008. *Propaganda. Konzepte und Theorien. Mit einem einführenden Vorwort von Peter Glotz*, 2nd ed. Wiesbaden: VS-Verlag.

Buttrey, T. V. 1973. "The *Spintriae* as a Historical Source." *The Numismatic Chronicle*, 7th Series 8: 52–63.

Champlin, E. 2003. *Nero*. Cambridge, MA: Belknap Press of Harvard University Press.

Champlin, E. 2008. "Tiberius the Wise." *Historia* 57: 408–25.

Champlin, E. 2011. "Sex on Capri." *Transactions of the American Philological Association* 141: 315–32.

Charles, M. 2002. "*Calvus Nero*: Domitian and the Mechanics of Predecessor Denigration." *Acta Classica* 45: 19–49.

Charles, M. 2006. "Domitianus 1.1: Nerva and Domitian." *Acta Classica* 49: 79–87.

Charlesworth, M. P. 1933. "Some Fragments of the Propaganda of Mark Antony." *Classical Quarterly* 27: 172–77.

Corbeill, A. 1996. *Controlling Laughter: Political Humor in the Late Roman Republic*. Princeton, NJ: Princeton University Press.

Craig, C. 2004. "Audience Expectations, Invective, and Proof." In J. Powell and J. Paterson, eds., *Cicero the Advocate*, 187–213. Oxford: Oxford University Press.

Demandt, A. 1997. *Das Privatleben der römischen Kaiser*, 2nd ed. Munich: C. H. Beck.

Döpp, S. 1972. "Zum Aufbau der Tiberiusvita Suetons." *Hermes* 100: 444–60.

Edwards, C. 1993. *The Politics of Immorality in Ancient Rome*. Cambridge: Cambridge University Press.

Eich, A. 2003. "Die Idealtypen 'Propaganda' und 'Repräsentation' als heuristisches Mittel bei der Bestimmung gesellschaftlicher Konvergenzen und Divergenzen von Moderne und römischer Kaiserzeit." In G. Weber and M. Zimmermann, eds., *Propaganda—Selbstdarstellung—Repräsentation im römischen Kaiserreich des 1. Jhs. n. Chr*, 41–84. Stuttgart: Franz Steiner Verlag.

Flach, D. 1972. "Zum Quellenwert der Kaiserbiographien Suetons." *Gymnasium* 79: 273–89.

Flaig, E. 2003. "Wie Kaiser Nero die Akzeptanz der Plebs urbana verlor. Eine Fallstudie zum politischen Gerücht im Prinzipat." *Historia* 52: 351–72.

Fraschetti, A. 1999. "Augusto e Vesta sul Palatino." *Archiv für Religionsgeschichte* 1: 174–83.

Fritz, K. von. 1957. "Tacitus, Agricola, Domitian, and the Problem of the Principate." In K. von Fritz, ed., 1976, *Schriften zur griechischen und römischen Verfassungsgeschichte und Verfassungstheorie*, 535–66. Berlin: De Gruyter.

Froissart, P. 2002. *La rumeur. Histoire et fantasmes*. Paris: Belin.

Funaioli, G. 1932. "C. Suetonius (4) Tranquillus." In *Paulys Realencyclopädie der classischen Altertumswissenschaften*, vol. 4A, 593–641.

Gascou, J. 1984. *Suétone historien*. Rome: École Française de Rome.

Greenidge, A. H. J. 1894. *Infamia: Its Place in Roman Public and Private Law*. Oxford: Clarendon Press.

Großmann, M. E. 2008. "Einige Überlegungen zur 'Basis von Sorrent.'" In G. Grabherr and B. Kainrath, eds., *Akten des 11. Österreichischen Archäologentages in Innsbruck 23.–25. März 2006*, 93–98. Innsbruck: Innsbruck University Press.

Hallet, J. P. and M. B. Skinner, eds. 1997. *Roman Sexualities*. Princeton, NJ: Princeton University Press.

Kapferer, J.-N. 1996. *Gerüchte. Das älteste Massenmedium der Welt*. Leipzig: Gustav Kiepenheuer Verlag.

Kienast, D. 1999. *Augustus. Prinzeps und Monarch*, 3rd ed. Darmstadt: Wissenschaftliche Buchgesellschaft.

Kim On Chong-Gossard, J. H. 2010. "Who Slept with Whom in the Roman Empire?" In A. J. Turner, J. H. Kim On Chong-Gossard, and F. J. Vervaet, eds., *Private and Public Lies: The Discourse of Despotism and Deceit in the Graeco-Roman World*, 295–327. Leiden, Netherlands: Brill.

Koch, C. 1958. "Vesta." In *Paulys Realencyclopädie der classischen Altertumswissenschaften*, vol. 8A, 1717–76.

Krenkel, W. A. 1980. "Sex und politische Biographie." *Wissenschaftliche Zeitschrift der Wilhelm-Pieck-Universität Rostock* 29: 65–76.

Langlands, R. 2006. *Sexual Morality in Ancient Rome.* Cambridge: Cambridge University Press.

Laurence, R. 1994. "Rumor and Communication in Roman Politics." *Greece & Rome* 41: 62–74.

Levick, B. 1999. *Vespasian.* London: Routledge.

Lunzer, D. von, 1948. "Valerius (120–122) Catullus." In *Paulys Realencyclopädie der classischen Altertumswissenschaften*, vol. 7A, 2352–53.

Mastino, A., and P. Ruggeri. 1995. "Claudia Augusti liberta Acte. La liberta amata da Nerone ad Olbia." *Latomus* 54: 513–44.

Meister, J. B. 2009. "Pisos Augenbrauen. Zur Lesbarkeit aristokratischer Körper in der späten römischen Republik." *Historia* 58: 71–95.

Meister, J. B. 2012. *Der Körper des Princeps. Zur Problematik eines monarchischen Körpers ohne Monarchie.* Stuttgart: Franz Steiner Verlag.

Meister, J. B. 2014. "Lachen und Politik. Zur Funktion von Humor in der politischen Kommunikation des römischen Principats." *Klio* 96: 26–48.

Meyer-Zwiffelhoffer, E. 1995. *Im Zeichen des Phallus. Die Ordnung des Geschlechtslebens im antiken Rom.* Frankfurt: Campus.

Murison, C. L. 1987. "Tiberius, Vitellius and the *spintriae.*" *The Ancient History Bulletin* 1: 97–99.

Osgood, J. W. 2008. "Caesar and Nicomedes." *Classical Quarterly* 58: 687–91.

Pina Polo, F. 2010. "*Frigidus rumor*: The Creation of a (Negative) Public Image in Rome." In A. J. Turner, J. H. Kim On Chong-Gossard, and F. J. Vervaet, eds., *Private and Public Lies: The Discourse of Despotism and Deceit in the Graeco-Roman World*, 75–90. Leiden, Netherlands: Brill.

Richlin, A. 1992/93. "Not before Homosexuality: The Materiality of the *cinaedus* and the Roman Law against Love between Men." *Journal of the History of Sexuality* 3: 523–73.

Scott, K. 1933. "The Political Propaganda of 44–30 B.C." *Memoirs of the American Academy in Rome* 9: 7–49.

Skinner, M. B. 2005. *Sexuality in Greek and Roman Culture.* Malden, MA: Blackwell.

Steidle, W. 1951. *Sueton und die Antike Biographie.* Munich: C. H. Beck.

Stein, A. 1899. "Claudia (392) Akte." In *Paulys Realencyclopädie der classischen Altertumswissenschaften*, vol. 3, 2888–89.

Stein, A. 1929. "Sporus." In *Paulys Realencyclopädie der classischen Altertumswissenschaften*, vol. 3A, 1886–88.

Wallace-Hadrill, A. 1995. *Suetonius*, 2nd ed. London: Bristol Classical Press.

Waters, K. H. 1964. "The Character of Domitian." *Phoenix* 18: 49–77.

Weber, G., and M. Zimmermann, eds. 2003. *Propaganda—Selbstdarstellung—Repräsentation im römischen Kaiserreich des 1. Jhs. n.Chr.* Stuttgart: Franz Steiner.

Williams, C. 2010. *Roman Homosexuality: Ideologies of Masculinity in Classical Antiquity*, 2nd ed. Oxford: Oxford University Press.

Winterling, A. 1999. *Aula Caesaris. Studien zur Institutionalisierung des römischen Kaiserhofes in der Zeit von Augustus bis Commodus (31 v. Chr.–192 n. Chr.).* Munich: Oldenburg Verlag.

Winterling, A. 2001. "'Staat', 'Gesellschaft' und politische Integration in der römischen Kaiserzeit." *Klio* 83: 93–112.

Winterling, A. 2009. *Politics and Society in Imperial Rome*. Malden, MA: Wiley-Blackwell.

Winterling, A. 2011. *Caligula: A Biography*. Berkeley: University of California Press.

Wiseman, T. P. 2007. "The Valerii Catulli of Verona." In M. B. Skinner, ed., *A Companion to Catullus*, 57–71. Malden, MA: Wiley-Blackwell.

Woods, D. 2009. "Nero and Sporus." *Latomus* 68: 73–82.

4

Creating Tyrants in Ancient Rome: Character Assassination and Imperial Investiture

Martijn Icks

Introduction[1]

Character assassination is not necessarily limited to the living. After all, someone's "character"—his or her good reputation—can endure long after the person in question has passed on. The Roman Empire offers many examples of posthumous character assassination. Since it was a risky business to antagonize living emperors, critics usually aimed their arrows at those rulers who were safely dead. Yet that did not make their attacks any less vicious—rather the opposite. The character assassinations of Caligula and Nero, in particular, have been so successful that both emperors are still household names in any list of "worst tyrants throughout the ages." Many of their colleagues did not fare much better. In this chapter, I will examine how and why Roman historians and biographers attacked the character of dead emperors in their works, presenting them to posterity as stereotypical tyrants. One event in an emperor's career lent itself particularly well to this purpose—namely, his investiture with imperial power at the hands of the army, the Senate, and the people of Rome.

An Unlikely Emperor

Before his rise to power, the Roman nobleman Tiberius Claudius Nero Germanicus had seemed an unlikely candidate for the imperial purple. Although he was a descendant of the empress Livia and an uncle of the emperor Caligula (AD 37–41), he commanded little respect. Claudius limped, drooled, and was widely considered to be half-witted. According to the biographer

Suetonius, he regularly fell asleep at the dinner table and was pelted with the stones of olives and dates by his fellow diners. Sometimes they put slippers on his hands as he lay snoring. In his younger years, his grandmother Livia found it beneath herself to talk to him, preferring to admonish him through short, sharp notes. Even his mother, Antonia, held him in contempt, calling him "a monster of a man, not finished but merely begun by Dame Nature." When she accused someone of dullness, she said that person was a bigger fool than her son Claudius—obviously a grave accusation.[2]

Nothing short of a "remarkable freak of fortune," it seems, could make Claudius the master of the Roman world. According to Suetonius, this was exactly what happened.[3] In the early afternoon of January 24, AD 41, a group of conspirators cut down the emperor Caligula when he left the theater. In the ensuing chaos, several other members of the imperial family were killed, while soldiers took the opportunity to loot the palace. Claudius, who was caught in the midst of all this blood and consternation, desperately tried to save his life by hiding behind a curtain. Suetonius describes what happened next:

> As he cowered there, a common soldier, who was prowling about at random, saw his feet and, intending to ask who he was, pulled him out and recognized him; and when Claudius fell at his feet in terror, he hailed him as emperor. Then he took him to the rest of his comrades, who were as yet in a condition of uncertainty and purposeless rage. These placed him in a litter, took turns in carrying it, since his own bearers had made off, and bore him to the Camp in a state of despair and terror, while the throng that met him pitied him, as an innocent man who was being hurried off to execution.[4]

Far from being executed, Claudius actually gained the support of the soldiers in the camp as well. Once he had them on his side, the Senate was forced to accept him as the new ruler. Rome's most famous fool became its emperor.

To what extent the account is reliable is up for debate, as is so often the case with Roman literary sources.[5] However, it is clear that Suetonius mocks the ludicrous way that Claudius supposedly gained the throne, using the moment of the latter's elevation as an opportunity for denigration.[6] Others had risen to power because of their personal achievements or because they had been appointed by previous rulers. Claudius, in contrast, stumbled across the principate purely by accident, as the unwitting tool of a riotous mob. Even while he ascended to the dignity of the highest office, he acted in an undignified manner, earning no respect, but only pity and ridicule.

Exemplary Discourses

Considering that he wrote his biography about seven decades after Claudius's death, Suetonius can hardly be accused of carrying a personal grudge against the emperor. Rather, he was adding to a hostile literary tradition that already existed.[7] Roman historians and biographers had a tendency to divide emperors into two categories: the good and the bad, with the latter encompassing the mad, the cruel, and the woefully incompetent. This was part of the exemplary discourse by which these authors linked actions, audiences, values, and memory. As the Romanist Matthew Roller has pointed out, the Romans considered it of vital importance to preserve the memory of the virtuous and, indeed, the wicked deeds of their ancestors, as they had been witnessed by both their countrymen and their enemies. These examples set the standard for admirable and despicable behavior and were supposed to inspire following generations to imitate, or avoid, certain actions. Naturally, the discourse was not static: value judgments differed from one interpreter to the next and could change over time, so that age-old *exempla* remained relevant for the social debates of later eras.[8]

From the moment that Octavian became the sole ruler of the Roman world in 31 BC, the emperor became the dominant figure in Roman historiography, eclipsing all others in importance. Inevitably, this turned him into the literary model of virtue or vice par excellence. The judges of his character and deeds were those who possessed the capabilities and leisure to write history—that is, the Greco-Roman elite: first and foremost, the senators. They determined if and how a ruler would be constructed as a "bad" emperor in Roman literature—posthumously, of course, because no one wanted to risk offending a living emperor.[9] However, the verdicts of these authors were not solely based on a ruler's actual character and deeds. Many external factors came into play, such as whether or not the emperor in question had ruled in living memory, which self-image he had broadcasted through coins and statues, which material monuments he had left behind, and last but not least, whether the Senate had deified him after his death or whether he had suffered *damnatio memoriae*, an official curse of his memory by senatorial decree.[10]

Despite these restrictions, Roman authors wielded considerable influence over an emperor's posthumous reputation, including the option of committing character assassination. In her book *The Art of Forgetting*, the historian Harriet Flower has coined the term "memory sanctions," which she defines as "deliberately designed strategies that aim to change the picture of the past, whether through erasure or redefinition, or by means of both."[11] For the Senate, *damnatio memoriae* was one of the prime instruments to achieve this, while historiography provided a useful tool for the development of individual initiatives. Since life expectancy and literacy were generally low, most Romans were doomed to oblivion after their death. "Memory space" was too small to preserve more than a tiny fraction of the past. For people of high status, being deprived of a place within Roman collective memory could be heavy punishment indeed. Even worse was being remembered as an unworthy individual. Flower remarks: "The deep-seated fear of the senators, that they would lose their status and their place in history, helped to make memory sanctions the ultimate tools of intimidation and of revenge in the Roman imperial period."[12]

To some extent, the same was true for emperors. Although they were unlikely to be completely forgotten anytime soon, they certainly ran the risk of being remembered for the wrong reasons—as a negative, rather than a positive, example.

Elevation and Denigration

Both in literature and in practice, an emperor's accession to the throne provided an important occasion for the assessment of his virtues and shortcomings. Evidently, imperial candidates used this event to present themselves as favorably as possible to their subjects. If all the relevant interest groups—the Senate, the soldiers, and the citizens of Rome—approved of their rise to power, their position was both legitimate and secure. In contrast, historians and biographers could use descriptions of imperial elevations to commit character assassination on emperors they disliked, as the case of poor Claudius amply demonstrates. By describing a ruler's conduct at his investiture in negative terms, authors signaled that an unworthy individual had risen to power and prepared their readers for what was to come—namely, a tyrannical, incompetent, and/or decadent reign.[13]

This chapter focuses on the investitures of two "bad" emperors: Otho (AD 69) and Didius Julianus (AD 193). Both seized power with the aid of the soldiers and only managed to stay on the throne for a few months. How did ancient authors turn the elevations of these men into exercises in denigration? Which traits and behavior of the new rulers did they target with their character attacks? What was the significance of the targeted behavior within the context of the ritual? And what does this ultimately tell us about Roman constructions of "bad" emperorship? Before we turn to these questions, though, a few words on imperial investiture are in order.

The Investiture Ritual(s)

Since the Roman Empire had evolved from the Roman Republic, the position of emperor as such was unconstitutional.[14] In practice, of course, emperors did reign, but the reality of monarchy was cloaked in a range of offices and mandates, all of which were bestowed on one man. Since the necessary titles could not simply be passed on from father to son, the principate could not be directly inherited from a predecessor. During the first centuries of imperial rule, a new emperor—who was usually either the (adopted) son of the previous emperor or the victor of a civil war—received his power through an acclamation by representatives of the Roman army, a vote by the Senate, and a *lex* (law) by the people's assembly.[15] If the investiture took place at Rome, the army as a whole was usually represented by the resident troops that guarded the emperor, the Praetorian Guard; if an emperor was elevated outside the capital, any legion could do the honors.

It is important to note that, strictly speaking, "the" investiture ritual did not exist during the principate. Until the end of the third century, there was no single ceremony that turned an individual into an emperor—and certainly nothing resembling a coronation. Rather, the man who claimed the throne had to interact with different groups at different places. These interactions could all take place on the same day, but they could also be spread over a longer period—even months, if the initial rise to power did not take place at Rome. But that does not mean the procedure was not ritualized. Each aspiring ruler had to perform particular actions in a more or less standardized sequence, to which particular responses from relevant groups were required. First, a candidate presented himself to the soldiers, who acclaimed him as emperor and swore an oath of loyalty to him. In response, he gave a speech (*adlocutio*) and promised them a donative. Next, the candidate presented himself to the Senate and made another speech. This was followed by a vote (later replaced by acclamations) by the senators and, ultimately, by the people's assembly.

The offices and mandates that the Senate and the people bestowed on an imperial candidate—most importantly the power of a proconsul and a tribune of the plebs—formed the legal foundation for his authority. However, the ruler of the Roman world was only considered legitimate as long as he enjoyed wide support among his subjects. He ruled not only by virtue of his proconsular and tribunician powers, but also by virtue of the notion that he was, in theory, considered the best man for the job. Due to his unique prestige (*dignitas*), he could lay claim to unique authority (*auctoritas*), sanctioned by the consent of men and gods. This consent had to be continuously earned through virtuous behavior and impressive achievements. The investiture of an imperial candidate therefore granted him authority in two different but complementary ways: it provided his emperorship with a legal foundation and signaled that vital groups supported his rise to power.[16]

The Accession of Otho (AD 69)

With Nero's suicide in AD 68, the Julio-Claudian dynasty came to an end, issuing in a period of civil war that has become known as the Year of the Four Emperors. The first of these was the 70-year-old general Galba. After he had been recognized as the new ruler, the senator Otho had high hopes that Galba would adopt him as his heir. However, the old man disapproved of Otho's loose morals and instead turned to the young senator Lucius Calpurnius Piso, whom he adopted on January 10, AD 69. Humiliated, Otho sought the favor of the Praetorian Guard. With their support, he staged a coup five days later and managed to seize the throne. We have four major accounts describing this affair—namely, those of Plutarch, Tacitus, Suetonius, and Cassius Dio.[17] Directly or indirectly, all these authors based themselves on the same source, the lost work of the contemporary historian Cluvius Rufus.[18] Their accounts of Otho's accession are hostile in tone and generally agree on the course of events, although each author places his own accents.

In his *Histories*, Tacitus paints an unfavorable picture of Otho, stating that he "had spent his boyhood in heedlessness, his early manhood under no restraint" and "had found favor in Nero's eyes by imitating his extravagance."[19] The pretender is contrasted with the virtuous Piso, whom Galba elected as his successor because he showed such high character and patriotism. In a telling speech, the emperor explains to his intended heir why adoption is the best method for selecting an emperor:

> Under Tiberius, Gaius, and Claudius we Romans were the heritage, so to speak, of one family; the fact that we emperors are now beginning to be chosen will be for all a kind of liberty; and since the houses of the Julii and the Claudii are ended, adoption will select only the best; for to be begotten and born of princes is mere chance, and is not reckoned higher, but the judgment displayed in adoption is unhampered; and, if one wishes to make a choice, common consent points out the individual [*si velis eligere, consensu monstratur*].[20]

Sentiments like these are to be expected from authors writing during the age of the adoptive emperors—that is, the period AD 96–180, when the rulers of Rome had no sons and therefore adopted the heirs of their choice. They were also in line with the ideals of the principate, which dictated that only those who excelled in virtue and abilities were *capax imperii*, capable of ruling the Empire. Otho fell far short of the mark. According to Tacitus, the treacherous senator did not conceive the principate in terms of duty, as a good ruler would, but as a luxury to be enjoyed. He records how Otho's slaves and freedmen "constantly held before his eager eyes Nero's luxurious court, his adulteries, his many marriages, and other royal vices, exhibiting them as his own if he only dared to take them, but taunting him with them as the privilege of others if he did not act."[21] We find a similar accusation in the account of Suetonius, who records that Otho had many debts, so that "he flatly declared that he could not keep on his feet unless he became emperor."[22]

Otho's unworthiness to rule is reflected in the way the authors describe his investiture with imperial power. According to Tacitus, whose account is the most elaborate, the ambitious senator sneaked away while Galba was performing a sacrifice. As an excuse, he told bystanders that he was going to examine some property he intended to buy. A small group of praetorians was waiting for him at the golden milestone and hailed him as emperor. The pretender was startled to see that they were only 23 in number and feared that he would be unable to muster the necessary support to overthrow Galba. According to the biographer Plutarch, he started to have second thoughts. "The soldiers who were there, however, would not suffer him to desist, but surrounding his litter with their swords drawn, ordered it to be taken up, while Otho urged the bearers to hasten, saying to himself many times that he was a lost man."[23] The scene is strongly reminiscent of the accounts of Claudius's kidnapping by the praetorians in the work of Suetonius and others, but with one important difference: Claudius had (supposedly) been an unwitting pawn in a game played by others, whereas Otho was personally responsible for the situation he was in.

Tacitus describes how the balance shifted in Otho's favor once he had gained access to the praetorian camp, where he was placed on a platform and surrounded with standards and ensigns. More and more soldiers now joined his side:

> There was utter confusion, with shouts and tumult and mutual exhortation—
> not such as one sees in a gathering of the people and populace, when there
> are various cries and half-hearted flattery, but they seized everyone they saw
> coming over to them, embraced them with their arms, placed them next to
> them, repeated the oath of allegiance, now recommending the emperor to
> the soldiers, now the soldiers to the emperor. Otho did not fail in his part: he
> stretched out his hands and did obeisance to the common soldiers, threw kisses,
> and played in every way the slave to secure the master's place [*omnia serviliter
> pro dominatione*].[24]

This is no carefully orchestrated investiture ritual in which the assembled
troops speak with one voice, reflecting their unanimous consent; this is an
agitated mob running wild. Tacitus underlines that Otho is not in control:
in his eagerness to gain military support, the pretender throws himself at the
mercy of the soldiers, begging for their approval. Hence he made himself sub-
servient to his inferiors—disgraceful behavior that did not befit an aspiring
emperor. Moreover, in the moral discourse of the principate, Otho's openly
flaunted desire to rule the Empire was disgraceful to begin with. "Good"
imperial candidates generally thought themselves unworthy to rule and only
accepted the throne because they were pushed by others or because they were
forced to do so by circumstances—for instance, because they had to avenge
a murdered predecessor.[25] The standard response to a military acclamation,
recorded for many emperors from the first century up to late antiquity, was a
recusatio imperii, a refusal of the throne. It signaled that one was modest and
untainted by a desire for power.[26] Not surprisingly, Tacitus never mentions
that Otho uttered such a *recusatio*—nor do Plutarch, Suetonius, or Cassius
Dio. The omission is significant, further cementing the image of the pretender
as an arrogant and power-hungry individual.

When Galba and Piso received word of what was happening in the praetorian camp, they were seriously alarmed. According to Tacitus, Piso climbed
the steps of the palace and gave a rousing speech to the assembled troops:

> I make no claim of high birth or character for myself, and I need not catalogue
> virtues when the comparison is with Otho. His faults, which are the only things
> in which he glories, were undermining the Empire even when he pretended
> to be the friend of the emperor . . . Adulteries and revelries and gatherings of
> women fill his thoughts: these he considers the prerogatives of imperial power.
> The lust and pleasure of them will be his, the shame and disgrace of them will
> fall on every Roman; for imperial power gained by wicked means no man has
> ever used honorably. The consent of all mankind [*consensus generis humani*]
> made Galba Caesar, and Galba made me so with your consent. If the state and
> the Senate and people are but empty names, it is your concern, comrades, that
> the emperor should not be made by the worst citizens.[27]

Piso's damning assessment of Otho's character is in accord with Tacitus's own
characterization of the pretender, so he appears to function as a mouthpiece
for the historian. Once again, the point is made that Otho is unworthy of

the purple and only craves it for selfish reasons—reasons for which he has betrayed the rightful emperor and is prepared to enforce his will upon the Senate and people of Rome.

In the praetorian camp, Otho also held a speech, as was expected of a newly acclaimed emperor. He, too, made an attempt at character assassination, listing Galba's many crimes and scorning the old emperor because he had never paid his soldiers the customary donative. In contrast, Otho would not fail to reward those who supported him. He remarked that, during his reign, the only rivalry between the army and the Senate would be to see who could put the emperor most in his debt.[28] Suetonius records that the pretender "made no further promises in the assembly to win the loyalty of the soldiers than to declare that he would have that—and only that—which they should leave to him." According to the historian Cassius Dio, "He bought them with many promises." As a consequence, Otho allegedly earned the almost universal hatred of his subjects, "because he had shown that the imperial office was for sale."[29] Both authors, then, appear to regard the donative as a mere bribe by which the loyalty of the soldiers was bought, rather than earned.[30] However, as Tacitus records, the aspiring emperor did not only dangle a juicy carrot in front of his men, he also made clever use of a stick. "Do you hear how men demand my execution and your punishment in the same breath?" the pretender exclaimed. "So clear it is that we can neither die nor be safe except together: and so merciful is Galba that perhaps he has already made promises such as befit the man who massacred all those thousands of innocent soldiers when no man demanded it."[31] Death, according to Otho, was unavoidable for anyone who abandoned him. This left the soldiers with but one viable option: to fight for their new master.

In the short run, at least, the pretender's gamble paid off. Galba and Piso could not muster enough military support to counter the rebellion and were killed in a bloody massacre, making Otho de facto emperor. However, he still needed the formal approval of the Senate and the people's assembly. Tacitus speaks with scorn of the senators, who "hurried to their places, and voted to give Otho the tribunician power, the title *Augustus*, and all the honours granted the other emperors; for all did their best to blot out the memory of their former abuse and insults." Plutarch shares the sentiment, recording how the senators, "as if they were now other men, or had other gods to swear by, . . . united in swearing an oath to support Otho—an oath which he himself had sworn in support of Galba, but had not kept."[32] In the eyes of these authors, the meeting of the Senate was a farce, an insincere expression of loyalty that was inspired by fear and opportunism. Suetonius and Cassius Dio both focus on the speech Otho held to the senators. According to Dio:

> He claimed, it is true, that he had acted under compulsion, that he had been taken into the camp against his will, and had there actually risked his life by opposing the soldiers. Furthermore he was kindly in his speech and affected modesty in his deportment, and he kept throwing kisses on his fingers to everybody and making many promises. But men did not fail to realize that his rule was sure to be even more licentious and harsh than Nero's.[33]

Just as Tacitus emphasized Otho's eagerness to please the soldiers, Dio emphasizes his eagerness to please the senators. Apart from this similarity in behavior, however, the emperor plays a very different role before the Curia than he did before the troops. He is no longer the rebellious commander urging his men to pick up arms against Galba, but a victim of circumstances, unwillingly swept up by the tide of revolt. Suetonius, too, notes that Otho claimed "that he had been carried off in the streets and forced to undertake the rule."[34] In all likelihood, this was indeed the version that the emperor presented to the Senate. Even as the initiator of the revolt against Galba, he made an attempt to model himself after the ideal of the reluctant prince. Unfortunately for him, the hostile chroniclers of his reign were not convinced.[35] As far as they were concerned, Otho's blatant attempts to distort the truth only strengthened his reputation for hypocrisy and untrustworthiness. In their accounts, he was turned into a prime example of the "bad emperor."[36]

The Accession of Didius Julianus (AD 193)

On March 28, AD 193, the Praetorian Guard revolted against the emperor Pertinax, provoked by the latter's attempt to restore military discipline after a period of laxity under his predecessors. The unfortunate ruler was unable to turn the tide and was murdered after a reign of just a few months. In the chaotic hours that followed, the senator Didius Julianus managed to gain the support of the praetorians and won the throne. Three ancient authors give a detailed description of Julianus's elevation.[37] The first is Cassius Dio, who was in Rome at the time and was one of the senators who voted Didius Julianus imperial powers. The second is Herodian, who used Dio's work as one of his sources.[38] The third is the life of Didius Julianus in the *Historia Augusta*, a series of imperial biographies that is of much later date and derives its information from a lost, contemporary source.

Cassius Dio, a personal acquaintance of Didius Julianus, did not think much of his fellow senator, claiming that "as advocate for others at trials I had frequently proved Julianus to be guilty of many offences." According to him, Julianus was "at once an insatiate money-getter and a wanton spendthrift, who was always eager for revolution." Herodian, too, paints an unflattering picture of the man, calling him "one of the Romans censured for an intemperate way of life."[39] The anonymous author of the *Historia Augusta* provides a counterview, denying all charges of extravagance and claiming that "Julianus was so frugal as to make a suckling pig or hare last for three days, if anyone by chance presented him with one; and often, moreover, even when there was no religious reason for it, he was content to dine on cabbages and beans without meat."[40] These different assessments of Julianus's character are reflected in the different representations of his investiture.

According to Dio, Didius Julianus immediately hastened to the praetorian camp when he heard of the death of Pertinax. The murdered emperor's father-in-law, the urban prefect Sulpicianus, was already present at the spot and tried to have himself acclaimed emperor. From outside the gates, Julianus started to make bids for the throne as well. This was an unprecedented situation: two rival claimants simultaneously attempting to win the support of the same group of soldiers. Dio relates:

> Then ensued a most disgraceful business and one unworthy of Rome. For, just as if it had been in some market or auction-room, both the City and its entire Empire were auctioned off. The sellers were the ones who had slain their emperor, and the would-be buyers were Sulpicianus and Julianus, who vied to outbid each other, one from the inside, the other from the outside. They gradually raised their bids up to twenty thousand sesterces per soldier. Some of the soldiers would carry word to Julianus, "Sulpicianus offers so much; how much more do you make it?" And to Sulpicianus in turn, "Julianus promises so much; how much do you raise him?"[41]

In the end, Julianus won the bid by offering each soldier a donative of 25,000 sesterces—an unprecedented sum. The aspiring ruler was received in the camp and greeted as emperor by the troops. As he had done with Otho, Dio thus presents Didius Julianus as a man who disgracefully bought his way to power.[42] Herodian goes even further. In his account, the praetorians locked themselves in the camp and placed the men with the loudest voices on the wall, where "they made proclamation that the Empire was for sale, promising to hand it over to the man who offered the highest price."[43] Undoubtedly, this ludicrous version of events is an embellishment of Dio's story.

Both authors mention that other factors also played a role in the election of Julianus, such as the fact that Sulpicianus was related to Pertinax and might wish to avenge the murdered emperor. Nowhere do Cassius Dio and Herodian suggest that Didius Julianus was chosen for his personal qualities. This notion is likewise absent in the *Historia Augusta*, which records that Julianus made "huge promises" to persuade the soldiers and wrote on placards that he would restore the good name of Commodus, a recent emperor whose memory had been condemned by the Senate.[44] However, the author does not claim that there was an "auction" in which Julianus managed to outbid Sulpicianus. Rather, he downplays the (alleged) fact that Julianus had bought the support of the praetorians. He even states that "Pertinax always spoke of [Julianus] as his colleague and successor"—a doubtful claim with the apparent aim of legitimizing the latter's elevation.[45]

If Dio is to be believed, Julianus's appointment by the Senate immediately laid bare the tension between his role as the champion of the praetorians and the role of modest prince that the Curia desired him to adopt. According to the senator, who was present at the occasion, the man was escorted by a great number of praetorians, "his object being to intimidate both us and the populace at the outset and thereby to secure our allegiance."[46] This was certainly not how a benevolent ruler was supposed to behave. Julianus's speech only strengthened the impression that he was thoroughly unsuited to wear the purple:

[We] heard him deliver a speech that was quite worthy of him, in the course of which he said: "I see that you need a ruler, and I myself am best fitted of any to rule you. I should mention all the advantages I can offer, if you were not already familiar with them and had not already had experience of me. Consequently I have not even asked to be attended here by many soldiers, but have come to you alone, in order that you may ratify what has been given to me by them."[47]

Unlike Otho, Didius Julianus did not even feign modesty when he was addressing the Senate. Rather than uttering a *recusatio imperii* or making excuses for his rise to power, as Otho had done, he committed the unpardonable faux pas of praising himself as the best man for the job.[48] Moreover, as Dio points out, the emperor was blatantly lying: he had not come to the Curia alone, as he said, but had surrounded the Senate house with heavily armed troops and had even taken many armed men inside with him. Thus, Julianus's military might forced itself on the Senate in a very direct and confrontational manner, leaving no doubt where his power base truly lay. The intimidated senators had no choice but to acknowledge him as emperor, but by his arrogant speech and brute display of force, the new ruler had alienated his former colleagues before his reign had good and well begun.[49]

The *Historia Augusta* gives a radically different version of events, stating that Julianus "came in the evening to the Senate, and entrusted himself to it without conditions; thereupon, by decree of the Senate he was acclaimed emperor and, after being raised to a place among the patrician families, he received the tribunician power and the rights of a proconsul." The next day, Julianus returned to the Senate house to deliver his first speech. Allegedly, he spoke in a calm manner, thanking the senators for choosing him as emperor and for granting his wife and daughter the honorary title of *Augusta*. He accepted the name *pater patriae*, "father of the country," but turned down the Senate's offer to erect a silver statue of him.[50] It is hard to imagine a greater contrast between this Julianus, who is behaving as the very model of a modest prince, and the version that Dio presents.

As with the accounts of Otho's investiture, all three authors fail to mention the confirmation of imperial powers by the people's assembly. However, they make it very clear that the people of Rome despised their new ruler. Dio claims that "all fell to shouting, as if by pre-concerted arrangement, calling him stealer of the empire and parricide." These words hinted at the rumor that Julianus had had a hand in the murder of Pertinax, collaborating with the praetorian prefect to get rid of his predecessor.[51] When the new emperor went from the praetorian camp to the palace, Herodian records, the soldiers had to form a phalanx to protect him from the gathered crowd, who did not cheer him, but shouted curses. Allegedly, they hated him "because he had purchased the empire shamefully, disgracefully, and fraudulently, using force and opposing the wishes of the people."[52] Even the *Historia Augusta* records that the populace "assailed [the emperor] with violent revilings, hoping that he might resign the sovereignty which the soldiers had given him; and they even launched a shower of stones." However, the anonymous biographer appears to side with Julianus against the rioting populace, claiming that "all this Julianus took with perfect equanimity; indeed all through the time he was on the throne he was exceedingly tolerant."[53]

Cassius Dio did not give the emperor so much credit. In his account, Didius Julianus could not endure the protests and ordered his soldiers to cut the people down, causing many Romans to be wounded or killed.[54] Once again, we have the contrasting images of the benign prince and the ruthless tyrant. Neither image ever came to dominate Julianus's reputation completely. But even if the attempts at character assassination by Dio and Herodian were not wholly successful, they certainly tarnished the memory of this short-lived emperor.

Creating Tyrants

Clearly, ancient authors went to great lengths to paint Otho and Didius Julianus as despicable individuals. With the exception of Cassius Dio, who spoke from personal experience about Julianus, it seems unlikely that these men had ever met the emperors they scorned. Indeed, some of Otho's critics had not even been born when he rose to power. Yet we need not be surprised by the hostility of the ancient accounts. As usurpers who only managed to stay on the throne for a few months, both Otho and Didius Julianus wound up on the losing side of history. Otho had been a close associate of Nero and was even acclaimed as "the new Nero" by the people—a clear sign that his notorious predecessor still enjoyed some popularity shortly after his death. However, when Vespasian emerged as the winner from the civil war of AD 69 and made an effort to distance himself from the last Julio-Claudian ruler, the reputation of Nero as a "bad" emperor was sealed—as was Otho's.[55] Didius Julianus, for his part, was overthrown by Septimius Severus, who marched on Rome to avenge the murder of Julianus's predecessor Pertinax.[56] The dynasty that Severus founded on this pretext still ruled the Empire when Dio was composing his history. This may well have influenced the historian's portrayal of Julianus, although personal enmity undoubtedly inclined him to cast the short-lived emperor in a negative light in any case.

Some of the personal attacks against Otho and Didius Julianus are very explicit. Tacitus in particular consistently portrays Otho as an extravagant and debauched individual who wallows in luxury and adulteries. Herodian applies the same commonplace to Didius Julianus by accusing him of an "intemperate way of life," although he does not elaborate on the accusation. In addition, the emperor's critics allege that he is "guilty of many offences," "an insatiate money-getter," "a wanton spendthrift," and "always eager for revolution." These attacks in themselves would be enough to establish that Otho and Julianus are unsuited to wear the imperial purple. However, the point is really driven home by the way their behavior during their investiture is portrayed. Both men are depicted as eager for power. They are not the intended heirs of their predecessors, nor are they widely considered as the best men to occupy the throne. Rather, they take power at their own initiative or because they are prompted to do so by associates of dubious moral stature, such as Otho's slaves and freedmen.[57] In their arrogance, they consider themselves worthy to rule the Empire, even when many others do not. Moreover, they are prepared to stoop to any means necessary to achieve their goal, be it bribery, deceit, violence, or intimidation.

Such immoral behavior undermined the meaning of the investiture ritual. Formally speaking, Otho and Julianus went through all the necessary steps to become emperor, gaining the consent of the army, the Senate, and the citizens of Rome. They were granted the powers of a proconsul and a tribune of the plebs. Their legal authority to rule was thus without question. Yet in the process of obtaining the necessary support, titles, and legal powers, the imperial candidates proved that they lacked a vital qualification: personal authority. At least, that is how their opponents presented them after their deaths. Time and time again, the hostile accounts emphasize that Otho and Julianus were not exemplary princes, inspiring loyalty through their virtuous behavior, but ruthless tyrants who forced others to comply with their rise to power. From the point of view of the senators who wrote most works of history, this immediately disqualified them as good rulers. As Tacitus knew, "imperial power gained by wicked means no man has ever used honorably."[58] It was not just the methods they allegedly employed that spoke against Otho and Julianus; equally condemning was the implication that they were so anxious to gain power in the first place. Those truly worthy of the purple were supposed to accept the burden of government reluctantly and only because they felt it was their duty to serve the state. Anyone who was actually eager to become emperor probably had selfish motives, such as the desire to dominate others—or, in case of Otho, to enjoy the luxuries and pleasures the principate provided.

In a discourse that judged the suitability of imperial candidates mainly in terms of morality and dignity, these attacks carried great weight. Yet not everyone agreed with the severe standards employed by senatorial and equestrian authors. Suetonius records how many soldiers kissed Otho's hands and feet at his funeral, "weeping bitterly and calling him the bravest of men and an incomparable emperor, and then at once slew themselves beside his bier."[59] Obviously, these men did not share the author's hostile attitude toward the deceased ruler. But apart from a few remarks in the literary sources, their sentiments have been lost. The soldiers may have had the power to make or unmake emperors, but a ruler's reputation was ultimately in the hands of historians.

Conclusion

In their efforts to cast imperial candidates in a negative light, Greco-Roman authors often showed only limited interest in the particular personalities and ideas of their victims. Although Tiberius, Caligula, and other early emperors were described as individuals with their own quirks, flaws, and vices, the portraits of many later rulers, especially minor ones, mostly consist of variations on established themes, with some individual touches. Otho and Julianus, as well as others whose attempts to seize the purple were unsuccessful or short-lived, are represented as more or less generic tyrants possessing the stereotypical traits of "bad" emperors.[60] (In Otho's case, however, there was a surprise ending, since authors admired the bravery with which he took his own life once his cause was lost, hence revealing a better side to his nature. As Plutarch states, "though he lived no more decently than Nero, he died more nobly."[61]) To what extent these usurpers were really as power hungry, decadent, and corrupt as our sources suggest is anyone's guess; the mere fact that they had seized the throne by force sufficed to paint them with the tyrant's brush.

The generic nature of such literary character assassinations is related to their lack of immediacy. In modern democracies, most character attacks take place in the context of political campaigning. Politicians and their spin doctors scrutinize every detail of their rivals' personalities, habits, convictions, actions, and past in search of weaknesses to exploit, so that they can launch their assaults with maximum effect. The historians and biographers of imperial Rome, in contrast, were not involved in a race for power or glory with the emperors they slandered, but aimed at victims who might have been dead for decades, if not centuries. Moreover, the "bad" imperial candidates in their accounts did not represent rivaling ideologies or sociopolitical movements that had to be discredited; they were merely usurpers who had failed to establish dynasties. Therefore, they could simply be labeled as "tyrants" and be hit with all the stereotypes and commonplaces that this label entailed, without much regard for the specifics of their persons and circumstances.

Clearly, ancient historians and biographers had greater concerns than destroying the reputations of sometimes long-dead rulers. In their writings, they formulated and reproduced a normative discourse that was widely shared by the Greco-Roman elite and was concerned with the preservation of political stability and the prestige of the Senate as the institute that had the right to appoint emperors. Imperial candidates who destabilized this order and bypassed the Senate in their quest for power were condemned in the harshest terms. Character assassination served to define the limits of good emperorship.

Notes

1. Parts of this article—in particular, the general discussion of imperial investiture rituals, and the analyses of the investitures of Otho and Didius Julianus—have been adapted from Icks 2011b, 350-62. In this article, the focus was on ritual failure, rather than on character assassination.
2. Suetonius, *Claudius* 8, 3.2. Unless indicated otherwise, all translated quotations of ancient sources are taken from the Loeb editions, sometimes with minor adjustments.
3. Suetonius, *Claudius* 10.1: *mirabili casu*.
4. Suetonius, *Claudius* 10.2.

5. Helmut Jung and Barbara Levick have argued that Claudius must at the very least have been aware of, if not actually complicit in, the conspiracy against Caligula: Jung 1972, 375, 382–86; Levick 1990, 35–39. See also Osgood 2011, 29–32.

6. Suetonius himself claims that someone mocked the emperor by publishing a book titled *The Elevation of Fools* (*Claudius* 38.3).

7. It is impossible to identify Suetonius's sources for the life of Claudius. The *Apocolocyntosis*, possibly written by Seneca, is a clear example of anti-Claudian sentiments not long after the emperor's death.

8. Roller 2004. See also Bücher 2006 (*exempla* in Cicero); Brenk 2008 (*exempla* in Plutarch).

9. For an analysis of the construction of a "bad" emperor—in this case, Elagabalus—see Icks 2008; expanded upon in Icks 2011a, 92–122.

10. For more on *damnatio memoriae*, see Varner 2004; Krüpe 2011.

11. Flower 2006, 2.

12. Flower 2006, 280.

13. Icks 2011b, 348.

14. I have already briefly discussed the imperial investiture ritual in Icks 2011b, 350–1 and—for investitures in late antiquity—Icks 2012, 464.

15. For a detailed analysis of the roles of the army, the Senate, and the *comitia* in the investiture of an emperor, see Parsi 1963.

16. Pabst 1997, 203–8: although I disagree with her thesis that the troops acclaiming an emperor gained the legal status of a people's assembly in late antiquity. Flaig (1992, 174–207) reduces imperial legitimacy to the consent of the governed, dismissing its legal components.

17. Plutarch, *Galba* 24.2–25.3, 28.1; *Otho* 3.1; Tacitus, *Historiae* 1.27–38, 47; Suetonius, *Galba* 19.1; *Otho* 6.17.1; Cassius Dio 63.5.1–3, 64.8.1–2. For a brief discussion of Otho, see Eck 2001.

18. See Peter 1965, 28–44: Plutarch, Tacitus, and Suetonius did not use each other's accounts for their treatment of Galba and Otho, but all used the work of Cluvius Rufus—in Plutarch's case exclusively. Cassius Dio probably based his accounts of Galba and Otho on Plutarch, or else on Cluvius Rufus as well.

19. Tacitus, *Historiae* 1.13. This characterization of Otho is a typical example of the predominance of moral discourses in the assessment of public figures in Roman literary culture. "Bad" rulers were not just corrupt or incompetent, but were invariably accused of effeminacy, deviant sexual behavior, extravagance, and related vices. For more on this, see Edwards 1993.

20. Tacitus, *Historiae* 1.16.

21. Tacitus, *Historiae* 1.22. The fact that Otho was prompted to seize power by lowly slaves and freedmen further illustrates the immorality of his motives.

22. Suetonius, *Otho* 5.1.

23. Plutarch, *Galba* 25.2. As Lukas de Blois has pointed out, Plutarch consistently emphasizes Galba's and Otho's failure to control the misbehavior of the soldiers to indicate their bad leadership (de Blois 2008).

24. Tacitus, *Historiae* 1.36.

25. Septimius Severus managed to muster a lot of military support during his march on Rome, "for he was universally considered as the avenger of Pertinax" (*Historia Augusta*, *Septimius Severus* 5.3–4). Herodian 2.9.10 criticizes Severus for using vengeance as an excuse to realize his own ambitions.

26. Béranger 1953, 137–69. See also Huttner 2004.

27. Tacitus, *Historiae* 1.30.

28. Tacitus, *Historiae* 1.37–38. Otho cannot be referring to a donative here, since senators by definition did not receive one. As Elizabeth Keitel has argued, Tacitus's renditions of Otho's speeches to the soldiers parody the regular exhortations of generals to their troops (Keitel 1987).

29. Suetonius, *Otho* 6.3; Cassius Dio 63.5.3, 9.1: ὅτι τήν τε ἀρχὴν ὤνιον ἀπεδεδείχει.

30. As Egon Flaig has argued, the granting of a donative by a new emperor should not be seen as a bribe, but as a symbolic gesture, confirming the affective bond between him and the soldiers (Flaig 1992, 451–59). See also Veyne 1976, 511–23.

31. Tacitus, *Historiae* 1.37.

32. Tacitus, *Historiae* 1.47; Suetonius, *Galba* 28.1.

33. Cassius Dio 64.8.1–2.

34. Suetonius, *Otho* 7.1: *quasi raptus de publico et suscipere imperium vi coactus.*

35. One might suppose that the hostile depictions of Otho in our sources are the result of negative propaganda by Vespasian, the ultimate victor of the civil war. However, Vespasian employed a—undoubtedly forged—letter by the dying Otho to justify his revolt against Vitellius (Suetonius, *Vespasian* 4.4.). Once he had established himself, the new emperor largely ignored Otho and Vitellius in his representation, in order not to antagonize the troops that had supported them; see Ferrill 1964/1965, 269.

36. It should be stressed, however, that Otho is not presented as without redeeming qualities. Even in Tacitus's hostile account, traces of a more positive tradition can be found (Shochat 1981, 377). In particular, the emperor's suicide is generally treated favorably: Plutarch, *Otho* 15.3–17.5; Tacitus, *Historiae* 2.47–49; Suetonius, *Otho* 10.1–11.2; Cassius Dio 63.13.1–15.2[2]. See also Braun 1992, 97–102.

37. Cassius Dio 74.11.1–13.1; Herodian 2.6.4–13; *Historia Augusta, Didius Julianus* 2.3–3.5. For a brief discussion of Didius Julianus, see Eck 1997.

38. Sidebottom 1998, 2792.

39. Cassius Dio 74.12, 11.2; Herodian 2.6.6. All translated quotations of Herodian are taken from the translation of E. C. Echols.

40. *Historia Augusta, Didius Julianus* 3.9. Evidently, the *Historia Agusta* preserves an alternative historiographical tradition that was more favorable to Julianus—an indication that his short reign may not have been as abysmal as Dio and Herodian would like us to believe. As J. B. Leaning suggests, "The tragedy of Didius Julianus was not so much the result of personal failings as of prevailing circumstances, and those same circumstances ensured that the calumny surrounding him was perpetuated long after his death" (Leaning 1989, 563).

41. Cassius Dio 74.11.3–5.

42. In fact, Dio may well have used Julianus's elevation as the inspiration for his account of Otho's elevation, as Flaig has claimed (Flaig 1992, 304–5n48).

43. Herodian 2.6.4.

44. *Historia Augusta, Didius Julianus* 2.6: *ingentia pollicentem.*

45. *Historia Augusta, Didius Julianus* 2.3.

46. Cassius Dio 74.12.

47. Cassius Dio 74.12.4.

48. As Anthony Birley has remarked, considering Julianus's impressive career and good connections, his claim to be the most *capax imperii* was "not as boastful or empty as Dio makes it sound" (Birley 1988, 96). Nevertheless, one was not supposed to boast about one's own suitability to rule.

49. According to Dio, the charm offensive that Julianus launched later failed to convince the senators because he was overcompensating: "For every act that goes beyond propriety, even though it seems to some to be gracious, is regarded by men of sense as trickery" (74.14.1).

50. *Historia Augusta, Didius Julianus* 3.3, 4.5. Cassius Dio mentions that Julianus refused a gold statue, asking for a bronze instead, but only because these presumably lasted longer than gold or silver statues. Dio comments: "In this he was mistaken, for it is virtue that preserves the memory of rulers" (74.14.2).

51. Cassius Dio 74.13.3: τῆς τε ἀρχῆς ἅρπαγα . . . καὶ πατροφόνον. The rumor is mentioned in the *Historia Augusta* (*Didius Julianus* 3.7) and is stated as undisputed fact by two fourth-century authors, Aurelius Victor (18) and Eutropius (8.16). Alan Appelbaum argues that it is a plausible possibility, although by no means a certainty (Appelbaum 2007, 204–6).

52. Herodian 2.6.12: μετά τε αἰσχρᾶς καὶ ἀπρεποῦς διαβολῆς.

53. *Historia Augusta, Didius Julianus* 4.8.

54. Cassius Dio 74.13.4.

55. Tacitus, *Historiae* 1.78. Vespasian's propaganda was targeted against Nero, rather than Otho; see note 33. Still, the defamation of an emperor with whom Otho had closely associated himself before and during his reign can hardly have had a positive effect on his memory. For Nero's ambiguous reputation in the Year of the Four Emperors, see Flower 2006, 197–233.

56. See note 25.

57. According to Herodian 2.6.7, Didius Julianus was persuaded to bid for the throne by his wife, his daughter, and "a number of parasites" (τῶν παρασίτων πλῆθος).

58. Tacitus, *Historiae* 1.30.

59. Suetonius, *Otho* 12.2. See also Plutarch, *Otho* 17.4-5; Tacitus, *Historiae* 2.51; Cassius Dio 63.15.1².

60. Prominent tyrannical commonplaces for Roman emperors included pride (*superbia*), lust (*libido*), cruelty (*crudelitas, saevitia*), and greed (*avaritia*); see Dunkle, 1971.

61. Plutarch, *Otho* 18.2.

Bibliography

Appelbaum, A. 2007. "Another Look at the Assassination of Pertinax and the Accession of Julianus." *Classical Philology* 102: 198–207.

Béranger, J. 1953. *Recherches sur l'aspect idéologique du principat*. Basel: Reinhardt.

Birley, A. R. 1988. *The African Emperor: Septimius Severus*, 2nd rev. ed. London: Batsford.

Blois, L. de. 2008. "Soldiers and Leaders in Plutarch's *Galba* and *Otho*." In H. M. Schellenberg, V. E. Hirschmann, and A. Krieckhaus, eds., *A Roman Miscellany: Essays in Honour of Anthony R. Birley on his Seventieth Birthday*, 5–13. Gdańsk: Foundation for the Development of Gdańsk University.

Braun, L. 1992. "Galba und Otho bei Plutarch und Sueton." *Hermes. Zeitschrift für klassische Philologie* 120: 90–102.

Brenk, F. E. 2008. "Setting a Good *exemplum*: Case Studies in the *Moralia*, the *Lives* as Case Studies." In A. G. Nikolaidis, ed., *The Unity of Plutarch's Work: 'Moralia' Themes in the 'Lives', Features of the 'Lives' in the 'Moralia'*, 237–54. Berlin: De Gruyter.

Bücher, F. 2006. *Verargumentierte Geschichte. Exempla Romana im politischen Diskurs der späten römischen Republik*. Stuttgart: Franz Steiner.

Dunkle, J. R. 1971. "The Rhetorical Tyrant in Roman Historiography: Sallust, Livy and Tacitus." *The Classical World* 65: 12–20.

Eck, W. 1997. "[II 6] M. Didius Severus Iulianus." In *Der neue Pauly. Enzyklopädie der Antike*, vol. 3, 542.

Eck, W. 2001. "Otho." In *Der neue Pauly. Enzyklopädie der Antike*, vol. 9, 107–8.

Edwards, C. 1993. *The Politics of Immorality in Ancient Rome*. Cambridge: Cambridge University Press.

Ferrill, A. 1964/1965. "Otho, Vitellius, and the Propaganda of Vespasian." *The Classical Journal* 60: 267–69.

Flaig, E. 1992. *Den Kaiser herausfordern. Die Usurpation im Römischen Reich*. Frankfurt: Campus Verlag.

Flower, H. I. 2006. *The Art of Forgetting: Disgrace & Oblivion in Roman Political Culture*. Chapel Hill: University of North Carolina Press.

Huttner, U. 2004. *Recusatio imperii. Ein politisches Ritual zwischen Ethik und Taktik*. Hildesheim: Olms.

Icks, M. 2008. "Heliogabalus, a Monster on the Roman Throne: The Literary Construction of a 'Bad' Emperor." In I. Sluiter and R. M. Rosen, eds., *KAKOS: Badness and Anti-Value in Classical Antiquity*, 477–88. Leiden, Netherlands: Brill.

Icks, M. 2011a. *The Crimes of Elagabalus: The Life and Legacy of Rome's Decadent Boy Emperor*. London: IB Tauris.

Icks, M. 2011b. "Elevating the Unworthy Emperor: Ritual Failure in Roman Historiography." In A. Chaniotis, ed., *Ritual Dynamics in the Ancient Mediterranean: Agency, Emotion, Gender, Representation*, 347–76. Stuttgart: Steiner.

Icks, M. 2012. "Bad Emperors on the Rise: Negative Assessments of Imperial Investitures, AD 284–395." *Klio. Beiträge zur alten Geschichte* 94: 462–81.

Jung, H. 1972. "Die Thronerhebung des Claudius." *Chiron* 2: 367–86.

Keitel, E. 1987. "Otho's Exhortations in Tacitus' *Histories*." *Greece & Rome* 34: 73–82.

Krüpe, F. 2011. *Die Damnatio memoriae. Über die Vernichtung von Erinnerung. Eine Fallstudie zu Publius Septimius Geta (198–211 n. Chr.)*. Gutenberg: Computus Druck.

Leaning, J. B. 1989. "Didius Julianus and His Biographer." *Latomus. Revue d'études latines* 48: 548–65.

Levick, B. 1990. *Claudius*. London: Batsford.

Osgood, J. 2011. *Claudius Caesar: Image and Power in the Early Roman Empire*. Cambridge: Cambridge University Press.

Pabst, A. 1997. *Comitia imperii. Ideelle Grundlagen des römischen Kaisertums*. Darmstadt: Wissenschaftliche Buchgesellschaft.

Parsi, B. 1963. *Désignation et investiture de l'empereur romain (Ier–IIe siècle apr. J.-C.)*. Paris: Sirey.

Peter, H. 1965. *Die Quellen Plutarchs in den Biographieen der Römer*. Amsterdam: Hakkert.

Roller, M. 2004. "Exemplarity in Roman Culture: The Cases of Horatius Cocles and Cloelia." *Classical Philology* 99: 1–56.

Sidebottom, H. 1998. "Herodian's Historical Methods and Understanding of History." In *Aufstieg und Niedergang der Römischen Welt* 2.34.4, 2775–836.

Shochat, Y, 1981. "Tacitus' Attitude to Otho." *Latomus. Revue d'études latines* 40: 365–77.

Varner, E.R. 2004. *Mutilation and Transformation: Damnatio Memoriae and Roman Imperial Portraiture*. Leiden, Netherlands: Brill.

Veyne, P. 1976. *Brot und Spiele. Gesellschaftliche Macht und politische Herrschaft in der Antike*. Transl. K. Laermann and H. R. Brittnacher, 1988. Frankfurt: Campus Verlag.

Editorial Reflections: Ancient Rome

Martijn Icks and Eric Shiraev

Both for the Roman Republic and the Empire, we are best informed about character attacks that occurred in elite circles, where power and prestige were viciously contested. Therefore, the means of defamation we are most familiar with are of an "elite" nature, as well. Only a privileged few had the rhetorical training to lambast their opponents in eloquent speeches or possessed the literary education and leisure necessary to write biting poems, satires, and histories. Since the nature of our evidence largely detracts the folklore of the lower classes from sight, we only catch occasional glimpses of more "popular" forms of character attacks. The biographer Suetonius records, for instance, how anonymous critics hung placards with defying texts on statues of Nero and how the emperor's musical aspirations were mocked in graffiti (*Life of Nero* 45.2). We can only guess who was responsible or how widespread such attacks were. Better attested are the chants that regularly broke out in theaters and amphitheaters, ridiculing or slandering public figures, sometimes while they were present. Still, the vast majority of our sources on defamation in ancient Rome concerns invective speeches, satirical works, and hostile historiographical and biographic accounts, written by members of the senatorial and equestrian orders.

The transition from republic to empire does not appear to have altered the favorite themes of character assassins, which included—among other things—sexual rhetoric and the mocking of physical disabilities. Although political competition was the domain of the elite, these themes were part of discourses that were widely shared among the different classes of Roman society (graffiti in Pompeii reflects similar lines of thinking). Many attacks were concerned with the private lives of victims, hinting at incest, passive homosexuality, excessive love of luxury, and other forms of immoral and extravagant behavior. The lives of the "bad" Roman emperors offer countless examples. Due to their nature, such accusations were usually impossible to check and therefore applicable to a wide range of victims. Nevertheless, if an attacker wanted to hit the mark, he could not simply say anything about anyone. Clever invectives took the target's reputation into account, playing on existing rumors to gain an air of plausibility. As we have seen, Cicero was frequently criticized for his execution of prisoners as consul and his purchase of a house on the Palatine, but not for gluttony or sexual extravagance, since such allegations would not have been credible to an audience that was familiar with the life and deeds of the famous orator.

Inevitably, the rise of the Empire triggered some changes in the practices of defamation. In the time of the Republic, there had been a fierce struggle for political office, influence, and prestige among senators. Slander was employed openly, often in the face of an opponent. As rhetorical handbooks indicate, it was regarded as perfectly acceptable to target any aspect of a rival's character, including his origins and physical attributes. Since most political offices were elected by the people's assembly, attackers made an effort to appeal to the expectations of the broader urban public. During the Empire, the people's assembly lost all of its political power, and the distribution of political offices came under the control of the emperor. From then on, many attacks launched by senators did not target fellow senators, but were aimed at the Caesars, whose might overshadowed even the most venerable and well-connected nobles. Scathing rhetoric, in large part, gave way to more "hidden" means of defamation, such as anonymous pamphlets circulating among the elite. Moreover, the posthumous character assassination of emperors gained ground, as attested in the histories and biographies of Tacitus, Suetonius, and others.

One important feature of such literary works is that they formulate an intra-elite discourse, reproducing and confirming the values of the upper classes. Of course, themes such as moral depravity were by no means the sole concern of the rich and literate, and many of the slanderous anecdotes recorded by our sources would have echoed widely circulating rumors. However, the ultimate yardstick of any emperor's memory was not his popularity with the general public, but his relation with the aristocracy and the extent to which he had looked after aristocratic interests. If the verdict was unfavorable, he was brandished as a tyrant and labeled with many negative commonplaces. Even in the highly individualized portraits of the Julio-Claudian emperors—such as Tiberius, Caligula, and Nero—recurring leitmotivs of cruelty, repression, and sexual deviance are easy to find. For the reader, there can be no doubt who the "bad" rulers were.

The Middle Ages

5

Falsifying the Prophet: Muhammad at the Hands of His Earliest Christian Biographers in the West

Kenneth Baxter Wolf

Introduction[1]

Arguably there is no better way to appreciate character assassination as practiced by medieval Christians than to consider early Christian biographies of Muhammad. One might think Muhammad would have rivals for this distinction among the Jews and the heretics, the two religious categories aside from Islam that played the biggest role in shaping early Christian identity. But as common as Christian treatises against the Jews were, their prophets were immune from Christian censure due to their perceived indispensability in corroborating Jesus's identity as the Messiah; Muhammad, whose prophecies postdated the Incarnation, was not afforded the same consideration. And while Christian writers regularly excoriated heresiarchs like Arius and Nestor, the reactions that Muhammad evoked were still more visceral, for, unlike Arius's innovation, Muhammad's never went away, and unlike Nestor's, it was linked to a polity that threatened to swallow Greek and Latin Christendom altogether. These circumstances combined to assure Muhammad the lion's share of attention from medieval Christian character assassins.

It took some time after the Muslim conquests before Christian biographies of Muhammad began to appear, but once they did, they never abated, appearing in all parts of the medieval Christian world, including those that ended up under Muslim rule. In fact it is among the lives of Muhammad written and manipulated by Christian *dhimmis* that we find the widest range of polemical strategies for discounting Islam by denigrating its prophet. In this chapter I will consider and contextualize two Latin portraits of Muhammad from early medieval Spain, each of which, in its own way, can be considered a product of the *dhimmi* experience. I will be examining these texts through the lens of "counterhistory," which turns out to be a particularly useful tool when the subject at hand is "character assassination."

The Notion of "Counterhistory"

Counterhistory, as defined by the late Amos Funkenstein, is the historiographical process whereby the events of an enemy's official history are maliciously reframed in an effort to create an alternative, subversive history for the purposes of internal consumption. In Funkenstein's own words, counterhistory involves "the systematic exploitation of the adversary's most trusted sources against their grain."[2] In its most "vicious" form, it can "deprive the adversary of his positive identity, his self-image, and substitute for it a pejorative counterimage."[3] Though it was the dueling histories of the Israelis and the Palestinians that inspired Funkenstein's thoughts on the subject, he traced the practice of counterhistory back to antiquity, pointing, for example, to the *Toldoth Yeshu*, the well-known Jewish revision of the biography of Jesus. True to the counterhistorical genre, this "antigospel" relied on (what I call) a "give-and-take" strategy. It gave (as in, "conceded") the basic facts that Jesus lived, worked wonders, attracted a following, and was ultimately betrayed and executed. But it took (as in, "took away") the sacral narrative by which these same events were invested with meaning. Hence the Jesus of the *Toldoth Yeshu* is depicted as the product of an illicit union who becomes a magician, dupes the ignorant into following him, and then dies at the hands of the Romans after being betrayed by a heroic infiltrator loyal to the Sanhedrin. Such a give-and-take strategy provided this Jewish counterhistorian with the rhetorical tactics necessary to infiltrate Christian sacred history and attack it from the inside.

Barbara Roggema has applied the idea of counterhistory—or, as she calls it, "parasitical historiography"—to the efforts of some of the earliest Syriac and Arabic Christian apologists who confronted the challenge of Islam.[4] One of them, for instance, described how Muhammad enticed the Arabs into conquering the "land of milk and honey," by claiming that it would be their reward for putting their faith in the One God. Note how in this case the Christian author accepts the Muslim claim that Muhammad brought monotheism to the Arabs, only to paint Muhammad's military success as the product of a ploy to entice the Arabs into taking up arms on his behalf.[5] Some aspects of Islamic history lent themselves so well to Christian counterhistory that the original narratives required little if any reworking. Such was the case of the Qur'anic account of Muhammad's marriage to Zaynab, the former wife of his adoptive son, Zaid. Though the Qur'an (specifically Sura 33.7) assured its Muslim readers that God had condoned the marriage, Christians treated the whole episode as proof that Muhammad, motivated by lust, was simply making up his "scriptures" as he went along.[6] Whether the Christian counterhistorian's hand was heavy or light, the tactics were the same: strategic acceptance of some aspect of Islam's sacred history so as to reframe the whole for Christian consumption.

Though Latin apologists naturally lagged a bit behind their Eastern counterparts when it came to crafting such counterhistories of Islam, Spain ultimately did produce a "modest dossier" of such texts,[7] including two Latin lives of Muhammad, to which I now turn.[8]

Two Early Latin Lives of Muhammad

The longer of these two anonymous lives, the *Storia de Mahometh*,[9] was written sometime between the mid-eighth and the mid-ninth centuries.[10] Beyond that, there is little that can be said with any certainty about its production and provenance. It is clear from the text that the author was quite familiar with the official biography of Muhammad. Specifically, he knew that Muhammad was an orphan, that he became a merchant, that he married his widowed patroness, that he claimed to be a prophet who received revelations from Gabriel, that he preached against idolatry, that he made reference to familiar Christian themes, that he led armies into battle, and that he married Zaynab.[11] These are the familiar bits and pieces of Muhammad's biography out of which the author of the *Storia* would construct his own caustic *counter*biography. Here is the first part:

> Muhammad's beginnings were these. As an orphan he was put under the charge of a certain widow. As an avaricious usurer, he travelled on business and began assiduously to attend assemblies of Christians. A shrewd son of darkness, he began to commit some of the sermons of the Christians to memory and became the wisest among the irrational Arabs in all things. Aflame with the fuel of his lust, he was joined to his patroness by some barbaric law. Soon after, the spirit of error appeared to him in the form of a vulture and, exhibiting a golden mouth, said it was the angel Gabriel and ordered Muhammad to present himself among his people as a prophet. Swollen with pride, he began to preach to the irrational animals and he made headway as if on the basis of reason so that they retreated from the cult of idols and adored the [in]corporeal God in heaven.[12] He commanded his believers to take up arms on his behalf, and, as if with a new zeal of faith, he commanded them to cut down their adversaries with the sword. God, with his inscrutable judgment . . . permitted them to inflict injury.[13]

It is easy to see how the Latin author twisted for polemical effect each and every historical datum that he pilfered from the official account of the Prophet. Muhammad the merchant is transformed into Muhammad the usurer. His marriage to Khadijah is illegitimate and "fueled by lust." Gabriel becomes a diabolical vulture that only pretends to be an angel, and so on and so forth. Beyond plugging actual events from Muhammad's life into a new, antagonistic story line, the author added "data" independent of the Islamic version of Muhammad's life. The insertion of Habakkuk's prophecy about the Chaldeans is a case in point, as is the part about Muhammad memorizing Christian sermons. But the most egregious example of such interpolation is the author's depiction of Muhammad's demise, a blatant parody of Jesus's resurrection that has nothing to do with any official version of the Prophet's death. The text reads:

> Sensing his imminent destruction and knowing that he would in no way be resurrected on his own merit, he predicted that he would be revived on the third day by the angel Gabriel, who was in the habit of appearing to him in the guise of a vulture, as Muhammad himself said. When he gave up his soul to hell, they ordered his body to be guarded with an arduous vigil, anxious about the miracle that he had promised them. When on the third day they saw that he was rotting, and determined that he would not by any means be rising, they said the angels did not come because they were frightened by their presence. Having found sound advice—or so they thought—they left his body unguarded, and immediately instead of angels, dogs followed his stench and devoured his flank. Learning of the deed, they surrendered the rest of his body to the soil . . . It was appropriate that a prophet of this kind fill the stomachs of dogs, a prophet who committed not only his own soul, but those of many others, to hell.[14]

This mixing of actual events from Muhammad's life with such a fanciful depiction of his death reminds us that, beyond some level of reliance on the official history, there are no rules when constructing counterhistorical narratives. The point is to disparage, and the author of the *Storia de Mahometh* must have felt that a combination of counterhistory and parody would best serve such a purpose.

*   *   *

The second and shorter of our two Latin lives diverges even more dramatically from the official biography of the Prophet. Compared to the *Storia de Mahometh*, the *Tultusceptru de libro domni Metobii* not only co-opts fewer actual pieces of Islamic history, but clothes them in a narrative that is barely even recognizable as a counterbiography of Muhammad.[15]

Everything about the *Tultusceptru* is a mystery, beginning with the title.[16] "Metobii" looks like a dyslexic version of "Metodii," suggesting some relationship to the famous seventh-century *Apocalypse of Pseudo-Methodius*, but the only parallels between the two texts are the mutual references to "Erribon," a distinctive form of Yathrib, the original name of the Arabian city Medina.[17] Pinpointing the date of composition is impossible.[18] The only hard evidence that we have is paleographic: based on the handwriting, the scribe who recorded the only extant version was most likely writing between 1030 and 1060.[19] But I believe it dates from as early as the ninth century, which will become clear as I go along.

The lack of a clear context does not take away from the value of the text as a fascinating piece of counterhistory in its own right.[20] It reads:

Father Bishop Osius, when he saw an angel of the Lord speaking to him . . . [21] The angel said to him: "Go and speak to my satraps who dwell in Erribon and are given to the northwest wind. With hard faces and indomitable hearts as if made of flint, so are the inhabitants who are in the desert. I send you to an apostate people. Their fathers have receded from me. They have violated my pact. Their children have persisted in perjuring my name in filth and business. So go and tell them, 'he who can hear, let him hear, and he who is still, let him be still. For lo, the house of the Lord is exasperated'.[22] And say to them: 'Be not unbelievers but believers.'"[23] So [Osius] set out to speak the words of the Lord to them. But he was weak and was about to be summoned by the Lord. So he ordered one of his monks named Ozim to go forth to Erribon [in his place] and speak to them the words that the angel of the Lord had ordered Father Bishop Osius to speak. The boy, whose name was Ozim, when he had heard the words of his teacher, [the words] which the angel of the Lord had narrated to him, set off to tell the satraps what had been commanded. When he got to Erribon, he found in an oak tree an angel of temptation that resembled the [other] angel. The evil angel who stood before him said to him: "What is your name?" [Ozim] responded: "I am called Ozim. I have been sent by my teacher Father Bishop Osius to speak the words that he spoke to me, the words that the angel of the Lord had ordered him to speak before the day of his summons came and his spirit was called to the celestial kingdom." Then the evil angel spoke to him, saying to him: "I am the angel who was sent to Father Bishop Osius. I will tell you the words that you are to preach to the satraps to whom you are being sent." And he said to him: "You will not be called Ozim but Muhammad." And so the angel who had revealed himself to him imposed this name on him and ordered him to say, so that [the satraps] might believe: "*Alla occuber alla occuber siti leila citus est Mohamet zazulille.*"[24] The monk did not know that [by so doing] he was invoking demons, for every *alla occuber* serves to conjure up demons.[25] Thus his heart was turned away by the unclean spirit and the words that the Lord had narrated to him through his teacher were lost to oblivion. And so what was to be a vessel of Christ became a vessel of Mammon to the perdition of his soul. All who were converted to this error and all those who, through his persuasion, shall be, are numbered among the company of hell.[26]

Even prima facie, it is obvious that we are dealing with a very different experiment in counterhistory than the one conducted by the author of the *Storia de Mahometh*. While both accounts posit some kind of Christian influence on the one hand and highlight the machinations of an evil angel on the other, the *Tultusceptru* exercises far greater independence from the official version of Islamic history. Were it not for its inclusion of the name "Mohamet" and the unmistakable attempt to transliterate the *adhān*, the traditional call to prayer, it would not be obvious that the *Tultusceptru* had anything to do with the origins of Islam at all. Closer inspection reveals two additional intersections with Islamic history. We have already noted the reference to "Erribon," or Yathrib. Equally obscure, especially out of context, is the use of "Ozim," which seems to me to be a form of Hashim, the Prophet's particular branch of the greater Quraysh tribe.[27]

Beyond its sheer distance from the standard narrative of Muhammad's career, the *Tultusceptru* also differs from the *Storia* in that it offers a much more positive spin on the origins of Islam. Whereas the *Storia* portrays Muhammad as an "avaricious usurer" and a "shrewd son of darkness," who is "swollen with pride" and "aflame with the fuel of his lust," the Muhammad of the *Tultusceptru* is described simply as a "monk" and a "boy," without such negative characterizations. Far from being inspired by a "spirit of error," the Muhammad of the *Tultusceptru* is delegated his missionary task by a Christian bishop who had been drafted for this purpose by a bona fide "angel of the Lord." Aside from anachronistically bearing the same name as a fourth-century Spanish bishop who, in a moment of weakness late in life, succumbed to imperial pressure and endorsed Arianism,[28] there is no hint in the text that this "father Bishop Osius" was anything but orthodox.[29] Not only do we see him being handpicked by God to bring the apostate[30] "satraps of Erribon" back into the fold, but his deputy repeatedly reminds us that he has been sent "to speak the words that [Osius] spoke to me, the words that the angel of the Lord had ordered him to speak." Following the logic of the story, if Osius had not become ill and died, or if his deputy had not, in his innocence, allowed himself to be duped by a second angel masquerading as the first, the message that the people of Yathrib would have received would have been a Christian one. Looked at from this perspective, the *Tultusceptru* is the tragic story of a pure revelation lost forever. Though the end result for the Muslims is the same as the one described at the end of the *Storia*—that is, that the 'ignorant' Arabs end up being "numbered among the company of hell"—the *Tultusceptru* stops well short of blaming Muhammad for leading them there.

*   *   *

One way of looking at the difference between these two counterhistories is to compare their levels of "give and take." Clearly both sought to "take" from Islam its legitimacy, depicting it as the work of the Devil in one form or another. But while the author of the *Storia* only "gave" (in the sense of "conceded") the historicity of certain facts of Muhammad's official biography, the author of the *Tultusceptru* "gave" not only the divine inspiration upon which Islam was based, but the purity of its original revelation and the innocence of its prophet's intentions! This is a remarkable set of concessions to say the least.[31]

In an effort to explain this difference, I will consider two contexts: one literary, involving the legendary Bahira figure, and the other sociohistorical, reflecting on the pressures faced by Christian communities living under Muslim rule.

A Literary Context

Though never mentioned in the Qur'an,[32] Bahira[33] played a key role in early biographies of the Prophet. According to the *Sirat* of Ibn Ishaq, for example, Bahira was a Christian monk living in a cell in Bosra who had in his possession an ancient book containing a description of a prophet to come. One day a Meccan caravan passed by, and Bahira saw, in one of the younger travelers, the telltale signs. He shared this insight with Muhammad's uncle Abu Talib, warning him about the Jews who would doubtless try to harm the young prophet if they realized who he was. Though the various Muslim accounts of this propitious meeting vary widely in terms of the details—including where Bahira was from, where and when he met Muhammad, and what signs he relied on to make his identification—the point of the story is always the same: to show Muhammad's status as a prophet being independently corroborated by a holy man—and a *Christian* holy man at that.

No sooner had the Bahira legend entered into the Islamic mainstream than Christian apologists in the East began to exploit its obvious counterhistorical potential.[34] There are as many variations in detail in the Christian versions as there are in the Muslim ones, but the basic story is the same. In the ninth-century Syriac renditions of the legend, a monastic narrator recounts his meeting in the Arabian desert with "Sergius Bahira," a monk living in a cell outside Yathrib, where he had been for the last 40 years, having fled persecution for his idiosyncratic ideas about the cross and its proper veneration. He came to be held in high esteem by the idolatrous Ishmaelites in the area because of his prophetic visions about the eventual rise of the Arabs. Sergius Bahira died a week after his visitor's arrival, forcing him to rely on a disciple to fill out the picture of the monk's career. The disciple told him how one day, when a group of Arabs came to refresh themselves at his well, Sergius Bahira recognized the young Muhammad as the one who would fulfil his prophecy. An extended dialogue ensued, during which Sergius Bahira agreed to mentor the unlettered and unsure Muhammad, teaching him by night what he would preach the following day. Sergius Bahira conspired to obscure his own role in the process by having Muhammad claim to be inspired by Gabriel. He went on, with some input from Muhammad, to define a heaven that would be attractive to an Arab audience and a regular system of fasts, prayers, and proscriptions that would not tax their endurance. He even suggested a way of adding authority to the Qur'an that he promised to write for Muhammad by tying it to the horn of a cow and having it delivered to the Arabs as if by a miracle.

The most surprising aspect of this Christian revision of the Bahira episode is its consistently sympathetic depiction of the monk and his protégé. True, Sergius Bahira's attitude toward the cross made him unwelcome in traditional Christian circles, but the author of the legend attributes his position to excessive zeal rather than heterodoxy.[35] Furthermore, there is nothing heretical about Sergius Bahira's answers to the questions posed by the young Muhammad,[36] which makes sense given the fact that God deemed him worthy of an important apocalyptic vision. The only place where Sergius Bahira seemed to overstep the bounds of propriety was when he set out to make Muhammad look like a prophet so as to ensure his success in fulfilling the prophecies about the Arab rise to domination. But even here the account—at least in its Syriac versions[37]—steers clear of any overt judgment, matter-of-factly depicting Sergius Bahira's subterfuge as if it were justifiable in light of its worthy end: the conversion of the Ishmaelites. Though Sergius Bahira's Qur'an was written with the intention of duping the Arabs, it is portrayed as being consistent with Christianity—at least in its original form.[38] Only after Sergius Bahira's death did it suffer adulteration, significantly enough at the hands of a Jew.[39] Thus, through no fault of Sergius Bahira, the Qur'an became the "confused" text that the Muslims would come to revere.[40] Consistent with the Syriac legend's exoneration of Sergius Bahira is its benign treatment of Muhammad. He comes across as a humble and simple boy, who is surprised but happy to learn of his role in sacred history and eager to get started by putting himself under Bahira's tutelage.[41]

The *Tultusceptru* never mentions Sergius Bahira. It does not even follow the basic story line of the Syriac legend. In fact the actual textual parallels between the legend and the enigmatic *Tultusceptru* go no further than the personification of "Awkbar" as a demon inadvertently invoked by the ignorant Arabs.[42] But if we compare the two texts from a more conceptual perspective, considering the forest as opposed to the trees, they turn out to be remarkably similar.[43] Like the Syriac Bahira legend, the *Tultusceptru* depicts Muhammad as an apprentice to a Christian holy man, and it manages to do so without blaming either one of them for the unintended results of their efforts to convert the Arabs.

A Sociohistorical Context

As illuminating as it would be to know the exact relationship between the *Tultusceptru* and the Syriac legend of Bahira,[44] it would get us no closer to answering what I regard as the more fundamental question: what did the author of the *Tultusceptru* have in mind when he crafted this unusually benign counterhistory, a counterhistory that not only countered the official Islamic history of the origins of Islam but countered the typical Christian counterhistories of the same? What were the conceptual needs of his audience that he aimed to address? Knowing something about the broader historical context of *dhimmi* Christians in Spain may help us understand the genesis of such "softer" approaches to Muhammad at both ends of the Mediterranean.

Though the corpus of Latin Christian apologetics is nowhere near as extensive as its Syriac and Arabic counterparts, one Andalusian Christian in particular left behind an extraordinarily vivid window into the complexities of *dhimmi* life under Muslim rule. Eulogius of Córdoba, the principal apologist for the so-called Córdoban martyrs, began his *Memoriale sanctorum* in the summer of 851, after the first modest wave of Christians were executed for publicly blaspheming Muhammad. Six or seven years later, when the number of decapitated Christians had risen above 40, he produced the *Liber apologeticus martyrum*. Eulogius wrote his treatises not only to record these executions for liturgical purposes, but to respond to the criticism levelled against the spontaneous "martyrs" by local Christians who felt that they were unnecessarily "rocking the boat" and incurring the wrath of the Muslim authorities against the Christian community as a whole. Though none of the Christians representing this more moderate point of view left any of their own writings behind, the logic of their position is easy to reconstruct from Eulogius's treatises thanks to his careful, point-by-point rebuttal. Eulogius took pains to counter three specific arguments against treating these Christians as martyrs of the ancient Roman type: one, that the executions were not graced with any miraculous signs; two, that the Christian community in Córdoba was not being persecuted; and three, that the Christians who died "suffered at the hands of men who venerated God and a law; they were not killed as ones summoned to sacrifice to the idols."[45]

For our purposes, Eulogius's response to the third of these accusations is the important one. It was precisely the claim that his "martyrs" were executed by monotheists as opposed to pagans that prompted Eulogius to share with his readers the contents of the *Storia de Mahometh* that he had discovered while visiting the monastery of Leyre in Navarre sometime between 848 and 850.[46] This caustic counterhistory of the rise of Islam served his own purposes well because, while it conceded that Muhammad had "made headway" in getting his Arab audience to "retreat from the cult of idols," it painted Muhammad in the darkest hues possible for a fellow monotheist—that is, as a diabolically inspired false prophet whose rejection of idolatry only served to disguise an even more insidious threat to the church. The implication of this argument: that all Christians living under Muslim rule should follow the example of the recent martyrs. Barring that, they should at least fall in line behind Eulogius and sing the martyrs' praises.

For Eulogius to have felt the need to appeal to a text as scurrilous as the *Storia de Mahometh*[47] to bolster his case that Islam posed a serious threat to Christians despite its monotheism, it follows that those Christians to whom he directed his remarks must have become accustomed to treating the monotheism of Islam as a justification for accepting their own political subordination. They had, in other words, come to see Muslims much as the Muslims famously regarded Christians: as fellow monotheists who, through no fault of their own, had been duped into accepting an adulterated version of an originally pure revelation.[48] Their willingness to explain away Islam in the same manner that the Muslims explained away Christianity underscores the utility of this strategy in a religiously pluralistic context, providing the theoretical scaffolding for a modus vivendi while at the same time leaving no doubt as to whose revelation was the pure one.

This is where the *Tultusceptru* comes in. Just as the *Storia de Mahometh* provided Eulogius with a counterhistory of the origins of Islam that justified the militancy of his "martyrs," so—I would argue—the *Tultusceptru* can be read as a counterhistory of the origins of Islam that would have helped Christian *dhimmis* justify their participation in Muslim society. While imagining Muhammad as a diabolically inspired, sexually profligate false prophet made sense to Eulogius, who was looking for a way to defend his "martyrs," imagining Muhammad as an innocent, well-meaning, but ultimately misguided Christian made sense to Christian *dhimmis* who were looking for a way of defusing their day-to-day interactions with Muslims.

I would go so far as to suggest that something akin to this situation—the one that led to the crafting of the *Tultusceptru* alongside the *Storia de Mahometh* in Spain—may account for the emergence and proliferation of the Christian Bahira legend alongside other less restrained Christian depictions of Islam in the East, such as those associated with John of Damascus in the mid-eighth century and Theophanes in the early ninth. The Christian Bahira legend would have filled a niche similar to that filled in Spain by the *Tultusceptru*, avoiding any overt demonization of Muhammad, providing Islam with a kind of Christian provenance, and, in the process, contributing to a sense of ultimate Christian priority. The end result was a conceptual package that allowed Christian *dhimmis* to relieve, in a quiet, undramatic way, some of the cognitive dissonance that came with life as a Christian living under Islamic rule.[49]

Counterhistory Revisited

Getting back to Funkenstein's conception of counterhistory, it turns out to be a bit too narrow when it comes to assessing early Christian views of Islam and the Prophet. His preoccupation with the more "vicious" forms of counterhistory—that is, those that "deprive the adversary of his positive identity, his self-image, and substitute for it a pejorative counterimage"[50]—fails to take into account other more benign versions of the process. This is not to say that the authors of the *Tultusceptru* and the Christian Bahira legend were any less intent on undermining the legitimacy of Islam. But when compared to Eulogius and the author of the *Storia de Mahometh*, their works stand out like sore thumbs, being much more forgiving of Muhammad's intentions, if not the end result of his mission.

If the well-documented divisions within the Christian community of mid-ninth-century Córdoba reflect the experiences of contemporary Christian *dhimmis* living under Muslim rule in other places, it is not hard to explain why we are faced with counterhistorical narratives with such varying degrees of bile. Beyond simply reflecting differences of opinion among subject Christians about Islam and Muhammad, it is likely that the two different "takes" on the subject were articulated and elaborated in direct response to one another, as part of an intramural *dhimmi* dialogue about the relationship between the two religions. Eulogius's brand of counterhistory, which by any standard would qualify as a form of character assassination, was polemically driven, designed to challenge the "complacency" of his coreligionists, who risked losing their religious identities altogether in the process of accommodating their lives within a non-Christian host society. Conversely, it was only in response to Eulogius's vitriol—and to the actions of his "martyrs," many of whom were executed precisely for their public assassination of Muhammad's character— that the less militant Christians felt obliged to articulate their contention that the Muslims, being neither pagans nor persecutors, should instead be treated as a neutral host society, one that permitted its *dhimmis* to render unto Caesar the things that were Caesar's and to God the things that were God's.[51]

Taking into account the steady decline in numbers of Andalusian Christians over the course of the century following Eulogius's death,[52] we might be tempted to credit a true "character assassin" like Eulogius with prescience: he knew that Christians could only maintain themselves as a separate community if they worked to maintain the boundaries and filters that protected them from being absorbed into the dominant culture.[53] On the other hand, if we are more interested in the process of boundary maintenance than the ultimate results, then the less militant *dhimmis* deserve just as much credit for managing to maintain their religious identity for as long as they did despite their proclivity to see Muslims as the Muslims saw them: as "worshippers of God and a law." When, for whatever reason, it no longer made sense to maintain that boundary, such Christians had a conceptual head start when it came to erasing it altogether.

Notes

1. This chapter is a modified version of "Counterhistory in the Earliest Latin Lives of Muhammad," delivered in July 2009 at the conference "Crossing Boundaries, Creating Images: In Search of the Prophet Muhammad in Literary and Visual Traditions," which took place in Florence, sponsored and hosted by the Kunsthistorisches Institut in Florenz / Max-Planck-Institut (Christiane Gruber and Avinoam Shalem). That paper will soon be published by De Gruyter as part of these proceedings. It is with the kind permission of De Gruyter that this form of the paper is being published as part of the present volume.
2. Funkenstein 1992, 69.
3. Funkenstein 1992, 79–80.
4. Roggema 2009, 30.
5. Roggema 2009, 33–34.
6. Roggema 2009, 30.
7. Díaz y Díaz 1970, 149.
8. Both of these texts are to be found in the *Codex of Roda, Biblioteca de la Real Academia de la Historia* (Madrid), 78: http://bibliotecadigital.rah.es/dgbrah/i18n/catalogo_imagenes/grupo.cmd?path=1000124. I have used the manuscript versions as the basis for my translations.
9. There are four extant manuscript versions of the *Storia Mahometh*, as well as one that was printed from a fifth manuscript version that is no longer extant (Díaz y Díaz 1970, 153–54). What appears to be a short recension of the *Storia* (or perhaps a summary based on a lost source common to both) has also come down to us in a letter from John of Seville to Paul Alvarus; this is the sixth letter of the Alvarus epistolary corpus (Cerro Calderón and Palacios Royán 1997, 9, 93). For a discussion of this version, see Díaz y Díaz 1970, 150–53.
10. We know that Eulogius of Córdoba consulted the *Storia* at the monastery of Leyre during his trip to Navarre, thus providing us with a firm *terminus ad quem*, since we know that Eulogius's journey fell somewhere between 848 and 850 (Wolf 1988, 54). The prologue of the *Storia* refers to historical events referenced in the *Mozarabic Chronicle*, which we know was written in 754, thus providing a potential *terminus a quo* (López 1982, 264). The text refers to Damascus as the Muslim capital, which might mean that it was written before the foundation of the Abbasid

capital in Baghdad in 762 (Franke 1958, 38–45). In the preface, the author of the *Storia* makes specific references to building projects in Toledo and Andújar, making it more likely that he hailed from one or the other city (the latter being perhaps a better candidate simply because it is a more obscure point of reference than Toledo).

11. The portion of the *Storia* dedicated to the Zaynab incident is actually a translation of Qur'an 33: 37, making it the first known Latin translation of a portion of the Qur'an (Franke 1958, 40).

12. The *Codex of Roda* version actually has it as *deum corporeum*, not *incorporeum*. Most commentators believe this to be a simple mistake on the part of the Roda scribe (Franke 1958, 39).

13. *Codex of Roda, Biblioteca de la Real Academia de la Historia* 78, 187r–188r.

14. The story of Muhammad's failed resurrection was a popular one in the East, judging from its inclusion in the Syriac versions of the Christian Bahira legend (Roggema 2009, 303n6) and the *Risalat al-Kindi* (Tartar 1985, 166). Neither of these, however, contains the part about the Prophet's body being eaten by dogs. As Franke has noted, it seems to be unique to the *Tultusceptru* (Franke 1958, 44; Tolan 2003, 91–93).

15. Díaz y Díaz 1970, 162; Vázquez de Parga 1971, 143–64; and López 1982, 253–71; Christys 2002, 62–64.

16. Vázquez de Parga speculated that *Tultusceptru* is a corrupt form of *tultum excerptum*, or "extract taken from" (Vázquez de Parga 1971, 152).

17. Vázquez de Parga 1971, 152; McGinn 1979, 74; Kedar 1984, 29.

18. Díaz y Díaz 1970, 160–63; González Muñoz 2004, 22.

19. Díaz y Díaz 1970, 161.

20. Here I part with Díaz y Díaz, who considered the *Tultusceptru* a "texto de escaso valor," notable primarily for its "curiosidad" (Díaz y Díaz 1970, 160).

21. This sentence is grammatically incomplete, one of a number of indications that the one who transcribed it into the *Codex of Roda* had difficulty reading the text from which he was working (Díaz y Díaz 1970, 160).

22. Ezechiel 2: 3–5.

23. John 20: 27.

24. Only the beginning (*Alla occuber alla occuber*) and the ending (*Mohamet razulille*) correspond to the actual wording of the *adhān*. Aside from "leila," the part in between reads more like Latin, indicating that something was "cited" (*citus est*) "in place" (*situ*) of something else. For attempts at reconstructing the Arabic original, see Díaz y Díaz 1970, 163; Hoyland 1997, 515.

25. This is consistent with Eastern Christian texts that treat "allah" and "akbar" as two different deities, hence undercutting the supposed monotheism of Islam (González Muñoz n.d., 5–6).

26. *Codex of Roda, Biblioteca de la Real Academia de la Historia* 78, 185v.

27. "Ozim" is also rendered "Ocim" in the *Tultusceptru*. The *Prophetic Chronicle*, produced in the Christian court of Asturias in 883, includes a Latin genealogy of Muhammad that renders "Hisham" as "Escim," making the connection between Hisham and Ozim/Ocim more obvious (Gómez-Moreno 1932, 624). Alternatively Hoyland has speculated that Ozim could be a form of the Arabic term *azim*, meaning "great," that was one of Muhammad's titles (Hoyland 1997, 516).

28. Hosius of Córdoba (c. 256–c. 358). After distinguishing himself as a staunch defender of orthodoxy against Arianism, Hosius ultimately endorsed the formula of the pro-Arian Third Council of Sirmium (357).

29. The choice of Hosius potentially allowed the author to build on connections (made by John of Damascus, among others) between Islam and Arianism, and to do so strategically for a Spanish audience used to conceiving of Arianism as a threat associated with the Visigoths prior to King Reccared's conversion in 586 (González Muñoz n.d., 7). As for the anachronism, there are times when "el razonamiento tipológico anula o neutraliza la razón cronológica" (González Muñoz n.d., 8). But González Muñoz is also willing to entertain the possibility that Osio is a corrupt form of "Sergius" (González Muñoz n.d., 9).

30. It is unusual to find the pre-Islamic Arabs described as "apostates," rather than pagans. This has a lot to do with the author's decision to tap into Ezechiel's mission to the wayward Israelites.

31. Previous historians who have considered the *Tultusceptru* have missed the substantial differences in tone between it and other anti-Islamic texts from Spain (López 1982, 260). Fernando González Muñoz is less sanguine about the difference in tone here since the "conversion" of Ozim, marked by his recitation of the *adhān* and the change of name, would have been interpreted as irredeemable steps in the direction of idolatry and hell. In other words, the end result of Ozim's corruption negates the promising beginnings. But González Muñoz still recognizes the influence of the Christian Bahira legend (González Muñoz n.d., 5, 9).

32. Qur'an 5: 82 has traditionally been read as a reference to Bahira: "You will find that the closest people in friendship to the believers are those who say, 'We are Christian.' This is because they have priests and monks among them, and they are not arrogant."

33. "Bahira" comes from the Syriac *bhira*, an honorific title given to monks who have been "tested," or "tried" (as by fire). The Islamic texts treat the adjective as a proper name.

34. "The genius of the author of the Christian Bahira legend was to have chosen the Islamic story on Muhammad's encounter with the monk as the center-piece for his work of apocalypse and apologetic" (Griffith 1995, 153). Though the earliest actual mention of Bahira in a Christian text can be dated to the 720s, it was not until the ninth century that a full-blown Christian interpretation of the Bahira-Muhammad encounter emerged and spread, surviving to this day in two Syriac and two Arabic forms. Griffith bases his positioning of the text in the ninth century not only on the allusions to Islamic history contained in the apocalyptic portion of the document, but on the nature of the apologetic arguments advanced in the Arabic version. He regards the Syriac version as anterior to the Arabic one (Griffith 1995, 156–57).

35. This places the author of the Syriac legend at odds with the majority of Christian opinions on the status of Muhammad's Christian mentor. Beginning with John of Damascus, who claimed that Muhammad had been mentored by an Arian, the list of apologists who posit the formative influence of a Christian heretic (Arian, Nestorian, or Jacobite) is long (Roggema 2009, 168–82).

36. As Roggema has observed, the various recensions each feature language that is specific to the Christological "flavor" of the imagined audience of that recension (Roggema 2009, 110–12). But the fact that the discussions of Christology are so brief makes it less obvious that any one interpretation was being favored over another (Roggema 2009, 112).

37. Only in the Arabic versions is any blame directed toward Sergius. The so-called long Arabic recension is framed as an extended confession on Bahira's part for his own "sinful" role in creating this "heretical invention": a false prophet (Roggema 2009, 435; cf. 415–19).

38. East-Syrian recension: "Not the slightest fear of God was to be found in it, because all that Sergius had handed down to them had been changed by Ka'b the Jew" (Roggema 2009, 307). West-Syrian recension: "However, because of their irrationality, they abandoned the words of Rabban Sergius Bahira, which were true, and accepted and adhered to this tradition which Kalb the Scribe had given them" (Roggema 2009, 335). As Roggema observed: "There is no insinuation that the monk taught something heterodox, or to be more concrete, it may be implied that the words used in the Qur'an can only derive from Christian teachings" (Roggema 2009, 110).

39. Identified as Ka'b or Kaleb. This is a clever tie-in to the Islamic version of the episode, in which Abu Talib is specifically warned to protect his nephew from the machinations of the Jews. Ka'b al-Ahbar was a name well-known in Muslim sources as an early Jewish convert to Islam. According to the Arabic versions of the Christian Bahira legend, Ka'b filled the Qur'an with "superstitions, ridiculous and arbitrary things, circumcision, ablution," and so forth, claiming that Muhammad was the Paraclete, whose coming Jesus had prophesied, and that, like Jesus, Muhammad would rise from the dead after three days, a claim that proved embarrassing to the Muslims when they realized it was not to be.

40. Roggema 2009, 303–5.

41. Roggema 2009, 285, 355.

42. As we saw before, the *Tultusceptru* describes how Ozim-Muhammad unwittingly corrupted the "satraps" by teaching them to say "*alla occuber*," not knowing that this invocation "conjured up demons." Similarly the Syriac text has the sons of Ishmael "provok[ing] the anger of God every day of their lives with their polytheistic worship of Awkbar, without being aware of it. [Indeed] the name Awkbar is proclaimed by them shamelessly with a loud voice" (Roggema 2009, 301).

43. González Muñoz refers to the *Tultusceptru* as "un extraño derivado latino del Apocalipsis de Sergio-Bahira," without elaborating on the connection between the two texts (González Muñoz 2004, 22).

44. It is certainly possible that the *Tultusceptru* is based, however loosely, on the Christian Bahira legend. There is plenty of evidence that contact and exchange between Spain and the Eastern Mediterranean continued and even increased after the Muslim conquest of 711, though it is hard to trace its actual mechanisms. The influx of Syrians under the Andalusian governor Balj in 741, the rise to power of the Syrian refugee Abd ar-Rahman in 756, and—more anecdotally—the presence of the monk George from St. Sabas (d. 852) among the martyrs of Córdoba stand out as the most salient markers of such ties between Al-Andalus and Syria (López 1982, 263).

45. Eulogius, *Liber apologeticus martyrum* 12; Gil 1973, 2.481.

46. Gil 1973, 2.483–86.

47. Richard Southern, and the many who have followed him, mistakenly interpreted Eulogius's use of the *Storia* as a sign of wilful ignorance on his part: "They were ignorant of Islam, not because they were far removed from it like the Carolingian scholars, but for the contrary reason that they were in the middle of it. If they saw and understood little of what went on around them, and if they knew nothing of Islam as a religion, it is because they wished to know nothing. The situation of an oppressed and unpopular minority within a minority is not a suitable one for scientific inquiry into the true position of the oppressor. Significantly they preferred to know about Mahomet from the meager Latin source which Eulogius found in Christian Navarre, rather than from the fountainhead of the Koran or

the great biographical compilations of their Moslem contemporaries" (Southern 1962, 25–26). Once one realizes the polemical task that Eulogius had assumed for himself, his use of this "meager" source makes more sense. Franke also misses the point here, seeing this as an example of a lack of engagement—specifically among Christians in the West—with Islam as a religion (Franke 1958, 45).

48. In other words, the author adopted and adapted the Muslim idea of *taḥrif* ("corruption"), this is, "falsification of the Bible," a concept developed in the seventh century (Roggema 2009, 12n7). Sayf ibn 'Umar, in the eighth century, described Paul as a Jew who deliberately corrupted Christian doctrine (Roggema 2009, 31). It should be remembered in this context that Muslim scholars did not blame Moses, Jesus, or any of the other prophets for later corruptions of their revelations. Compare, in this regard, the *Tultusceptru* to the *Summary of the Ways of Faith*, a Christian Arabic text from the early Islamic period, where we find references to Christians who strategically downplayed the distinctively Christian aspects of Jesus's career and adopted a Father-centric notion of divinity that they justified on the grounds of consistency with the Old Testament. The author of the text was as critical of them as Eulogius was of his coreligionists (Griffith 1995, 58–59).

49. This interpretation helps fill out Sidney Griffith's own observations about the Christian Bahira legend. In his own words, "The Christian story is a clever construct, not lacking in verisimilitude, which builds on well-known Islamic lore, to serve as a literary vehicle for a Christian response to the civil and religious pressures of Islam. And it provides the Christian reader not only with a way religiously to account for the rise of Islam and the course of its history, but it also suggests that Islam is actually a misunderstood form of Christianity. And it provides the Christian reader with apologetic strategies for rebutting Islamic objections to Christian doctrines" (Griffith 1995, 148). Griffith stops just short of exploring the less aggressive implications of seeing Islam as a "misunderstood form of Christianity."

50. Funkenstein 1992, 79–80.
51. Matthew 22: 21.
52. Bulliett 1979.
53. Glick and Pi-Sunyer 1969.

Bibliography

Bulliet, R. W. 1979. *Conversion to Islam in the Medieval Period: An Essay in Quantitative History*. Harvard: Harvard University Press.

Cerro Calderón, G., and J. Palacios Royán, eds. 1997. *Epistolario de Álvaro de Córdoba*. Córdoba: Universidad de Córdoba.

Christys, A. 2002. *Christians in al-Andalus: 711–1000*. Richmond, UK: Curzon.

Díaz y Díaz, M. C. 1970. "Los textos antimahometanos más antiguos en códices españoles." *Archives d'histoire doctrinale et littéraire de Moyen Age* 37: 149–68.

Franke, F. R. 1958. "Die freiwilligen Märtyrer von Córdoba und das Verhältnis der Mozaraber zum Islam." In E. Schramm, G. Schreiber, and J. Vives, eds., *Gesammelte Aufsätze zur Kulturgeschichte Spaniens*, vol. 13, 1–170. Münster: Aschendorffsche Verlagsbuchhandlung.

Funkenstein, A. 1992. "History, Counterhistory, and Narrative." In S. Friedlander, ed., *Probing the Limits of Representation: Nazism and the "Final Solution,"* 66–81. Cambridge, MA: Harvard University Press.

Gil, J., ed. 1973. *Corpus Scriptorum Mvzarabicorum*. 2 vols. Consejo superior de investigaciones científicas. Madrid: Instituto Antonio de Nebrija.

Glick, T., and O. Pi-Sunyer. 1969. "Acculturation as an Explanatory Concept in Spanish History." *Comparative Studies in Society and History* 11: 136–54.

Gómez-Moreno, M. 1932. "Las primeras crónicas de la Reconquista: el ciclo de Alfonso III." *Boletín de la Real Academia de la Historia* 100: 562–628.

González Muñoz, F. 2004. "*Liber Nycholay*. La leyenda de Mahoma y el cardenal Nicolás." *Al-Qantara* 25: 5–43.

González Muñoz, F. n.d. "La nota del códice de Roda sobre el obispo Osio y el monje Ozim" (unpublished paper).

Griffith, S. 1995. "Muhammad and the Monk Bahira." *Oriens Christianus* 79: 146–74.

Hoyland, R. 1997. *Seeing the Islam as Others Saw It: A Survey and Evaluation of Christian, Jewish and Zoroastrian Writings on Early Islam*. Princeton, NJ: Princeton University Press.

Kedar, B. Z. 1984. *Crusade and Mission: European Approaches toward the Muslims*. Princeton, NJ: Princeton University Press.

López, J. E. 1986. "La cultura del mundo árabe en textos latinos hispanos del siglo VIII." In A. Sidarus, ed., *Islão e Arabismo na península ibérica. Actas do XI congresso da União Europeia de arabistas e Islamólogos*, 253–87. Évora: Universidade de Évora.

McGinn, B. 1979. *Visions of the End: Apocalyptic Traditions in the Middle Ages*. New York: Columbia University Press.

Roggema, B. 2009. *The Legend of Sergius Bahira: Eastern Christian Apologetics and Apocalyptic in Response to Islam*. Leiden, Netherlands: Brill.

Southern, R. W. 1962. *Western Views of Islam in the Middle Ages*. Cambridge, MA: Harvard University Press.

Tartar, G., ed. 1985. *Dialogue Islamo-Chretien sous le calife Al-Ma'mun (813–834). Les épîtres d'Al-Hashimî et d'Al-Kindî*. Paris: Nouvelles Editions Latines.

Tolan, J. 2003. *Saracens: Islam in the Medieval Imagination*. New York: Columbia University Press.

Vázquez de Parga, L. 1971. "Algunas notas sobre el Pseudo-Metodio y España." *Habis* 2: 143–64.

Wolf, K. B. 1988. *Christian Martyrs in Muslim Spain*. Cambridge: Cambridge University Press.

6

Louis of Orléans, Isabeau of Bavaria, and the Burgundian Propaganda Machine, 1392–1407

Tracy Adams

Introduction

Character assassination and public opinion are closely connected in the modern era, with defamation generally presupposing a public capable of reacting in such a way as to promote the agenda of the attacker.[1] Of course, attackers sometimes fail to turn public opinion against their target, bringing opprobrium on themselves instead, but modern publics, informed by media, polls, and election results, usually are able to judge whether an attack achieves its mark or backfires. In contrast, the success of a premodern act of character assassination is hard to analyze. We cannot easily distinguish between a report of an attack in contemporary documents, like chronicles, and a public's reaction to an attack. A chronicler's description of an "unpopular" individual may prove only that someone was slandering him or her; that is, such a description may represent an act of character assassination rather than a public's response to an act of character assassination.

The campaign of character assassination perpetrated between 1392 and 1407 by the Dukes of Burgundy against the Duke and Duchess of Orléans—that is, Louis, brother of mad King Charles VI of France, along with his wife, Valentina Visconti—and the queen of France, Isabeau of Bavaria, exemplifies this problem. The campaign must in one sense be regarded as among the most successful in history: many historians, popular and scholarly, believe to this day that two of the victims, Louis of Orléans and Isabeau of Bavaria, were detested by their contemporaries. And yet, it is not at all clear that this was the case. In this essay I examine how the attack was carried out in this period before the press made wide and rapid circulation of defamatory stories possible. Moreover, I use the case to highlight the need for caution in our modern historical approach to defamation in the premodern era.

The Context

Some recent scholarship describes Duke Louis of Orléans as a cartoonishly debauched character involved in a love affair with the queen. Gossip supposedly circulated about "the relations between the queen and the duke of Orleans, a liaison that lasted until the duke's assassination in a Paris street near the queen's residence in November 1407"; throughout his lifetime, he and Isabeau allegedly were "fleecing the kingdom for their pleasures."[2] True, many scholars recognize these stories to be modern vestiges of the campaign of character assassination orchestrated by the Dukes of Burgundy. Still, most continue to assume that even if they were not guilty as charged, Louis and Isabeau suffered from black reputations during their lifetimes, that "the unscrupulous Louis and the questionable Isabeau had been garnering ill repute for massive debauchery and financial greed, both individually and, supposedly, as a couple."[3]

The story of this campaign of character assassination and its continued influence begins with the onset of the madness of King Charles VI. This debilitating mental illness, probably schizophrenia, struck him first in 1392, when he was just 24, and afflicted him with increasing frequency and severity throughout his life.[4] During these episodes he attacked members of his family and entourage, refused to eat or wash, and suffered from hallucinations.[5] Although chroniclers record periods of remission, it is unlikely that the king ever regained his full mental capacity. From the initial episode, Louis vied with the young man's uncle, Philip of Burgundy, for regency of the kingdom when the king was indisposed. Historians often assume an equivalency between the dukes' claims, describing both as ambitious and greedy.[6] However, this is not accurate; Philip had no legitimate claim to regency. Charles VI's father, Charles V, mistrustful of collateral male relatives, attempted to avoid the power struggles that marked the early Valois kingships by relying on a small group of non-nobles as his most intimate advisors, while appeasing his three brothers with appanages that kept them wealthy and occupied.[7] Moreover, anticipating the struggle that would arise among the brothers if he died early, leaving a minor king, he created a regency ordinance in August 1374, to set the age of majority at 14. In the ordinance he specified his second son, Louis, by name, as next in line after the dauphin, Charles.[8] In another ordinance of October 1374, Charles V further attempted to ward off potential danger by awarding primary *tutelle*, or guardianship, of the dauphin to the queen, who would be assisted by his youngest brother, Philip of Burgundy, and his brother-in-law, Louis of Bourbon. Furthermore, Charles V specifically placed the guardians under surveillance of his closest advisor, to whom he gave veto power over their decisions.[9] In another document of the same day, he appointed his eldest brother, Louis of Anjou, regent of the realm during the minority of the dauphin, but placed him too under the watch of the same advisor.[10]

When Charles V died in 1380, leaving a minor heir, his two younger brothers ejected the eldest brother, Louis of Anjou, from the position assigned him, along with Charles V's advisors, and seized power for themselves.[11] They remained until Charles VI, then 20 years old, dismissed them from his Royal Council in 1388 and took control of his kingdom. At the same time, the king reinstalled the advisors and strengthened his brother's position. With Charles VI's first bout of insanity, however, Philip returned to power.[12] The king attempted several times to insure Louis's primacy in the government of the kingdom during his periods of mental illness. An ordinance promulgated in 1393 (temporarily supplanted by Philip and then restored in 1403) named him regent in the case of the death of the king before the majority of his heir.

That Philip would be appointed regent during the lifetime of a competent brother of the king—that is, a man more closely related to the reigning king than Philip—was quite simply impossible. As Bernard Guenée has demonstrated, a fixation on rank developed throughout the reign of Charles V, so that by the reign of Charles VI a cluster of some 70 "cousins" were minutely ordered on the basis of how closely they were related to the reigning king.[13] Philip thus made the only plausible case that he could to increase his share of the power, arguing that the kingdom should be governed by a council, headed by himself, and, to reinforce his argument, he worked hard to discredit Louis, depicting him as too young (even when he was into his thirties) and accusing him of oppressive taxation.[14] Philip's son, Jean of Burgundy ("Jean sans Peur," or "John the Fearless") continued the process after Philips's death in 1404.[15] Louis, in contrast, confident of the righteousness of his position, waged no countercampaign beyond a series of letters to the cities of the kingdom during an attempt at a coup by Jean.[16] This lack of counterattack undoubtedly accounts to a large extent for the success of the Burgundian propaganda among later historians, who see only Philip and Jean's attacks and no defense.

The Character Assassination

This is the context within which the campaign took place. I now turn to the campaign itself. On November 23, 1407, Jean of Burgundy had Louis of Orléans assassinated. Just days before, the dukes had publicly proclaimed their friendship.[17] But although the act was considered all the more heinous for having been carried out treacherously, Louis's terrified male relatives did not react immediately. Jean, initially denying involvement, quickly fled to his own territories when the truth was revealed. It was late December before the king summoned him to Paris to account for his actions. When he did not turn up, the king sent his uncles to Amiens to confront him. The result was that Jean agreed to present himself in Paris if he were guaranteed that no armed men would guard the gates to the city, and he returned to Paris in March 1408, along with Jean Petit, theologian at the University of Paris, who declaimed a justification of the assassination before the court. Because Louis had been a tyrant, he had deserved to die, and Jean therefore had acted in the interests of the kingdom. In addition, Louis had been greedy (he had tried to take over Normandy and had helped himself to the taxes raised for the war), and he had tried for years to kill the king by poison or sorcery in such a way as to arouse no suspicion of murder.[18]

Insane during the discourse, the king was functional the next day, and he issued Jean of Burgundy a pardon when informed of the justification. A spokesman for the Duchess of Orléans responded to the justification; this elicited a second justification by Jean Petit. Copies of the first justification circulated widely in Europe, and, because Jean took control of the government in 1409, the Burgundian perspective initially prevailed.[19] A Burgundian chronicle, the verse *Geste des ducs de Bourgogne*, circa 1412, described Louis as a necromancer and poisoner attempting to do away with his brother. True, after the Orléanists gained power in 1413 following a revolt in Paris, encouraged by Jean of Burgundy, the doctrines expressed by Jean Petit were condemned, in February 1414, by the bishop of Paris, although Petit himself had died in 1411.[20] But in March 1414 Jean of Burgundy appealed the condemnation to Rome, and in September 1414, Pope John XXIII appointed three cardinals to examine the appeal.[21] Jean of Burgundy in the meantime proclaimed his innocence before assemblies throughout his territories. A delegation headed by University of Paris chancellor Jean Gerson attempted to get Petit's justification condemned at the Council of Constance (1414–18) but was countered by a Burgundian embassy that was more "focused, methodical, political and perfidiously political."[22] Although the council pronounced against tyrannicide in general, swayed by the Burgundian embassy, it refused to name names.[23] Moreover, on January 15, 1416, the cardinals annulled the condemnation by the bishop of Paris. In response, on September 16, 1416, the Parlement de Paris made illegal the publication of anything supporting tyrannicide or Petit's justification.[24] But in March 1419, with Jean of Burgundy back in power in Paris after the infamous massacre of the Orléanists by the Burgundians in 1418, the Parlement de Paris revoked all condemnations of Jean Petit's doctrines.[25] It mattered little by this time because Jean of Burgundy was himself assassinated by men of the dauphin Charles, later Charles VII, in October 1419.

Although Jean of Burgundy's character assassination of Louis is well known and his motive obvious, its place in the long-term program of character assassination carried out by the Burgundians has not been studied systematically. The first Burgundian attack against Louis of Orléans is generally considered to date from 1401, nearly ten years after the king's first episode of madness, taking the form of a letter of complaint by Philip that Louis was mismanaging the realm. The context for the complaint was Philip's flight from the royal court in Paris, itself occasioned by the revelation that he was plotting to create a confederation with the Holy Roman Emperor, Robert of Bavaria, against Duke of Milan Giangaleazzo Visconti, father-in-law to Louis. Specifically, Robert, encouraged by his understanding with the Duke of Burgundy, decided to descend on Milan. When Louis got wind of this, he was outraged, and Philip became an enemy at court. In reaction, Philip sent an open letter to the Parlement in October 1401, implicitly attacking Louis by expressing his concern about the state of the kingdom: it was a great pity to hear what he had heard, and he could hardly believe that things were in the state that they were in.[26] The dukes' rivalry is first noted explicitly in chronicles at about the same time. In 1401 we read that in "the face of the constant excessively jealous and stubborn struggle for superiority, courtiers ceaselessly attempted through spouting flattery to ignite into a giant fire the sparks of hatred hiding under the embers of dissimulation, with the object of provoking the dukes to shows of public enmity."[27] In December 1401, the dukes almost came to arms.

However, I suggest that Burgundian character assassination began earlier, shortly after the king's first episode of madness, in 1393, when the king awarded regency to Louis. This is compatible with Jean Petit's justification, which accuses Louis of sorcery beginning around the time of Charles VI's madness.[28] True, Burgundian-leaning chronicler Michel Pintoin, also known as "the Monk of St. Denis," recounts that a certain magician who failed to cure the king defended himself by claiming that the cure was being interfered with by the Duchess of Orléans.[29] But we can infer from Jean Petit's justification that Louis, too, was targeted, although Pintoin mentions only Valentina. In 1395 and 1396, Pintoin mentions that many others throughout the kingdom began to suffer from the same disease as the king and that they blamed magical spells.[30] Once again, suspicion fell on Valentina, a suspicion shared by the people and the nobility. The chronicler Froissart notes that her alleged motive was that she coveted the throne for Louis.[31] Pintoin insists that the charges against the duchess were without foundation, professing to believe, along with doctors and theologians, that the king's youthful excesses had come back to haunt him. But in any case, someone powerful was behind the rumors, because the Duke of Orléans finally was persuaded to send his wife from court to avoid scandal.[32] Pintoin depicts further attacks in 1398. The constable of France, Louis of Sancerre, sent two Augustinians, called Pierre and Lancelot, to cure the king through magic.[33] Unsuccessful, they blamed Louis for blocking attempts at a cure with his own magic. Pintoin explains that the Augustinians frequented the Duke of Burgundy, a strong suggestion that Philip was behind the attacks.[34]

After Philip's death, in the spring of 1404, attacks against Louis increased. Jean, a mere cousin of the king, had yet less claim to regency than his father and therefore continued all the more vigorously to push for a governing council, led by himself, that excluded Louis and Queen Isabeau, who had allied herself with her brother-in-law after the death of Philip. The Orléanist-leaning chronicle attributed to Pierre Cousinot mentions that the Duke of Burgundy spread lies about Louis and Isabeau among vagabonds and in taverns.[35] But

Jean went much further than this, summoning the citizens of Paris to rise up against Louis. In August 1405, Jean kidnapped the dauphin in an attempt to seize power, justifying his actions in a discourse by his counselor Jean de Nielles before a group of notables assembled at the Louvre. The Duke of Burgundy was interested only in the good of the kingdom, not in power for himself. He was obliged to act because the kingdom was not being well tended: the king's *officiers* were corrupt; the domain was in a state of disrepair; the Church was being oppressed with taxes; and the taxes supposedly collected for the war against England were lining the pockets of the Duke of Orléans.[36] Both Louis and Jean called their men to arms, and, during the standoff that followed, Jean called on the Parisians to join him against the Duke of Orléans. They refused, explaining that they answered only to the king, or in his absence, to the dauphin.[37]

We have seen how and why Louis and Valentina were targeted by the Dukes of Burgundy. I now consider attacks made by Jean of Burgundy on the queen, Isabeau of Bavaria. Attacks upon her were mild in comparison to those waged against Louis and Valentina. Also, the queen is attacked only in tandem with Louis, never alone. But two sources, both referring to the years 1405–06—when, as we have seen, Jean took up his father's struggle with Louis—show her falling victim to the Burgundian propaganda machine.

In the first source, Pintoin's chronicle for 1405, the monk reports popular discontent against Louis and the queen, describing the French army's inability to protect the people from the English, who were marauding the coastline. According to Pintoin, the French blamed their general misery on the queen and the Duke of Orléans, whom they saw as the cause of their financial worries and the war.[38] Pintoin's second report of discontent features an Augustinian monk, Jacques Legrand, who scolds Isabeau and her courtiers in a sermon in the spring of 1405. Once again, the root of the complaint is the war. The monk refers to her soldiers as devotees of Venus (rather than Mars)—that is, emasculated lackeys. Pintoin reports that the king asked Legrand for a repeat performance; Legrand explains to the king that during the time of Charles V, heavy taxes were imposed for the war, but at least the French won sometimes! The monk records another instance of character attack in the midst of Jean's coup attempt in early autumn of 1405, writing that noble seigneurs asked that the kingdom be watched over, because the queen and Louis, by virtue of the rights they enjoyed as the nearest relatives of the king, were deciding things on their own without consulting the uncles and cousins of the king, or other members of the Royal Council. It is not clear who was speaking and where, but the noble seigneurs must have been Jean and possibly other Burgundian members of the Royal Council, and the audience seems to have been the king. Just afterward some unnamed people tell the king that the queen was neglecting to caress the dauphin.[39]

The second source is the anonymous allegorical poem known as the "Songe véritable," composed circa 1406. Like Pintoin's chronicle for 1405, it can only have been motivated by Burgundians: two of the poem's main villains are Louis of Orléans and Jean de Montaigu, master of Charles VI's household, both killed at Jean's orders. Isabeau figures as well, as one whose good reputation will be destroyed in the near future. The character Fortune claims to have become angry at Isabeau one year ago—at just the time that Jean of Burgundy turned against her. However, most important for this study of character assassination, Fortune further clarifies that she has not yet managed to produce the desired result: to blacken the queen's reputation. When she refers to what she has in store for the queen, Fortune uses the future tense: "I will bring such shame to her / and such damage and loss / that in the end she will be ruined by it" (lines 1736–38). The poem thus dramatizes the Burgundian goal to defame the queen, but not its accomplishment.

Continuation of the Black Legends

If the defamation of Louis and Isabeau was energetic, it is not clear that it was successful during its own time because accounts of their lack of popularity are found only among authors with a Burgundian bias. In the context of a feud, attacks by enemies are the norm, and, as is the case in deeply polarized political scenarios today, they serve simply to deepen already-existing divisions. Different from the modern scenario where "independent" voters up for grabs form the audience for character assassination, there was no public in the modern sense to be usefully attracted to one side or the other. Individual loyalties were mediated by corporate bodies, as we have seen in the case of the Parisians whom Jean attempted to persuade to take arms against the Duke of Orléans. At higher levels, individual lords could be attracted by personal promises from the individual feuders, and changing sides was frequent. However, both the Orléanists and the Burgundians always retained sufficient support to remain in a stalemate. Although Philip, the son of Jean of Burgundy, continued to produce anti-Orléanist propaganda, by the late fifteenth century, Jean's justification of the assassination of Louis had lost credibility to the extent that even chronicles written in Burgundian territories describe the act as dreadful, the catalyst for decades of civil strife.[40]

And yet, the character assassination must be regarded as successful, at least regarding Louis and Isabeau, in the sense that they are still characterized as frivolous spendthrifts in many modern histories. Although the charge that Louis tried to kill the king through witchcraft or poison has been laid to rest, the other elements of Burgundian propaganda continue to hold force in many recent studies.[41] In particular, a story based on a misunderstanding of one bit of Burgundian propaganda is today widespread: that a rumor linking the two in an affair circulated during their lifetimes. The notion of a romantic liaison between the duke and his sister-in-law arose from a misreading of the second negative mention of Isabeau in Pintoin's chronicle, referred to above, Jacques Legrand's complaint about the queen and her courtiers. Although scholars today no longer believe that Isabeau and Louis were romantically involved, many continue to assume that gossip about them was rife. However, no contemporary chronicle, not even those of Burgundian bias, mentions such a rumor.[42]

Finally, I will consider how the bad reputations of Louis and Isabeau have been carried into the modern era by historians, who, divorced from the original context of a particular act of character assassination, mistake it for the widespread dislike of a figure. To begin, we can explain quite easily how Louis's and Isabeau's bad reputations were transmitted to the present day. As for Louis, as Françoise Autrand explains,[43] most nineteenth-century historians were influenced by the Revolution to dislike the monarchy, and they accepted uncritically the image of Philip of Burgundy—man of the people denouncing taxes levied by Louis for the war against the English—promoted by the most widely read chroniclers of the period of Charles VI, Pintoin and Monstrelet, who like Pintoin was Burgundian-leaning during the years in question.[44] As Jean-Michel Dequeker-Fergon points out, chroniclers under Armagnac king Charles VII and his descendants tended to write polemical histories that favored Louis.[45] However, these were not the sources to which nineteenth-century historians turned for information on the reign of Charles VI, and nineteenth- and early twentieth-century historians Michelet, Guizot, Martin, Colville, and Thibault set in place narratives about the court of King Charles VI and his relatives that continue to hold force. True, monarchist historians viewed the royal family positively, but they were few.[46] In addition to the discernible partisanship in the chroniclers most familiar to historians, another important source of the modern anti-Orléans bias is noted by Élisabeth Gonzalez: the difficulty of gathering sources on the House of Orléans, since they are spread throughout France. The result has been that histories treating Louis have often lacked a critical perspective.[47]

The transmission of Isabeau's black legend to the present is more complex. During her lifetime, except for the couple of attacks we have discussed, chronicles indicate that she was respected, and royal ordinances assigning her positions of real authority during the mad king's periods of indisposition demonstrate Charles VI's great trust in her. Even the now infamous Treaty of Troyes, making Henry V the king's legal heir in place of her own son, was not widely held against her, but was often seen as an attempt to put an end to a conflict between implacable enemies. After the Burgundian attacks, the oldest layer of character assassination is her alleged promiscuity, created shortly before her death by the English to justify Henry VI's kingship. This was closely followed by her image as a novice interfering in politics, appearing for the first time in some late sixteenth-century treatises on female regency—an image based on the derogatory mentions in Pintoin's chronicle that we have examined. Increasingly distant from the ideology of feuding that had dominated the fifteenth century and guided by stereotypes of feminine fickleness, some of the treatises condemned the queen as manipulating the dukes for her own gain.[48] The next development of the queen's bad reputation came when she was associated with the *Cour amoureuse*, the Court of Love, whose charter was discovered in the early eighteenth century. These different pieces were gathered together by Louise de Kéralio in her diatribe against the queens of France.[49] Kéralio's Isabeau as a prototype of Marie-Antoinette was then taken up by nineteenth-century historians, prone themselves to anti-German sentiment. This is the Isabeau whom twentieth-century historians, popular and scholarly, have had to extract from the legends in which she was long embedded.

And yet, the evil reputations of Louis and Isabeau endure even in recent histories. Both have been the object of some measured studies, but these seem to have had little impact on the way they are represented.[50] Why? I would suggest that a major cause of historical character assassination is the tendency to adopt historical figures as "bundles" of stereotypical traits to help to flesh out historical narratives. For such purposes there is no need to unpack the bundle and verify the various strands that it contains. In the case of Louis of Orléans, the notoriously complicated and still relatively little-understood Armagnac-Burgundian feud has been simplified for easy comprehension into a series of personal conflicts waged by two ambitious and greedy competitors for a prize to which they had an equal claim.[51] Conceived of in this way, the feud requires no further investigation and allows us to ignore the issue of rank, always problematic for modern readers. Bernard Guenée has argued that by the time of Charles VI, the royal family was a massive and hierarchized body with those most closely related to the current king occupying the highest ranks;[52] Charles V's ordinances show a similar attention to the degree of relation, awarding his wife the first place among guardians of the dauphin and royal children and making his second son the successor after his first son. Charles VI follows a similar pattern, naming his brother regent and treating his Burgundian uncle and cousins as valued counselors, but not as potential regents. Obviously Burgundian perspectives on the situation ignore nuances of rank, which modern readers are inclined to do, as well. For example, we find in Pintoin's chronicle that the Duke of Orléans had no patience for sharing power (*impaciens consortis*) and claimed that his right was greater because he was closer to the throne.[53] Pintoin (and modern readers) disapprove of what the monk describes as Louis's arrogance. And yet, Louis's position corresponds precisely to Charles VI's construal of his brother's role.

Isabeau has been bundled as an antitype in a similar way, standing in as a metonymy for court life in the scholarship on Christine de Pizan. Christine wrote about the court, and she has been viewed as a scandalized moralist critiquing the queen.[54] References to the queen's supposed affair with Louis of Orléans and Christine's imagined disapproval are common.[55] Indeed, a whole narrative has been invented around Christine's early "courtly" writings that rewrites the poet's observations about the woes of love as discreet criticisms aimed at the supposedly promiscuous Isabeau. But most enduring of all, Isabeau has been made into the traitor who ceded France to the English, declaring her own son a bastard, with the Treaty of Troyes. This same Isabeau has been bundled as an antitype in Joan of Arc scholarship, sometimes against Yolanda of Aragon, the "good" mother-in-law of Isabeau's son, Charles VII, sometimes against Joan herself, as the Eve who lost France in contrast to the Virgin who restored it. This vision of the queen has been stubbornly persistent because it is entwined with a powerful foundational myth, that of French nationalism as spawn of the Treaty of Troyes.

Conclusion

Although their motives are not nefarious, recent scholars have continued the character assassination begun by the enemies of Louis and Isabeau. Similar to the criticism leveled against Michel Foucault that he created a monolith of sexual behavior during the Middle Ages to use as a foil for his argument about the discursive nature of modern sexuality, my argument is that Louis and Isabeau have been used as useful foils in many cases—that is, their stories too often have not been unpacked.

I conclude this essay with the observation that Valentina Visconti, heavily targeted with her husband by Burgundian propaganda, has avoided the calumny so often attached to Louis and Isabeau, as well as the assumption that her contemporaries hated her, even enjoying a positive image in modern scholarship. The reason is pure serendipity: the Duchess of Orléans received the support of Pintoin, skeptical about witchcraft in general, who remarks in his chronicle that surely she was not guilty. The sympathetic portrait of the slandered duchess was lent further appeal when Pintoin described Valentina's great distress after Louis's assassination. Valentina, not a queen, avoided the fury of Madame de Kéralio, who mentioned only that Isabeau chased her into exile, and she has endured in the popular imagination as a likeable character.[56] She was even given a glowingly positive biography by Émile Collas and is often deployed as a foil for the rapacious Isabeau.[57] And yet, her positive image surely is attributable to good historical luck, just as the negative images of Louis and Isabeau are also the result of historical hazard.

Notes

1. The concept of "public opinion" deserves a detailed discussion. The work of Habermas on the concept has been critiqued and adapted, especially for the Middle Ages. See Gauvard 1985, for one such example. In this essay, however, I use the term only in the restricted sense of a large group of people as opposed to a relatively small opposing faction.
2. Willard 1984, 150; Previté-Orton 1978, 976.
3. Margolis 2011, 93.
4. On the king's madness, see Guenée 2004. On the power struggle, see Autrand 1986; Famiglietti 1986; Nordberg 1964; Schnerb 1988; Vaughan 2002a and 2002b.
5. For details, see the first chapter of Famiglietti 1986.
6. For example, Knecht 2004, 51–52; Neillands 1993, 186–88; Smith and De Vries 2005, 75.
7. Autrand 1994, 523–28, 661–68.
8. Heckmann 2002, vol. 2, 758–62.
9. Heckmann 2002, vol. 2, 763–73. See 770 for veto power.
10. Heckmann 2002, vol. 2, 773–78.
11. Autrand 1986, 20–21.
12. Froissart 1867, vol. 3, 164.
13. Guenée 1988, 456.

14. For Louis's youth, see Pintoin 1994, vol. 3, 12 and Juvénal des Ursins 1836, 421. The topic of youth as a means of delegitimation of late-medieval rulers is explored further by Gilles Lecuppre in this volume. On Louis's taxes, see Philip's self-serving letter, which he had read to discountenance a tax levied at the order of the Royal Council, in Cochon 1870, 205. In another letter read before the Parlement de Paris, Philip explains that he had heard bad things about the way that the kingdom was being governed. See Douët-d'Arcq 1863, vol. 1, 213.

15. Throughout I refer to "Jean sans Peur" rather than "John the Fearless" to avoid inconsistency: Jean Gerson, whom I discuss, is routinely referred to by modern scholars as "Jean."

16. Autrand 2009, 271–73.

17. Vaughan 2002a, 44–48, 67–68 offers a good summary of this episode.

18. Vaughan 2002a, 70–72 summarizes the charges. Monstrelet records the discourse: Monstrelet 1857, vol. 1, 217–21, 224–34.

19. Willard 1969.

20. *Chartularium*: Denifle 1897, vol. 4, 283, no. 2015.

21. Coville 1932, 504.

22. Coville 1932, 513.

23. Valois 1902, vol. 4, 324–30.

24. Baye 1885, vol. 2, 270–71.

25. Guenée 1987, 244–45, 252.

26. See note 13, above.

27. Pintoin 1994, vol. 3, 12.

28. Monstrelet 1857, vol. 1, 217–21, 224–34. Vaughan 2002a, 70–72 offers a summary of Jean Petit's main charges.

29. Pintoin 1994, vol. 2, 88.

30. Pintoin 1994, vol. 2, 404–6.

31. Froissart 1867, vol. 15, 352–25. See also the chronicle of Monstrelet 1857, vol. 1, 228–29, which reports that Jean Petit made the same accusation during his justification of Jean of Burgundy's assassination of Louis.

32. Pintoin 1994, vol. 2, 406.

33. Pintoin 1994, vol. 2, 544.

34. Pintoin 1994, vol. 2, 542.

35. Cousinot 2002, 109.

36. Mirot 1914, 403.

37. According to Pintoin 1994, vol. 3, 340, on September 24 a group of the ruling men of Paris refused Jean's request that they take arms against Louis: they did not answer to Jean but to the king or the dauphin. Juvénal des Ursins 1836, 437 reports that the Parisians honored each of Jean's requests except for one, that they take arms and follow him.

38. Pintoin 1994, vol. 3, 228.

39. Pintoin 1994, vol. 3, 288–90.

40. For the continued propaganda, see the *Pastoralet*, dated sometime after 1422: Anonymous 1983, 26. For the ultimate victory of the Orléanists on the propaganda front, see Dequeker-Fergon 1986, 62–68.

41. Except in the case of Huizinga (1921), who appears to have taken Petit's justification at face value. See 206, 271–73, 287–88.

42. The story of the rumor has been dispelled by several historians. See Famiglietti 1986, 42–43.

43. Autrand 2009, 271–72.

44. Louis was attacked savagely by Kéralio (1791, 132–93).
45. Dequeker-Fergon 1986, 62–68.
46. Michelet 1840, 93–158; Guizot 1873, vol. 2, 209–84; Martin 1886; Colville 1888; Thibault 1903. These early works set in place narratives about the court of King Charles VI and his relatives that continue to hold force. Nineteenth-century monarchists viewed the royal family more positively. See Jarry 1889. Recently Gonzalez (2004) and Autrand (2009, 271–73) have cautioned against taking criticisms of Louis at face value.
47. Gonzalez 2004, 14.
48. See Adams 2010, 38–72, for more detail on what follows.
49. Kéralio 1791, 132–93.
50. Jarry 1889; Famiglietti 1986; Gibbons 1997.
51. For a more thorough investigation of the feud, see the PhD dissertation of Pollack-Lagushenko (2004), although the feud is not the central interest of the study.
52. Guenée 1988, 456.
53. Pintoin 1994, vol. 3, 12.
54. The black legend of the queen entered Christine de Pizan studies through the biography of Willard (1984). Although this biography was important for having introduced the poet to a wide audience, the assessments of historians upon which Willard relied for depictions of Isabeau and Charles VI's court were those cited here.
55. Willard 1994, 39.
56. Kéralio 1791, 145–46.
57. Collas 1911, 219–30. For another example, see Thibault 1903, 340–44 and, most recently, Veenstra 1998, 81.

Bibliography

Adams, T. 2010. *The Life and Afterlife of Isabeau of Bavaria*. Baltimore: The Johns Hopkins University Press.

Anonymous, 1873. "Geste des ducs de Bourgogne." In J. Kervyn de Lettenhove, ed., *Chroniques relatives à l'histoire de la Belgique sous la domination des ducs de Bourgogne*, vol. 2, 259–572. Brussels: Hayez.

Anonymous, 1890. "Le songe véritable." Ed. H. Moranvillé. *Mémoires de la Société de l'histoire de Paris et de l'Ile de France* 17: 217–438.

Anonymous, 1983. *Le Pastoralet*. Ed. and introd. J. Blanchard. Paris: Presses Universitaires de France.

Autrand, F. 1986. *Charles VI. La folie du roi*. Paris: Fayard.

Autrand, F. 1994. *Charles V*. Paris: Fayard.

Autrand, F. 2009. *Christine de Pizan. Une femme en politique*. Paris: Fayard.

Baye, N. de. 1885. *Journal de Nicolas de Baye, Greffier de Paris 1400–1417*. Ed. Alexandre Tuetey, 2 vols. Paris: Renouard.

Collas, E. 1911. *Valentine de Milan. Duchesse d'Orléans*. Paris: Plon.

Cochon, P. 1870. *Chronique normande de Pierre Cochon*. Ed. C. Robillard de Beaurepaire. Rouen: A. Le Brument.

Colville, A. 1888. *Les Cabochiens et l'ordonnance de 1413*. Paris: Hachette.

Cousinot, G. 2002. *Chronique de la Pucelle ou chronique de Cousinot, suivie de la chronique Normande de Cochon, relatives aux régnes de Charles VI et de Charles VII, restituées à leurs auteurs et publiées pour la première fois intégralement à partir de l'an*

1403, d'après les manuscrits, avec notices, notes, et développements. Ed. A. Vallet de Viriville, 2nd ed. Paris: Elibron Classics.

Coville, A. 1932. *Jean Petit. La question du tyrannicide au commencement du XVe siècle.* Paris: Picard.

Denifle, E. H., ed. 1889–97. *Chartularium Universitatis Parisiensis,* 4 vols. Paris: Delalain.

Dequeker-Fergon, J.-M. 1986. "L'histoire au service des pouvoirs." *Médiévales* 10: 51–68.

Douët-d'Arcq, L. C. 1863. *Choix de pièces inédites relatives au règne de Charles VI,* 2 vols. Paris: Renouard.

Famiglietti, R. C. 1986. *Royal Intrigue: Crisis at the Court of Charles VI, 1392–1420.* New York: AMS Press.

Froissart, J. 1967. *Chroniques.* Ed. J. Kervyn de Lettenhove, 26 vols., 2nd ed. Osnabrück: Biblio Verlag.

Gonzalez, E. 2004. *Un prince en son hôtel. Les serviteurs des ducs d'Orléans au XVe siècle.* Paris: Publications de la Sorbonne.

Gauvard, C. 1985. "Le Roi de France et l'opinion publique à l'époque de Charles VI." In Centre National de la Recherche Scientifique, 1985, *Culture et idéologie dans la genèse de l'état modern,* 353–66. Rome: École Française de Rome.

Gibbons, R. C. 1997. "The Active Queenship of Isabeau of Bavaria, 1392–1417." PhD diss., University of Reading.

Guenée, B. 1987. *Between Church and State: The Lives of Four French Prelates in the Late Middle Ages.* Transl. A. Goldhammer, 1991. Chicago: University of Chicago Press.

Guenée, B. 1988. "Le roi, ses parents et son royaume en France au XIVe siècle." *Bulletino dell'Istituto Storico Italiano per il Medio Evo et Archivio Muratoriano* 94: 439–70.

Guenée, B. 2004. *La folie de Charles VI, roi bien-aimé.* Paris: Perrin.

Guizot, F. 1873. *Vol. 2: L'histoire de France depuis les temps les plus reculés jusqu'en 1789 racontée à mes petits-enfants.* Paris: Hachette.

Heckmann, M.-L. 2002. *Stellvertreter, Mit- und Ersatzherrscher. Regenten, General-statthalter, Kurfürsten und Reichsvikare in Regnum und Imperium vom 13. bis zum frühen 15. Jahrhundert,* 2 vols. Warendorf: Fahlbusch.

Huizinga, J. 1921. *The Autumn of the Middle Ages.* Transl. R. J. Payton and U. Mammitzsch, 1996. Chicago: University of Chicago Press.

Jarry, E. 1889. *La vie politique de Louis de France, duc d'Orléans, 1372–1407.* Paris: A. Picard.

Juvénal des Ursins, J. 1836. *Histoire de Charles VI, roy de France, et des choses mémorables advenues durant quarante-deux années de son règne. Depuis 1380 jusqu'à 1422. Nouvelle collection des mémoires pour servir à l'histoire de France.* Eds. J.-F. Michaud and J.-J.-F. Poujoulat, 1st series, vol. 2. Paris: Editions du commentaire analytique du Code civil.

Kéralio, L. de. 1791. *Les crimes des reines de France depuis le commencement de la monarchie jusqu'à Marie-Antoinette.* Paris: Prudhomme.

Knecht, R. J. 2004. *The Valois: Kings of France, 1328–1589.* London: Hambledon and London.

Margolis, N. 2011. *An Introduction to Christine de Pizan.* Gainsville: University Press of Florida.

Martin, H. 1886. *L'histoire de France populaire depuis les temps les plus reculés jusqu'à nos jours,* vol. 1. Paris: Furne.

Michelet, J. 1840. *L'histoire de France,* vol. 4. Paris: Hachette.

Mirot, L. 1914. "L'enlèvement du dauphin et le premier conflit entre Jean sans Peur et Louis d'Orléans (1405)." *Revue des questions historiques* 95: 329–55; and 96: 47–88, 369–419.

Monstrelet, E. 1857–62. *La chronique d'Enguerran de Monstrelet, 1400–1444*. Ed. Louis Claude Douët-d'Arcq, 2 vols. Paris: Renouard.

Neillands, R. 1993 (reprint). *The Hundred Years War*. London: Routledge.

Nordberg, M. 1964. *Les ducs et la royauté. Étude sur la rivalité des ducs d'Orléans et de Bourgogne 1392–1407*. Uppsala: Svenska Bokförlaget.

Pintoin, M. 1994. *Chronique du Religieux de Saint-Denys contenant le règne de Charles VI, de 1380–1422*. Ed. and transl. L. Bellaguet, 6 vols., 2nd ed. Paris: Editions du Comité des travaux historiques et scientifiques.

Pizan, Christine de. 1994. *The Writings of Christine de Pizan*. Selected and ed. C. C. Willard. New York: Persea Books.

Pollack-Lagushenko, T. R. 2004. "The Armagnac Faction: New Patterns of Political Violence in Late Medieval France." PhD diss., Johns Hopkins University.

Previté-Orton, C. W. 1978 (reprint). *The Shorter Cambridge Medieval History*, 2 vols. Cambridge: Cambridge University Press.

Schnerb, B. *Les Armagnacs et les Bourguignons. La maudite guerre*. Paris: Perrin.

Smith, R. D., and K. R. DeVries. 2005. *The Artillery of the Dukes of Burgundy: 1363–1477*. Woodbridge, Suffolk, UK: The Boydell Press.

Thibault, M. 1903. *Isabeau de Bavière. Reine de France. La Jeunesse (1370–1405)*. Paris: Perrin et Cie.

Valois, N. 1896–1902. *La France et le grand schisme d'Occident*, 4 vols. Paris: Picard.

Vaughan, R. 2002. *John the Fearless: The Growth of Burgundian Power*, 2nd ed. Woodbridge, Suffolk, UK: The Boydell Press.

Vaughan, R. 2002. *Philip the Bold: The Formation of the Burgundian State*, 2nd ed. Woodbridge, Suffolk, UK: The Boydell Press.

Veenstra, J. R. 1998. *Magic and Divination at the Courts of Burgundy and France*. Leiden, Netherlands: Brill.

Willard, C. C. 1969. "The Manuscripts of Jean Petit's Justification: Some Burgundian Propaganda Methods of the Early Fifteenth Century." *Studi Francesi* 3: 271–80.

Willard, C. C. 1984. *Christine de Pizan: Her Life and Works*. New York: Persea Books.

7

A Newcomer in Defamatory Propaganda: Youth (Late Fourteenth to Early Fifteenth Century)

Gilles Lecuppre

Introduction[1]

"Woe to thee, O land, when thy king is a child."[2] This quotation from the Book of Ecclesiastes, which was used by chroniclers Thomas Walsingham and Adam Usk against Richard II of England, could be considered a late-medieval slogan.[3] Things not only tended to be rather tense during periods of formal minorities,[4] but many times child kings were dethroned by ambitious and charismatic uncles with the assent—and to the great relief—of the political community.[5] After all, the crown remained within the royal family; a form of continuity with the preceding reign was established. Such crises reveal unspoken rules against children, women, and foreigners as kings. Kingship combined with virile charisma mattered more than the rules of succession.

In addition, something new occurred in the 1380s, when youth ceased to be a mere matter of chronological age and became a sort of personal trait, a negative psychological profile. A man in his thirties, like King Richard, might nonetheless be described as young, an assessment based on his foolish behavior. The frequent recurrence of this theme throughout the major Western kingdoms down to 1420 is striking. Youth was a favorite insult in defamatory propaganda, proving highly corrosive and personally damaging to legitimate holders of power.

Although the word *propaganda* did not exist at the close of the Middle Ages, the phenomenon itself was widespread.[6] Naturally, we are better informed about the various forms of written propaganda than we are about oral forms. Written propaganda was aimed at particular audiences. Treatises were broadly circulated and had a genuine impact, although only in the necessarily restricted milieu of princes, nobles, and royal officers. Circumstantial Latin lampoons and polemical texts were intended primarily for an audience of clerics. But the standard medium was the royal letter, read aloud at crossroads by heralds and sometimes posted on the doors of cathedrals or in other prominent places.[7] All in all, propaganda was circulated in many genres: historical works; prophecies; Latin, French, or English poetry; clandestine bills; and so on. As for oral and visual propaganda, although they were important, we know less about them because they have left only indirect and often fragmentary traces. Princes were able to communicate with their people and even, in some cases, advertise their political programs through royal entries.[8] Speeches and sermons of preachers were often critical toward royal power when they were delivered by mendicants, who rarely minced words. The songs of travelling singers and works of profane drama were significant, as well. Thus, it can be said that something like an emergent public opinion was shaped by a constant flow of propaganda, both positive and negative.

This chapter intends to focus on five cases—I do not claim that my list is exhaustive. Richard II, king of England, was the first of those princes who allegedly never managed to grow up. Deposed in 1399, he was probably killed in his jail cell, one year later, at Henry IV's instigation.[9] The latter waged a campaign of character assassination aptly summed up in a phrase of his supporter, Archbishop Thomas Arundel: Richard was a boy, not a man.[10] Scotland experienced comparable events in 1402. David, Duke of Rothesay, was Robert III's first son and ruled Scotland as lieutenant of the realm, since his father had been removed from government because of his disability. David was kidnapped and starved to death at the order of Robert, Duke of Albany, his jealous uncle, who later blamed this regrettable misfortune on his nephew's uncontrollable frivolity.[11] In France, Charles VI's close relatives were in turn accused of youthful vices. His brother, Louis of Orléans, acting as a regent during the king's mental crises, was a target for his "beloved" Burgundian uncle and cousin, John the Fearless, who blamed him for being a big spender, particularly during his "jeunesses étranges"—his strange youth. John the Fearless had him assassinated in 1407 and reactivated the charge against Louis in order to account for his regicide.[12] In a very similar way, the dauphin Louis, Duke of Guyenne, was not very popular among his subjects, who were enduring a new phase of the Hundred Years War and the beginnings of a destructive civil war, while he was painting the town red. Luckily for him, he died in 1415, when he was 18, putting a stop to his many critics.[13] Burgundian chroniclers briefly made fun of Louis of Guyenne's younger brother, Charles, who would become Charles VII, in 1418, when he had to flee from Paris. He was then in the care of the Armagnacs, the opposite party, which hardly loosed the bridle on his neck. But the young pup was transformed into someone far more dangerous as he took part in John the Fearless's murder in 1419. Youth was definitely over.[14]

To guide this investigation of character assassination, I propose to examine the following three issues:

1. What did "youth" mean? Why was it suddenly a crime to be or to remain a young prince? Where did that peculiar idea come from? And to what extent did those five victims fit this new stereotype? What was really at stake with those charges?
2. How did such campaigns work? Where were they launched? Which media were used? For whose ears was such defamation intended?
3. How did those accusations find their way to people who counted? What can they teach us about the political issues of that time?

Youthfulness as a Negative Character Trait:
The Emergence of a New Theme

The background of political suspicion regarding youthful faults is to be found in a moralized medical theory that slowly spread through encyclopedias, mirrors for princes—that is, didactic politicomoral treatises—and even literary works.[15] By the end of the fourteenth century, the idea of youthfulness as a shortcoming was both readily accessible and commonplace. Medieval Western medical representations could be ultimately traced back to Hippocrates and rested on the famous theory of the four humors.[16] That leads us to a conception of the human body based around the four humors (phlegm, blood, yellow bile, and black bile) and four essential qualities (heat, cold, wetness, and dryness). Basically, men are hot and dry, which is why they are so vigorous and, above all, constant in their will, their morality, and their speech. Women are cold and wet; they are therefore weak and physically, morally, and sexually inconstant.[17] Young people share hotness with men and wetness with women. Interesting inferences could be drawn from this established fact: youths, like men, are strong, but, being wet like women, they often prove sensual, lazy, changeable, gullible, and so on. Through Aristotle and Aegidio Romano, Giles of Rome, whose late thirteenth-century mirror for princes became a best-seller, medieval political thought was imbued with those beliefs. Even a female writer like Christine de Pizan adhered to the tradition.[18]

Of course, all this provided ready arguments for anyone who wanted to attack real princes. A wide range of criticism was formulated at the expense of Richard II, who seemed to possess every characteristic of evil youth. According to aristocratic and, later, Lancastrian vituperations, the king lacked reason. Thus, he neglected good and wise counselors and, being highly suggestible, favored immoral and hypocritical advisers.[19] His temper and energy were chaotic, although now and then he would dig in his heels.[20] His excessive pride and his love of the flesh led him to greed, lust, and dissoluteness.[21] He had a tendency to delusions of grandeur. Nineteenth- and twentieth-century historians, taking such vitriol seriously, related Richard's peaceful and Francophile diplomacy to his so-called effeminate inclinations.[22] As for the Scottish heir David of Rothesay, he was summarily dismissed by an English chronicler,

John Shirley, who wrote in the 1440s that the prince's life had been "openly known vicious." This shows that the allegations of David's uncle, Robert of Albany, who coveted the throne for himself, had hit their target.[23]

As one might expect, the French princes Louis of Orléans and his nephew Louis of Guyenne were revelers and had a taste for wasteful gambling, balls, and feasts, the latter obviously confusing days and nights.[24] During the Bal des Ardents (the "Ball of the Burning Men"), which took place in 1393, Louis of Orléans, who was 21, accidentally set merry masqueraders on fire with his torch; among them was his own brother, King Charles.[25] He was also known as a great womanizer, which caused scandals, according to the austere Monk of St. Denis. The theologian Jean Petit even alleged that, being a slave of Venus, Louis possessed a ring that could subject women to his unclean desires.[26] As a statesman, he was credited with ambition, impulsiveness, and greed, faults that were linked to his prolonged youth. What is more, he was interested in magic, especially in nigromancy, or black magic. Those forbidden rites were used to alter his brother's mental health, if we are to believe widespread rumors that were soon relayed by the English king Henry IV and, naturally, by Burgundian propaganda.[27] Interestingly enough, when trying to defend the duke's reputation, the aforesaid monk referred to Charles VI's physicians, who merely explained his illness by the excesses he had committed during his youth.[28] As for his younger son, Charles VII, he was described as a creature in the hands of the Armagnacs, mortal enemies of the Burgundians during the civil war, or as a foal, pulled along by its bridle.[29]

Of course, what was at stake was the princes' ability to assert themselves and effectively to take power. On the one hand, they felt they had to behave in a way appropriate to their position. They shared such aristocratic values as *largesse* or *liberality*. Pomp and circumstance were as necessary as a crown or a throne. Fine clothes and high standards of living really made kings. When trying to raise funds to establish their household, they could not be blamed for acting frivolously, unless they were precisely shown as obstinate teenagers or childish adults. On the other hand, most of their supposed vices derived from court culture.[30] The chronicler Thomas Walsingham deprecated Richard II's entourage, in which he saw "knights of Venus and not of Bellona" (Venus clearly reigned over young hearts, both in France and England) and pretended that the king was surrounded by spineless and decadent youths.[31] That was not true, of course, and among Richard's near relations, Simon Burley, for example, had already served during the reign of Edward III, Richard's grandfather.[32] He nevertheless was impeached for treason, along with other favorites, and executed at the request of the Merciless Parliament in 1388.

However, Richard's close friends and kindred spirits, who happened to be quintessential courtiers and not only self-interested sycophants, also enabled him to resist the tutelage that had been imposed on him through various forms of councils, one of them being incidentally called the "Continual Council," as though his minority had no end.[33] English historians nowadays are used to interpreting the famous *Wilton Diptych* in this way. The bombastic altarpiece is a visual depiction of Richard II's kingship at its very beginning; but it was painted at the end of his reign, between 1397 and 1399, after he had crushed his old enemies, the former Lords Appellant. He now longed for a personal rule. The *Diptych* is therefore an indirect allusion to the indignities he had suffered in his later adolescence and early adulthood and a clear reminder of the heavenly mandate he had been given at his coronation, since it depicted Richard on his own, as if he had been an autonomous ruler from the start.[34]

Details and Targets of Propaganda Campaigns

Now that we have learned a little more about the contents of that specific form of character assassination, it is high time for us to gain insight into its mechanisms. Most of the time, the right moment to launch attacks corresponded to the end of the victims' legal youth. By the standards of the fourteenth century, princes came of age at 13 or 14. Nevertheless, Richard II's troubles in this respect began in 1387,[35] when he was 20, and came to an end with his death at 33. Character assassination thus counteracted the princes' aspiration to be self-sufficient and to be in authority. David, Duke of Rothesay, was 23 and had been lieutenant of the realm for three years, when his uncle Albany decided that he had become uncontrollable after the death of his influential mother, Annabella, one year before, in August/September 1401. Nearly four decades later, Walter Bower's *Scotichronicon* still blamed the prince for his moral failures and his debauched way of life in the same manner.[36] Louis of Orléans was 21 when he set his brother on fire and consequently sparked off controversy.[37] Louis of Guyenne was 16 when he had to face disparaging remarks along with a major rising in Paris. The Cabochian movement, a popular uprising, incited by John the Fearless and made up of members of the butchers' and skinners' guilds, held the capital at the time, and various orators kept harping on Louis of Guyenne's orgies and misconduct. Master Eustache de Pavilly, Carmelite friar and supporter of the Burgundians, patiently explained to him that his father's insanity and his uncle's ignominious death had been caused by their tumultuous youth. To this his mother Isabeau of Bavaria added a threat of disinheritance, unless he changed his bad behavior.[38] Finally, Léon of Jacqueville, the Burgundian captain of Paris, made a terrible scene when he came upon Louis in the middle of his "indecent" nighttime dances. The boy was so affected that he suffered from spitting blood for three days.[39] Burgundians started mocking his brother, the dauphin Charles, when he was 15, even though some months later he styled himself regent, led Armagnac armies, and conquered several major towns.[40] They must have thought he stooped to conquer.

Sometimes, defamation raged after the fact, or at least after the princes were dead, to convince the political community that their deaths had been a good thing. At least half of anti-Ricardian literature emerged after Richard had already been deposed. Character assassination became the official version of his reign as a consequence of Archbishop Arundel's speeches in front of members of Parliament.[41] Robert of Albany was cleared of all blame for the Duke of Rothesay's abduction and death by a general council, to which he had explained how perverted his nephew was.[42] In 1407, Jean Petit praised John the Fearless, Louis of Orléans's murderer, in the Hôtel de St. Pol, before an assembly of the royal court. He thus tried to enumerate and establish once and for all Louis's vices and crimes.[43] In contrast, there was no need for polemists to let loose on Louis of Guyenne, because he was immediately succeeded by another dauphin, Jean of Touraine, and political life simply went on. In a somewhat biased funeral oration, Michel Pintoin, the Monk of St. Denis, stated simply that the inhabitants of the realm did not regret the death of Louis very long.[44]

Understanding the development of defamatory campaigns was no easy task for medievalists, who heavily depended on chronicles that, by definition, reassembled facts at the end of the whole process and stole liberally from each other. By reading them, one can guess there were many snakes in the grass, but it remains difficult, if not impossible, to account for the huge amount of tittle-tattle and rumors that must have underlain and strengthened more public announcements. There is no doubt that the deeds of womanizers created much gossip in Paris, although the Monk of St. Denis proved a little more discreet about them. Thus, he mentioned Charles VI's carnal desires but put things into perspective by acknowledging that the king never caused any scandal.[45]

As for spectacular speeches and noticeable milestones in smear tactics, let us focus on Richard II's case, which is by far better documented. The theme of youth first appeared in 1387 in a sermon preached at St Paul's Cross by a Dominican friar named Thomas Wimbledon. He fustigated the foolish behavior of Rehoboam, son of Solomon, who turned down the good advice of old wise men, preferred the counsel of his youthful playfellows, and scornfully dismissed the complaints of the people of Israel. As a result, the people rebelled, and the kingdom split in two parts.[46] The parallel with Richard was evident. Insinuations and attacks then moved from churches to Parliament. The 1388 session, known as the Merciless Parliament, denounced the traitors who took advantage of the king's suggestibility.[47] Then, 11 years after, Thomas Arundel reunited both rhetoric genres by preaching a sermon to the estates of the realm, which had just approved Richard's deposition and accepted Henry, Duke of Lancaster, as his replacement. He lengthily portrayed Richard as a boy, whereas his successor was a man.[48] He repeated his demonstration during the opening of Henry IV's first parliament some days later.[49] He at last basically gave the floor to chroniclers—Thomas Walsingham, Adam Usk, the continuator of the *Eulogium historiarum*, and so on—and even to poets like John Gower, who rewrote Richard's reign with hindsight.[50]

When it comes to the social impact of character assassination, one is tempted to mention primarily clerics and monks. They represented an important part of the body politic and still had the biggest share in cultural life. Through preaching, academic speeches, and mastery over historical writing, they could impose their point of view, which could not but condemn youthful faults. To say the least, actual rulers did not look like the mature and wise princes who were to be found in traditional mirrors. Well aware of medical theory and deliberately confusing politics with morality, churchmen had to be the masterminds—and the general handymen—of the whole insidious conspiracy. High aristocracy and oppositional party leaders followed close behind. They could not be satisfied with princes who wanted to free themselves from their supervision and expel them from counsel. They simply converted youthful faults into serious professional misconduct in order to keep their influence over daily governance. Fear entered into consideration too: for example, Richard II had managed to destroy some of his enemies—Woodstock, FitzAlan, and Beauchamp, the former Lords Appellant.[51] Robert of Albany had every reason on earth to be on the outs with his royal nephew, the Duke of Rothesay. There had been frequent family rows about the formation of counsel, the distribution of lands, or episcopal nominations. That is why he made a point of being in cahoots with Archibald, Earl of Douglas, and in conceiving the incredible story about Rothesay's habits.[52] Anyway, the harsh criticisms formulated by clerics and lay nobility finally struck a chord with other groups inside the political community. Kingship was a sort of common patrimony, and economic elites had their say in the matter. The English bourgeois MPs and the Parisian mob of the 1400s could be very receptive to backbiting—especially, as was the case with the latter, when they felt that princes despised them and lorded it over them. Louis of Orléans was regularly depicted as haughty, particularly toward his creditors, on whom he played many tricks.[53]

Success and Eventual Disappearance of the Theme

Behind debates about youth, one can discover deep-rooted political issues, which waited for such opportunities to reveal themselves. Many taxpayers remained touchy about the final destination of their money, which they felt should have been used to wage war, instead of being wasted in a hypothetic growth of royal household expenditure or in showy gifts and feasts. It is therefore with good reason that, in his chronicle, Michel Pintoin multiplied passages in which Louis of Orléans is denounced for his exactions,[54] his carelessness and profligacy,[55] and, as a result, cursed by the little people without ceremony.[56] Most ratepayers shared a desire for reform, a trend of public opinion that appeared during the fourteenth century in reaction against the rising modern state.[57] That is why demagogic or popularity-seeking rumors could be so devastating.

The attacks against youthful rulers did not suddenly appear by accident. From the thirteenth century on, kingly power kept growing, as did theoretical and practical resistance to that trend. Many works were devoted to the opposite of good kingship—tyranny.[58] According to Aristotle, a tyrant ruled for his own sake and to fulfill his desires. Because of these secret and violent desires, young capricious princes were believed to resemble ancient and modern tyrants. They shared uncontrollable appetites, according to the *sanior pars* of the political community. Viewed from a political angle, they upset the balance by claiming personal power or by transferring power to a new generation or a new social group. The entire body politic was at risk during that adventurous trip. Viewed from a moral angle, male youths, just like women, could be seen as men who were not fully formed; it would have been criminal to give free rein to their dangerous whims. Thus, the time was perfectly ripe for anti-youth propaganda and for its recycling to achieve character assassination. Youth had become the new deceptive face of tyranny. Authors hardly ever resorted to the very word—Thomas Walsingham and Michel Pintoin did[59]—but the notion was obvious to their contemporaries.

It is a matter of fact that the theme did not survive after 1419. The dauphin Charles substituted lèse-majesté for youthful inconstancy. With the murder of John the Fearless on the bridge at Montereau on September 10, 1419, he proved that he had come of age. His father—or his Anglo-Burgundian entourage—understood perfectly that something had changed, and he more or less declared that one should not take account of the youth of the dauphin because he was quite old enough to tell good from evil.[60] His reign, as Charles VII, lasted 39 years, and when his son Louis XI came to the throne, he was already 38. He could be compared to a tyrant, and so he was by the former bishop of Lisieux, Thomas Basin,[61] but in no way to a childish sovereign.[62] The Scottish kings James II and James III went through long minorities without being accused of remaining minors.[63] In England, Henry VI ruled only nominally: his uncles, his cousin, and his wife reigned instead of him.[64] He demonstrated, as his kingdom sank into civil war, that a *rex inutilis*, a shadow king,[65] was more dreadful than a young would-be autocrat. At the end of the fifteenth century, the ideal king in contemporary minds was still middle-aged or old enough to be said to be well experienced. But the cause of young princes had gained some ground. The tragic deaths of the Princes in the Tower aroused some compassion,[66] whereas the young French king Charles VIII's dreams of glory led a rather enthusiastic aristocracy to Italian battlefields.[67]

Moreover, the old-fashioned theme of the child king was now and then turned against its instigators. Boys would be boys anew. That is, at least, what a miniature from a 1484 manuscript of the *Vigiles de Charles VII* seems to indicate.[68] It illustrates Martial d'Auvergne's long poem in praise of Charles VII, Charles VIII's grandfather and propitiatory eponym, and especially, as far as we are concerned, the very moment where the young dauphin was taken to the Bastille to get away from Burgundian massacre. Charles is depicted as a tiny child, in the middle of a huge group of adults. He wears a gown decorated with fleurs-de-lis and a red hat. He is carried by a man who is calmly walking toward the gate of a fortress, which is hardly bigger than him. This man is Tanneguy du Châtel, one of the Armagnac leaders, who was then provost of Paris. The scene cannot but conjure up the traditional image of St. Christopher with the child Jesus on his shoulder. However puny he might have looked, the dauphin was a 15-year-old man in 1418. But a comparison with the Holy Child made sense; glamorization helped to forget character assassination.

Conclusion

Spare the rod and spoil the child. The end of the fourteenth and the beginning of the fifteenth century were not the golden age of young ambitious princes. Character assassination was often followed or preceded by physical assassination. A mutation had occurred: on both sides of those 40 years, there was nothing in youthful behaviors to make a fuss about, but around 1400, youth was a political blunder in itself. Above all, it had become a slanderous leitmotiv, comparable to the accusations of sodomy that had been all the rage one hundred years earlier. Everyone could understand how close to one another the abstract but trendy notions of tyranny and youth had come. The way a young prince could disturb and corrupt the monarchical system was patently obvious. That is why reformers and veteran politicians met with success when they launched their attacks. Such charges were radical because they put a question mark over the princes' competence and ability to govern.

Some historical and literary works of the sixteenth century were reminiscent of that tremendous clash of generations. Shakespeare credited his Henry V with a riotous youth, although his biography clearly disproves this misinterpretation. Chroniclers insisted on his morality and severity. The legend of the young hedonist is a later invention.[69] But it was after all only a reasonable extrapolation from other medieval princely fates. Shakespeare's tour de force consisted in the way he reconciled a dissolute youth with a kingly adulthood. Richard, David, and Louis were not even given the opportunity to take up the challenge.

Notes

1. I am very grateful to Tracy Adams for her kind proofreading.
2. Ecclesiastes 10: 16.
3. *The Saint Albans Chronicle*: Taylor, Childs, and Watkiss 2003, 690; *The Chronicle of Adam of Usk*: Given-Wilson 1997, 68.
4. Beem 2008.
5. Lecuppre 2010.
6. See, for example, Guenée 2002.
7. Lecuppre-Desjardin 2011.
8. Lecuppre-Desjardin 2004.
9. Saul 1997; Bennett 1999; Dodd 2000; Tuck 2004.
10. On this seminal sermon, see Fletcher, 1–3. Of course, I am very much indebted to Christopher Fletcher's work. Although he is mainly concerned with a renewed gender studies approach and mostly interested in masculinity per se, as well as in the fact that Richard II's "reign can be seen as a clash between opposed ideals of masculinity," he remains the first theoretician of youth with regard to medieval politics.
11. Boardman 1992; Boardman 1996, 234–47.
12. Coville 1974; Jarry 1976; Guenée 1992.
13. Autrand 1986, 512–16.

14. Du Fresne de Beaucourt 1881; Vale 1974; Autrand 1986, 548–76.

15. Sears 1986; Fletcher 2008, ch. 4; Reinle 2008.

16. Arikha 2007.

17. Jacquart and Thomasset 1988; Cadden 1995.

18. Ribémont 2000.

19. *Wimbledon's Sermon*: Knight 1967, 328–29; *Rotuli parliamentorum*: Strachey 1783, 229–38; *Historia siue narracio de modo et forma mirabilis parliamenti*: McKisack 1937, 1–2; *Historia vitae et regni Richardi secundi*: Stow 1977, 166.

20. *The Saint Albans Chronicle*: Taylor, Childs, and Watkiss 2003, 702.

21. *Historia vitae et regni Richardi secundi*, 156, 167. Such criticisms are scattered throughout the alliterative poem "Richard the Redeless" in Barr 1993.

22. Fletcher 2008, 7–9.

23. *The Dethe of the Kynge of Scotis*: Connolly 1992, 49: "soare dreding yf he hadde regned aftur his fadur, that many inconveniences, infortunes and vengeances myght owe fyllonye and fallen uppon al that region by cause of his lyff soo opnly knowen vicious."

24. The charges against Louis of Orléans are summed up by Autrand 1986, 368–74. As for Louis of Guyenne, see the *Chronique du Religieux de Saint-Denys*: Bellaguet 1994, vol. 3, V, 28–31, 78–81, 586–89.

25. *Chronique du Religieux de Saint-Denys*: Bellaguet 1994, vol. 2, II, 64–71; *Œuvres complètes de Jean Froissart, Chroniques*: Kervyn de Lettenhove 1967, XV, 84–92.

26. *Chronique du Religieux de Saint-Denys*: Bellaguet 1994, vol. 2, III, 758.

27. *Chronique du Religieux de Saint-Denys*: Bellaguet 1994, vol. 2, III, 58–60, 756–58.

28. *Chronique du Religieux de Saint-Denys*: Bellaguet 1994, vol. 1, II, 407.

29. *Extrait d'une chronique anonyme*: Douët d'Arcq 1857, 257.

30. On Richard's court, see Saul 1997, 332–46.

31. *The Saint Albans Chronicle*: Taylor, Childs, and Watkiss 2003, 814.

32. Leland 2004.

33. Dodd 2008.

34. Dodd 2008, 105–6.

35. Christopher Fletcher tellingly called the chapter he devoted to the period 1386–1388 "The Return of the King's Youth" (Fletcher 2008, 151).

36. *Scotichronicon*: Watt 1987, 39.

37. See above, note 25.

38. *Chronique du Religieux de Saint-Denys*: Bellaguet 1994, vol. 3, V, 28–31. For a reassessment of the much slandered queen: Adams 2010.

39. *Chronique du Religieux de Saint-Denys*: Bellaguet 1994, vol. 3, V, 78–81.

40. Armagnac chroniclers were delighted with this transfiguration. See *Chronique de la Pucelle ou chronique de Cousinot*: Vallet de Viriville 1859, 175.

41. *Rotuli parliamentorum*, vol. 3, 415–53.

42. *Scotichronicon*, vol. 8, 39; *Acts of the Parliaments of Scotland*, vol. 1, 572.

43. *La chronique d'Enguerran de Monstrelet*, vol.1, 177–244.

44. *Chronique du Religieux de Saint-Denys*: Bellaguet 1994, vol. 3, V, 586–89.

45. *Chronique du Religieux de Saint-Denys*: Bellaguet 1994, vol. 1, I, 566.

46. Knight 1967, 328–29.

47. McKisack 1937, 1–2.

48. *Rotuli parliamentorum*: Strachey 1783, 423.

49. *Rotuli parliamentorum*: Strachey 1783, 415.

50. *Continuatio eulogii*: Haydon 1863, 384; Macaulay 1902, 555–71.

51. Saul 1997, 278–79.
52. Boardman 1992, 7–11.
53. *Chronique du Religieux de Saint-Denys*: Bellaguet 1994, vol. 2, III, 282–85.
54. *Chronique du Religieux de Saint-Denys*: Bellaguet 1994, vol. 2, III, 26, 141, 229, 232, 266, 330, 434, 458–61.
55. *Chronique du Religieux de Saint-Denys*: Bellaguet 1994, vol. 2, III, 229, 232, 266, 282–85, 458–61.
56. *Chronique du Religieux de Saint-Denys*: Bellaguet 1994, vol. 2, III, 232.
57. Contamine 1992.
58. Turchetti 2001.
59. *Annales Ricardi Secundi*: Riley 1866, 199 (*tyrannizare*, "tyrannize") and 223 (*propter Regis tyrannidem et malitiam*, "because of the King's tyranny and malice"). See also Barron 1968. *Chronique du Religieux de Saint-Denys*: Bellaguet 1994, vol. 2, III, 232 ("Many humbly begged Jesus-Christ to send someone to rescue the people from his tyranny"—note the post-factum prophecy!) and 266, where the queen is associated with Louis's tyranny.
60. *Mémoires de Pierre de Fénin*: Dupont 1837, 119–20.
61. Thomas Basin, *Histoire de Louis XI*: Samaran 1963–72.
62. Favier 2001.
63. McGladdery 1992; Macdougall 1982.
64. Griffiths 1981.
65. The notion was studied by Edward Peters, although his book did not investigate the problem further than 1327: Peters 1970.
66. Pollard 1991.
67. Yvonne Labande-Mailfert's first biography was adorned with a telling subtitle, in relation to our subject: Y. Labande-Mailfert, *Charles VIII et son milieu (1470–1498). La jeunesse au pouvoir* (Paris: Klincksieck, 1975). It was succeeded by Y. Labande-Mailfert, *Charles VIII. Le vouloir et la destinée* (Paris: Fayard, 1986).
68. Paris, Bibliothèque Nationale de France, Fr 5054, f. 16.
69. Fletcher, forthcoming.

Bibliography

Sources

Barr, H., ed. 1993. *The Piers Plowman Tradition: A Critical Edition of* Pierce the Ploughman's Crede, Richard the Redeless, Mum and the Sothsegger *and* The Crowned King. London: Dent.

Bellaguet, M. L., ed. 1994. *Chronique du Religieux de Saint-Denys contenant le règne de Charles VI de 1380 à 1422*, vol. 3. Paris: Éditions du comité des travaux historiques et scientifiques.

Connolly, M. 1992. "*The Dethe of the Kynge of Scotis*: A new edition." *Scottish Historical Review* 71: 46–69.

Douët d'Arcq, L., ed. 1857. *La chronique d'Enguerran de Monstrelet en deux livres avec pièces justificatives, 1400–1444*, vol. 1. Paris: Madame veuve Jules Renouard.

Douët d'Arcq, L., ed. 1862. "Extrait d'une chronique anonyme." In *La chronique d'Enguerran de Monstrelet en deux livres avec pièces justificatives, 1400–1444*, vol. 6, 181–327. Paris: Madame veuve Jules Renouard.

Dupont, L., ed. 1837. *Mémoires de Pierre de Fénin*. Paris: Jules Renouard.

Given-Wilson, C., ed. 1997. *The Chronicle of Adam of Usk, 1377–1421*. Oxford: Clarendon Press.

Haydon, F. S., ed. 1863. "*Continuatio eulogii.*" In *Eulogium historiarum sive temporis*, vol. 3, 323–421. London: Longman, Brown, Green, Longmans, and Roberts.

Kervyn de Lettenhove, J., ed. 1967. *Œuvres complètes de Jean Froissart, Chroniques*, vol. 15. Osnabrück: Biblio Verlag.

Knight, I. K., ed. 1967. *Wimbledon's Sermon: Redde rationem villicationis tue: A Middle English Sermon of the Fourteenth Century*. Pittsburgh: Duquesne University Press.

Macaulay, G. C., ed. 1902. *The Complete Works of John Gower*, vol. 4. Oxford: The Clarendon Press.

McKisack, M., ed. 1926. *Historia siue narracio de modo et forma mirabilis parliamenti*. *Camden Miscellany*, vol. 14. By Thomas Favent. London: Offices of the Society.

Riley, H. Th., ed. 1866. *Annales Ricardi Secundi*. In Idem, ed., *Johannis de Trokelowe, et Henrici de Blaneforde, monachorum Sancti Albani, necnon quorundam anonymorum, chronica et annales regnantibus Henrico Tertio, Edwardo Primo, Edwardo Secundo, Ricardo Secundo et Henrico Quarto: A.D. 1259–96; 1307–1324; 1392–1406*, 153–420. London: Longmans, Green, Reader, and Dyer.

Samaran, C., ed. 1963–72. *Histoire de Louis XI*, 3 vols. By Thomas Basin. Paris: Les Belles Lettres.

Stow, G. B., ed. 1977. *Historia vitae et regni Richardi secundi*. Philadelphia: University of Pennsylvania Press.

Strachey, J., ed. 1783. *Rotuli parliamentorum: ut et petitiones et placita in Parliamento, Volume 3: Tempore Ricardi R. II*. London: publisher unknown.

Taylor, J., W. Childs, and L. Watkiss, eds., 2003. *The Saint Albans Chronicle: The Chronica maiora of Thomas Walsingham, Volume 1: 1376–1394*. Oxford: Clarendon Press.

Thomson, T., ed. 1844. *Acts of the Parliaments of Scotland, Volume 1: 1124–1423*. Edinburgh: publisher unknown.

Vallet de Viriville, M., ed. 1859. *Chronique de la Pucelle ou chronique de Cousinot*. Paris: A. Delahays.

Watt, D. E. R., ed. 1987. Scotichronicon *by Walter Bower, in Latin and English*, vol. 8. Aberdeen: The University Press.

Secondary Literature

Adams, T. 2010. *The Life and Afterlife of Isabeau of Bavaria*. Baltimore: The Johns Hopkins University Press.

Arikha, N. 2007. *Passions and Tempers: A History of the Humours*. New York: Ecco.

Autrand, F. 1986. *Charles VI. La folie du roi*. Paris: Fayard.

Barron, C. M. 1968. "The Tyranny of Richard II." *Historical Research* 41: 1–18.

Beem, C., ed. 2008. *The Royal Minorities in Medieval and Early Modern England*. New York: Palgrave Macmillan.

Bennett, M. J. 1999. *Richard II and the Revolution of 1399*. Stroud: Sutton Publishing.

Boardman, S. 1992. The Man Who Would Be King: The Lieutenancy and Death of David, Duke of Rothesay, 1378–1402. In R. Mason and N. MacDougall, eds., *People and Power in Scotland: Essays in Honour of T. C. Smout*, 1–27. Edinburgh: John Donald.

Boardman, S. 1996. *The Early Stewart Kings: Robert II and Robert III, 1371–1406*. Edinburgh: Tuckwell Press Ltd.

Cadden, J. 1995. *Meanings of Sex Difference in the Middle Ages: Medicine, Science, Culture.* Cambridge: Cambridge University Press.

Contamine, P. 1992. "Réformation: un mot, une idée." In Idem, ed., *Des pouvoirs en France, 1300–1500*, 37–47. Paris: Presses de l'École Normale Supérieure.

Coville, A. 1974. *Jean Petit. La question du tyrannicide au commencement du XVe siècle.* Geneva: Slatkine.

Dodd, G. 2000. *The Reign of Richard II.* Stroud, UK: Tempus.

Du Fresne de Beaucourt, G. 1881. *Histoire de Charles VII, t. 1: Le dauphin, 1403–1422.* Paris: Librairie de la Société Bibliographique.

Favier, J. 2001. *Louis XI.* Paris: Fayard.

Fletcher, C. 2008. *Richard II: Manhood, Youth and Politics, 1377–99.* Oxford: Oxford University Press.

Fletcher, C. "King as Man, King as King: The Case of Henry V." In E. Bousmar, H. Cools, J. Dumont, and A. Marchandisse, eds., *Le corps du prince au cœur des rituels de la cour. Autour des travaux d'Agostino Paravicini Bagliani.* Forthcoming.

Griffiths, R. A. 1981. *The Reign of Henry VI: The Exercise of Royal Authority, 1422–1461.* Berkeley: University of California Press.

Guenée, B. 1992. *Un meurtre, une société. L'assassinat du duc d'Orléans, 23 novembre 1407.* Paris: Gallimard.

Guenée, B. 2002. *L'opinion publique à la fin du Moyen Âge d'après la Chronique de Charles VI du Religieux de Saint-Denis.* Paris: Perrin.

Jacquart, D., and C. Thomasset. 1988. *Sexuality and Medicine in the Middle Ages.* Translated by M. Adamson. Princeton, NJ: Princeton University Press.

Jarry, E. 1976. *La vie politique de Louis de France, duc d'Orléans: 1372–1407.* Geneva: Slatkine-Megariotis Reprints.

Labande-Mailfert, Y. 1975. *Charles VIII et son milieu (1470–1498): la jeunesse au pouvoir.* Paris: Klincksieck.

Labande-Mailfert, Y. 1986. *Charles VIII. Le vouloir et la destinée.* Paris: Fayard.

Lecuppre, G. 2010. "L'oncle usurpateur à la fin du Moyen Âge." In M. Aurell, ed. *La parenté déchirée. Les luttes intrafamiliales au Moyen Âge*, 147–56. Turnhout, Belgium: Brepols.

Lecuppre-Desjardin, E. 2004. *La ville des cérémonies. Essai sur la communication politique dans les anciens Pays-Bas bourguignons.* Turnhout, Belgium: Brepols.

Lecuppre-Desjardin, E. 2011. "Des portes qui parlent. Placards, feuilles volantes et communication politique dans les villes des Pays-Bas à la fin du Moyen Âge." *Bibliothèque de l'Ecole des Chartes* 168: 151–72.

Leland, J. L. 2004. "Burley, Sir Simon (1336?–1388)." *Oxford Dictionary of National Biography.* http://www.oxforddnb.com/view/printable/4036 (accessed May 30, 2011).

Macdougall, N. 1982. *James III: A Political Study.* Edinburgh: John Donald Publishers Limited.

McGladdery, C. 1992. *James II.* Edinburgh: John Donald Publishers Limited.

Peters, E. 1970. *The Shadow King: "rex inutilis" in Medieval Law and Literature, 751–1327.* New Haven, CT: Yale University Press.

Pollard, A. J. 1991. *Richard III and the Princes in the Tower.* Stroud, UK: Alan Sutton.

Reinle, C. 2008. "Jugend als Typus—Jugend als Topos. Stereotype Vorstellungen bis zur Mitte des 16. Jahrhunderts." In I. Kwiatkowski and M. Oberweis, eds., *Recht, Religion, Gesellschaft und Kultur im Wandel der Geschichte.* Ferculum de cibis spiritualibus. *Festschrift für Dieter Scheler*, 393–414. Hamburg: Dr. Kovačs.

Ribémont, B. 2000. "Le regard de Christine de Pizan sur la jeunesse (à propos du Charles V)." *Cahiers de recherches médiévales et humanistes* 7: 255–60.

Saul, N. 1997. *Richard II*. New Haven, CT: Yale University Press.

Sears, E. 1986. *The Ages of Man: Medieval Interpretations on the Life Cycle*. Princeton, NJ: Princeton University Press.

Tuck, A. 2004. *Richard II (1367–1400)*. Oxford: Oxford University Press.

Turchetti, M. 2001. *Tyrannie et tyrannicide de l'Antiquité à nos jours*. Paris: Presses Universitaires de France.

Vale, M. A. G. 1974. *Charles VII*. London: Methuen.

Editorial Reflections: Medieval Cases

Martijn Icks and Eric Shiraev

It would be unwise, to say the least, to attempt to extract general character-istics of medieval character assassination from the three preceding chap-ters. After all, the Middle Ages were a long, multifaceted period, and the differences between eight- or ninth-century Spain, on the one hand, and late-medieval England and France, on the other, are undoubtedly much greater than the similarities. Nevertheless, it is possible to compare and reflect on these three cases on a more conceptual level. When we do so, one of the most striking things is that defamation was employed for wholly different purposes in these examples. The posthumous attacks on the Prophet Muhammad by anonymous Christian writers targeted him not as a personal opponent, but as the constituent and symbol of a different worldview—namely, Islam. The intended audience of these counterhistories consisted of Christians: rather than seeking to convert Muslims, the authors strove to strengthen the faith of their fellow *dhimmis*. In contrast, different world views were not an issue in the slander campaigns launched against Louis of Orléans and other late-medieval kings and princes. Here, naked power was at stake, and the perpe-trators did not attack their victims as symbols of one thing or another, but as rivals for the power and influence they desired for themselves.

Despite these wholly different purposes, and the wholly different his-torical contexts of the attacks, the detractors of Muhammad and those of late-medieval kings employed some of the same techniques. As the "give-and-take" strategy of counterhistories illustrates, character attacks were often most effective when they mixed (perceived) truth with falsehoods. Hence the detractors of Muhammad "conceded" some well-known facts about the life of the Prophet, but mixed these with slanderous details of their own invention. Although it would go too far to regard the hostile chronicles concerned with the reigns of Louis of Orléans and other rulers as "counterhistories," a mix of truth and falsehood is in evidence here, as well—just as it can be found in other forms of attack against late-medieval rulers. For instance, the fact that Louis thanked his powerful position to the insanity of his brother, King Charles VI, was exploited to suggest that he was somehow responsible for the king's mental condition. Likewise, the heavy taxes that the Duke of Orléans levied to wage war against the English fed rumors that he squandered money for his personal pleasure. This employment of facts and half-truths made slanderous allegations sound more credible. Attacks that diverged too far from the truth often failed; hence the defamation of the dauphin Charles as an incompetent child was untenable once he started conquering major towns.

The exploitation of fears, taboos, and stereotypes was another effective way to destroy character. Such labels provided attackers with a convenient short-cut, since they confirmed existing biases and were thus often accepted without question. In many, they triggered an immediate emotional response, link-ing the target to a whole range of negative associations. Hence the *Storia de Mahometh* played on Christian fears of demonic forces, presenting Muham-mad as a "son of darkness" who was in league with the Devil and would lead his followers straight to hell. Needless to say, only "irrational Arabs" would be credulous enough to fall for this obvious ploy. Likewise, Burgundian propa-ganda linked Louis of Orléans to the taboo of practicing sorcery. Yet perhaps the best example of a negative label is the accusation of youth made against several late-medieval rulers, implying that they were unmanly, chaotic, sen-sual, and even tyrannical. Interestingly, this label was only effective during a certain period. As soon as its underlying assumptions were no longer gener-ally accepted, it lost its power as a weapon of character attack.

Even though there is little doubt about the general effectiveness of the defamation strategies described above, their success in particular cases is harder to establish. Here, we are confronted with the difficult question of to what extent our sources are reliable and representative. When a chronicler mentions that negative rumors circulated about a ruler, it is often unclear whether he is merely reporting a fact, unwittingly reproducing an invented or embellished fact, or deliberately inventing or embellishing a fact. As the fates of Louis of Orléans and Isabeau of Bavaria—among many others—show, historians who fail to address these questions adequately can unintentionally perpetuate slander from the past, brandishing their subjects with much worse reputations than they actually deserve.

The Early Modern Age

8

The Ass in the Seat of St. Peter: Defamation of the Pope in Early Lutheran *Flugschriften*

Bobbi Dykema

Introduction[1]

On October 31, 1517, Martin Luther addressed a letter to Archbishop Albrecht of Mainz, enclosing his 95 Theses, with their challenge to the Roman Church's cult of indulgences.[2] While his posting of the theses on the door of the Schloβkirche[3] had perhaps more symbolic impact, Luther's invitation to the supranational scholarly community to a disputation on the doctrine of indulgences[4] was indeed construed as an attack on the papacy by at least some of his respondents.[5] The Church had long offered indulgences—remission of temporal punishment for sin granted for specific good works and prayers, drawing on the treasury of merit laid up by Christ's sacrifice—but by the early sixteenth century the practice had become a widespread, unabashed, and much-abused fundraising technique.

According to Gordon Rupp, "Luther did not set out to oppose papal authority."[6] Nor was Luther's conflict with the Holy See central to his program of reform.[7] Rather, Luther's opposition to the papacy grew organically out of his doctrine of justification by faith, which posed a direct challenge to the penitential system of the Roman Catholic Church.[8] Luther felt that the system of confession, penance, and good works was unbiblical and unnecessary; his substitute doctrine of *sola fide*—"faith alone"—meant that the only act required to merit salvation was to place one's faith in Christ. Luther and his followers were not solely or even primarily focused on a negative campaign against the religion of Rome, but instead on the positive goal of reforming the German church to conform to the true religion of Christ. The depth of corruption, which Luther saw in the papacy, lent urgency to his task, for he came to believe that the Devil was at work in the office of the bishop of Rome, to the extent that that office had become the prophesied figure of Antichrist and that the endtimes were at hand.[9] Indeed, Luther's innovation in antipapal rhetoric was the distinction that the office, and not the person of the pope, was in effect the Antichrist.[10]

The Roman Catholic Church's devotional practices, piety, theology itself were in many ways primarily image based, a condition necessitated by the illiteracy of the overwhelming majority of the laity. To communicate the evangelical message to the populace, Luther and his followers employed a variety of strategies, including popular sermons, printed texts, and images. As the Lutheran Reformation unfolded, cheaply printed pamphlets (*Flugschriften*) and broadsheets, in tandem with evangelical preaching, were the engine that drove the movement.[11] In cities across Germany, the diffusion of evangelical ideas was accomplished by preachers who considered themselves in solidarity with Luther proclaiming the Word of God to the people;[12] many of these additionally published their sermons in printed form. Hundreds of such sermons, treatises, pamphlets, and tracts, which served as a tangible record whose impact endured beyond that of oral forms of communication, were printed and sold. For many of the single-page broadsheets, the primary mode of communication was the image. Fortunately for Luther, a powerful image maker devoted to his cause was able to skillfully combine medieval conventions of devotional imagery with polemical images of the pope to create a visual theology that complemented Luther's verbal theology. That artist was Lucas Cranach the Elder. This essay will examine three of Cranach's early contributions to the Lutheran case against the papacy: visual denunciations of Popes Julius II and Leo X in *Passional Christi und Antichristi* (1521), depictions of the pope as the Whore of Babylon and Beast of Revelation in Luther's translation of the New Testament (1522), and the Papal Ass (1523).

The German Laity and the Papacy

Those living in the first quarter of the sixteenth century had a long list of reasons to view the office of the papacy as antithetical to true Christian religion. The fifteenth century had seen the Great Schism of the papacy, the prodigious growth of curial bureaucracy, the Sack of Rome, and Church funds and energies devoted to defending papal lands and expensive building projects.[13] The German people had particular cause to be affronted by papal activities, as more of the money to fund papal wars and building projects "came from the Germans than from any other nationality within the Church."[14]

Luther himself had visited Rome and "seen some of the squalor firsthand";[15] he had come to believe that there was in the papacy an "unholy satanic power" raging against Christendom and heralding "the approach of the Day of Judgment."[16] In these activities Luther saw a papacy that was arrogating to itself the powers and privileges of secular rule and thus violating the distinction between spiritual and temporal power that had been ordained by God, while simultaneously neglecting its spiritual duties and even suppressing evangelical preaching.[17]

Luther's theology of the two kingdoms, spiritual and temporal, was central to his case against the papacy.[18] While it would not be fully articulated until 1523 with *Temporal Authority*, this theology, in which the governance of earthly realms and of the spirit must be kept firmly separate, was already taking shape as early as his 1515–16 lectures on the book of Romans.[19] For Luther, the authority of both church and state were ordained by God for the ordering of human affairs, and the distinctions between the two spheres corresponded to that between Law and Gospel. The task of the spiritual kingdom is "to hallow us in Christ through preaching and the Word," while the temporal kingdom serves to "sustain justice and peace through the power of the sword."[20] The mingling of the two kingdoms taking place in the papacy's assertion of power over temporal matters was for Luther the Devil's work,[21] which he called on the Christian princes of Germany to oppose in his open letter to them of 1520 (*To the Christian Nobility of the German Nation*). The pamphlet *Passional Christi und Antichristi*, appearing in the spring of 1521, employs many of the same arguments against the papacy as *To the Christian Nobility of the German Nation*[22] and in effect serves as the corresponding work aimed at the third estate.

Lucas Cranach the Elder

In 1505, a young Franconian artist, Lucas Cranach, was named court painter to the elector of Saxony, Frederick the Wise. Cranach was an accomplished portraitist and depicter of animal scenes, as well as a sought-after painter of mildly erotic Venus, Lucretia, and nymph paintings created to suit the tastes of the Saxon nobility.[23] Cranach was an important woodcut artist as well as upper Germany's most prodigious painter. Print technology had taken off in Germany with the introduction of Gutenberg's press, and numberless broadsheets and pamphlets, known as *Flugschriften*, or "flying writing," were produced in addition to books. Both a sympathizer and a friend of Martin Luther,[24] Cranach, uniquely among creators of evangelical *Flugschriften*, enjoyed the imprimatur of the Saxon reformer himself.

In a letter to Georg Spalatin dated March 7, 1521, Luther described a pamphlet in prepublication as *bonus et pro laicis liber*,[25] "a good book for the laity." That work, *Passional Christi und Antichristi*, was published in May 1521 by Johann Rhau Grünenberg of Wittenberg, in a succession of German, as well as one Latin, editions. It is a 19-centimeter quarto booklet of 28 pages, with woodcuts on each page by Cranach. The accompanying text, drawn almost entirely from scripture and canon law, was selected and edited by Philipp Melanchthon and canon lawyer Johann Schwerdtfeger.[26] *Passional* consists of 13 images of Christ paired with texts quoted from scripture; on each facing page is a contrasting image of the pope paired with quotations from canon law. This strategic combination of text and image could appeal to a wide spectrum of literacy.

Luther himself did not have a hand in its creation, but he was aware of and approved of the pamphlet prior to its publication—a second letter to Spalatin,

Paſſional Chriſti und

Chriſtus

Die füchß haben yre gruben / vnd die fogell der lufft yre neſter/
Aber d ſon des menſchen hat nicht do er ſeyn heubt legte. Lu.9.
Dieſſer ab er woll reich war / dennoch vmb vnſert willen iſt er
arm worden/ vnd ſeyn armut hat vns reich gemacht. z. Cor. 8.

Figure 8.1a   A woodcut from the 1521 pamphlet *Passional Christi und Antichristi*.

Courtesy of the Richard C. Kessler Reformation Collection, Pitts Theology Library, Candler School of
Theology, Emory University.

Antichristi.

Wir loßen auff alle eyde die die geystlichen zu gefengknis gelo=
bet haben vnnd gebieten das mann nit allein mit geystlichem/
sonder auch mit dem weltlichem schwerdt yre gütter beschutzē
sall/ so lang biß das sie yr etwandt gutt widder haben 15.q.6
c. Auctoritatem/vnd der yn dießem krieck stirbt adir vordirber
wirt erlangen das ewig leben 23.q.5.c. Simet q.8.c. Omni/
das heyst seyns guts gewiß sein/ das mans auch vor gut acht=
ob schon christenblüt daruber vorgossen wirdt.   C

Figure 8.1b   A woodcut from the 1521 pamphlet *Passional Christi und Antichristi*.

of April 14, 1521, refers to antithetical figures of Christ and the pope by Cranach; *Passional* was printed in May.[27] *Passional* relies heavily on Luther's "two kingdoms" theology, which argues that while both secular and spiritual governments are necessary, they must be kept firmly separate. Secular authority cannot lead people to righteousness, and spiritual authority "cannot maintain external peace and order in human affairs."[28] Temporal, secular rulers uphold their authority through wielding the physical sword; the "sword" of spiritual leaders is the Word of God.

The pamphlet seeks actively to efface the image of the pope in the mind of its reader-viewer and to lead him or her toward a doubled vision, which sees both the pretense to spiritual leadership and the diabolical reality beneath it. Unlike most of the rest of the illustrated Lutheran *Flugschriften* produced in the sixteenth century, *Passional*'s depictions of the pope are not generic images of a man in a triple tiara and cope; rather, 12 of the papal images recognizably depict Leo X (Giovanni di Lorenzo de'Medici), who reigned from March 1513 to December 1521. The thirteenth papal image depicts Leo's predecessor, Julius II (Giuliano della Rovere), who reigned from November 1503 to February 1513.

Chronological exactitude was not a concern in the creation of *Passional*. Cranach's woodcut of the nativity of Christ occurs on page 15, and across the gutter, the lone image of Julius II can be seen (Figures 8.1a–b). As the Prince of Peace enters into the world in incarnate human form, naked and impoverished, his vicar on earth prepares to personally lead an army into battle against the rebel fiefdoms of Perugia and Bologna, an unprecedented act that Julius announced to a thunderstruck college of cardinals on August 17, 1506.[29] In Cranach's woodcut, Julius is depicted wearing both the triple tiara and a suit of armor. He is at the foreground of a group of soldiers readying for war, bearing halberds, spears, and cannon. A group of knights on horseback completes the scene, with a walled city in the background. The accompanying text, quoting from canon law, commands that the property of clergy be protected by the sword and decrees that anyone who should perish in this struggle will be considered a martyr.

One of the most fascinating aspects of *Passional* is its use of canon law. While the text contains a few editorial comments on the part of Melanchthon, most of the verbal explication of Cranach's papal pictures is taken directly from the words of the papacy itself; thus, the *Passional* editorial team allows the Holy See to convict itself of its excesses and wrongs, in much the same way as a twenty-first-century social media meme might quote a politician or pundit to underscore his or her hypocrisy, malice, or lack of common sense.

The image of the nativity of Christ juxtaposed with the warrior pope makes a point that may not be initially clear. The text accompanying the Christ image refers the viewer to Luke 9, where Jesus indicates to his disciples that "Foxes have holes and the birds of the air have nests, but the Son of Man has nowhere to lay his head."[30] In contrast, the pope has at his disposal not only spiritual but temporal power to protect both his and the clergy's vast worldly wealth.

The reader-viewer might also be inclined to note that whereas Christ comes as the Prince of Peace,[31] the pope has become a man of war. The relationship of the reader-viewer to each figure is also set in contrast: while Christ commands the Christian's worship and adoration, the pope demands men, money, and materiel to carry out his imperial ambitions. Luther's resentment of Julius II was revealed even in his university lectures, where he referred to the Rovere pope as a figure of cruelty who aspired to saintliness,[32] a person "mighty in wickedness,"[33] and an "enemy of the cross."[34] Luther's call to arms in *To the Christian Nobility of the German Nation* was itself motivated by the bloodthirstiness of Julius II.[35]

Even so, Julius's successor, Leo X, the papal thorn in Luther's side whose reign would last another six months beyond the publication of *Passional*, comes in for a much more severe skewering. At every turn of the page, his behavior and the canon-law excuses for it are seen to be in 180-degree opposition to the life and teachings of Christ: Christ is tortured with the crown of thorns, while Leo receives the splendid papal triple tiara; Christ carries the cross, while Leo is carried in a luxurious litter; and so on. On the last pair of facing pages, the ultimate fates of the two figures are revealed, as Christ ascends into heaven, and Leo the papal Antichrist is cast into the flames of hell.

By way of illustration, a single example will suffice: On page 6 of *Passional*, Leo is enthroned beneath his baldachin, with an array of mitered bishops and tonsured monks, as well as nobles and princes, clustering around the throne. The pope extends his shod foot for one of the princes to kiss and raises his right hand in blessing. Cardinals, scholars, and other members of the three estates are included in the group waiting to pay homage to the Vicar of Christ, who is seated on a richly brocaded throne atop two steps. The Ionic column in the upper right underscores the rich ornamentation of the space.

Across the gutter, the role of Christ is a mirror image of the pope's. Christ washes feet; Leo's feet are kissed. Christ is a humble servant; Leo, a proud ruler. The leader of the Christian hurch has succumbed to the attractions of the deference of all men, rather than being the servant of all, as Christ himself was. The text accompanying the image of papal foot kissing references Revelation 13: 15, correlating this display of deference with the worship of the Beast of Revelation. *Passional Christi und Antichristi* as a whole thus serves as an iconoclastic gesture against such idolatrous behavior. Unlike destructive iconoclasm, works of creative iconoclasm, such as *Passional*, bypass the act of destruction and proceed directly to making a new image that reveals the emptiness of that which it effaces and critiques: the pope as spectacle becomes the pope as object of scorn and derision. Having laid bare the depth of iniquity to which the papacy had sunk—so far that to Luther's mind, at least, the office had itself become the prophesied Antichrist—Cranach and Luther continued at key times to issue joint efforts of image and text to further drive home the point.

Cranach's Woodcuts for Luther's New Testament:
The Beast and the Whore of Babylon

The edict of the Diet of Worms—the formal assembly of the Holy Roman Empire that tried and found Luther heretic and outlaw—was presented on May 25, 1521,[36] at nearly the exact moment that *Passional Christi und Antichristi* appeared in Wittenberg bookshops. Luther became an outlaw; his literature was officially banned, and anyone sighting him was required to apprehend him. On his way back to Wittenberg, Luther was intercepted by masked horsemen, who conveyed him to the Wartburg Castle at Eisenach,[37] under the protection of the lector Frederick III (the Wise) of Saxony, who, while a devout Catholic himself, apparently approved of Luther's program of reform.

One of Luther's projects while in hiding was the translation of the New Testament from the original Greek, as edited by Erasmus in the second edition (1519) of the *Textus receptus*, into German.[38] This translation became known as the *Septembertestament*, as it was published initially in September 1522. To facilitate his translation, Luther made forays into nearby towns and markets to listen to the colloquial language of the people,[39] in order to make for a truly populist translation, which would serve to give the German laity personal access to the Word of God.

Luther's interpretation of the papacy as Antichrist developed further over the course of his translation efforts. While the word "Antichrist" (ἀντίχριστος) appears five times in the New Testament, all in the Johannine epistles, it was Luther's work on 2 Thessalonians and Revelation that most influenced his continued thinking on the papacy as Antichrist.[40]

In his description of the eschatological battle between good and evil in 2 Thessalonians, Paul refers to a key figure whom he calls at one point the "Man of Sin" (ὁ ἄνθρωπος τῆς ἁμαρτίας) and at another the "Son of Perdition" (ὁ υἱός τῆς ἀπωλείας). This figure will overthrow worship of the one true God and demand that he himself be worshipped. When Christ returns, however, the Man of Sin will be revealed and overthrown.[41] Luther's introduction to 2 Thessalonians makes clear that he is both reading Paul's prophecy apocalyptically and applying it specifically to the papal Antichrist, interpreting the events foretold there as a sort of curriculum vitae of the final traitor of Christendom: the Antichrist, identified by Paul as the Man of Sin, will betray the Church from within, undermine the Roman Empire, mislead the faithful through false signs and doctrines, and usurp the place of God.[42] Luther uses the German *Endchrist* ("final Christ") to refer to this figure, which is the same term used in all of his original writings to refer to the papal Antichrist (as opposed to the more literal translation of "Antichrist," *Widerchrist*, or "against Christ," which he uses in his writings about a quarter as often).[43] When Luther examined the actions and decretal self-justifications of the papacy's many unscriptural and self-serving excesses, he found the realization of the Pauline prophecies unfolding. Luther was inspired by Lorenzo Valla's *Discourse on the Forgery of the Alleged Donation of Constantine*,[44] as well as the writings of the

Bohemian protoreformer Jan Hus.[45] By 1530 he was entirely convinced that the New Testament book of Revelation was a guide to the end-times and the acts of the papal Antichrist.[46] Already in 1521, however, Luther's illustrator—Cranach—seems to have suffered no compunctions on this score.

The book of Revelation (German *Apokalypse*) in the *Septembertestament* is accompanied by 21 full-page woodcuts by Cranach.[47] Among these, two in particular carry an antipapal message: the image accompanying Rev. 11: 1–8, of the Beast who menaces the prophetic witnesses sent by God to measure the Temple (Figure 8.2); and that which appears alongside Rev. 17, of the Whore of Babylon. Both of these figures—the Beast and the Whore—are crowned in Cranach's renditions with the papal triple tiara.[48]

In Revelation 11, the narrator is asked to measure the Temple, while two witnesses are given authority to prophesy for a period of three and a half years. At the end of this period, the "Beast from the pit" will arise and kill them.[49] Their bodies will lie unburied in the street for three and a half days, after which the breath of God will revive them. Cranach depicts the two witnesses in contemporary sixteenth-century German dress, conferring together before the Temple, which is represented as a long hallway supported by narrow interior Ionic columns, culminating in an altar graced with a single, slender golden candlestick. Meanwhile St. John is diligently measuring the Temple with builders' tools in the middle right. The right foreground is occupied by a fearsome dragon, which seems to have arisen from below a displaced floor slab of the Temple sporting the papal crown, whose hot breath is directed at the two witnesses.

Revelation 17 describes the great Whore who appears riding a seven-headed Beast and carrying a golden cup of abominations. While the scriptural passage depicts her as bearing the name "Babylon" inscribed on her forehead and refers to her as a personification of the great city,[50] Cranach depicts her as a literal woman dressed in fine courtly garments with golden choker and chain; on her head is not a name but the papal crown. In terms of defamation of the pope, these images represent a move away from the direct indictment against Julius II and Leo X in *Passional Christi und Antichristi*, toward a metaphorical attack on the papacy in general, extending backward and forward to include its occupants from all generations. Whereas in *Passional*, the Pope is *named* as Antichrist and depicted engaging in all manner of anti-Christlike behavior, in the *Septembertestament*, Antichrist, in his various guises, is visually coterminous with the crowned head of the Christian Church, whoever he may be at any given moment. The defamation in the *Septembertestament* smears the papacy as an office, rather than its particular officeholders. However, the officeholders themselves do not, in Luther's reckoning, escape condemnation. By promulgating the notion that the papacy was and is Antichrist, Luther and his colleagues by implication indicted all of its officeholders, past, present, and future, as being in league with the Devil—possibly the most damning assassination of character possible, particularly for those who ostensibly were tasked with the care of the souls of all of Christendom.

Figure 8.2 A woodcut from the *Septembertestament*.

Courtesy of the Richard C. Kessler Reformation Collection, Pitts Theology Library, Candler School of Theology, Emory University.

According to Mark U. Edwards Jr., Cranach's images of the crowned figures of the Beast and the Whore of Babylon not only "provoked considerable
outcry,"[51] but were highly influential in terms of both the sheer number of editions and copies of the *Septembertestament* that were produced, as well as the
re-creation of the images themselves by numerous Cranach imitators.[52] The
September edition sold out almost at once; a total of 43 editions appeared from
September 1522 to December 1525,[53] representing no less than 86,000 total
copies.[54] The offending papal tiara, but not the introductions to 2 Thessalonians
and the Apocalypse, was excised from the Whore and the Beast in many of
these editions—in Albertine Saxony, at the behest of Duke Georg;[55] slightly less
than a quarter included the antipapal imagery initiated by Cranach.[56] However,
those that kept the visual papal defamations in some cases actually heightened
the insult: Hans Holbein the Younger produced versions for the Basel edition
published by Thomas Wolff in 1523, with the triple tiaras made distinctly larger
and more obtrusive.[57] This change was carried over into the anonymously produced woodcuts for the 1534 Wittenberg edition of Luther's translation of the
complete Bible.[58] While Carl C. Christensen argues that the visual identification
of the Beast and the Whore with the papacy was less polemical than incultura-
tional,[59] and Robert W. Scribner suggests that the identification of the papacy
specifically with the Whore of Babylon may have been an outgrowth of the
legend of Pope Joan,[60] in light of Luther's ongoing efforts and Cranach's visual
collaboration, in publicizing his identification of Antichrist with the papacy
during this period, it seems more likely that the papal tiaras on the Whore of
Babylon and the Beast of Revelation were primarily defamatory in nature and
intent. In them, Luther and his colleagues lent the weight of additional biblical
eschatology to their theological case against the papacy, as begun with the publication of *Passional*. A third insult, both more metaphorical and more direct,
more pointed and yet more esoteric, was to appear in 1523.

The Papal Ass

In Matthew 24: 24, Jesus warns his disciples of the "signs and wonders" that
will herald the close of the age. Luther's interpretation of biblical apocalyptic
literature as foretelling events unfolding in his own time and referring in veiled
terms to the corruption of the papacy was accompanied by the appearance of
signs and wonders in the natural world. One of these was the Papal Ass, a
monstrously amalgamated creature whose corpse had reportedly washed up
on the banks of the Tiber following a flood in 1496.[61] As Luther's antipapal
eschatological thinking evolved toward the end of the first quarter of the sixteenth century, he and his colleagues, Lucas Cranach as well as Philipp Melanchthon, seized upon this strange portent as a further exemplification of the
papal Antichrist enthroned in Rome.

While some scholars have asserted that concern with the imminent end
of historical time and the apocalyptic crises foretold by scripture were not
potent features of late-medieval life,[62] the themes of death, judgment, heaven

and hell, as well as specific figures and episodes from the book of Revelation, can be seen to have reached new heights of significance in the first quarter of the sixteenth century, especially in Germany. Luther's sense of the urgency of his mission was impelled by a belief that a level of crisis had been reached in current events such that the end of time could not be far off.[63]

Earlier theologians, such as Bernard of Clairvaux (1090–1153) and Joachim of Fiore (1135–1202), had emphasized an apocalyptic understanding of scripture being fulfilled by specific, proximate events in human history.[64] As early as 1514, Luther in his lectures referenced Bernard's epochal sequence in his growing concern regarding the portent of the Church's sale of indulgences: "The way I see it, the Gospel of St. Matthew counts such perversions as the sale of indulgences among the signs of the Last Days."[65]

While Luther's prior rhetorical explications of the papal Antichrist can be seen to have emerged from his study of scripture and of papal decretals—letters of the popes that formulate decisions in ecclesiastical law—it is somewhat unclear what inspired him and Melanchthon to take up the Papal Ass (a term that may well have been coined by Luther himself).[66] Johann Carion's illustrated *Prognosticatio* appeared in 1521,[67] and there is some evidence that Melanchthon and Luther had received a prepublication copy of the anonymous Bohemian treatise entitled *Anatomy of the Antichrist*;[68] both documents dealt to some extent with the 1496 Tiber monster.[69]

Cranach's woodcut depiction of the Papal Ass (Figure 8.3) closely follows an earlier version by Wenzel von Olmütz. The donkey-headed beast stands on its hind legs on the banks of the Tiber, with the Castel Sant'Angelo visible in the background, flying the papal flag with its crossed keys of St. Peter. The ass has a long flowing mane, suggestive of unbound female human hair, and the breasts and rounded belly of a female human torso. Its tail terminates in two heads, those of a dragon and an old man, and its body is covered with scales. The extremity of each leg is that of a different creature: the right foreleg ends in an elephant's foot, while the left bears a female human hand; the right hind leg is an ox's hoof, and the left a griffin's foot.

Half of the pamphlet in which this freak appears is devoted to another monstrous creature, the deformed fetus of a calf that appeared in Freiberg in December 1522. Luther provided the textual explication for this animal, which he dubbed the Monk-Calf—and which may have also inspired the entire pamphlet.[70] Melanchthon wrote the expository material for the Papal Ass. He discusses each body part of the beast individually, incorporating scriptural references to make clear their eschatological significance; in particular, the strange ram and goat that appeared to King Belshazzar in Daniel 8 are cited throughout as evidence of God's utilization of the natural order of creation to reveal his messages to humankind.[71]

Beginning at the top, the head of the monster signifies the pope. Exodus 13: 13 is quoted by way of highlighting the low regard in which the donkey, among animals, is held by God: while the firstborn male of all other livestock is to be dedicated to the Lord, the donkey's firstborn must either be redeemed with a sheep or have its neck broken. Likewise, the body of Christ, which

Figure 8.3   Cranach's 1523 woodcut depiction of the Papal Ass.

Courtesy of the Richard C. Kessler Reformation Collection, Pitts Theology Library, Candler School of Theology, Emory University.

should have no earthly head, is instead governed and controlled by the bray-ing ass of a pope.[72]

The elephant foot at the end of the creature's right forelimb signifies the spiritual power of the papacy, by which the faithful are trampled via their fear of eternal punishment.[73] The left forelimb terminates in a human hand, which connotes the papacy's secular power.[74] This power, which in Luther's two kingdoms theology properly belongs only to the secular rulers whom God has placed in authority over the people, has been acquired by the papacy via human means—thus, the human hand.

The Papal Ass's female breasts and belly allude to the carnality and bodily lusts—for sumptuous food, illicit sex, lavish wealth, and pompous regalia—evidenced in the excesses of the church hierarchy: bishops, cardinals, and priests.[75] Melanchthon cites Matthew 24: 4, Jesus's warning to the disciples to not let anyone lead them astray, in his discussion of the monster's (right) ox hoof. This appendage signifies the teachers, preachers, pastors, and especially scholastic theologians who deviously lead the faithful astray, just as an ungoverned ox will veer with its plough off toward the ditch.[76]

The creature's left foot, a griffin's claw, connotes the canon lawyers, those servants of the pope's secular power who repress the entire world.[77] The scaly skin of the monster is compared with the description of Leviathan in Job 41: 7; these scales are the secular princes and lords who defend and support papal wrongdoings.[78] Finally, the bizarre tail of the creature, which terminates in the heads of both a dragon and an old man, is held to be the prophets of Israel named in Isaiah 9: 15, the tail which was cut off by dint of having led the people astray.[79] The dragon head is the plethora of papal bulls and pronouncements that oppress Christendom; the aged man's head signifies the decline of the Roman pontiff's power. That the creature was found dead is a sign of the corrupt and false church's ultimate demise.

The Papal Ass, like the defamatory imagery of the *Septembertestament*, enjoyed fairly extensive popularity. The figure was revisited by Luther in 1545 in his *Depiction of the Papacy*, and its publication saw 14 editions—9 with the Monk-Calf, and 5 without.[80] Its creation can be seen as the zenith (or perhaps nadir) of Luther, Melanchthon, and Cranach's visual and textual program of defamation of the papacy in the early 1520s, which began with the human Antichrist Popes Julius II and Leo X in *Passional Christi und Antichristi*, continued with the Whore of Babylon and Beast of Revelation popes of biblical eschatology in the *Septembertestament*, and concluded with the monstrous Papal Ass.

Conclusion

Thousands of other works of defamatory antipapal *Flugschriften*, mostly produced anonymously, were circulated during the early years of the Protestant Reformation. The particular images discussed here have the distinction of having been produced and signed by a well-known master artist, in direct collaboration with the evangelical movement's primary reformer, for the purpose not merely of denigrating the pope, but to advance a particular theological argument—namely, that the papacy itself was the scripturally prophesied Antichrist. Luther found no justification for even the existence of a papacy in scripture, and the monstrous arrogation of power to that office, culminating in the Borgia and Medici popes in his lifetime, confirmed his suspicion that the very man tasked with overseeing the care of all Christian souls was instead in deliberate and conscious league with the Devil. The earliest Cranach works of Lutheran pictorial character assassination were directed specifically against

Julius II and Leo X; later works besmeared the office as a whole, in the present and all preceding generations. Accepting coronation as pope meant joining the forces of darkness in a powerful leadership role that threatened the foundations of Christian faith and heralded the prophesied end times.

This shift in emphasis, from current papal officeholders to the office itself, had the effect of giving antipapal sentiments greater intensity and staying power. As recently as the 1960s, the Irish folksingers The Clancy Brothers had audiences shouting, with fervor, "Up the long ladder and down the short rope, to hell with King Billy and God bless the Pope"—for which the Protestant Irish version was "God bless King Billy, to hell with the Pope."[81] The notion that the pope was Antichrist, in league with the Devil (and sure to meet his just end), turned out to be incredibly enduring. Witness the current broad brush with which all of the U.S. Congress is tarred, regardless of political party: "If pro is the opposite of con, what's the opposite of progress?" is a popular bumper sticker, and standing for high office renders an otherwise esteemed person immediately suspect.

Sixteenth-century apologists for the Catholic Church produced counterpropaganda, but nowhere near on the order of magnitude and originality as the Lutherans. Jan L. de Jong has recently demonstrated how the propaganda campaign of the Vatican itself was carried out not in the accessible medium of printed *Flugschriften*, but in frescoed and sculpted artistic efforts displayed in the interiors of lavish and exclusive spaces where papal visitors would be received.[82] Whereas Cranach's defamatory images were seen by tens of thousands, the numbers of those able to view the papal counterpropaganda campaigns numbered perhaps in the dozens. It may well be that the success and long-lasting resonance of the Protestant Reformation owes as much to the sheer numbers, availability, and cleverness of its negative portrayals of the Catholic hierarchy as it does to the attractiveness of its own theology.

Notes

1. I would like to thank Anitra Kitts and Olga Ostash for their invaluable assistance in helping me obtain research materials for this project.
2. Brecht 1981, 190–92.
3. Leppin 2007, 145–50.
4. Brecht 1981, 199.
5. Hendrix 1981, 32.
6. Rupp 1983, 262.
7. Rosin 2003, 409.
8. Hendrix 1981, 394.
9. Oberman 1966–1984, 30.
10. Rosin 2003, 424.
11. Scribner 1981, 1; Edwards 1994, 1–2.
12. Lau and Bizer 1964, 32–33, cited in Karant-Nunn, 82. Scholars disagree as to how unified "Lutheran" teaching may have been in the early years of the movement; see also Moeller and Stackman 1996 and Edwards 1994, 1–2.

13. Rosin 2003, 412ff.
14. Rosin 2003, 413.
15. Rosin 2003, 415.
16. Hamm 2007, 251.
17. Spitz 1985, 129.
18. The term "doctrine of the two kingdoms" was coined in 1922: Lohse 1981, 188.
19. Luther 1970.
20. Nygren 1949, 305.
21. Prill 2005, 18.
22. Fleming 1973, 358; Luther 1966.
23. Snyder 1985, 383.
24. Cf. Tacke 1992.
25. Luther 1825.
26. Luther 1933b.
27. Luther 1933a.
28. Estes 2005, 39.
29. King 2003, 34.
30. Luke 9: 58.
31. Isaiah 9: 6.
32. Luther 1911, lines 14–17.
33. Luther 1897, 18–20.
34. Luther 1938.
35. Luther 1888, line 2.
36. Bratcher n.d.
37. MacCulloch 2003, 132.
38. Brecht 1990, 46.
39. Zecher 1992; Hasty 2009, 458.
40. Whitford 2008, 31.
41. Whitford 2008, 32.
42. Whitford 2008, 37.
43. Whitford 2008, 36.
44. Whitford 2008, 28.
45. McGinn 2000, 203.
46. Backus 2000, 8. See also Hofmann 1982.
47. Edwards 1994, 123. See also Martin 1983.
48. Scribner 1981, 169–70.
49. Rev. 11: 7.
50. Rev. 17: 18.
51. Edwards 1994, 123.
52. Scribner 1981, 173ff.
53. Edwards, o cit.
54. Edwards 1994, 126.
55. Koerner 2004, 173.
56. Edwards 1994, 127.
57. Scribner 1981, 173–4.
58. Christensen 2005, 403.
59. Christensen 2005, 404.
60. Scribner 1981, 171.
61. Buck 2011, 361.
62. Cf. Holeton 1994, 29.

63. Oberman 1982, 68ff.
64. Emmerson and Herzman 1992, 4.
65. Luther 1885, line 7f.
66. Ibid.
67. Spinks 2009, 60.
68. Buck 2011, 363.
69. Scribner 1981, 131.
70. Spinks 2009, 63.
71. Scribner 1981, 132.
72. Spinks 2009, 67.
73. Buck 2011, 364.
74. Scribner 1981, 131.
75. Buck 2011, 365.
76. Spinks 2009, 68.
77. Scribner 1981, 132.
78. Buck 2011, 365.
79. Buck 2011, 366.
80. Scribner 1981, 132.
81. Bentley 2009.
82. De Jong 2013.

Bibliography

Backus, I. 2000. *Reformation Readings of the Apocalypse: Geneva, Zurich, and Wittenberg.* Oxford: Oxford University Press.

Bentley, K. 2009. "The Clancy Brothers and Tommy Makem." *Global Rock Legends of the 60s and 70s: A Unique South African Perspective on the Artists Who Shaped a Generation* (blog). January 7, 2009. http://globalrocklegends.blogspot.com/2009/01/clancy-brothers-and-tommy-makem.html (accessed October 23, 2013).

Bratcher, Dennis. n.d. "The Diet of Worms (1521)." In *The Voice: Biblical and Theological Resources for Growing Christians.* http://www.crivoice.org (accessed September 28, 2013).

Brecht, M. 1981. *Martin Luther, Volume 1: His Road to Reformation, 1483–1521.* Transl. J. L. Schaaf, 1985. Philadelphia: Fortress Press.

Brecht, Martin, 1990. *Martin Luther, Volume 2: Shaping and Defining the Reformation, 1521–1532.* Transl. J. L. Schaaf, 1994. Minneapolis: Augsburg Fortress.

Buck, L. S. 2011. "*Anatomia Antichristi*: Form and Content of the Papal Antichrist." *Sixteenth Century Journal* 47 (2 Summer): 349–68.

Christensen, C. C. 2005. "Luther and the Woodcuts to the 1534 Bible." *Lutheran Quarterly* 19 (4 Winter): 392–413.

de Jong, J. L. 2013. *The Power and the Glorification: Papal Pretensions and the Art of Propaganda in the Fifteenth and Sixteenth Centuries.* University Park: The Pennsylvania State University Press.

Edwards Jr., Mark U. 1994. *Printing, Propaganda, and Martin Luther.* Minneapolis: Fortress Press.

Emmerson, R. K., and R. B. Herzman. 1992. *The Apocalyptic Imagination in Medieval Literature.* Philadelphia: University of Pennsylvania Press.

Estes, J. M. 2005. *Peace, Order and the Glory of God: Secular Authority and the Church in the Thought of Luther and Melanchthon, 1518–1559.* Leiden, Netherlands: Brill.

Fleming, G. 1973. "On the Origin of the *Passional Christi and Antichristi* and Lucas Cranach the Elder's Contribution to Reformation Polemics in the Iconography of the *Passional.*" *Gutenberg Jahrbuch* 48: 351–68.

Hamm, B. 2007. "Luther's Freedom of a Christian and the Pope." Transl. H. Heron and M. J. Lohmann. *Lutheran Quarterly* 21 (3 Autumn): 249–67.

Hasty, W. 2009. "The Singularity of Aura and the Artistry of Translation: Martin Luther's Bible as Artwork." *Monatshefte* 101 (4 Winter): 457–68.

Hendrix, S. H. 1981. *Luther and the Papacy: Stages in a Reformation Conflict.* Philadelphia: Fortress Press.

Hofmann, H.-U. 1982. *Luther und die Johannes-Apokalypse. Dargestellt im Rahmen der Auslegungsgeschichte des letzten Buches der Bibel und im Zusammenhang der theologischen Entwicklung des Reformators.* Tübingen: Mohr.

Holeton, D. R. 1994. "Revelation and Revolution in Late Medieval Bohemia." *Communio viatorum* 36 (1): 29–45.

Karant-Nunn, S. C. 1988. "What Was Preached in German Cities in the Early Years of the Reformation? *Wildwuchs* versus Lutheran Unity." In N. Bebb and S. Marshall, eds., *The Process of Change in Early Modern Europe: Essays in Honor of Miriam Usher Chrisman,* 81–96. Athens, OH: Ohio University Press.

King, R. 2003. *Michelangelo and the Pope's Ceiling.* New York: Penguin Books.

Koerner, J. L. 2004. *The Reformation of the Image.* Chicago: University of Chicago Press.

Lau, F., and E. Bizer. 1964. *Reformationsgeschichte Deutschlands bis 1555.* Göttingen: Vandenhoeck & Ruprecht.

Leppin, V. 2007. "Geburtswehen und Geburt einer Legende. Zu Rörers Notiz von Thesenanschlag." *Luther* 78 (3) 145–50.

Lohse, B. 1981. *Martin Luther: An Introduction to His Life and Work.* Transl. R. C. Schultz, 1986. Philadelphia: Fortress Press.

Luther, M. 1883–1978. *D. Martin Luthers Werke, Kritische Gesamtausgabe.* Eds. R. Hermann, G. Ebeling, et al. 127 vols. Weimar: H. Bohlau.

Luther, M. 1883. "Letter to Georg Spalatin; March 7, 1521." In *D. Martin Luthers Werke,* vol. 1, 571.

Luther, M. 1885. "Lectures on the Psalms." In *D. Martin Luthers Werke,* vol. 3, 435.

Luther, M. 1888. "To the Christian Nobility of the German Nation. In *D. Martin Luthers Werke,* vol. 6, 404–69.

Luther, M. 1897. "Lectures on the Psalms." In *D. Martin Luthers Werke,* vol. 19, 569.

Luther, M. 1911. "Lectures on Genesis." In *D. Martin Luthers Werke,* vol. 42, 237.

Luther, M. 1933a. "Letter to Georg Spalatin; Frankfurt/Main, April 14, 1521." In *D. Martin Luthers Werke,* vol. 2, 298.

Luther, M. 1933b. "Letter to Philip Melanchton; Warburg, May 26, 1521." In *D. Martin Luthers Werke,* vol. 2, 347.

Luther, M. 1938. "Lectures on Romans. Rom. 5: 3." In *D. Martin Lutherse Werke,* vol. 56, 301–2.

Luther, M. 1970. "Lectures on Romans." In *D. Martin Luthers Werke,* vol. 56, 481–82.

MacCulloch, D. 2003. *Reformation: Europe's House Divided, 1490–1700.* London: Allen Lane.

Martin, P. 1983. *Martin Luther und die Bilder zur Apokalypse. Die Ikonographie der Illustrationen zur Offenbarung des Johannes in der Lutherbibel 1522 bis 1546.* Hamburg: F. Wittig.

McGinn, B. 2000. *Antichrist: Two Thousand Years of the Human Fascination with Evil.* New York: Columbia University Press.

Moeller, B., and K. Stackmann. 1996. *Städtische Predigt in der Frühzeit der Reformation. Eine Untersuchung deutscher Flugschriften der Jahre 1522 bis 1529*. Göttingen: Vandenhoeck & Ruprecht.

Nygren, A. 1949. Luther's Doctrine of the Two Kingdoms. *Ecumenical Review* 1 (3 Spring): 301–10.

Oberman, H. A. 1966–1984. *The Reformation: Roots and Ramifications*. Transl. A. C. Gow, 1994. Grand Rapids, MI: Eerdmans.

Oberman, H. A. 1982. *Luther: Man between God and the Devil*. Transl. E. Walliser-Schwarzbart, 1982. New Haven, CT: Yale University Press.

Prill, Th. 2005. Martin Luther, the Two Kingdoms, and the Church. *Evangel* 23 (1 Spring): 17–21.

Rosin, R. 2003. The Papacy in Perspective: Luther's Reform and Rome. *Concordia Journal* 29 (4 October): 407–26.

Rupp, G. 1983. "Luther against 'The Turk, the Pope, and the Devil.'" In N. Brooks, ed., *Seven-Headed Luther: Essays in Commemoration of a Quincentenary, 1483–1983*, 255–73. Oxford: Clarendon Press.

Scribner, R. W. 1981. *For the Sake of Simple Folk: Popular Propaganda for the German Reformation*. Oxford: Clarendon Press.

Snyder, J. 1985. *Northern Renaissance Art: Painting, Sculpture, the Graphic Arts from 1350 to 1575*. New York: Harry N. Abrams.

Spinks, J. 2009. *Monstrous Births and Visual Culture in Sixteenth-Century Germany*. London: Pickering & Chatto.

Spitz, L. W. 1985. "The Christian in Church and State." In M. Hoffmann, ed., *Martin Luther and the Modern Mind: Freedom, Conscience, Toleration, Rights*, Toronto Studies in Theology, vol. 22, 125–61. Toronto: Edwin Mellen Press.

Tacke, A. 1992. *Der katholische Cranach. Zu zwei Grossaufträgen von Lucas Cranach d.Ä. Simon Franck und der Cranach-Werkstatt (1520–1540)*. Mainz: von Zabern.

Whitford, D.M. 2008. "The Papal Antichrist: Martin Luther and the Underappreciated Influence of Lorenzo Valla." *Renaissance Quarterly* 61 (1 Spring): 26–52.

Zecher, H. 1992. "The Bible Translation That Rocked the World." *Christian History* 11 (2): 35–37.

9

Odious and Vile Names: Political Character Assassination and Purging in the French Revolution

Mette Harder

Introduction[1]

Character assassination has always been a very effective weapon to win political battles or settle personal scores. This assertion is certainly true regarding the French Revolution (1789–99), in whose political culture and practices attacks on character, identity, and private life played a key part. Character assassinations in journals, pamphlets, caricatures, and by word of mouth, a habit which had already flourished under the prerevolutionary governments of Louis XV and XVI, targeted almost all leading political figures after 1789: from Marie-Antoinette to Robespierre.[2] Readers might be familiar with famous eighteenth-century caricatures depicting Louis XVI as a gluttonous pig and his wife as a spoiled, promiscuous foreigner who took little interest in the country's well-being.[3] Throughout the early 1790s, similar smear campaigns were directed at whole groups of undesirables: foreigners, often accused of forming a fifth column, and nobles, labeled as traitors and parasites to the nation.[4] Character assassination equally targeted the revolutionary camp: abroad, where the British press portrayed the sans-culotte movement as cannibals, and from inside France, where false claims could quickly end politicians' lives and careers. Even such a man of exemplary conduct as Maximilien Robespierre, nicknamed the *Incorruptible*, became the victim of character assassination after his fall on 9 Thermidor year II (July 27, 1794) when his enemies painted him as a bloodthirsty tyrant who had harbored shameful private vices.

As part of this volume on character assassination, my chapter investigates how political and personal attacks on individuals, especially politicians, worked in the French Revolution and what kind of role they played in the escalating political violence during this time. Which methods did character assassins use against their targets, what were their most common accusations, and was there any way to successfully defend oneself against their attacks?[5] To what extent did attacks on character contribute to the many cases of political purging during this time? Character assassination in the Revolution is mostly associated with the Terror (1793–94), which unleashed massive purges based on malicious accusations against politicians in the press and the legislature. As full-scale parliamentary warfare between different political factions erupted in the early republic, the safeguards of parliamentary immunity were gradually removed, and hundreds of legislators were denounced, arrested, imprisoned, and, in some cases, executed or deported for alleged political crimes. The practice of purging, or *l'épuration*, of leading politicians, most of whom became in turn both perpetrators and victims, affected continuously revolutionary politics at the highest level. From the persecution of the Girondins between June 1793 and early 1794, the show trial of Danton and Camille Desmoulins in the spring of 1794, to the fast-track execution of Robespierre, Saint-Just, and their allies in Thermidor II (July 1794), character assassination functioned as a major tool of political purging. Politicians regularly fell victim to slander, false allegations about their private and political conduct, and willful misinterpretations of their words and actions. Corruption and treason were common themes in character assassinations during the Terror, as was the accusation of wearing a mask to deceive the public and the issue of a lack of virtue (the latter particularly hard to prove or disprove).[6] As the personal became confused with the public, private acts were invested with political meaning in order to taint the enemy's reputation. In the spring of 1794, for instance, Robespierre's ally Saint-Just was able to ruin the political reputation of the veteran revolutionary Danton by calling him a "bad citizen," a "bad friend," and an "evil man."[7] Danton's subsequent political trial and execution, resulting from Saint-Just's accusations, signaled that character assassination had become a deadly business, more often than not resulting in capital sentences against leading revolutionaries, who were powerless to counter the allegations made against them.

While character assassination formed an important part of the political culture of the Terror, the practice also continued in the Thermidorian Reaction, the troubled period between 1794 and 1795 that followed Robespierre's fall from power. During this time, Robespierre, especially, became the victim of a posthumous, sustained assault on his character, which led to the creation of a dark legend around the politician that has endured to this day. Reactionaries eager to whitewash their own *terroristes* pasts also targeted many of Robespierre's former political allies: through smear campaigns in the legislature, the revolutionary press, and pamphlets, which compared their targets to Sulla and Catiline,[8] and promised that their "odious and vile names" would soon replace those of "the most execrable and hypocritical tyrants in history."[9]

Just as in the Terror, reactionary character assassinations led to numerous purges and trials of revolutionary politicians, who were imprisoned and often convicted on the basis of very little evidence. Character assassinations in the Reaction were made possible by the revival of a free press and reached a climax during the 1795 inquest into the responsibility of four Jacobin politicians for the Terror: the *Conventionnel* Barère, denounced as a spineless opportunist, and his colleagues Billaud-Varenne (labeled a ferocious tiger), Collot d'Herbois (accused of having been a *mitrailleur* of innocent citizens in the Terror), and Vadier (blamed for the "rivers of blood" of the year II).[10] The inquest attracted much public attention and resulted in new waves of persecution against revolutionary politicians in the Reaction that were comparable to the great show trials of the Terror.

While character assassination had played a key role in the Terror, it continued to be an equally strong feature of French politics in later years. The Thermidorian period, in fact, saw a veritable second Terror among revolutionaries, which drew heavily on attacks on character and libelous practices. As in the year II, character assassination in the Reaction was used, particularly, to attack politicians against whom there was little actual evidence of political misconduct. As in the Terror, libel remained a useful tool whenever the real reason for attacking one's opponents was that they held a different political opinion. The long-term use of this practice in the Revolution, particularly in connection to political purging and trials, highlights the extent to which revolutionary politicians struggled to distance themselves from the legacy of the Terror and its dubious political practices. The problem of character assassination in this period also reveals deeper political issues facing the French revolutionaries: how to have open yet fair debates on politicians' responsibility, how to balance freedom of the press with the need to protect politicians against calumny and slander,[11] and how to define an appropriate register for political debate. Character assassinations severely damaged individual revolutionary politicians' lives and careers during the Terror. The revolutionaries' continued use of this practice in later years highlighted major difficulties in their experiment with democratic practices, political contestation, and political responsibility in the aftermath of the Terror and beyond.

Character Assassination in the Early Revolution and the Terror: 1789 to 1794

The practice of character assassination in French politics preceded the Revolution, as Robert Darnton's work on slander in the eighteenth century has shown.[12] The publication of individuals' *private* or *secret lives*, for example— short biographical texts that alleged dark, humiliating or shameful secrets in someone's past so as to damage his or her reputation—had been a common tactic in the Old Regime, used against ministers, kings' mistresses, and other public figures.[13] The tone of pre-1789 character assassinations was astonishingly frank and frequently pornographic. Their usually anonymous authors focused on the alleged low or illegitimate origins, "perverted" sex lives (accusations of homosexuality, orgies, and—in women—a voracious sexual appetite were particularly frequent), and greediness and corruption of their victims, as Colin Jones's work on caricatures depicting Madame Pompadour has shown.[14] Many of the authors of character assassinations were struggling writers, trying to make a living by attracting as large a readership for their scandalous accounts as possible.[15] But, as Darnton has pointed out, even Enlightenment greats, such as Voltaire, engaged in libeling to settle personal scores with former friends and ideological opponents.[16]

The Revolution saw a continuation of Old Regime traditions of calumny and slander. In the "virtually unregulated revolutionary press" of 1789, character assassinations flourished, and many journals and pamphlets adopted or went beyond the irreverent tone of previous publications.[17] Familiar themes, such as sex scandals and gluttony, went hand in hand with allegations of corruption and treason. In his famous 1789 *Discours de la lanterne aux Parisiens*, the radical journalist Camille Desmoulins, for instance, appealed to his audience's empty stomachs and their inherent distrust of Versailles politics by suggesting that members of the court were plotting France's ruin over "delicious suppers." He also cheekily denounced the corruption of a system that allowed certain society women to receive state pensions "for having slept with a Minister."[18] Alongside the court and the nobility, the royal family, of course, remained a key focus of character assassination in the early Revolution. As Antoine de Baecque has highlighted, the hit series *Historical Essays on the Life of Marie-Antoinette*, first published before 1789, continued to enjoy tremendous success. The 16 reprints of this text, which focused on the queen's alleged promiscuity and the king's (also alleged) inability to satisfy her, were published between 1789 and 1790, and six forgeries with titles such as *The Private, Libertine, and Scandalous Life of Marie-Antoinette of Austria* (1792) were put on the market from 1791 to 1793.[19] Other antiroyalist publications, such as Lavicomterie's series *The Crimes of the Kings of France, from Clovis to Louis XVI*, which inculpated Louis on the basis of his predecessors' supposed wrongdoings, also enjoyed a large readership.[20]

Revolutionary writers, such as Desmoulins and Lavicomterie, quickly learned to use the weapon of character assassination very effectively. Yet the revolutionaries themselves soon became the targets of attacks on character in the counterrevolutionary press of 1789 and the early 1790s. Demonstrating a marked obsession with birth and social origin, royalist journalists denounced leaders of the Revolution as either high-born traitors of their noble caste or low-life, common parvenus. The royalist and "razor-sharp" journal *Actes des Apôtres* was one example for this treatment. Using "wit and satire," it "made fun of real or imagined physical weakness, marital trouble, and political failure, focusing on the pornographic and scatological aspects where possible."[21] The journal made a particular habit of ridiculing the young radical Maximilien Robespierre for his Northern French accent, provincial mannerisms, and overlong speeches. It also made unflattering comparisons between "Robertspierre" (a deliberate misspelling to suggest the politician's insignificance) and

Robert Damiens, the failed regicide executed in 1757, by playing on similarities in their names and making much of the fact that both had been born in Arras. At the same time, the paper attacked pro-revolutionary noblemen by suggesting that their support for the Revolution resulted from the fact that they were really the illegitimate (and hence disgruntled) biological sons of their families' servants.[22]

Following these and similar damaging attacks on character, the early Revolution saw numerous debates on setting limits on press freedom and punishing those who slandered their political enemies—efforts discussed in detail by Charles Walton. Some journalists, Desmoulins, Marat, and Loustalot among them, faced serious accusations of calumny and slander during this time.[23] By 1792, Robespierre was warning the Jacobin Club against the "power of calumny."[24] He described the practice as a shameful feature of Old Regime antechamber politics, fit only to "topple ministers or chase courtesans." The circumstances of the Revolution had unfolded calumny's power to the fullest extent, with dangerous and damaging consequences. Yet Robespierre himself could not resist denouncing his political enemies in the same speech by accusing various factions of using calumny against "liberty" and "patriots."

Robespierre's opposition to the practice of character assassination, in fact, clashed uncomfortably with the Jacobins' belief in the need to unmask traitors and test the revolutionary commitment of their members by digging around in their personal and political pasts. As the Revolution radicalized under the Jacobins' leadership, attacks on character did, in fact, not stop, but intensify. What had been a common, half-humorous, half-damaging exercise in the pre- and early Revolution, now "became a matter of unveiling, unmasking, tearing away curtains, and exposing secret lives hidden behind the false fronts turned toward the public."[25] As such, character assassination developed into a key feature of the politics of the Terror of 1793 and 1794. While in the early years of the Revolution, the practice had served to ruin public figures' reputations, it became a fatal weapon in the Terror's rigid political climate that insisted on virtue, transparency, and selfless conduct.[26] The perpetrators of character assassinations had also changed: the revolutionary government now frequently used the practice to damage the opposition, rather than the other way around. It deployed an eclectic mix of familiar themes, such as gluttony, sexual conduct, and keeping the wrong company, and more serious accusations, such as involvement in counterrevolutionary words and deeds, corruption, and being part of a faction. Many attacks made on the character of these targets during the Terror were vague and unsubstantiated. At her trial in October 1793, for instance, Marie-Antoinette faced allegations of sexual misconduct with her son, a false claim that infuriated serious politicians, such as Robespierre, who recognized that it undermined the government's reputation far more than it did that of the accused.

The Jacobin era was particularly haunted by the idea that its politicians wore masks, pretended to be virtuous when they were not, and led private lives that contradicted their official, civic rhetoric.[27] This made the period particularly susceptible to character assassination. As revolutionary France

faced the dual pressures of external war and civil war, and as political alle-
giances and borders shifted, threats to unmask the traitors, as well as personal and political character denunciations among politicians, multiplied.
Use of this practice reached extremes during the rapidly escalating factional
conflict between moderate (Girondin) and radical (Montagnard) deputies at
the National Convention in 1793 and again during the crisis of the factions,
which resulted in Danton's trial and execution in early 1794. Marisa Linton
has investigated the unscrupulous ways in which French revolutionaries took
aim at former friends and collaborators about whom they had intimate and
damaging knowledge.[28] Camille Desmoulins's 1792 pamphlet *Jean-Pierre
Brissot démasqué* [sic], for instance, mercilessly slandered the reputation of
the Girondin leader. Mixing "personal and political allegations," Desmoulins
portrayed Brissot as a "self-seeking and duplicitous villain."[29] Shortly after,
in early 1793, Brissot's allies counterattacked with equally malicious accusations of revolutionary dictatorship against Desmoulins's friends Danton and
Robespierre.

In June 1793, the Girondins lost the battle for power against the Montag-
nards and were purged from the legislature. During their political trial a few
months later—the first grand-scale prosecution of elected representatives—
the Girondins not only stood accused of forming a faction (which they vehe-
mently denied), but also saw their personal and political lives grossly distorted
in slanderous publications flooding the capital. Pierre Turbat's *Vie secrète et
politique de Brissot*, for example, portrayed Brissot as a "modern villain," a
"hypocrite," a "man with two faces," and (irony!) a libeler. Brissot, the pamphlet alleged, had used his "Tartuffe-like genius" to obtain money and public offices from the Revolution.[30] A second publication, by the same author,
attacked the former Duke of Orléans, a Girondin sympathizer who was executed in November 1793. The author warned the reader not to confuse his
own with another slanderous work of the period, the *Vie secrète et privée du
duc d'Orléans*, which he denounced as a "disgusting fable, written in an even
more disgusting manner." His own text, he claimed, was "perfectly informed
of all that concerns the former house of Orléans," and all its anecdotes had
been verified.[31] Turbat then described the duke as being descended from a
family of poisoners, monsters, and cross-dressers, who had been debauched,
incestuous, and immoral. The duke himself, Turbat speculated, was either the
result of his mother having prostituted herself to one of her valets or the illegitimate son of the Count of Melfort, a "young libertine." Perhaps, the text
speculated maliciously, the duke's mother herself did not know? The rest of
the pamphlet focused on painting its victim as beset by vice and crime, with
"pores [that] oozed perversity," who had engaged in "infamous orgies."

Following the fall of the Girondins, a second wave of character assassinations hit the Revolution in the spring of 1794. The crisis of the factions, which
saw radical Hébertistes pitched against moderate followers of Danton—with
the revolutionary government stuck uncomfortably in between—resulted in
vicious attacks from all sides. One pamphlet from this time was directed at
Hébert, the radical leader and author of the famously foulmouthed journal

Père Duchesne It described Hébert as having had, since childhood, "a sullen and sly character," which had "developed in the most hideous way." It also alleged that he had relationships with prostitutes, a habit of stealing from friends and benefactors, and that he was an ingrate, a hypocrite, and a traitor.[32] The politicians involved in the crisis of the factions also engaged directly in attempts at character assassination. In their report on the Dantonistes, Saint-Just and Robespierre, for example, spoke of their enemies' lack of virtue, political and sexual misconduct, and hypocrisy.[33] Danton and Desmoulins struck back by alleging that Saint-Just, though seemingly burning with revolutionary fervor, was actually a closet nobleman, who led a secret life of luxury and wrote accusations against his colleagues while relaxing in his "bath" and his "boudoir."[34] Desmoulins insisted on addressing the revolutionary, who was the son of a soldier decorated with the cross of Saint-Louis, as *Monsieur le chevalier Saint-Just*, alleged that he harbored selfish ambitions, and called into question his Republicanism.[35] Returning to the theme of personal habits, Danton claimed that Saint-Just regularly frequented the expensive Chinese Baths on the Boulevard des Italiens (an institution associated with the Old Regime and perhaps also suggesting an excessive need for cleanliness in a person who used dirty political practices).[36] Saint-Just responded, famously, by having the accused excluded from their trial.

The Character Assassination of Robespierre and His Allies after 9 Thermidor

Only a few months after Danton's death, Robespierre and Saint-Just themselves became the victims of a political purge. Arrested in the middle of the National Convention on 9 Thermidor, the deputies were not granted a hearing, and there was little time for their enemies to slander them before their fast-track execution on the tenth (July 28, 1794). Character assassination, however, was much in evidence in the new government's efforts to justify the Robespierristes' arrest and execution in the days, weeks, and months that followed. In his seminal study of the Thermidorian republic, Bronisław Baczko relates how, already in the night of 9 to 10 Thermidor, Robespierre's enemies disseminated the rumor that the *Incorruptible* had planned to marry the daughter of Louis XVI and become king of France.[37] How, Baczko asks, could this "absurd" idea of "Robespierre-roi" have fallen on such fertile ground, especially given that he had been one of the republic's most respected politicians?[38] Part of the answer lies in France's long prerevolutionary and revolutionary history of character assassination. Sustained slander campaigns not only against the Girondins in 1793, but also against popular public figures, such as the Hébertistes and Dantonistes in 1794, had suggested that politicians were naturally untrustworthy. The pamphlet *Vie secrète, politique et curieuse de M. J. Maximilien Robespierre*, for example, lamented that "one has made the sad experience that the nation has almost always been fooled and betrayed by men whom it entrusted with its government." Robespierre, this publication argued, was no exception. The self-proclaimed defender of democracy had, in reality, been a "modern Catiline," a "new Cromwell," and at least as bloodthirsty as Charles IX.[39] A report on the papers of Robespierre and his allies, given to the Convention by Courtois, a former Dantonist deputy, made similar claims: it suggested that Robespierre had, already in childhood, exhibited ambitious and domineering character traits: "An anxiety, a vague and restless desire, avid for domination and renown, devoured him." Robespierre, the schoolyard tyrant, Courtois concluded, had grown up to become cruel as Sulla.[40]

Thermidorian attacks on the *Incorrutible* frequently focused on the idea that Robespierre had deceived the French people. Rather than virtuous, Robespierre had been a "false and somber man . . . incapable of having a friend, proud to excess, a flatterer, treacherous, in one word."[41] There had been many disquieting contradictions in his character that he had sought to hide: he had been "feeble yet vengeful, abstinent yet sensual, chaste by temperament, yet a libertine in his imagination." Over time, more and more accusations of the *Incorruptible*'s voracious sexual and sensual appetites were added to the character assassination mix. This was especially surprising, as Robespierre's public image up to this point had been that of an abstinent man, sacrificing his private life to revolutionary politics, and suspected of impotency. Now he was portrayed as a "monster" who had frequented orgies and indulged in expensive, exotic fruit during times of shortages: "He was insatiable for them; no one dared touch this sacred fruit."[42] He had "imprisoned women just to take pleasure in giving them their freedom" and had enjoyed seeing victims of the Terror cry.[43] Out of these various claims grew the creation of what Julia A. Douthwaite has called "Gothic Robespierre": "From cannibalism, torture, and intimidation to petty criminality, this Robespierre incarnate[d] the awful." The pamphlet *La vie et les crimes de Robespierre*, for instance, alleged that Robespierre had turned victims' skins into shoes and that his supporters had drunk human blood.[44] Similar allegations would be repeated in generations of literature on the French Revolution and still form part of persistent historical myths about Robespierre.[45]

Robespierre's allies, friends, and family also became the targets of character assassination after Thermidor. These attacks focused on presenting those who had been close to the *Incorruptible* as collaborators in his allegedly tyrannical regime and as partakers in his "perverted" private life. The deputy Couthon, executed with Robespierre on 10 Thermidor, might have "affected virtue," one publication declared, but "his half-dead body" (he had been paralyzed from the waist down) suggested a sinister character. His gentle features and manners had merely been a mask hiding "the most ferocious and completely perverse soul that [had] ever sullied humanity." His disability was used against him as a sign of duplicity: "Under seductive traits and in a body half destroyed and deprived of life, Couthon carried a heart closed to any kind of sensibility." His real character had been ambitious and cowardly.[46] Robespierre's other close ally, Louis-Antoine Saint-Just, was ridiculed in pamphlets as having been a mere child who had "only just escaped" from the schoolyard (he had been 26 at his execution) when entering government.[47] He was described as an immature, "apocalyptic," and brooding youth who had done Robespierre's bidding without understanding the political consequences. He had "guillotined poor Camille [Desmoulins]" because he had envied his talents.[48] Alongside "Robespierre-Catiline," Couthon and Saint-Just were now labeled "Antony" and "Lepidus," and all three were accused of having formed a "triumvirate."[49] A few days after 9 Thermidor, investigations were also launched into so-called orgies that the triumvirate was said to have organized at the residence of the mayor of Choisy sur Seine, a former friend of Robespierre.[50] Members of the mayor's family were accused of being bad characters ("inept" and "evil by nature") and arrested.[51] Friends, former servants, and hosts of the Robespierristes all became the targets of sustained slander and calumny campaigns resulting in prison sentences and ruined lives and careers.

Character Assassination: A Specialty of the Reaction?

While 9 Thermidor was a tragedy for those close to Robespierre and his allies, it was celebrated throughout France not only as the official end of the Terror, but also of the practice of political denunciation, character assassination, and purging. The Thermidorian Convention, seeking a radical break with the recent past, quickly denounced the purges of the year II as part of Robespierre's "system of Terror" and attempted to reverse their effects as much as possible.[52] Following this initial period of restraint, the Convention, however, denounced and decreed the arrests of at least 78 of its members—a substantial number. As Michel Biard has illustrated, accusations against the so-called tail of Robespierre started a few weeks after his fall and were heavily based on the practice of character assassination.[53] Pamphlets targeted former associates of Robespierre, members of the governing committees of the year II, and Montagnard representatives on mission. They also led to a series of mass purges of politicians in the spring and summer of 1795. Despite their scale and importance, little attention has been paid to these Thermidorian purges during this time, and no comparisons have been made between them and the more high-profile cases of the Terror. This is surprising, not only because the Thermidorian purges played a pivotal role in the politics of the Reaction, but also because they occurred as the French revolutionaries tried to move away from the Terror, establish a constitutional regime, and safeguard elected representatives from violence.

The tactic of character assassination played a key role in the attacks on radical legislators in the Reaction. Many accusers used language reminiscent of the Terror in denouncing their colleagues. They likened them to notorious historical or biblical figures, arguing that "Cromwell's court [was] not yet fully destroyed" or that their targets were "marked on their foreheads with the sign of crime."[54] Apart from associating their victims with the Terror and Robespierre, they also attempted to dehumanize them: as "monsters," "tigers," "impurities," and "stains" on the nation's honor. Such accusations reached a climax during the campaign against the "four"—the deputies Barère, Billaud-Varenne, Collot d'Herbois, and Vadier, who were accused of being responsible (alongside Robespierre) for the Terror. While the four defended their lives and careers in publications, such as the *Réponse de J.-N. Billaud, représentant du peuple, à Laurent Lecointre, représentant du peuple*, and during long, drawn-out hearings at the Convention, character assassinations against them flooded the capital.[55] In them, Barère, for instance, was portrayed as a hypocritical turncoat, who had lived as a nobleman before the Revolution and had only supported the government of the Terror for personal gain. He was said to have owned a "house of pleasure" at Clichy, where "des jeux d'amour" had taken place and which had also served as an "odious lair" where he and others had conspired against the people. He was supposed to have had a mistress named la Demahy (which might or might not have been a reference to Thomas de Mahy, a former agent of the Count of Provence, executed in 1790), and his sexual misdemeanor was alleged to have been shocking even compared to the "nocturnal scenes of the gardens of Versailles and the petit Trianon." Barère was also accused of having received petitioners dressed "in the robes of a Sybarite" and of having callously thrown their petitions into the fire, saying, "Voila ma correspondance faite."[56]

Barère's colleagues fared little better. Vadier was accused of speaking badly and with contempt of the people by calling them "a vile horde" and "imbeciles."[57] He was described as a glutton who had consumed meals worth 60,000 livres while on mission in the provinces.[58] Collot d'Herbois was attacked by his colleagues in aggressively titled pamphlets, such as *Collot mitraillé par Tallien*, which held him and Billaud-Varenne responsible for crimes committed during the Terror.[59] The latter was described as a ferocious "tiger" in the Thermidorian press, as a "man of blood" and a scoundrel, who had shared in the evil projects of Robespierre.[60] Over time, publications discussing Barère's, Billaud's, Collot's, and Vadier's responsibility for the Terror became increasingly polemic and violent: "The infamous trio Collot, Barrère [sic], Billaud is subject to public execration, crime is painted on their livid features; death has marked their fronts . . . Innocent blood wakes in the night to trouble their sleep. Miserable tyrants, tigers who degraded humanity, hangmen of my country, do you hear your death sentence declared on the public squares?"[61] In one of his defense statements, Billaud expressed his belief that "calumnies pass, while truth remains."[62] In his case, calumny won the day: despite the four's best efforts to defend themselves, they were deported to French Guyana without a trial in the spring of 1795.

Character assassinations against the four deputies in Paris soon prompted provincial pamphleteers to also call for the prosecution of the "monsters" at the Convention.[63] Petitioners from the provinces called for the punishment of additional deputies, such as the former "terrorist Moltedo"[64] or the *Conventionnels* Amar, Javogues, Albitte, and Meaulle, who "should be purged, because their presence sullied the sanctuary of the law."[65] A citizen from Bayonne asked for the removal of the politician Monestier, who was "unworthy of sitting in the French Senate." If the Convention "continue[d] to forget [about] men sullied by crime and blood, it nourishe[d] vipers within its midst and expose[d] the *patrie* to new dangers."[66] The Convention should strike, argued the citizens of Sedan, "their cruelest tyrant," the "apostate Massieu," and other "impure reptiles who must neither sully the soil of liberty nor the French Senate."[67] Familiar terms such as "scoundrel," "monster," and "tiger" repeated themselves in hundreds of Thermidorian petitions against politicians with little means to defend their reputations and their careers.[68]

Character assassination remained a key form of political violence in the Reaction—partly inspired by practices adopted during the Terror, partly made possible by the return of a free press in this period—and contributed a great deal to the political purges of this era.[69] It was used by the government and by ordinary citizens wishing to get revenge against a former representative on mission. Rampant attacks on character led to renewed debates among legislators concerning the regulation of calumny and slander. The deputy Laignelot, for instance, complained about being a victim of character assassination: "For too long have they tried to tear the republic apart, have conspirators attacked the reputations of honest men through small intrigues and defamations."[70] His colleague Léonard Bourdon complained that his political enemy Fréron had falsely accused him of "theft and assassinations." Bourdon denounced these accusations as calumnies and asked for a law against them. There was also much discussion on whether politicians should be allowed to own journals and use them as weapons against their colleagues—an issue touching on fundamental questions facing revolutionary democracy at this time.[71] But taking action against defamatory publications was extremely difficult, especially as journals did not always indicate their authors, and politicians distanced themselves from their own journal when the latter were accused of calumny. The writers of character assassinations also claimed that their victims, after all, had the right to defend themselves. This was to ignore, however, the fact that victims' defenses tended to attract less readers and less public attention. Character assassinations thus continued throughout the Reaction, and into the Directory, until Napoleon's laws put a stop to free press and limited this particular kind of political conflict.

Conclusion

The practice of character assassination—already a common feature of politics in the Old Regime—played an important part in the power struggles between French revolutionaries in 1789 and the 1790s. As Charles Walton has argued, the practice also presented the revolutionary government with serious challenges in terms of dealing with calumny and slander while maintaining freedom of speech and democratic dialogue.[72] The new, liberated press of the early Revolution made rampant attacks on character by both revolutionaries and counterrevolutionaries possible. Victims' personal and political lives were mercilessly distorted and mined for infractions or weaknesses that would tarnish their reputations. Their political actions and words were taken out of context, blown out of proportion, or, in some cases, entirely made up. They were compared to Roman dictators and conspirators (Sulla, Catiline). Revolutionary audiences were very receptive to character assassinations, revealing a deep distrust of politicians as well as a degree of gullibility concerning the written word. Whenever a sufficient number of pamphlets attacked a particular politician, and, especially, whenever the government itself engaged in such an attack, the result was often the abrupt end of a revolutionary life and career.

It is difficult to determine what the authors of revolutionary character assassinations thought of their own texts. Did they cynically make up their content, or did they believe it was based on facts? The form that assaults on character took often revealed anxieties that seemed specific to a period: during the Terror, denunciations focused on a lack of virtue, on deception and treason, and on the need to unmask those who misled the people. A 1793 pamphlet on Brissot, for instance, claimed that "posterity and the entire universe will one day admire a nascent republic for being able to distinguish between perverse men and those who truly wanted to serve it."[73] In the Reaction, authors made frequent, obsessive references to their targets' monstrous political crimes and terror, to sexual depravity, and tyranny. It is these elements of (possibly) true fear, paranoia, and trauma in the character assassinations of the Revolution that leave historians of the period with a difficult legacy when dealing with such texts. As the revolutionary Dubois-Crancé suggested: "I have seen so many people of good faith led astray by perfidious suggestions, that it would not be surprising if a historian, even if he was completely impartial, were led astray over the results."[74]

After the collapse of the First French Republic (1799) and the Empire (1815), many revolutionaries who had been the victims of character assassination hoped that history would be able to separate the "facts from the clouds with which they have been covered."[75] In the introduction to his memoirs, the revolutionary Levasseur (de la Sarthe), for instance, expressed the hope that "a young generation, who has not seen our days of thunder" would regard the French revolutionaries as "historical personalities who do no longer attract any living passions." Some revolutionaries also wished to distance themselves from previous character assassinations that they had engaged in. In writing his memoirs, Marc-Antoine Baudot, for instance, promised that "in discussing the Girondins' politics, I don't intend to attack their character or their talents . . . This is an abstract question, not a gladiator's fight." This did not, however, prevent him from labeling his former colleague Saint-Just an "exterminator."[76] The moderate revolutionary La Revellière-Lépeaux could, similarly, not let go of his dislike for Lazare Carnot, hoping that, one day, "the vice and lies" of the "impostor" would be fully exposed.[77] In the revolutionaries' memoirs, the frequent attacks on their colleagues' character show the extent to which they were unable to let go of the Manichean worldviews, the personal and political hatreds, and the willingness to save their own reputations by ruining those of colleagues that had driven character assassinations throughout the Revolution.

Perhaps unsurprisingly, historians of the Revolution also struggled with the legacy of hundreds of denunciations and counterdenunciations produced in the 1790s. Both the nineteenth and the twentieth centuries saw historians take sides regarding the revolutionaries' mutual character assassinations.[78] In 1857, the daughter of the revolutionary Merlin de Thionville, for instance, complained to Jules Michelet about several historians who cast a "bad light . . . over the memory of Danton's friends" because they wanted to "sanctify" Robespierre.[79] The widow and the son of Philippe Lebas, a deputy who had died alongside Robespierre on 9 Thermidor, similarly criticized Lamartine's partial approach to the Revolution, covering the historian's work with comments such as "How do you know?," "Error," "False," "Invention," "Fable."[80] A few generations later, Alphonse Aulard, the great historian of the Revolution who was sympathetic to Danton's cause, would describe the revolutionary Marat as "one of the innately bloodthirsty figures of the Revolution" and Collot d'Herbois as "a coarse, loud-voiced, vindictive, ferocious person."[81] Albert Mathiez, by contrast, devoted much of his professional career to rescuing the reputation of one revolutionary (Robespierre) by undermining that of another (Danton). In 1969, the famous English historian of the French Revolution, Richard Cobb, wrote that there was "no historical personage" he found "more repellent" than Robespierre, "save possibly Saint-Just."[82] The practice of character assassination, which had wreaked havoc among the Revolution's contemporaries, remained equally tempting to its historians.

Notes

1. The author would like to thank the editors of this volume, Martijn Icks and Eric Shiraev, for their thoughtful comments, as well as Charles Walton for his continuous support and Katie Jarvis for her help with finding out more about the Chinese Baths of eighteenth-century Paris.
2. Hunt 2003, 117–38.
3. Baecque 1993, 68–72.
4. Higonnet 1981; Rapport 2000, 2.
5. In 1795, the revolutionary Jean-Marie Collot d'Herbois, for instance, published his *Défense particulière de J. M. Collot, représentant du peuple* (Paris: De l'Imprimerie de Guerin, 1795) in which he defended his role in the Terror and accused his enemies of calumny. Like many other defenses published by victims of character assassination in the Revolution, Collot's was, ultimately, unsuccessful.
6. Linton 2013, 13, 36, 48–49.
7. Higonnet 1981, 170.
8. References to Roman (and Greek) figures in French revolutionary discourse were extremely frequent. While the Roman Republic, as well as Athens and (in some cases) Sparta, served as models for the French Republic, the revolutionaries also referred to Roman and Greek precedents of betrayal, tyranny, and abuse of power. See, for example, Mossé 1989.
9. Courtois 1794. All translations from the French by the author, unless otherwise indicated.

10. Anonymous 1795.
11. Walton 2009.
12. Darnton 2010.
13. Darnton 2010.
14. Jones 2002.
15. Darnton 1971, 81–115.
16. Darnton 2010, 22–23.
17. Darnton 2010, 424; Popkin 1990, 32.
18. Desmoulins 1789, 6, 14.
19. Baecque 1993, 52–53.
20. Baecque 1993, 59.
21. Osen 1995, 32.
22. Pellet 1873, 86–87, 104–5.
23. Walton 2009, 115–6.
24. Robespierre 1792, 1.
25. Darnton 2010, 424.
26. Linton 2013.
27. Linton 2013.
28. Linton 2013.
29. Linton 2013, 130.
30. Turbat 1793a.
31. Turbat 1793b.
32. Turbat 1794.
33. Robespierre 1794; 1841; Saint-Just 1794.
34. Desmoulins 1794; 1865, 179.
35. Desmoulins 1794; 1865, 179, 185.
36. See Monar 1993, 590–91; Anonymous 1794a.
37. Baczko 1989, 11, 15.
38. Baczko 1989, 21.
39. Duperron 1794; Baczko 1989, 19.
40. Courtois 1828; 1978, 24–5.
41. Duperron 1794.
42. Courtois 1828; 1978, 154–59. McPhee 2012, 33, 187.
43. Duperron 1794.
44. Douthwaite 2012, 196.
45. Jones 2012; Baczko 1996.
46. Anonymous 1794b.
47. Anonymous 1794b.
48. Courtois 1828; 1978, 24.
49. Baczko 1989, 27–28.
50. Anonymous 1794c.
51. Commune de Choisy 1794.
52. Steinberg 2013, 177–83.
53. Biard 1997, 201–13.
54. Dumont 1794; 1847, 366–67.
55. Billaud-Varenne 1794.
56. Vilate 1794.
57. Vilate 1794.
58. Anonymous 1795.
59. Tallien 1795.

60. La Touche 1794.
61. Anonymous, *Le Messager du Soir*, 1794d.
62. Billaud-Varenne 1794.
63. Les citoyens de la commune de Bourg 1795a.
64. Anonymous 1795.
65. Les citoyens de la commune de Bourg 1795b.
66. Barterreche De Bayonne 1795.
67. Les citoyens de Sedan 1795.
68. Darnton 2010, 426.
69. Popkin 1990, 39.
70. Laignelot 1795.
71. Bourdon 1795; 1847, 252.
72. Walton 2009.
73. Turbat 1793a.
74. Dubois-Crancé 1830–1835; 2003, 27.
75. Barère 1842–1844; 1896, 12.
76. Baudot 1893, 136, 154.
77. La Revellière-Lépeaux 1895.
78. Baudot 1893, 203.
79. Le Barbier de Tinan 1857–1858.
80. Stéfane-Pol 1901, 326–31.
81. Aulard 1901, 60–61.
82. Cobb 1969; 1998, 22.

Bibliography

Anonymous. 1794a. *Notes et observations (16 germinal l'an 2)*. Paris: Archives Nationales de France. F/7/4443.

Anonymous. 1794b. *Supplices des scélérats Couthon, Saint-Just, Payan, Henriot, Dumas, Coffinhal & Fleuriot-Lescot; tous dignes associés & complices de Maximilien Robespierre*. Grenoble: Chez Ferry.

Anonymous. 1794c. *Rapport ou Résumé sur chaque prevenu d'après les dénonciations. Vaugeois fils, Vaugeois, femme du Maire… (Thermidor II)*. Paris: Archives Nationales de France. A.N. W/ 79.

Anonymous. 1794d. *Le Messager du Soir ou Gazette générale de l'Europe*. No. 835, 12 Frimaire III. Paris: Bibliothèque Nationale de France. LC2-682.

Anonymous. 1795. *Juste courroux du peuple contre Vadier et les autres décemvirs*. Paris: De l'Imprimerie de Pain.

Anonymous. 1795. *Aux représentants du peuple composant le Comité de Sureté Générale*. Paris: Archives Nationales de France. D/III/354-355.

Aulard, A. 1901. *The French Revolution: A Political History 1789–1804*, vol. 1. Transl. B. Miall, 1910. New York: Charles Scribner's Sons.

Baczko, B. 1996. "Comment est fait un tyran … Thermidor et la légende noire de Robespierre." In J. Ehrard, A. Ehrard, and F. Devillez, eds., *Images de Robespierre. Actes du colloque international de Naples, 27–29 septembre 1993*, 3–10. Naples: Vivarium.

Baczko, B. 1989. *Comment sortir de la Terreur. Thermidor et la Révolution*. Paris: Gallimard.

Baecque, A. de. 1993. *The Body Politic: Corporeal Metaphor in Revolutionary France, 1770–1800*. Transl. C. Mandell, 1997. Stanford, CA: Stanford University Press.

Barère, B. 1842–1844; 1896. *Memoirs of Bertrand Barère, Chairman of the Committee of Public Safety during the Revolution*, vol. 2. Transl. V. Payen-Payne. London: H. S. Nichols.

Barterreche De Bayonne, L. 1795. *Dénonciation des crimes de Monestier du Puy de Dôme. Aux membres composant les Comités de gouvernement.* Paris: Archives Nationales de France. D/III/354–355.

Baudot, M. A. 1893. *Notes historiques sur la Convention Nationale, le Directoire, l'Empire et l'exil des votants.* Ed. H. Quinet. Paris: D. Jouaust.

Biard, M. 1997. "Après la tête, la queue. La rhétorique antijacobine en fructidor an II et vendémiaire an III." In M. Vovelle, ed., *Le tournant de l'an III. Réaction et Terreur blanche dans la France révolutionnaire*, 201–13. Paris: Éditions du CTHS.

Billaud-Varenne, J. N. 1794. *Réponse de J.-N. Billaud, représentant du peuple, à Laurent Lecointre, représentant du peuple.* Paris: Imprimerie de R. Vatar.

Bourdon, L. C. N. 1795; 1847. "Convention nationale (24 Vendémiaire III), MON 27, 27 Vendémiaire III." In L. C. A. G. Gallois, ed., *Réimpression de l'Ancien Moniteur*, vol. 22, 252. Paris: Plon Frères.

Les citoyens de la commune de Bourg. 1795a. *A la Convention nationale.* Paris: Archives Nationales de France. D/III/354-355.

Les citoyens de la commune de Bourg. 1795b. *Dénonciation des citoyens de la commune de Bourg, chef lieu du département de l'ain. Contre Amar, Javogues, Albitte et Meaulle. A la Convention Nationale, 28 Floréal III.* Paris: Archives Nationales de France. D/III/354-355.

Les citoyens de Sedan. 1795. *Dénonciation que les citoyens de Sedan adressent a la Convention nationale, contre leur plus cruel Tyran, l'apostat Massieu, Sedan, 18 Prairial III.* Paris: Archives Nationales de France. D/III/354–355.

Cobb, R. 1969; 2004. "Experiences of an Anglo-French Historian." In R. Cobb and D. Gilmour, eds., *Paris and Elsewhere: Selected Writings*, 7–69. New York: New York Review Books.

Collot d'Herbois, J. M. 1795. *Défense particulière de J.M. Collot, représentant du peuple.* Paris: De l'Imprimerie de Guerin. Paris: Bibliothèque nationale de France.

Commune de Choisy. 1794. *Rapport ou Résumé sur chaque prevenu d'après les dénonciations. Vaugeois, père, maire de Choisy; Vaugeois fils, Vaugeois, mere, Vaugeois, filles…(Thermidor II).* Paris: Archives Nationales de France. W/80.

Courtois, E. B. 1794. *Ma Catilinaire, ou Suite de mon rapport du 16 nivôse, sur les papiers trouvés chez Robespierre et autre conspirateurs.* Paris: Desenne. Paris: Bibliothèque nationale de France.

Courtois, E. B. 1828; 1978. *Papiers inédits trouvés chez Robespierre, Saint-Just, Payan, etc. supprimés ou omis par Courtois, précédes du rapport de ce député à la Convention nationale*, vol. 1. Geneva: Mégariotis.

Darnton, R. 1971. "The High Enlightenment and the Low-Life of Literature in Pre-Revolutionary France." *Past & Present* 51: 81–115.

Darnton, R. 2010. *The Devil in the Holy Water, or The Art of Slander from Louis XIV to Napoleon.* Philadelphia: University of Pennsylvania Press.

Desmoulins, C. 1789. *Discours de la lanterne aux Parisiens.* Paris: Chez Le Jay fils, Libraire, rue de l'Echelle S. Honoré. Paris: Bibliothèque nationale de France. NUMM-6457978.

Desmoulins, C. 1794; 1865. "Notes de Camille Desmoulins sur le Rapport de Saint-Just." In Anonymous, *Oeuvres de Camille Desmoulins*, vol. 3, 179–85. Paris: Lucien Marpon.

Douthwaite, J. A. 2012. *The Frankenstein of 1790 and Other Lost Chapters from Revolutionary France.* Chicago: The University of Chicago Press.

Dubois-Crancé, E.-L.-A. 1830–1835; 2003. *Analyse de la Révolution Française.* Cler-mont-Ferrand: Editions Paleo.

Dumont, A. 1794; 1847. "Convention nationale (13 Thermidor II), MON 315, 15 Ther-midor II." In L. C. A. G. Gallois, ed., *Réimpression de l'Ancien Moniteur*, vol. 21, 366–67. Paris: Plon Frères.

Duperron, L. 1794. *Vie secrette, politique et curieuse de M.J. Maximilien Robespierre, député à l'Assemblée constituante en 1789, et à la Convention nationale jusqu'au 9 thermidor l'an deuxième de la République, veille de son exécution et de celle de ses complices. Suivie de plusieurs anecdotes sur cette conspiration.* Paris: De l'Imprimerie de Chambon. Paris: Bibliothèque Nationale de France. NUMM-41117.

Higonnet, L. R. 1981. *Class, Ideology, and the Rights of Nobles during the French Revolu-tion.* Oxford: Clarendon Press and Oxford University Press.

Hunt, L. A. 2003. "The Many Bodies of Marie-Antoinette: Political Pornography and the Problem of the Feminine in the French Revolution." In D. Goodman, ed., *Marie-Antoinette: Writings on the Body of a Queen*, 117–38. New York: Routledge.

Jones, C. 2002. *Madame de Pompadour: Images of a Mistress.* London: National Gallery Company, distributed by Yale University Press.

Jones, C. 2012. "French Crossings: III. The Smile of the Tiger." *Transactions of the Royal Historical Society* (Sixth Series) 22: 3–35.

Laignelot, J. F. 1795. "Convention nationale (23 Vendémiaire III), MON 26, 26 Ven-démiaire III." *Réimpression de l'Ancien Moniteur*, 242. Paris: Plon Frères.

La Touche, J. C. H. Méhée de. 1794. *L'Ami des Citoyens. Journal du commerce et des arts.* No. LII, 22 Frimaire III. Paris: Bibliothèque Nationale de France. MFICHE LC2-638.

Linton, M. A. 2013. *Choosing Terror: Virtue, Friendship, and Authenticity in the French Revolution.* Oxford: Oxford University Press.

McPhee, P. 2012. *Robespierre: A Revolutionary Life.* New Haven, CT: Yale University Press.

Monar, J. 1993. *Saint-Just. Sohn, Denker und Protagonist der Revolution.* Bonn and Paris: Bouvier Verlag Bonn and Deutsches Historisches Institut Paris.

Mossé, C. 1989. *L'Antiquité dans la Révolution française.* Paris: Albin Michel.

Osen, J. L. 1995. *Royalist Political Thought during the French Revolution.* Westport, CT: Greenwood Press.

Pellet, M. 1873. *Un journal royaliste en 1789. Les Actes des apôtres (1789–1791).* Paris: Armand Le Chevalier.

Popkin, J. D. 1990. *Revolutionary News: The Press in France, 1789–1799.* Durham, NC: Duke University Press.

Rapport, M. 2000. *Nationality and Citizenship in Revolutionary France: The Treatment of Foreigners, 1789–1799.* Oxford: Clarendon.

La Revellière-Lépeaux, L. M. de. 1895. "Observations essentielles sur mes mémoires." In O. de La Revellière-Lépeaux, ed., *Mémoires, publiés par son fils sur le manuscrit autographe de l'auteur et suivis des pieces justificatives et de correspondances inédites*, vol. 1, II–IV. Paris: E. Plon; Nourrit.

Robespierre, M. 1792. *Discours de Maximilien Robespierre, Sur l'influence de la cal-omnie sur la révolution, prononcé à la société, dans la séance du 28 octobre 1792, l'an premier de la république.* Paris: De l'Imprimerie de Pierre-Jacques Duplain. Paris: Bibliothèque Nationale de France. NUMM-6257831.

Robespierre, M. 1794; 1841. *Projet rédigé par Robespierre du Rapport fait à la Con-vention nationale par Saint-Just, contre Fabre d'Eglantine, Danton, Philippeaux, Lac-roix, et Camille-Desmoulins.* Paris: Chez France, libraire-éditeur. Paris: Bibliothèque Nationale de France. MFICHE 8-LE38-743.

Saint-Just, L. A. 1794. *Fragment de Saint-Just*. Paris: Bibliothèque Historique de la Ville de Paris. Correspondance et papiers de Camille Desmoulins. MS 985 (Rés 24).

Stéfane-Pol, 1901. *Autour de Robespierre. Le Conventionnel Le Bas d'après des documents inédits et les memoires de sa veuve*. Paris: Ernest Flammarion.

Steinberg, R. 2013. "Trauma before Trauma: Imagining the Effects of the Terror in Post-Revolutionary France." In D. Andress, ed., *Experiencing the French Revolution*, 177–83. Oxford: Voltaire Foundation, University of Oxford.

Tallien, J. L. 1795. *Collot mitraillé par Tallien. Éclaircissemens véridiques de Tallien, représentant du peuple, envoyé en mission à Bordeaux, en réponse aux "Eclaircissemens necessaries" de Collot, ancien membre du Comité de salut public*. Paris: Bibliothèque nationale de France. 8-LB41-1676.

Tinan, Le Barbier de (née Merlin de Thionville, M. L.). 1857–1858. "Lettres à Jules Michelet." In *Papiers Michelet, correspondance*, vol 16. Bibliothèque Historique de la Ville de Paris. Liasse A 4796 (4).

Turbat, P. 1793a. *Vie secrette et politique de Brissot*. Paris: L'Imprimerie de Franklin.

Turbat, P. 1793b. *Vie de L.-J. Capet, ci-devant duc d'Orléans; ou mémoires pour servir à l'histoire de la Révolution française*. Paris: L'Imprimerie de Franklin.

Turbat, P. 1794. *Vie privée et politique de J.-R. Hébert, auteur du Père Duchène. Pour faire suite aux Vies de Manuel, Pétion, Brissot et d'Orléans*. Paris: L'Imprimerie de Franklin.

Vilate, J. 1794. *Causes secrètes de la revolution du 9 au 10 thermidor, par Vilate, ex-juré au tribunal révolutionnaire de Paris, détenu à la Force*. Paris: Bibliothèque nationale de France. NUMM-41180.

Walton, C. 2009. *Policing Public Opinion in the French Revolution: The Culture of Calumny and the Problem of Free Speech*. New York: Oxford University Press.

10

"As Awkward and Deficient as His Wife Is Amiable and Accomplished": The Character Assassination of the Dutch Statesman Rutger Jan Schimmelpenninck (1761–1825)

Edwina Hagen

Introduction[1]

In history Dutch politicians have a longstanding reputation for their tendency of always avoiding conflict, adhering to a certain kind of tolerance that historians have subscribed to the influence of the age-old phenomenon of the consensus-based "polder model."[2] However, early modern politics in the Netherlands is definitely a rich source of striking examples of character assassination. In 1672, for instance, hostile rumors and royal propaganda spread via numerous pamphlets resulted in the character assassination of the brothers De Witt, two leading statesmen of the Dutch Republic and opponents of William III, the Prince of Orange from 1672 to 1702. The accusations against them (of betraying the fatherland and conspiring against William) even led to their actual physical assassination. Both were dragged out of prison to be killed, hung, and mutilated by an angry mob.[3]

The study of the character assassination of political figures in early modern times demands the recognition that the media of those days played a role of cardinal importance in society—that is, not just in public debates, but also in politics. Today, most Dutch political and cultural historians, at least those who are working on the late eighteenth century, accept that both spheres were closely interlinked as parts of wider intertextual webs that involved, for instance, not only the political and parliamentary press, but also theater plays, poems, and cultural or spectatorial weeklies.[4] While former poets, actors, and playwrights became important parliamentary members (and vice versa), literary genres as well as formal political writings all continuously helped to shape and reshape policy discourses and the political culture as a whole. During the early modern period, and even more so toward the end of the eighteenth century, the media and public opinion became political actors in their own right.[5]

This effect of reading and writing was so powerful that to the American cultural historian Robert Darnton, the continuous publishing of French libels, which was meant to destroy the public trust in Louis XVI, perpetuated a "negative mythology" that "undercut the monarchy of the Ancien Régime."[6] This historical tendency of deliberate malicious slander also went on after the French Revolution. As a matter of fact, a shift took place from attacks all directed against the figurehead of the king and his court in prerevolutionary times, to mutual attacks among political factions in postrevolutionary times.[7] To a less drastic extent, Darnton's thesis on the impact of slander before and—in a different way—after the French Revolution, also seems to bear some similarities to the Dutch situation. Here defamation also played a critical role in the propaganda of the revolutionary period, which started with the Patriotic Revolt of 1781–87 and continued after the Batavian revolution of 1795.[8] Although the last Dutch *stadholder*, William V of Orange, was less authoritarian than the king in France before the Revolution, he also became the target of many attempts at character assassination. In his anonymously published pamphlet *To the People of the Netherlands* (1781), which started the Dutch revolution, Joan Derk van der Capellen tot den Pol reclaimed a democratic form of government and the end of the *stadholder* regime. He blamed William V for the Dutch military defeat by the English in the Fourth Anglo-Dutch War (1780–84). Moreover, in the same pamphlet, Van der Capellen also attacked William V personally by defamation, as he accused him of extramarital sexual debauchery and permanent drunkenness.[9]

In general, the Dutch slanderous publications of the 1780s are, however, more comparable to those of the postrevolutionary years in France. After 1789 the French libelers aimed at unmasking the conspirators among the leading political figures of the Revolution by exposing the intimate life behind the public person.[10] In the Netherlands, the different political factions were made up of the Patriots and their opponents, the Orangists. But here also the different parties attacked each other by making their respective victims' private lives an issue of public debate.[11] Such attempts at character assassination also kept flourishing during the years of the Batavian Republic (1795–1806), but then between the revolutionary politicians themselves as well.[12]

This chapter will explore a striking example of this latter kind (of attacks among factions), in the final months of the Batavian Republic (then called the Commonwealth), when revolutionary politicians wrecked the public reputation of their leader of that time: Rutger Jan Schimmelpenninck. Rutger Jan started out as an advocate of the patriotic ideology, became a member of the first National Assembly in 1796, and then went to Paris as the Dutch ambassador to France, finally ending up as the head of state. He was appointed by Napoleon Bonaparte, who viewed Schimmelpenninck as the right person to rule the Dutch satellite of France. The emperor gave him all of the executive power with the title of *raadpensionaris* (grand pensionary), in spite of Rutger Jan's own wish to introduce a form of government similar to that of the United States of America, with himself at the head of it, in the capacity of a Republican president. However, his position did not last for very long. Only 13 months later, he was removed because Napoleon had a new strategy for his empire: to put his family members in charge of the vassal states. He transformed the Batavian Commonwealth into the Kingdom of Holland, with his brother, Louis Bonaparte, as king.

Ultimately, Napoleon's political powers brought Rutger Jan's regime down. But, as will be argued in this chapter, his fall from power was also accelerated by a gossip and slander campaign stirred by his own Batavian colleagues, who strategically leaked rumors to the international press. While such leaks were partially directed against Rutger Jan's wife, Catharina Nahuys (1770–1844), their main goal was to undermine the moral basis of Schimmelpenninck's public reputation and, with that, his grip on power.

In order to analyze the different stages in the process of Rutger Jan's character assassination, firstly, attention will be given to the core elements that constituted the esteem in which Rutger Jan himself wanted to appear in the public eye. Second, the case will be looked at from the angle of the perpetrators, or the character assassins, and the nature of their attacks. Who were they, what encouraged them, in which political climate did they operate, and by which means did they commission their attacks? And, third, what was the credibility of their slander to the public or audience whose estimation they apparently wanted to change?

Introduction to the Victim

Rutger Jan was originally trained as a lawyer at the University of Leiden, but his real interest was politics. From his student years on, he participated in the revolutionary movement. In 1795 he took a leading role in the "velvet" revolution, which brought him and his fellow Republicans to power. The French army had helped them to overthrow the government. As the troops marched into the Republic, the *stadholder* William V fled to England. A year later Rutger Jan became one of the 126 elected members of the first Dutch democratic parliament, which was founded after general elections in 1796. He was known for his eloquence and acted successfully as the Speaker of parliament several times. Moreover, he gained influence as the political leader of the moderate Unitarians, who were advocates of a central government. Being highly critical of the more radical Republicans, he left The Hague just before a coup d'état took place on January 22, 1798. The coup was directed against the federalists, who were opposed to the formulation of a more democratic, centralistic constitution. On June 12, 1798, a second coup d'état was engineered, this time by moderates. By then, Rutger Jan already had become a rising diplomatic star in Paris.

In 1802, Rutger Jan Schimmelpenninck served as a plenipotentiary to the Amiens negotiations, which temporarily ended the hostilities between the French Republic and the United Kingdom.[13] When Napoleon Bonaparte indicated that he preferred a centralized organization of the Dutch state, Rutger Jan constructed a new constitution in close consultation with the Dutch government. Soon after, he presented his draft to Napoleon and his minister of foreign affairs, Talleyrand, who came to a quick decision. On the fifteenth of May 1805, the Batavian Republic, now renamed as the Commonwealth, had a new constitution and government, with Rutger Jan at its head. Officially he was given the title of "grand pensionary," but in political practice he had the executive powers of a republican president, the first and only one (so far) in Dutch national history.[14]

Reputation

Self-made man

The political powers that Rutger Jan gradually gained were largely the result of his strong personality. This had much to do with his political ideology, as he promoted Republicanism. Central to this ideology was the conviction that power came from the people. This in a way introduced a note of heroism into the lives of ordinary citizens. A republic could only be as strong as the virtue of its inhabitants.[15] Unlike the old ruling elite, the new social groups the Patriots belonged to exercised their powers on the basis of education and personal devices, rather than, as under the Old Regime, hereditary ascension or church membership.

Like most other politicians of his generation, Rutger Jan was a political newcomer. His social background was rather ordinary, though not very common. His father, Gerrit, was a wine merchant from Deventer, a city in the Dutch province of Overijssel. He did very well, but because he belonged to the Mennonite Church, or *doopsgezinden*, as they called themselves, he was considered a second-class citizen. Being a nonreformed citizen, he had been excluded from full citizenship. Rutger Jan himself was baptized in the reformed church of his mother, but from his father, who also joined the Patriotic Movement, he knew that times needed changing.

Because most revolutionary politicians were self-made men, self-presentation and self-representation, or "self-fashioning" as Stephen Greenblatt has called it, became very important to them.[16] And this was exactly where Rutger Jan's special talent lay. He presented himself extremely well and knew how to step into the spotlight, but he also knew how to self-represent by the use of powerful instruments of self-assertion. As the ambassador to

France, he convincingly constructed his own identity—a public persona—through ceremonies, art, the monumental buildings in which he lived, the finest clothing, and also by the self-promoting use of the press and the media of the time.[17]

This mastery of spin was demonstrated by Schimmelpenninck's insistence that the Dutch media celebrate the Treaty of Amiens, which was signed on March 25, 1802, as a great diplomatic victory. Even though he actually did not have much to show for it, he asked the minister of foreign affairs, Maarten van der Goes, to organize publicity in order to manage the public's perception of the outcome of the peace treaty to be as positive as possible,[18] with the desired result: soon after Rutger Jan was glorified by many journalists, as well as theater makers and poets, as an important European peacemaker.[19]

In his role as an ambassador representing a close and dependent ally of France, he had not much formal power, but Rutger Jan still managed to gain a good deal of status, just on the basis of his own personal social skills. Colonel Nightingall wrote about the French negotiator in Amiens, Joseph Bonaparte: "He has not at all the manner of a gentleman." The Dutch ambassador, on the other hand, he thought was "rather above par."[20] The exquisite dinners that Rutger Jan served his guests were even mentioned and praised in *The Times*. This newspaper wrote that, regarding the luxuries of the table and the choice of his wines, he outdid all competition. He had his turbot and eels from Holland, pike and perch from the Rhine; and the heaths and woods of Provence supplied him with game.[21]

Gentlewoman

Rutger Jan's representational qualities were legendary, but his greatest trump card was his wife, Catharina. Among the beau monde in Paris, she was celebrated for her extraordinary beauty. Talleyrand, Madame de Staël, Lucien, and Joseph Bonaparte were said to be among her greatest admirers. Catharina was, as much as her husband, a high-profile public figure, as she became more and more professionally involved in his career. Much evidence for this can be found in their marital correspondence, in which the couple exchanged not just private messages, but also (secret) political information.[22] Catharina helped Rutger Jan with his public image, presided over the receptions, managed their staff, and did the finances. Her influence, however, went beyond the classic status of the ambassador's wife—namely, she also acted as Rutger Jan's biggest political confidant. During the times when they were apart because he had to be in Paris, and she in Amsterdam or The Hague, or vice versa, Catharina served as his local special assistant, passing on his messages, which were important to his work on reforming the state, to politicians and diplomats.

Where he operated on the front lines, she did the necessary networking behind the scenes. But Catharina also fulfilled an increasingly public role. In Amiens she made her debut on the international stage, where she was publicly visible next to her husband. According to Colonel Nightingall, she was the prettiest and best of all the wives attending the conference: "She has more the manners of a gentlewoman than anyone here."[23] Claude Francois de Méneval, Napoleon's private secretary, remembered her especially because of her tea parties, at which she and her daughter, Kitty, did the honors. Even years later he remembered her vividly: "She knew how to unite the domestic virtues and the duties of good mother with her worldly successes."[24] In 1805 she attended Rutger Jan's inauguration as grand pensionary and fulfilled the role of hostess in the Huis ten Bosch (House in the Woods), the palace in The Hague, the official residence of the Schimmelpenninck family.

Family Man

The Schimmelpennincks not only knew very well how to present themselves, they also knew how to *represent* themselves. The year in which the Treaty of Amiens was signed has also become the quantitative high point in the Schimmelpenninck iconography. In this period, as a manner of underpinning his self-declared diplomatic successes, Rutger Jan started to use art as an effective form of self-advertising. He ordered many artists to produce portraits of him and his relatives. He at first instructed the French painter Pierre-Paul Prud'hon to portray him, together with his wife and their 12-year-old daughter and 8-year-old son, Gerrit, who also accompanied him to Amiens. Preoccupied as Rutger Jan was with his self-representation, Prud'hon's painting, known under the title *Réunion de famille*, could very well be seen as a consciously constructed public profile (see Figure 10.1). Prud'hon had a reputation for creating sensuous, intimate works.[25] What is most striking about this visual representation is that Rutger Jan did not have himself portrayed as a diplomat, but rather as a husband and father. The portrait is, however, not apolitical. As he is surrounded by nature and his family, it could easily be regarded as a depiction of the Roman virtue of resignation, personified by the Roman statesman Cincinnatus, who happily returned to his farm and family after his public services were no longer required.

Cincinnatus was also prominent in the iconography of George Washington, a personal hero of Rutger Jan.[26] Like the American president, Rutger Jan was very good at the political game of gaining authority by downplaying his eagerness for power. Yet, the portrait clearly relates him to the Republican discourse of norms of manhood exemplified by the "Family Man," empowering him in his (future) leadership. The portrait seems to confirm how De Méneval experienced Rutger Jan and his wife during their stay in Amiens. In his eyes they were a model patriarchal family: "All in this family breathed the spirit of patriarchal simplicity."[27] But Prud'hon portrayed Rutger Jan clearly not as a traditional patriarchic authority with little

Figure 10.1   Art can be an effective form of self-advertising. Artist Pierre-Paul Prud'hon depicts Schimmelpenninck and his family in 1802.

Source: Rijksmuseum website. Portrait of Rutger Jan Schimmelpenninck and his Family, Pierre Prud'hon, 1801–1802.

visible emotion. In fact, he looks exactly the opposite: understanding and affectionate.[28]

Rutger Jan carefully cultivated a rather emotional or sensitive image. This also helped his popularity as the head of state, that is to say, at least among his political friends. In many Dutch and French poems, and historical accounts of the time, he was particularly praised for striking the right balance between the head and the heart. The inauguration speech he delivered in 1805 as the new head of state was particularly well received because people felt it came straight from the heart.[29] Many poets—among whom Rhijnvis Feith, a Dutch literary author and sentimentalist par excellence—dedicated poems to their new political leader. Strikingly, they all characterized him as meek, but without being weak. In their eyes he was a supremely warm and emotionally empathic man. As Anna Catharina Brinkman, a journalist, wrote, full of admiration, he managed to "let tears flow, and hearts glow" with his speeches.[30] Above all, he was humanitarian. His political dynamism was not weakened but strengthened by his sensitive capacity to put himself in the place of another person. Just because of this special personal quality he could really make a difference.[31]

Rutger Jan's ceremonial talent, his perfect and close working relationship with his wife, his trustworthy fatherhood, and his understanding and humanitarian sensitiveness, all served as crucial elements in the public image he created of himself. However, the qualities he initially was extensively praised for ultimately became his weak spots to his opponents.

The Attacks

As the head of state, Rutger Jan's position was that of a one-man executive, with the assistance of a "Staatsraad," resembling the French Conseil d'État. The democratic basis of his regime was notably weak. There was a Legislative Corps, but this body only consisted of 19 men, who came together once every six months and who had no powers beyond approving or rejecting constitutional laws.[32] Right from the beginning, Rutger Jan was openly criticized for the dictatorial powers he possessed. It was widely and repeatedly written in all kinds of Dutch and French publications that even William V had not wielded as much power as the grand pensionary. According to a missive signed by a group of 12 Dutch noblemen, his far-reaching powers made him even more "despotique" than the *stadholders* of the past or a "constitutional king."[33] "The Grand Pensionary has more power than the King in England, he has even more power than the Emperor of France; or the Sovereign has in any country," the French newspaper *The Moniteur* wrote.[34] *The Universal Magazine* pejoratively called him "an advocate of some note" and wrote that it would be ridiculous to consider the acceptance of his constitution as the act of free people.[35]

Nevertheless, Rutger Jan's autocratic regime made it possible to accomplish more than the previous chaotic regimes had accomplished in the ten years since 1795. His regime particularly implemented important tax and education reforms.[36] Still, public opinion turned against him from the moment he assumed power. Above all, this had to do with the growing public suspicion that Rutger Jan allowed himself the status of a sort of king. According to his critics, the audiences at the Huis ten Bosch were marked by an offensive level of pomp and ceremony, etiquette, and dress.[37] There is no doubt Rutger Jan adopted Napoleon's Empire style, which in turn was heavily influenced by the splendid court culture of the Sun King.[38] The grand pensionary carefully chose his own costumes and was escorted by a uniformed guard. The disapproving opinions were also voiced in English periodicals, which certainly must be seen within the context of anti-Napoleonic propaganda.[39] As *The*

Gentleman's Magazine put it bluntly: "He [Rutger Jan] is endeavouring to dazzle the eyes of the frugal citizens of that unhappy country, by the splendour of his equipages and the grandeur of his processions."[40]

Rutger Jan's detractors were given a greater level of freedom to defame him after it was made public that he was slowly going blind. Around the same time, rumors also started to circulate that Napoleon was considering making his brother Louis Bonaparte the new ruler of the Batavians. In the spring of 1806, an influential pamphlet appeared—*Convocation of the Batavian People* by the Dutch Republican Maria Aletta Hulshoff. She warned that the Republic was threatened by a "foreign despot" and characterized Schimmelpenninck as an incompetent traitor of Republicanism, whose power hunger and blindness had brought the Republic to the brink of disaster.[41] It was not Hulshoff's anti-French Republican message but the fact that she linked his visual disability to his failing statesmanship that Rutger Jan thought was defamatory. Hulshoff was taken to court and condemned to two years at her own expense in the city house of correction.[42]

From then the attacks became more virulent. "It appears," *The Moniteur* wrote a month later, "the Grand Pensionary entirely has lost his sight. Who is to be his successor?"[43] The attacks no longer came solely from individual dissidents but were for the most part orchestrated by Batavians of Rutger Jan's own inner circle of colleagues, whom he had been close to in Paris. Carel Hendrik Verhuell, the secretary for the navy, had supported Rutger Jan while they both stayed in France, but now he started secret talks with Talleyrand and Napoleon about the future of the Batavian Republic without Rutger Jan. In the winter of 1805, Verhuell showed Louis Bonaparte round in the south of the Netherlands, officially to inspect the French army troops stationed in the Republic. They also paid a visit to the Huis ten Bosch. Afterward Verhuell reported back to the Parisian embassy that Rutger Jan was too ill to receive them properly and that Catharina had been extremely rude to their French royal guest.[44]

While Verhuell conducted the (unfair) negotiations with the emperor in Paris, he and Gerard Brantsen, Rutger Jan's successor as the ambassador to France, generated a stream of negative publicity about the grand pensionary, which found its way to the French and English press.[45] In many letters to other Batavian officials, Brantsen also attacked Rutger Jan for his refusal to resign. He blamed this on Catharina's influence upon him. Within the French government, it was said, according to Brantsen, that they did not know anymore what sex they were dealing with. It was like Rutger Jan had undergone a sex change.[46] Meanwhile spies reported to Paris that Catharina was after a life of great luxury and ordered others to address her as "Her Excellency."[47]

International Slander

Rutger Jan's hold on power rapidly weakened with Napoleon's changed focus on the European continent, as well as Verhuell's and Brantsen's smear campaigns against him. Interestingly, because of the transnational nature of Rutger

Jan's political career, as he acted within the Batavian, French, and English political cultures, he is probably the only eighteenth-century Dutch states-man who was targeted in political fiction filled with sexual or pornographic elements. This was a genre that did not develop in the late eighteenth-century Netherlands, at least not to a significant extent. Texts such as the farce *William V's Disturbed Bout of Bonking* were rather rare.[48] The English society author H. Stewarton, who wrote about the beau monde of Paris, became Rutger Jan's biggest tormentor. In the year he was installed as the head of state, Stewarton published *The Secret History of the Court and Cabinet of St. Cloud in a Series of Letters from a Gentleman at Paris to a Nobleman in London*. It must have been a best-seller: the British Library has a fourth American reprint from 1807, German and French translations from 1816, and many English reprints, even from the beginning of the twentieth century.[49]

The author did not reveal any information about his true identity. The only thing he said about himself was that he was a great friend of Joséphine de Beauharnais, who was having marital problems with Napoleon at the time and conceived an illegitimate child in 1805. Stewarton was clearly part of Napoleon's inner circle as he possessed an awful lot of inside information.[50] About Rutger Jan he wrote that only twice in his life had he been in the Dutch-man's company. He thought of Rutger Jan as both "timid and reserved." From what little he said, the author "could not possibly judge his character and capacity." Yet, he claimed that "his portrait and its accompaniments" had been presented and delivered to him by "a Mr. M (formerly an ambassador also), who was both his schoolfellow and his comrade at the university." The way this man, Mr. M, was described, coming from the same province and with a similar career, has to be taken with a grain of salt, but it seems again to point in the direction of Rutger Jan's own Batavian colleagues. It could have been Brantsen or Verhuell, but also Carel de Vos van Steenwijk, another political rival, whom Schimmelpenninck could not stand.[51]

Stewarton quoted the words of his Dutch informant "as near as pos-sible." By summing up his "traits," he assassinated Rutger Jan's character in the most thorough way. *Reputation* was the keyword: "More vain than ambi-tious, Schimmelpenninck from his youth, and, particularly, from his entrance into public life, tried every means to make a noise, but found none to make a reputation." Backboneless as he was, he "caressed in succession all the sys-tems of the French Revolution" and became "immediately a partisan" of every important king or notorious great man. Their "virtues or the vices, the merit or defects," were of no consideration to him. He just wanted to be "famous." Stewarton, on behalf of his informant, also predicted Rutger Jan's downfall, on the grounds of his failing personality: "Without acquired ability, without natural genius, or political capacity, destitute of discretion and address, as confident and obstinate as he is ignorant, he is only elevated to fall and to rise no more."[52]

Then Stewarton goes on about another important and cherished feature of Rutger Jan's reputation: his wife. He praised her heavily, but just to hit Rutger Jan as hard:

> Madame Schimmelpenninck, I was informed, is as amiable and accomplished as her husband is awkward and deficient; though well acquainted with his infidelities and profligacy, she is too virtuous to listen to revenge, and too generous not to forgive. She is, besides, said to be a lady of uncommon abilities, and of greater information than she chooses to display. She has never been the worshipper of Bonaparte, or the friend of Talleyrand; she loved her country, and detested its tyrants.[53]

Depicting Catharina as an overly ambitious almost equal copresident next to Rutger Jan, who exercised the real political power, was only done in order to make him look even more weak and silly. It resembles what was said about Abigail Adams. Her husband's opponents called her "Mrs. President." Stewarton's words about Catharina were of the same kind: "Had she been created a grand pensionary, she would certainly have swayed with more glory than her husband; and been hailed by contemporaries, as well as posterity, if not a heroine, at least a patriot."[54]

Disgraced by Debauchery

Stewarton took the cumulative impact of the rumors, lies, and distortions spread by Batavians to destroy Rutger Jan's national and international reputation and to prompt him to resign to a whole new level. The personalized way in which Rutger Jan conducted his politics by carefully cultivating his personal reputation now backfired. Stewarton followed the well-proven formula of the French libelers: he distorted the public picture of the identity of his victim by reducing his political identity to his private personality, which he exposed to the outside world. Wrecking Rutger Jan's proud picture of himself as a perfect and enlightened father, he unmasked him as a hypocrite by depicting him as a regular client of prostitutes. Stewarton really believed in the power of information to change the attitude of the Dutch, as he predicted that the Batavians with "patriotic and honourable sentiments" would certainly start to resent their grand pensionary if they only realized how much he was a slave of Napoleon and, moreover, "disgraced by debauchery."[55] From his Dutch informant, Stewarton had heard that when it was known in Paris that Rutger Jan had set out for his new sovereignty, "no less than sixteen girls of the Palais Royal demanded passes for Holland."[56]

In a second publication written by Stewarton that was as successful as the first one, *The Revolutionary Plutarch: Exhibiting The Most Distinguished Characters, Literary, Military and Political in The Recent Annals of The French Republic*, Rutger Jan also visited the "French Belles." He now kept a Dutch woman, a certain "Madame Lacken," as well. She was the "young and gallant wife of an old and rich sugar boiler at Amsterdam, who exchanged the dullness of the French capital, leaving her honest husband, of whose embraces she was unworthy to pay her numerous debts as a consolation for her infidelity."[57] The truth of this story about Madame Lacken, which was, according to Stewarton, also a hot topic in the French press, is very difficult to check, since courtesans very often worked under several nicknames. However, it does resemble the story of the Dutch courtesan Elseline Versfelt, or Ida Saint-Elme, whom Rutger Jan, according to her *Mémoires* (written to derive success from the described scandals), had known quite well, as she insinuated, in a sexual way.[58]

The result of all of these revelations of Rutger Jan's supposed sexual (mis)conduct was that he came across as a man who was not in control of his own needs and feelings, which was exactly the opposite of the image he promoted of himself as a statesman who was morally strong, not because he ignored his soft side, but because he fully embraced his sensitivity. To add insult to injury, Catharina's political talent, "morality and prudence," Stewarton ascribed not to "virtuous principles" but to her "native insensibility and Batavian phlegm."[59] Stewarton's writings must of course all be seen in the light of the aforementioned English anti-Napoleonic rhetoric. But that does not mean that it could not have been true. Joseph Fouché, the minister of police, spent six million francs on attractive women working for him as political spies.[60] Rutger Jan's predecessors, the Dutch ambassadors Gerard Brantsen, Jacobus Blauw, Caspar Meyer, and Jan Eykenbroek, were all known for their frequent and intensive contacts with Parisian women and prostitutes.[61]

It is difficult to say whether the character assassins succeeded in changing the public perception of the political discourse. Like Stewarton, they aimed at an international audience, most likely to influence the Parisians directly connected to Napoleon. Of all of Stewarton's writings, only his *Secret History of The Court* was published in the Netherlands. In 1814 a Dutch translation came out, but heavily censored. The most scandalous text fragments were left out, including the lines about his 16 prostitutes. With this, the worst slander did not reach Rutger Jan's own country.[62] The writings of the courtesan Elseline Versfelt about her acquaintances with important makers of French history and of her opinions about them were published in the 1820s. They therefore cannot be considered as part of the political campaign of slander against Rutger Jan.[63]

Conclusion

Nine months after Rutger Jan was installed as the head of state, Talleyrand officially informed him that he was going to be replaced by Louis Bonaparte. *The Gentleman's Magazine* reported: "Schimmelpenninck retired in disgust."[64] Six days after his dramatic fall from power, on the thirteenth of June 1806, Catharina wrote to her husband: "This is the first time my friend, that I can write to you, without fearing being read by everyone else, how happy I am that you have left The Hague. You were not made for being the subordinate of someone like Verhuell."[65] Here Catharina's words testify how much she personally suffered from the constant governmental spying on her and her husband, and how glad she was to be freed from Verhuell, whom she always (and rightly) had suspected of political disloyalty. Still, as indicated before, it is difficult to establish to what extent the attempts to destroy Rutger

Jan's and Catharina's reputation were a contributory factor to their downfall. In the longer term, however, the attacks against them have definitely had damaging effects. Within Dutch history writing, it is only recently that the Schimmelpennincks, like the Batavian revolutionaries in general, are proudly depicted as "constitution makers" and "political pioneers."[66] In their own time, and even long after they died, however, the image of the Schimmelpennincks as money-grabbing pseudoroyals was entrenched in the mind of the public. This was done by disappointed Republican authors, but later also by triumphant Orangists and many nineteenth- and twentieth-century historians.[67]

Gerrit Schimmelpenninck, Rutger Jan's only son, published a biography on his father in 1845. As it was partially based on interviews with Rutger Jan, the biography offered in retrospective a justification for his actions, thoughts, and intentions. He did not respond directly to the allegations of too much courtly grandeur. Instead, he stressed that his ceremonial representation had, indeed, been crucial to the way he handled politics, so that he had sometimes even paid for it out of his own pocket.[68]

Rutger Jan's case thus provides an early modern Western illustration of the danger that a state built upon a "cult of personality" is likely to be vulnerable to personal attacks.[69] Whereas the French state at the time was built on the personality cult of Napoleon, whose character was very heavily attacked by the English, Rutger Jan's case shows us a unique European example of the fact that republican "presidents" of the late eighteenth century also had to be alert to the undermining force of publicity concerning (supposed) scandals about their private lives.[70] However, Rutger Jan was clearly more prone to the damaging effects of character attacks than the emperor, who seemed to be immune to them. Rutger Jan was, of course, more vulnerable because his regime depended greatly on Napoleon's capricious policy. He had not much in the way of formal foreign power, hence the reason he was desperate to keep up his personal friendship with the emperor. Schimmelpenninck's personality, reputation, and representation were extremely important to his hold on power. But there were also Dutch internal factors at play. One influential factor might have been problems within the sphere of the "cultural transfer" of Rutger Jan's and Catharina's Napoleonic style of ceremonial representation, which did not fit in the context of the perception of the Batavian Republicans, who still cherished the Dutch virtue of simplicity.[71]

The effectiveness of the slander could perhaps also be understood in the light of Catharina's public prominence, which conflicted with the new political culture of the revolution. In the Netherlands, women lost their indirect political influence because of the professionalizing influence that politics underwent by the democratic changes.[72] Catharina's visibility in the political sphere could be regarded as an unwanted relic from prerevolutionary times. In any event, there is more than a hint of irony in the fact that the very traits and tools that launched Rutger Jan's successful political career were also used to end it.

Notes

1. This chapter is largely based upon the research I did for the biography Hagen 2012 (reprinted in 2013).
2. Van Sas 2004, 41.
3. Reinders 2013, 149–72.
4. Deen, Onnekink, and Reinders 2010, 15; Van Sas 2002; Grijzenhout, Van Sas, and Velema 2013; Kloek and Mijnhardt 2004.
5. Oddens 2012; Van Sas 2005, 195–221; De Vries 2013, 243–73.
6. Darnton 2010, 299.
7. Darnton 2010, 422–38.
8. Some key publications on the history of the Dutch revolution: Colenbrander 1908; Colenbrander 1905–1922; Geyl 1948–1959; Jourdan 2008; Leeb 1973; Palmer 1959–1964; Rosendaal 2004; Schama 1977; de Wit 1969.
9. Klein 2008, 132–33.
10. Darnton 2010, 422–38.
11. See for a striking example of character assassination (of the Orangist author Johannes Le Francq van Berkhey) in the 1780s Honings 2011, 92–96.
12. Meijer Drees and Nieuwenhuis 2010, 205–6.
13. Grainger 2003; van Hall 1847.
14. A selection of the main literature on Rutger Jan Schimmelpenninck (1761–825): Schimmelpenninck 1845; van Hall 1847; Colenbrander 1911; de Vries 1941; Kronenberg 1950; Sixma van Heemstra-Schimmelpenninck 1961; Rogier 1964; Plemp van Duiveland 1971; Klein 1993; van Sas 2005, 293–313; Hagen 2012.
15. Klein 1993; Velema 1998; Velema 2007.
16. Greenblatt 1980. Greenblatt's concept of self-fashioning has also been successfully applied to eighteenth-century political case studies. See, for instance, Osborne 2008.
17. Hagen, *President*, passim, 148.
18. He failed, for instance, to sign an agreement upon the indemnification of the deposed House of Orange for its losses in the Netherlands, which would have been satisfying to the Dutch. His claim that the Batavian Republic was not to furnish any part of the indemnity did not tell the whole truth. In reality, the Dutch still bore the costs of the French military operations, but Schimmelpenninck presented it as a great achievement, which he took all the credit for: Hagen 2012, 143–45, 148; Schama 1977, 528–9.
19. Hagen 2012, 150.
20. Grainger 2003, 68.
21. Alger 1904, 21.
22. The marital letters of Rutger Jan and Catharina, about 180 in total, are kept in a private archive, which is stored in the castle of the Schimmelpenninck family in the Dutch province of Overijssel.
23. Grainger 2003, 68.
24. De Méneval 1910.
25. Staring 1947; van Thienen 1963; Wolleswinkel 1995.
26. Wills 1984.
27. De Méneval 1910.
28. Hunt 1992. For the Dutch discourse on the compassionate father, see Lok and Scholz 2012, 19–44.
29. Loosjes 1811, 86.
30. Brinkman 1805. See also Feith and Kantelaar 1805; Lublink de Jonge 1805; Kemper 1805.

31. I am currently working on a scholarly publication on Rutger Jan's use of emotional culture to fashion his political identity. I have been inspired to enter this new direction in research, which in the context of the Batavian Republic is still in an experimental phase, by Reddy 2000; Reddy 2001; Lewis 1998.
32. A plebiscite was duly organized, which elicited 14,903 yes votes (against 136 nos) from an electorate of 353,322. The abstentions were counted as "tacit affirmatives" in the now well-established tradition.
33. Colenbrander 1905–1922, vol. 4, 594.
34. Schama 1977, 562–63.
35. *The Universal Magazine*, 1805, 461.
36. van Sas 2005.
37. Colenbrander 1905–1922, vol. 4, 597; van Limburg Brouwer 1846, 180.
38. See, for instance, Nouvel 2007.
39. Burrows 2006.
40. *The Gentleman's Magazine*, June 1805, 573.
41. Hulshoff 1806; Poell 2008, 301.
42. Stouten 1984; Joor 2000, 292–94, 307, 357, 460, 481, 484–90, 492, 537, 568, 690.
43. Schama 1977, 562–63.
44. Turksma 1991; Verhuell 1847, vol. 1, 351, 355.
45. Schama 1977, 562
46. Colenbrander 1905–1922, vol. 4, 614. Brantsen to Van der Goes, April 17, 1806. Colenbrander 1905–1922, vol. 4, nos. 650, 630.
47. Vreede 1865, vol. 2, 115–28.
48. Klein 1993, 133; Mijnhardt 1993, 283–300.
49. Stewarton 1806, vol. 2, 34–44.
50. There is no biographical information available about Stewarton. He has been often identified with Lewis Goldsmith (1763–1846), but this seems not to be right: Burrows 2006, 155.
51. Colenbrander 1905–1922, vol. 4, 419–20, 425.
52. Stewarton 1806, vol. 2, 34–44.
53. Stewarton1806, vol. 2, 34–44.
54. Stewarton 1806, vol. 2, 34–44.
55. Stewarton 1806, vol.3, 411–21.
56. Stewarton 1806, vol. 2, 34–44.
57. Stewarton 1806, vol. 3, 411–22.
58. Saint-Elme 1827–1828, 216–19; Ostendorf-Reinders 2009; Samplonius 2006.
59. Stewarton 1806, vol. 3, 421.
60. Groenewegen and Hallema 1976, 112.
61. Stewarton 1807, 183; Colenbrander 1905–1922, vol. 2, 743; Koenes 2013.
62. Stewarton 1814. By whom and why this translation was censured could not be traced.
63. Samplonius 2006.
64. *The Gentleman's Magazine and Historical Chronicle*, June 1806, 570.
65. Colenbrander 1905–1922, vol. 1, LV.
66. See, for instance, Oddens 2012.
67. See, for instance, van der Aa 1806, 595–97.
68. Schimmelpenninck 1845.
69. Based on a statement made in Darnton 2010, 437.
70. Paraphrase of Darnton 2010, 437.
71. Jourdan 2009, 559–80.
72. Dekker 1989. See for the historiographical debate on this: Hagen 2012, 352.

Bibliography

Aa, C. van der. 1806. *Geschiedenis van het leven, character en lotgevallen van wijlen Willem den Vijfden, Prinse van Oranje en Nassau*, vol. 1. Amsterdam: Allart.

Aa, C. Van der. 1808. *Geschiedenis van het leven, character en lotgevallen van wijlen Willem den Vijfden, Prinse van Oranje en Nassau*, vol. 4. Amsterdam: Allart.

Alger, J. G. 1904. *Napoleon's British Visitors and Captives: 1801–1815*. Westminster: A. Constable.

Brinkman, A. C. 1805. *Dichtregelen aan zijne excellentie den heere raadpensionaris R.J. Schimmelpenninck*. The Hague: Erven Isaac van Cleef.

Burrows, S. 2006. "Britain and the Black Legend: The Genesis of the Anti-Napoleonic Myth." In M. Philp, ed., *Resisting Napoleon: The British Response to the Threat of Invasion, 1797–1815*, 141–57. Aldershot: Ashgate.

Colenbrander, H. T. 1905–1922. *Gedenkstukken der algemeene geschiedenis van Nederland van 1795 tot 1840*, 22 vols. The Hague: Nijhoff.

Colenbrander, H. T. 1908. *De Bataafsche Republiek*. Amsterdam: Meulenhoff.

Colenbrander, H. T. 1911. *Schimmelpenninck en koning Lodewijk*. Amsterdam: Meulenhoff.

Darnton, R. 2010. *The Devil in the Holy Water, or the Art of Slander from Louis XIV to Napoleon*. Philadelphia: University of Pennsylvania Press.

Deen, F. D. Onnekink, and M. Reinders. 2010. *Pamphlets and Politics in the Dutch Republic*. Leiden: Brill.

Dekker, R. 1989. "Revolutionaire en contrarevolutionaire vrouwen in Nederland, 1780–1800." *Tijdschrift voor geschiedenis* 102: 545–63.

Feith, R., and J. Kantelaar. 1805. *Aan R.J. Schimmelpenninck in mei 1805*. Amsterdam, Johannes Allart.

Geyl, P. 1948–1959. *Geschiedenis van de Nederlandse stam*, 3 vols, rev. ed. Amsterdam: Wereldbibliotheek.

Grainger, J. D. 2003. *The Amiens Truce: Britain and Bonaparte, 1802–1803*. Woodbridge: Boydell.

Greenblatt, S. 1980. *Renaissance Self-Fashioning: From More to Shakespeare*. Chicago: University of Chicago Press.

Groenewegen, N., and A. Hallema. 1976. *Van nachtwacht tot computermacht. Vijftig eeuwen politie en justitie*. Zaltbommel: Europese Bibliotheek.

Grijzenhout, F. N. van Sas, and W. Velema, eds. 2013. *Het Bataafse experiment. Politiek en cultuur rond 1800*. Nijmegen: Vantilt.

Hagen, E. 2012. *President van Nederland. Rutger Jan Schimmelpenninck 1761–1825*. Amsterdam: Uitgeverij Balans.

Hall, M. C. van. 1847. *Rutger Jan Schimmelpenninck voornamelijk als Bataafsch afgezant op het vredescongres te Amiens, in 1802. Eene bijdrage tot zijn leven en karakter*. Amsterdam: Schleijer.

Honings, R. A. M. 2011. *Geleerdheids zetel, Hollands roem! Het literaire leven in Leiden 1760–1860*. Leiden: Primavera Pers.

Hulshoff, M. A. 1806. *Oproeping van het Bataafsche volk, om deszelfs denkwijze en wil openlijk aan den dag te leggen, tegen de overheersching door eenen vreemdeling, waarmede het vaderland bedreigd wordt*. Amsterdam: Gedrukt voor rekening van de schrijfster, en alöm te bekomen.

Hunt, L. 1992. *The Family Romance of the French Revolution*. Berkeley: University of California Press.

Joor, J. 2000. *De adelaar en het lam. Onrust, opruiing en onwilligheid in Nederland ten tijde van het Koninkrijk Holland en de inlijving bij het Franse Keizerrijk (1806–1813)*. Amsterdam: De Bataafsche Leeuw.

Jourdan, A. 2008. *La révolution batave entre la France et l'Amérique*. Rennes: Presses Universitaires de Rennes.

Jourdan, A. 2009. "Politieke en culturele transfers in een tijd van revolutie: Nederland 1795–1805." *BMGN—Low Countries Historical Review* 124: 559–80.

Kemper, J. M. 1805. *Lierzang, ter gelegenheid der aanspraak van zijne excellentie den raadpensionaris R. J. Schimmelpenninck, bij het aanvaarden van zijn waardigheid*. S.l.

Klein, S. R. E. 1993. "Republikanisme en patriottisme. Rutger Jan Schimmelpenninck en de klassieke wortels van het republikeinse denken (1784–1785)." *Tijdschrift voor geschiedenis* 106: 179–207.

Kloek, J. J., and W. W. Mijnhardt. 2004. *1800: Blueprints for a National Community*. Assen: Royal van Gorcum / Basingstoke: Palgrave Macmillan.

Koenes, B. 2013. *Schijngestalten. De levens van diplomaat en rokkenjager Gerard Brantsen (1735–1809)*. Hilversum: Uitgeverij Verloren.

Kronenberg, H. 1950. "Waar is Rutger Jan Schimmelpenninck geboren?" *Vereeniging tot Beoefening van Overijsselsch Regt en Geschiedenis (VORG), Verslagen en Medeelingen* 65: 238–40.

Leeb, I. L. 1973. *The Ideological Origins of the Batavian Revolution: History and Politics in the Dutch Republic 1747–1800*. The Hague: Nijhoff.

Lewis, J. 1998. "Those Scenes for which Alone My Heart Was Made: Affection and Politics in the Age of Jefferson and Hamilton." In N. Stearns and J. Lewis, eds., *An Emotional History of the United States*, 52–66. New York: New York University Press.

Limburg Brouwer, van. 1846. *Het leven van M. Samuel Iperuszoon Wiselius*. Groningen: van Zweeden.

Lok, M., and N. Scholz. 2012. "The Return of the Loving Father. Masculinity, Legitimacy and the French and Dutch Restoration Monarchies (1813–1815)." *BMGN— Low Countries Historical Review* 127 (1): 19–44.

Loosjes, P., and J. Wagenaar. 1811. *Vaderlandsche historie, vervattende de geschiedenissen der Vereenigde Nederlanden, zints den aanvang der Noord-Americaansche onlusten, en den daar uit gevolgden oorlog tusschen Engeland en deezen staat, tot den tegenwoordigen tyd. / Uit de geloofwaardigste schryvers en egte gedenkstukken zamengesteld. . . . Ten vervolge van Wagenaars Vaderlandsche historie*, vol. 47. Amsterdam: Allart.

Lublink de Jonge. 1805. *Hulde aan zijne excellentie R. J. Schimmelpenninck, bij zijne terugkomst uit Parijs*. S.l.

Méneval, C. F. baron de. 1910. *Memoirs of Napoleon Bonaparte: The Court of the First Empire*, vol. 1. New York: F. Collier & Son.

Meijer Drees, M., and I. Nieuwenhuis. 2010. "De macht van satire: grenzen testen, grenzen stellen." *Nederlandse letterkunde* 15 (3): 193–220.

Mijnhardt, W. W. 1993. "Politics and Pornography in the Seventeenth- and Eighteenth-Century Dutch Republic." In L. A. Hunt, ed., *The Invention of Pornography: Obscenity and the Origins of Modernity (1500–1800)*, 283–300. New York: Zone Books.

Nouvel, O. 2007. *Symbols of Power: Napoleon and the Art of the Empire Style, 1800–1815*. New York: Abrams.

Oddens, J. 2012. *Pioniers in schaduwbeeld. Het eerste parlement van Nederland 1796–1798*. Nijmegen: Vantilt.

Osborne, J. 2008. "Benjamin Franklin and the Rhetoric of Virtuous Self-Fashioning in Eighteenth-Century America." *Literature and History* 17 (2): 14–30.

Ostendorf-Reinders, G. "Versfelt, Maria Elselina Johanna." *Digitaal Vrouwenlexicon van Nederland*. http://www.inghist.nl/Onderzoek/Projecten/DVN/lemmata/data/versfelt (accessed April 7, 2009).

Palmer, R. R. 1959–1964. *The Age of the Democratic Revolution: A Political History of Europe and America, 1760–1800*, 2 vols. Princeton: Princeton University Press.

Plemp van Duiveland, L. 1971. *Schimmelpenninck 1761–1825. Levensverhaal en tijdsbeeld*. Rotterdam: Donker.

Poell, Th. 2008. "The French Occupation and the Transformation of the Dutch Public Sphere (1795–1813)." In C. Nubola and A. Würgler, eds., *Ballare con nemico? Reazioni all' espansiane franscese in Europa tra entusiasmo a resistenza (1792–1815). Mit dem Feind tanzen? : Reaktionen auf die französische Expansion in Europa zwischen Begeisterung und Protest (1792–1815)*, 283–306. Bologna and Berlin: Il Mulino / Duncker & Humblot.

Reddy, W. 2000. "Sentimentalism and Its Erasure: The Role of Emotions in the Era of the French Revolution." *The Journal of Modern History* 72 (1): 109–52.

Reddy, W. 2001. *The Navigation of Feeling: A Framework for the History of Emotions*. Cambridge: Cambridge University Press.

Reinders, M. 2013. *Printed Pandemonium: Popular Print and Politics in the Netherlands, 1650–72*. Leiden: Brill.

Rogier, L. J. 1962. "Rutger Jan Schimmelpenninck, 31 oktober 1761 te Deventer geboren." *Vereeniging tot Beoefening van Overijsselsch Regt en Geschiedenis (VORG), Verslagen en Medeelingen* 77: 144–202.

Rosendaal, J. 2004. *Bataven! Nederlandse vluchtelngen in Frankrijk 1787–1795*. Nijmegen: Vantilt.

Saint-Elme, I. 1827–1828. *Mémoires d'une contemporaine, ou Souvenirs d'une femme sur les principaux personnages de la République, du Consulat, de l'Empire, etc.*, vols. ¾. Paris: Ladvocat.

Sas, N. C. F. van. 2002. "The Netherlands, 1750–1813." In H. Barker and Simon Burrows, eds., *Press, Politics and the Public Sphere in Europe and North America, 1760–1820*, 48–68. Cambridge: Cambridge University Press.

Sas, N. C. F. van. 2004. "The Netherlands: A Historical Phenomenon." In D. Fokkema and F. Grijzenhout, eds., *Dutch Culture in a European Perspective 1650–2000: Accounting for the Past*, 41–92. London: Palgrave Macmillan.

Sas, N. C. F. van. 2005. *De metamorfose van Nederland. Van oude orde naar moderniteit, 1750–1900*. Amsterdam: Amsterdam University Press.

Samplonius, E. J. M. 2006. "Ida Saint-Elme: Girl power anno 1800." http://www.cubra.nl (accessed August 10, 2011).

Schimmelpenninck, G. 1845. *Rutger Jan Schimmelpenninck, en eenige gebeurtenissen van zijnen tijd*, 2 vols. The Hague: Van Cleef.

Schama, S. 1977. *Patriots and Liberators: Revolution in the Netherlands, 1780–1813*. New York: Knopf.

Sixma van Heemstra-Schimmelpenninck, A. 1961. *In de schaduw van Napoleon. Uit het persoonlijk leven van raadpensionaris Rutger Jan Schimmelpenninck*. The Hague: Voorhoeve.

Staring, A. 1947. *Fransche kunstenaars en hun Hollandsche modellen in de 18ᵉ en in den aanvang der 19ᵉ eeuw*. The Hague: A. A. M. Stols.

Stewarton. 1806. *The Secret History of the Court and Cabinet of St. Cloud in a Series of Letters from a Gentleman at Paris to a Nobleman in London, Written during the Months of August, September, and October, 1805*, vol. 2. London: John Murray.

Stewarton. 1806. *The Revolutionary Plutarch: Exhibiting the Most Distinguished Characters, Literary, Military, and Political in the Recent Annals of the French Republic: The Greater Part from the Original Information of a Gentleman Resident at Paris*, 4th ed., vol. 3. London: John Murray.

Stewarton. 1807. *A Picture of the Empire of Buonaparte: And His Federale Nations, or The Belgium Traveller through Holland, France and Switzerland during the Years 1804–1805 in a Series of Letters from a Nobleman to a Minister of State*. Middletown, CT: Alsop, Rilet, and Alsop.

Stewarton. 1814. *De geheime geschiedenis van het Hof en Kabinet van St. Cloud, in eene reeks van Brieven, van eenen Heer van Aanzien in Frankrijk, aan eenen Engelschen Edelman. In III Deelen*, 3 vols. Amsterdam: H. Gartman.

Stouten, J. 1984. "Maria Aletta Hulshoff (1781–1846), dweepster of idealiste?" *Literatuur. Tijdschrift over Nederlandse letterkunde* 1 (2): 72–79.

The Gentleman's Magazine (June 1805).

The Gentleman's Magazine and Historical Chronicle (June 1806).

The Universal Magazine (May 1805).

Thienen, W. S. van. 1963. "Pierre-Paul Prud'hon (1758–1823). Rutger Jan Schimmelpenninck met zijn familie." *Openbaar kunstbezit* 7: 19.

Turksma, L. 1991. *Admiraal van Napoleon Bonaparte. Het leven van Carel Hendrik graaf Verhuell, 1764–1845*. Zutphen: Walburg Pers.

Velema, W. 1998. "Beschaafde republikeinen. Burgers in de achttiende eeuw." In R. Aerts and H. te Velde, eds., *De stijl van de burger. Over Nederlandse burgerlijke cultuur vanaf de middeleeuwen*, 80–99. Kampen: Kok Agora.

Velema, W. 2007. *Republicans: Essays on Eighteenth-Century Dutch Political Thought*. Leiden: Brill.

Ver Huell, Q. M. R. 1847. *Het leven en karakter van Carel Hendrik graaf Ver Huell*, 2 vols. Amsterdam: Beijerinck.

Vreede, G. W. 1863–1865. *Geschiedenis der diplomatie van de Bataafsche Republiek*, 3 vols. Utrecht: Broese.

Vries, Th. U. de. 1941. *Rutger Jan Schimmelpenninck*. The Hague: Leopold.

Vries, M. de. 2013. "De geboorte van de moderne intellectueel. Literatuur en politiek rond 1800." In F. Grijzenhout, N. van Sas, and W. Velema, eds., *Het Bataafse experiment. Politiek en cultuur rond 1800*, 243–73. Nijmegen: Vantilt.

Wit, C. H. E. de. 1965. *De strijd tussen aristocratie en democratie in Nederland, 1780–1848*. Heerlen: Winants.

Wills, G. 1984. *Cincinnatus, George Washington and the Enlightenment*. Garden City, NY: Doubleday and Company, Inc.

Wolleswinkel, J. 1995. "Nieuwe portretten van Rutger Jan Schimmelpenninck en zijn gezin door Ch. H. Hodges, bezien in hun tijd." *De Nederlandsche leeuw. Maandblad van het Nederlandsch Genootschap voor Geslacht-en Wapenkunde* 112: 374–80.

Editorial Reflections: Early Modern Cases

Martijn Icks and Eric Shiraev

The invention of the printing press opened up a whole new world for character attackers. It was now possible to reach much wider audiences in a much shorter time—the start of a development that is still ongoing and has only accelerate since the invention of radio, TV, the Internet, and other mass media in recent times. However, the new possibilities that opened up also brought new challenges and pitfalls with them. For one thing, it became necessary to develop new "languages" that were not just comprehensible to cultured elites, but could be understood by the masses, as well. Luther and his sympathizers proved to be masters at this. Deftly combining images and words in their pamphlets, they employed the conventions of devotional imagery to get their point across. The counterattacks of their Catholic opponents were not nearly as widespread and imaginative. The *availability* and *appeal* of character attacks thus became crucial factors in wars of slander; much more so than before, one needed to know how to "sell" one's message.

In a world in which pamphlets, broadsheets, and, later, newspapers circulated widely, and in which literacy was steadily on the rise, a growing group of people started to take an active interest in political and religious matters. In late eighteenth-century France, revolutionaries of different affiliations launched numerous attacks against each other—as did Orangists and Patriots in the final years of the Dutch Republic. As all three chapters show, political and religious leaders became ever more dependent on the emergent public opinion. Throughout northern Europe, Renaissance popes lost millions of former supporters to Protestantism. In the years of turmoil following the French Revolution, French and Dutch politicians lost popular support as quickly as they had gained it. The introduction of democratic systems of government further strengthened this trend: contrary to the kings and dukes of the Old Regime, whose positions were hereditary and seldom questioned by the majority of their subjects, democratically elected leaders were—and are—directly dependent on the continued approval of voters to maintain their position. This made—and makes—them all the more vulnerable to character attacks.

Confronted with more vocal and informed audiences, leading figures had to make an effort to create appealing public personae. Even though Rutger Jan Schimmelpenninck had not been democratically elected as grand pensionary of the Batavian Republic, he still took care to cultivate the image of the gentle family man—meek, but not weak—to win the consent of Dutch citizens. At the same time, however, these carefully cultivated personae became favorite targets of attackers. Schimmelpenninck learned this, to his detriment, when his enemies portrayed him as a lecherous hypocrite who engaged in secret debaucheries, hence destroying the cherished image of the family man. Both in pre- and postrevolutionary France, allegations of scandalous private lives were oft-used tools to undermine the reputations of public figures. Particularly in the chaotic period of the early 1790s, when public trust in politicians was at an all-time low and the general public was willing to believe just about anything about their leaders, numerous revolutionaries were "unmasked" as deceivers, whose noble outward appearances only served to hide the licentious pleasures they secretly indulged in. Often, they paid with their lives.

This brings us to one last aspect of the ever-increasing importance of public opinion in the early modern age, a matter that particularly vexed the French revolutionaries who attempted to reshape their world—namely, the question of free speech versus protection against calumny. For the Renaissance popes, who attempted to quell the rise of Protestantism by all means possible, this was not an issue: anyone who slandered the Church, its officials, or its doctrines was automatically guilty of blasphemy and would be punished, either in this life or the next. Several centuries later, when the French king was overthrown and the notion of free speech was formulated, things were no longer as simple. On the one hand, everybody was free to have their say, and public figures were by definition open to criticism. On the other hand, defending oneself against malicious allegations often proved a difficult, if not impossible, task—especially if the allegations concerned private affairs that could not be verified or disproven. A balance had to be struck to reign in slander while at the same time giving free range to the voicing of critical opinions. This was easier said than done. In fact, it is an issue that is still with us today.

The Modern Age

11

Character Attacks and American Presidents

Jason Smart and Eric Shiraev

Introduction

In 1776, near the New Jersey shore, the advancing British army, aided by their American loyalists, captured George Washington's manservant. His name was Billy Lee. On him, the captors found a portmanteau with the general's personal belongings and several letters addressed to his family. In these letters, the future first president of the United States expressed deep regrets about the war he had waged against his fellow British. He worried about his fate. He felt that he was a coward. He wanted to strike a peace deal with the king, whom he loved, as the letters revealed.[1] The British and the loyalists could not believe their luck. They thought that the seized documents would deliver the fatal blow to Washington's reputation and might accelerate the end of the rebellion in North America.

In fact, Washington did not write these letters, and Billy Lee did not surrender to the British. The letters were fakes. They had apparently been made up by a group of loyalists. Eager to attack and disgrace Washington, they had taken a shot at the general's character before he was to be defeated, as they hoped, on the battlefield. Although the British quickly discovered that the letters were fraudulent, they were later published and sold very well.[2] General Washington tried to ignore such a brazen attempt on his character. Yet almost two decades after this incident, the same lies would reemerge, and a new wave of character attacks would target the first president again.

Many years later, during the 2004 presidential elections in the United States, a document was reportedly found that, as some hurryingly claimed, could have ruined the incumbent president's chances for reelection. This document revealed that President George W. Bush had avoided active duty during the Vietnam War due to his father's political connections. The file appeared real to those who claimed that they had discovered it. Famed U.S. news anchorman Dan Rather of CBS quickly announced the existence of this document. He also claimed that there were other new documents showing that young George W. Bush had had a lackluster performance during his time in the Texas Air National Guard. Those who for some time had questioned the president's integrity and character felt vindicated. However, they quickly realized that these alleged files were fakes. Dan Rather's 50-year journalistic career came to a sudden end.[3]

The United States' president, who is the head of state, head of government, and the commander-in-chief of the armed forces, has been one of the most obvious and convenient targets of character attacks. Such attacks become particularly unkind during the presidential campaigns that take place once every four years. They are significantly longer than similar campaigns in most European democracies. In the United States, no federal agency directly manages the elections. Each state uses its own laws to elect a president. Of course, there are federal and state statutes against defamation, libel, and electoral perjury. Yet the law does not generally protect public figures from criticisms, accusations, or slander the way it protects most ordinary citizens.

A comprehensive analysis of character attacks against U.S. presidents is beyond our modest goals in this chapter. We will focus instead on several types of attacks that have emerged over the years and provide noticeable examples of them. At least three types of character attacks have been selected for review: cheap shots, falsifications, and direct character assassination attempts. They differ in terms of the initial intention, the scope and variety of the methods used, and the most anticipated effect. There is no clear demarcation line between these types. Table 11.1 provides a brief description of these three types of attacks.

Table 11.1   Three types of character attacks

Types	Description	Attackers' Goals	Defenders' Challenges
Cheap Shots	Focus on an episode, an action, or statement of a candidate that may raise questions about this person's credibility, honesty, integrity, generosity, or decency.	Annoy and distract opponents and their supporters so that the attacks can cause cumulative damage or push the victim to overreact.	To ignore or not to ignore such cheap shots? There are two undesirable outcomes: appearing weak and overreacting.
Falsifications	Based on lies, which by the time they are spread are difficult to distinguish from facts.	To deliberately associate an opponent's political message with his or her alleged immoral acts or other serious character flaws.	To ignore may appear as acceptance of the falsifications. Rebuttal takes time and resources and may cause speculations.
Character Assassination Attempts	Serious and direct accusations, claims, charges, statements, or other information that is based on certain known facts.	Attacks should result in immanent moral damage and unavoidable political defeat of the opponent.	How to defend without appearing defensive, apologetic, or shielding the victim of the attacks.

Cheap Shots

This is a relatively simple yet potentially hurtful form of attack, which emphasizes an episode, an action, a statement, or a biographical fact in the life of a politician that alludes to this person's individual features, including but not limited to his or her credibility, competence, honesty, integrity, generosity, or decency. Such attacks can be either deliberate or spontaneous. Cheap shots occur in the context of certain political, social, or economic developments, but for the attackers, their target is the opponent's character. "Character defenders" have to face a difficult dilemma: to ignore such cheap shots or not? A reasonable action would be to simply ignore them. Yet the defenders, if they are not paying attention to the attacks, may appear weak and afraid to respond. They also may look as if they are hiding something important. Those who launch cheap shots try to annoy and distract their opponents, and maybe cause them to overreact. To illustrate: in 1991, presidential candidate Bill Clinton was openly mocked for his adulterous past.[4] He spent significant time defending against the rumors. Cheap shots are usually brief and often appear spontaneous (which they may or may not be). They include critical remarks involving name-calling, insulting, and ridiculing, which may constantly overlap.

Insults and Name-Calling

Insults do not require factual proof. That is why this technique is often the easiest to use in an attack: one throws slurs, insults, and accusations against an opponent without backing them with facts. Name-calling usually is a quick, short insult. Personal insults create problems for the targeted victims because they often do not know how to respond to insults that appear particularly outrageous. If you are a presidential candidate, a small misstep or a lack of clarity in your statements may trigger cheap shots aimed at your character.

Name-calling is obviously not an invention of contemporary politics. The Founding Fathers of the United States and their political "teams" were quite unceremonious in their political campaigns. During the 1800 presidential election, John Adams had established himself as the likely victor: after all, he was the incumbent president. To undermine this advantage, Thomas Jefferson, who had run against Adams four years earlier, sought the assistance of a political hack, James Callender.[5] He was then a well-known journalist and a pamphlet writer.[6] Callender obliged: his pamphlets called Adams different names and attacked his character in many ways. One called Adams a "hideous hermaphroditical character, which has neither the force nor firmness of a man, nor the gentleness and sensibility of a woman."[7] Adams responded in kind. As the campaign continued, both candidates tirelessly insulted each other. Adams was "labeled a fool, a hypocrite, a criminal, and a tyrant, while Jefferson was branded a weakling, an atheist, a libertine, and a coward."[8] Jefferson was publicly attacked as an "anarchist" and "liar." Not to be outdone,

Adam's team referred to Jefferson as "a mean-spirited, low-lived fellow, the son of a half-breed Indian squaw, sired by a Virginia mulatto father." One newspaper stated that with Jefferson as commander-in-chief, "murder, robbery, rape, adultery, and incest will be openly taught and practiced, the air will be rent with the cries of the distressed, the soil will be soaked with blood, and the nation black with crimes."[9] In the end, Jefferson stomached the attacks and became the third president.

The 1860 presidential campaign was one of the most contentious and divisive in the history of the United States. The march toward the Civil War was underway. Together with boiling political tensions, name-calling against candidate Abraham Lincoln became vicious. His physical appearance became a common theme of attacks. A newspaper called him a "horrid-looking wretch . . . sooty and scoundrelly [sic] in aspect; a cross between the nutmeg dealer, the horse-swapper, and the night man."[10] He was cursed in the opposition media as an ape, a baboon,[11] a monster, a Negro,[12] an idiot, and a buffoon. Comparisons to Robespierre[13] of France and Charles I of England—two individuals who had been executed—occurred repeatedly and deliberately.

Name-calling was a continuing feature in the twentieth century's elections. During the 1930s Franklin D. Roosevelt was branded as a "destroyer of capitalism." Other common insults included "Fascist" or "dictator." He as a person and his New Deal policies were regularly compared to Adolf Hitler and Nazism, Benito Mussolini and Fascism, and Joseph Stalin and Communism. More than 80 years later, a Google search for "Franklin Roosevelt was a Communist" (calling someone a "Communist" was and is considered slanderous in the United States) yields 233,000 hits. Harry Truman was relentlessly attacked for being soft on Communism and Communists.[14] Richard Nixon in 1968 labeled his Democratic opponent George McGovern with three A's: "amnesty, abortion and acid."[15]

Bill Clinton faced numerous cheap shots and insults for his lack of military service during the Vietnam War (as George W. Bush experienced later on). Clinton's opponents in 1992 and 1996 were seasoned war veterans, and this certainly gave them obvious advantage. Clinton's long and complicated story of why he was avoiding the military draft emboldened his opponents in calling him a "felon." "Draft dodger" was probably the most common insult. Clinton's murky explanations about his real and alleged sexual relationships, his draft avoidance, and his use of marijuana (he admitted smoking pot while he was in Europe, but added an infamous caveat: "I did not inhale") again made him an easy target of name-calling. "Slick Willy" is among the most memorable. Former President Ford echoed a widespread sentiment among Clinton's ardent critics by calling him a "pathological liar."[16]

The education, age, origin, and wealth of a candidate are common targets of cheap shots as well. Biographers of Lyndon Johnson admit that he, as vice president, produced many cheap shots directed at President Kennedy because of his youth, apparent naiveté, and inexperience. (There was no love lost between these two men.)[17] Wealthy candidates are commonly scorned for their financial success and affluence. The Democratic Party's 2004 presidential hopeful, Senator John Kerry, had a difficult campaign against the incumbent president, George W. Bush. As a multimillionaire, Kerry was relentlessly painted as being "out of touch" with ordinary people and being a "limousine liberal."[18] Mitt Romney, another wealthy candidate, in 2012 faced similar types of attacks.

Candidates' specific decisions and actions quickly become targets of cheap shots. In 2004, Senator Kerry's attempts to explain why his voting pattern in the Senate was inconsistent resulted in the label "flip-flopper," which began to circulate on the web.[19] Similar cheap shots followed. A television advertisement showed Kerry windsurfing in the ocean. The narrator says that Kerry had voted "for" the war in Iraq before voting "against," then "for," now "against." The narrator then points out that Kerry voted similarly in relation to Medicare, defense, and education. "In each case the surfboard turns a new direction." The portrayal is perfect as the narrator ends with the line, "John Kerry: whichever way the wind blows." Cheap shots against George W. Bush during the 2000 and 2004 presidential elections were particularly plentiful and relentless. Bush was repeatedly called a drunk and an alcoholic. (He had had a drinking problem in the past, but had been sober for years.) One of the most vivid phrases against his candidacy for the second term was "Bush lied, people died." It referred to the allegedly falsified intelligence information that led to the Iraq War. Bush's occasional difficulties with grammar resulted in numerous cheap shots alleging his "stupidity" and "illiteracy." A 2004 interned ad read: "Voting for Bush is like running in the Special Olympics. Even if you win, you're still retarded." U.S. organizations running the Special Olympics protested, but the ad went viral on the web. "George Bush is retarded" gets 84,100 hits in a Google search. It is interesting that the phrase "Barack Obama is retarded" gets 2,360,000 hits. It looks like this word has become a common form of unspecified insult, comparable to "fool" or "idiot." Accusations of Bush being a "draft dodger"[20] and a "chicken hawk"[21] remained common cheap shots directed at him during his presidency.

Hillary Clinton as a presidential candidate in 2008 faced a barrage of cheap shots and insults. Her age (she was born in 1947) was a common theme in caricatures and photoshopped pictures portraying her as an old, tired woman. From the very beginning of her presidential run, rumors circulated that Hillary was a lesbian, which is a common personal insult against assertive, powerful, and successful women.[22] Her alleged sexual partners included some Russians,[23] her top aide (Huma Abedin),[24] and a few unidentified others.

Barack Obama was a target of name-calling when he was a candidate and president. His family was not spared either. His mother was called a "hippie." His father was berated as a Marxist (in fact, he was). Obama appeared as a "Communist," a "Socialist," or a "leftist." Caricatures and profiles of Marx, Engels, Lenin, Stalin, Mao, and Obama together were commonplace. Captions such as "spreading wealth since 1917"[25] pointed at him as a Socialist (and referred to the Russian Revolution of that year). There were pictures of Obama as a Soviet general in Red Square[26] and as a Soviet propagandist.[27]

The fact that Obama was regularly portrayed dressed in a Nazi uniform should not be surprising: this is a generic form of insult. (His predecessor Bush was customarily depicted this way.) Depictions appeared of Obama as an SS officer,[28] Obama associated with Hitler,[29] as a Brown Shirt,[30] as a Brown Shirt leader,[31] and as Hitler himself.[32] A 2013 Google search for Barack Obama gets 12,100,000 hits for "Barack Obama is a Fascist" and 1,250,000 hits for "Barack Obama is a Communist." Google hits for "Barack Obama is a terrorist" number 2,390,000. Obama was attacked in the conservative press for not wearing a U.S. flag lapel pin. Statements about him lying about his birthplace were common. (A president must have been born in the United States, and Obama, in fact, was born in Hawaii, which is a U.S. state). "Obama was born in Kenya" produces about 1.5 million hits through Google search.

Ridiculing

Ridiculing is a purposeful and contemptuous exaggeration or distortion in a comical context. The humorous nature of ridiculing helps attackers to portray their victims as weak, lightweight, dumb, unbalanced, irrational, or hypocritical so that they and their policies appear less meaningful or important than they actually are. Ridiculing is often sarcastic in tone. Personal looks, manners, and habits—all matter in such character attacks. President Andrew Jackson was derided in the press for acting like royalty and was depicted in political cartoons as being King Andrew I of Britain.[33] President Coolidge was infamously mocked for taking afternoon naps. Al Smith, a governor of New York and Democratic presidential candidate in 1928, was ridiculed as a person with an Irish background, his attackers remarking that the White House would smell like "corned beef, cabbage, and home brew."[34] President Ford was frequently mocked for his clumsiness after several accidental falls during his domestic and foreign public appearances.[35] Opponents eagerly turned to the remark of former president Johnson, who had allegedly mocked Ford by saying that "Jerry Ford is so dumb he can't fart and chew gum at the same time."[36] (Although the verb "fart" in most commentaries was naturally replaced with "think" as a form of self-censorship.) In the same vein, Johnson had also quipped, "Jerry Ford is a nice guy but he played too much football with his helmet off."[37] President Clinton in May of 1993 was mocked by almost every mainstream media outlet, and particularly by his opponents, for his $200 haircut, which he had received aboard *Air Force One* (the presidential aircraft) before taking off. At that time, coincidentally, Clinton himself was arguing against the government's wasteful spending.

When Senator Barack Obama entered the presidential race, he was frequently criticized for not appearing "presidential" enough. Ridiculing became relentless. A photo of Obama (accompanied by sarcastic remarks) wearing traditional Kenyan clothing went viral. His seemingly positive traits were turned inside out to ridicule him. His constant promises of change were ridiculed as "messianic"; his opponents called his a "messiah." A Google search related to the words "Obama + messiah" returns about 23 million references (in comparison, the "Clinton + messiah" combination yields only 2.5 million references, almost ten times fewer).

Incompetence is a favorite theme of ridiculing. George H. W. Bush in 1992 was relentlessly ridiculed as an ignorant politician who was out of touch with ordinary Americans after he had been visibly amazed by an electronic scanner in a supermarket.[38] The press immediately went after Bush's character: if this old president does not know how modern stores work, how could he possibly understand the larger issues in people's lives? Independent candidate H. Ross Perot regularly used this method of ridiculing against Bush.

Editorial cartoons and drawings are among the most common means of ridiculing. Dwight Eisenhower's apparent inaction during the rise of civil rights discord was a source of mockery, as editorials insinuated his indecisiveness. John Kennedy was portrayed as soft for his appeal to Democrats who opposed some policies of his administration, to the gain of the Republicans.[39] Richard Nixon was depicted as being paranoid and secretive, hiding like a hoarder in a pile of junk in his office, behind the flag,[40] and, later in his term, as a crook.[41] Reagan was mocked as an angry warmonger[42] and for being an empty shell attempting to project a strong image.[43] George H. W. Bush's denial of his knowledge about the secret deal between the U.S. and Iranian governments (the Iran-Contra scandal) was an easy source of mockery: he was portrayed as an ignorant fool.[44] For his adulterous affairs, Bill Clinton was constantly mocked in sexually suggestive caricatures.[45] Cartoons of a clueless George W. Bush having left the United States in disarray after his eight years of presidency were very common.[46] Barack Obama has been ridiculed for a range of missteps. For instance, he was frequently depicted in cartoons as Pinocchio—a powerful symbol attached to liars—for his infamous statement "If you like your doctor, you can keep your doctor," the promise he could not deliver in the early process of implementation of his health reform.[47] His indecisiveness in foreign policy, especially in dealing with the Syrian genocide, was emphasized in cartoons picturing him as an indecisive, immature person. One amateur cartoon that went viral on the web portrayed him as a prissy girl, with whom other kids (Iran, Russia, and China) do not want to play.

On the whole, cheap shots against Republicans tend to paint them as "rich," "elites," and "caring for the wealthy," who survive off the back of the power classes.[48] Hypocrisy and elitism are commonly attached to liberals as well, who are often portrayed as "limousine liberals."[49] In one cartoon, presidential candidate Kerry is saying, while leaning on his huge luxury car, "Bush is extreme. I am mainstream." Democrats are routinely painted as tree-hugging hippies; whereas Republicans are likely to appear as pro-big-business warmongers. In both cases, the goal of this type of ridiculing is to create a perception that the opponent is an elitist, a radical, an extremist, and a zealot. Bottom line, the opponent is out of touch with the American people.

Falsifications

Falsifications are lies, which by the time they are spread are often difficult to distinguish from facts. Unfounded rumors were circulating in 1987 about presidential candidate Michael Dukakis's alleged serious mental health problems.[50] When Hillary Clinton was the first lady in the 1990s, rumors circulated about her promiscuous behavior and lethal actions: she was rumored to have a male lover, Vincent Foster, who had been a White House counsel and who—also allegedly—had been murdered on her orders.[51] Falsifications are usually planned and tend to be more sophisticated than cheap shots. Falsifications are lies. Yet because they are often hard to immediately distinguish from facts, character assassins use them as a powerful means to associate the victim's character with certain alleged immoral or inappropriate acts.

Let us return to the opening of this chapter and the two falsification cases against Presidents Washington and Bush. The falsified letters appeared in 1776. Washington re-experienced the painful impact of falsifications in 1795, when he was serving his second terms as president. While attempting improvements in the relations with Great Britain, he met fierce domestic opposition. His political opponents, for a host of reasons, hoped to prevent a new treaty between the two countries. Some of them turned to character attacks, using newspapers and pamphlets in which they were calling Washington arrogant, self-loving, aloof, and selfish. His character was labeled as "fraudulent." Then, the bogus letters from the Revolutionary War were republished. Although some informed individuals knew the letters were fakes, many others did not. Washington again was openly called a British sympathizer, which was a nasty accusation against any politician at that time. The president tried to ignore this slanderous assault, as he had done 20 years earlier. This time he could not. Historians admit that as a victim of character attack, he felt increasingly helpless, angry, and embittered.[52] In the case involving George Bush, even though the letters accusing him of inappropriate behavior were quickly recognized as fakes, Bush's opponents remained relentless in their criticisms of the president: they argued that, although the letters could be forged, there must have been some other documents showing Bush's indecency and cowardliness. The old proverb, "Where there's smoke, there's fire" illustrates why some forms of character attacks are effective.

Attackers often use falsifications about presidents or candidates having inappropriate ties with certain "undesirable" political groups or countries. For example, in the past, an alleged association with Communists could have ruined a person's professional career. In 1944, supporters of presidential candidate Thomas Dewey attempted to associate their opponent, Vice President Harry Truman, with Sidney Hillman, a labor leader and an alleged agent of the Communist Party.[53] By making such accusations, Dewey's supporters hoped to provoke popular dismay and to incite voters' disappointment with Vice President Truman and his party.

Astrology has almost no connection to Communism, yet a president's supposed association with this pseudoscience may affect his reputation. President Ronald Reagan's wife, Nancy, had a strong interest in astrology. This passion had such a sturdy grip on her that she allegedly insisted that her husband did not give important speeches or make key decisions on dates when the stars did not "align."[54] Fortunately for Reagan, these allegations came out only in 1988, after he'd left the White House. Reagan's critics expectedly used this information to attack him for being shallow and absentminded.

Billionaire candidate Ross Perot made serious accusations during his race against George H. W. Bush and Bill Clinton in 1992. Among Perot's assertions was that Bush was in fact such a morally corrupt man that he had commissioned CIA operatives to tap Perot's computers and to disrupt Perot's daughter's wedding. These accusations did not have evidence to support them, but they drew great media attention. Other accusations were more serious. George H. W. Bush and his son, George W. Bush, as presidents were scorned for their close ties with the Saudi royal family and for personally profiting from these ties. Accusations were made, countless cheap shots were fired, and dozens of articles were written on this subject. Both presidents were accused of being dishonest and greedy sellouts.[55] The journal *Salon* asked, "Did the Saudis buy a President?"[56] Accusations linking the bin Laden family with the Bush family have been a continuing source of accusatory fodder.[57] A Google image search for "George Bush bin Laden" returns numerous depictions of both of them as friends and partners.

Falsifications refer to big as well as small issues. Franklin D. Roosevelt, for instance, was relentlessly attacked for the alleged inappropriate use of the United States' Navy for personal business. In 1944, his political opponents claimed that he had left his dog, Fala, on some remote island in the Pacific and then ordered a big navy vessel to retrieve his beloved pet. Similar accusations haunted president Obama: most common were statements about his dog flying solo and separately from the president's family.[58]

Why are many falsifications and outrageous accusations not rejected by the public outright? Why do character attacks that use lies become effective? The context in which the attacks take place should help in addressing these questions. When one candidate's resume appears superior to that of his or her opponent's, then the attackers feel emboldened to attack the weaker opponent. To illustrate, bashing George W. Bush's unimpressive military record and attacking his competency as a commander-in-chief was somewhat easy when he ran against John Kerry in 2004. John Kerry had been in active duty during the Vietnam War, while Bush had not. Falsifications may implant doubts about the victim of attacks ("Is he the right person?") and strengthen the attacker's own base ("That's a good person compared to the opponent."). An effective defense against falsifications tends to be difficult. For example, complete silence about outrageous allegations may be perceived as an attempt to hide facts. An emotional rejection of the falsification may be perceived as a person's overreaction and a weakness.

Direct Character Attacks

This type of attack involves strong accusations about a person's character flaws. Direct attacks may overlap with falsifications. Yet they tend to be different from falsifications because the latter are lies and the former are based on facts or apparently reliable evidence. Direct character attacks typically exaggerate this evidence to harm a victim as much as possible. Such attacks tend to be planned and coordinated. The defenders have to find a right balance in their responses: to deny some of the attackers' damaging information is no longer possible because it is factual; yet to unconditionally defend the victim of the character assassination may not be effective or appropriate. To exemplify, we have chosen just several common topics of attacks.

Religious Identity

The religious identity of any presidential candidate is an established fact. Attackers therefore link their victim's religious identity to certain alleged character features or behaviors that the public may find inappropriate. In 1908, some Evangelical Protestants openly yet falsely accused presidential candidate William Taft in the press, calling him a Catholic and an infidel. (He attended All Souls Church, which is Unitarian, not Catholic.) In 1928, presidential candidate Al Smith was attacked as a Catholic, which was a huge liability at that time. He was portrayed as a dutiful puppet of the Catholic Church, who would obey the pope if he was elected. During the 1960 presidential campaign, John Kennedy's opponents did not wait long and routinely warned the public that if Kennedy were elected, then he, as a Catholic, would take direct orders from the pope in Rome.[59]

Similar doubts and attacks appeared when Senator Joseph Lieberman—an Orthodox Jew—won the vice presidential nomination for the Democratic Party in August 2000. Critics raised concerns about whether the senator, if elected, would put the interests of his religion and the state of Israel before the interests of the American people. Mitt Romney was a Mormon, and his identity was used in attacks as well. The attacks were frequent and typically involved polygamy (practiced by Mormons in the past), their conservatism, and even their long underwear.[60] The Huffington Post ran an article asking, "Did anti-Mormonism cost Mitt Romney the 2012 election?" It showed that a small proportion of people considered his religious affiliation a negative factor for his candidacy.[61]

Attacks against President Obama's religious identity were perhaps among the fiercest. His father was a Kenyan agnostic (or atheist) with Muslim family roots.[62] The fact that Barack and Hussein are common Muslim names helped to spur many of the attacks against Obama, as one could point to his names as undeniable evidence of what his origin was. Despite Obama's statements about his Christian faith, accusations were persistent that that he was no Christian. In Google searches, "Barack Obama is Christian" appears in

600,000 hits. "Barak Obama is Muslim" reveals 400,000 hits. A Google image search of the words "Barack Obama" and "Muslim" leads to hundreds of depictions of Obama in traditional Islamic garb, appearing as an imam,[63] hanging out with Bin Laden,[64] and similar depictions. One of the most frequently reposted photos has Obama, wearing Arab-Muslim dress, with a beard, an Obama campaign pin, and the White House in the background. The caption reads, "So America you want change? . . . Just wait."[65]

Sexual Misconduct

The intimate lives of politicians are a common theme of character attacks. We have seen several examples earlier in this book. Sexual misconduct, real or alleged, has been a convenient threat playing a major part in character assassination. James Callender, whose name has already appeared in this chapter, successfully produced a number of attacks against Alexander Hamilton, including a pamphlet of letters revealing that Hamilton had been engaged in an extramarital affair with Maria Reynolds. Moreover, it became known that Hamilton had been paying hush money to Maria's husband, James, to keep the relationship secret. The purpose of this pamphlet served no public benefit other than the defamation of Hamilton's character, which, Callender hoped, would help advance his political objectives. Accurate to Callender's hopes, following this series of attacks, Hamilton's political career waned. Callender, after spoiling his relationship with Jefferson, launched rumors that the president had had an affair with a slave named Sally Hemmings. Jefferson denied the rumors. Today we know that there was perhaps some evidence in support of that accusation.[66]

When President Kennedy was alive, his powerful family vigorously protected his reputation, and only few potentially disturbing facts about his sexual life have leaked in the form of rumors. Moreover, following his death in 1963, it was unpopular for some time to speak poorly of the slain president. Some detailed allegations of Kennedy's affairs came up in the 1970s, including claims by Judith C. Exner, published in her book.[67] Endless rumors about Kennedy's relationship with actress Marilyn Monroe abound. Multiple sources continuously put forward various assumptions and some alleged eyewitness accounts for several decades, such as a book by Mimi Alford, a White House intern working for Kennedy. The "womanizer" label has been permanently attached to the former president.

Senator Gary Hart was a strong and popular contender for the Democratic Party's 1988 presidential nomination. His bid for the White House went awry when rumors began to circulate that Hart, a married man, was having an affair. Hart confronted the rumors in a press conference challenging the reporters.[68] The same day that the dare ran in the newspapers, a story broke of Donna Rice visiting the senator's home late at night. Though Hart at first denied any relationship with Rice, a photograph surfaced showing both of them on a yacht. (For a bit of irony: the yacht was named "Monkey Business.")

Hart's political ambitions were forever dashed. A womanizer and liar were not the features that the future president was willing to associate with his character. When searching "Gary Hart" and "Donna Rice" together 25 years later, 34,300 Google hits appear.

Bill Clinton was under constant attack after he entered the national political scene. Rumors about Clinton's multiple affairs with women appeared during his 1992 race for the White House. Names were popping up, including Kathleen Wiley, Judy Gibbs, and Sally Perdue.[69] During an investigation of his relationship with Paula Jones, the name of Monica Lewinsky came to the forefront, and her affair with the president was exposed. Clinton was relentlessly attacked as a "womanizer."[70] Even in his postpresidency, most character attacks are associated with his sexual behavior.[71] The most serious attacks called him a "sex offender."[72] A 2013 Google search revealed 46,900 hits for "Bill Clinton is a womanizer." To compare, there were zero hits for "George Bush is a womanizer."

Deceitful Behavior

Woodrow Wilson won reelection using the slogan (referring to himself) "He kept us out of the War." Despite this popular isolationist view, it did not hold up for long. Wilson eventually decided to engage the United States in the war that he had promised to avoid. This led to attacks on his character, in which his opponents portrayed him as a liar.[73] Richard Nixon's career in politics was always tainted with two types of attacks directly referring to his character. The first was the claim that he was paranoid (that is, pathological suspiciousness of other people). The other was the claim that Nixon was a pathological liar. These attacks were especially massive during the Watergate crisis in the early 1970s, when he and his close associates attempted to cover up the details of an unfolding scandal involving the Republican Party operatives. The facts of the cover-up and the president's involvement in it have appeared in the press—which from the beginning was very unsympathetic toward Nixon— and Nixon was directly accused of being a liar. Under the pressure of new facts and relentless attacks against him, Nixon lost the support of his party and became the only president in American history to resign from office. The charges that Nixon was extremely suspicious of people, and even paranoid, appeared after his resignation in several political biographies.[74] Nixon earned the nickname "Tricky Dick," and Bill Clinton, "Slick Willy," due to his perceived lack of honesty and ability to get in and out of political scandals.

During the 2004 presidential election, President Bush's opponent, Senator Kerry, suffered one of the most prominent concerted character attacks of recent time. Despite the fact that Bush had a less than valorous record from the Vietnam War era, and John Kerry had served in combat (and was awarded three Purple Hearts), the anti-Kerry organization Swift Boat Veterans for Truth was extremely active and effective in defaming Kerry's military service. In the televised attack ads, Kerry's service was mocked as a mere political stunt. His criticisms of the U.S. war in Vietnam were especially emphasized. The attacks against Kerry were so successful that the term "swiftboating" came into modern American vocabulary. It means "conducting an unfair or untrue political attack."

Mental Capacity

Ridiculing another person's mental capacity and psychological health can be particularly damaging to that person's reputation because the victim appears incapable of rational thinking and coherent behavior. For years, the status of the mental health of presidents and presidential candidates was unknown to the public and the press. The fact that President Woodrow Wilson had apparently suffered multiple strokes that left him mentally handicapped at the end of his term in 1919 was essentially hidden from the public.[75] After the 1960s, private information about the personal life of presidents and presidential candidates became increasingly public.

Richard Nixon's mental state was a common target of attacks. His personality was frequently associated with labels such as "paranoia," "paranoid schizophrenic," and "paranoid personality." (At least 29 books related to his presidency mention accusations about Nixon having some pathological mental traits.) In fact, Nixon faced these allegations even earlier when he served as senator and vice president. These attacks often annoyed Nixon. He blamed the media for these accusations, which he considered absurd.[76]

One of the most remembered cases involved Senator Thomas Eagleton, who was vice presidential candidate in 1972. From the start of the campaign, rumors appeared that he had some sort of a "medical history." Eagleton publicly announced that, in the previous decade, he had sought, on three separate occasions, mental health assistance for his depression. Almost immediately, his party's support evaporated. Top Democratic advisers believed that the average voter would see Eagleton's psychological problems as a serious character deficiency. Within a few days, Eagleton was forced to withdraw his candidacy.[77]

Mental health was used in attacks during Reagan's presidency. Not only did Reagan's opponents openly mention his advanced age, they also discussed whether his physical decline negatively affected his mental abilities. Reagan was frequently referred to as an "unintelligent actor," an "ignorant cowboy," and an "absentminded old man." During a 1984 presidential debate, Reagan, who was 74 and running against a 52-year-old Walter Mondale, was already prepared for defending his age against attacks. When asked whether he thought, perhaps, his old age could be a problem for him as president, Reagan responded, "I want you to know that also I will not make age an issue of this campaign. I am not going to exploit, for political purposes, my opponent's youth and inexperience."[78] After Reagan left the office in 1989, multiple sources discussed whether he had already had Alzheimer's while in the White House. (At least six books related to his political career highlight this serious illness affecting memory and many other cognitive functions.)

George W. Bush was called a "drug addict" for his well-known problems with alcohol in the past.[79] In 2004, a popular online essay analyzed his actions and declared that Bush had Narcissistic Personality Disorder.[80] Research articles focused on his IQ (intelligence quotient) to launch attacks on his mental capabilities. Although the direct measurement of any president's IQ is impossible, various indirect assessments of the quotient abounded. Although Bush's assumed IQ was higher than the average, this did not prevent the attackers from labeling him as having the lowest IQ of all presidents since the 1950s.[81] Though George W. Bush had not been a stellar student during college, he had completed his undergraduate degree at Yale and his master's in business administration at Harvard. When entering Yale, his SAT scores were 1,206 (out of 1,600).[82] Attacks against Bush also claimed that Kerry was intellectually more capable than the president. In fact, Bush's GPA at Yale was slightly better (a high C) than Kerry's, who had graduated from the same school two years earlier.[83] This did not matter. Senator Kerry quipped in 2004, referring to Bush, "I cannot believe that I am losing to this idiot."[84] Other attackers were more blatant. One book author repeatedly addressed Bush as the most psychologically damaged president since Nixon.[85] Another book referred to Bush's mental state as "a madness" (an old term for a range of severe psychological problems) and suggested a new diagnosis for Bush, that is "*malignant egophrenia,*" or a psychospiritual disease of the soul.[86]

What Was the Logic behind the Attacks?

With a few exceptions, character attacks are generally driven by the zero-sum logic of politics: to win, you have to defeat your opponent. The attackers strike on behalf of political parties or special interests and simultaneously target two opposite groups of people. One group, the supporters of the victim of an attack, are expected to be discouraged and weakened. A successful attack should damage the reputation of a person (such as a president or a presidential candidate) by distracting, annoying, and angering him or her. This should damage public support for the victim. It should also take the victim's time, energy, and resources to respond, to decide about whether or not to launch a response, and if doing so, which response should be given, when, and how. The attackers, or those acting on their behalf, are supposed to be encouraged by the negative impact of a character attack on the victim, who is their opponent.

A successful character attack should negatively affect not only the victims, but also their close associates and supporters. They too could be distracted, frustrated, and even confused, for at least some time. They may have to mobilize additional financial resources and consult with their associates about an effective response to the attacks. Others may respond quickly yet inappropriately, thus creating more problems for the victim of the attack. Attacks may increase a candidate's public visibility and bring backing from interest groups or political donors. Relatively unknown or so-called independent candidates (in the United States, those who typically do not belong to the Democratic or Republican Parties) commonly launch character attacks against their powerful opponents simply to get noticed. In 1992, a little known independent candidate, Ross Perot, attacked incumbent president George H. W. Bush's character, emphasizing Bush's profound incompetence. Perot's weakening of Bush strengthened candidate Clinton, who became president.

The attackers may also target a larger base of the victims' supporters and those who may vote for them in the future. As was mentioned in Shiraev's chapter on the psychology of character attacks, a sliver of doubt in an unsure supporter or an undecided voter, caused by a character attack, may affect these individuals' voting preferences and intentions. Even the smallest decline of public support for a candidate can be judged as a significant success of a character attack. Five days before the 2000 presidential elections, George W. Bush's opponents leaked rumors about his 1976 arrest for driving under the influence of alcohol. Although we do not know if these damaging facts directly affected voters' intentions, Gallup polls showed a clear tightening of the race between Bush and Gore.[87] Gore supporters, whose candidate was behind in most polls, immediately began to claim that the race had reached a turning point. The media, especially the three biggest television networks that were largely sympathetic toward Gore, quickly focused on the apparent tightening of the race. We can only speculate how this news might have affected the 2000 presidential elections, the tightest in U.S. history. But we know that personal attacks are probably most effective when they are intended to influence the least informed and unaffiliated citizens and voters. If a person has a strong political affiliation or knows where the candidates stand on important issues, a character attack—no matter whether it be slander or name-calling—is unlikely to change this person's opinion. In contrast, an uninformed voter is more susceptible to character attacks against his or her chosen political candidate.

Attackers also expect that, in case of a successful strike against an opponent, they can strengthen their own candidate's position simply because of the falling support of their rival. Attacks may also help in consolidating the political base and can attract new support as soon as a character attack is underway (as has already been discussed in this book). But an attack may misfire and thus harm the attacker and his or her political team. In the 2008 race, presidential candidate John McCain openly criticized one of his supporters, who had referred to their opponent, candidate Obama, as "Barack Hussein Obama" (thus emphasizing his Muslim middle name and probably assuming that most Americans had only heard the name "Hussein" in the context of "Saddam Hussein").[88] The McCain campaign felt that by pointing at Obama's middle name, they would push away some independent voters who might become upset by this persistent reference to Obama's origin. The McCain campaign therefore did not use Obama's middle name in its political advertisements.

There is an old American political adage that "mudslinging is as American as Mississippi mud." It seems that the experiences of the past two and a half centuries of American political campaigns support that assertion. The Internet has only generated new opportunities for character attacks. Today, a political cartoon, a piece of gossip, any dirt about a candidate or a contender can be disseminated in seconds and spread globally. Any slander can be easily designed and then posted with a few strikes on the keyboard. An uninformed person remains a desired prize for an attacker.

Notes

1. See Ford and Randolph 2012, for details.
2. See Lengel 2011, for details.
3. See Kurtz 2004.
4. Online image at http://bit.ly/18J33lP.
5. See Remer 2010.
6. See Monticello 2013.
7. See Swint 2008.
8. Ibid.
9. See Miller Center, 2013.
10. Guelzo 1999, 247.
11. See History Channel 2013.
12. Petersen 1949, 21.
13. See Benson 1999.
14. Mitchell 1998, 40–42.
15. Novak 2008, 225.
16. See in DeFrank 2007.
17. Caro 2012, 85, 95–96.
18. See Luskin 2004.
19. Online video at http://www.youtube.com/watch?v=pbdzMLk9wHQ.
20. See Moore 2003.
21. See Liberals Like Christ 2008.
22. Shiraev and Hooper discussed this issue at the First Colloquium on Character Attacks and Defamation, Heidelberg, Germany.
23. See Newsguy 2012.
24. See Political Night Train 2007.
25. Online image at http://bit.ly/18qc6tW.
26. See Sodahead 2013.
27. See Shorttimer 2012.
28. See Thehappydare 2013.
29. See Nowtheendbegins 2013.
30. Online image at http://toddkinsey.com/blog/wp-content/uploads/2012/03/Obama_Communist_Red.jpg
31. Online image at http://eurokulture.missouri.edu/wp-content/uploads/2012/09/obama-nazi.jpg
32. Online image at http://bit.ly/1iVpIiH
33. See James 2010.
34. Cumins 2007, 181.
35. See in Iaspace 2008.
36. *The Guardian* 2006.
37. Reeves 1975, 40.

38. Rosenthal 1992.
39. Online image at http://www.loc.gov/rr/print/swann/herblock/images/s03474u.jpg
40. Online image at http://www.loc.gov/rr/print/swann/herblock/images/s03469u.jpg
41. Online image at http://www.loc.gov/rr/print/swann/herblock/images/s03536u.jpg
42. See Darnovsky 1982.
43. Online image at http://www.loc.gov/rr/print/swann/herblock/images/s03284u.jpg
44. Online image at http://www.loc.gov/rr/print/swann/herblock/images/s03459u.jpg
45. Online image at http://www.loc.gov/rr/print/swann/herblock/images/s03502u.jpg
46. Wasserman 2008.
47. Online image at http://bit.ly/18J9Rjm
48. See Sack 2013.
49. See Luskin 2004.
50. See PBS 2008.
51. See Smith 2008.
52. Lengel 2011.
53. Fraser 1993.
54. Reagan Chief of Staff, Don Regan, stated, "Virtually every major move and decision the Reagans made during my time as White House Chief of Staff was cleared in advance with a woman in San Francisco who drew up horoscopes to make certain that the planets were in a favorable alignment for the enterprise." See Walder 1998.
55. Online image at http://www.michaelmoore.com/books-films/fahrenheit-911
56. See Unger 2004.
57. Global Research 2013.
58. See Gizzi 2013.
59. Dudley and Shiraev 2008, 89.
60. See *The Sun* 2012.
61. See in Knoll 2013.
62. See in Snopes.com 2008.
63. Online image at http://itmakessenseblog.com/files/2012/07/obama-muslim11.jpeg
64. Online image at http://goatmilk.files.wordpress.com/2008/10/barack_obama_muslim.jpg
65. Online image at http://www.exposebarackobama.com/image/muslim.jpg
66. See Monticello 2013.
67. Exner 1978.
68. See in *New York Times* Editorial Board 1987.
69. See Smith 1998.
70. Online image at http://on.fb.me/1dCrt4v
71. Online image at http://strandedalien.files.wordpress.com/2012/04/bill-clinton-prostitutes.jpg
72. Online image at http://politicalhumor.about.com/library/blclintonsexoffender.htm
73. See in Scher 2013.
74. Reeves 2002.
75. Berg 2013.
76. Online video at http://www.youtube.com/watch?v=_RMSb-tS_OM
77. See in NPR 2012.
78. See in Reagan Foundation 2013.
79. See Green 2013.
80. See Minot 2007.
81. Simonton 2006, 511.
82. Online image at http://www.iuptown.com/YaleProtest/bushs_yale_transcript.htm

83. See Bendetto 2005.
84. Ibid.
85. Frank 2007.
86. Levy 2006.
87. See Moore 2000.
88. See Parker 2008.

Bibliography

Bendetto, R. 2005. "Who Is Smarter, Kerry, or Bush?" *USA Today*. http://usatoday30. usatoday.com/news/opinion/columnist/benedetto/2005-06-10-benedetto_x.htm (accessed November 26, 2013).

Benson, A. 1999. "Abraham Lincoln—An American Robespierre." *The Copperhead Chronicle*. http://www.csa-dixie.com/copperheadchronicle/article12.htm (accessed November 26, 2013).

Berg, A. S. 2013. *Wilson*. New York: Penguin.

Cummins, J. 2007. *Dirty Tricks, Cheap Shots, and October Surprises in US Presidential Campaigns*. Philadelphia: Quirk Books.

Darnovsky, M. 1982. "Let's Fake a Deal! A History of Arms Control." FoundSF. http://bit.ly/1b5SJAw (accessed November 26, 2013).

DeFrank, T. 2007. *Write It When I Am Gone*. New York: Putnam Adult.

Dragoo, P. 2012. "Twelfth Imam." It Makes Sense Blog (online image). http://itmakes-senseblog.com/files/2012/07/obama-muslim11.jpeg (accessed November 26, 2013).

Dudley, R., and E. Shiraev. 2008. *Counting Every Vote: The Most Contentious Elections in American History*. Washington DC: Potomac Books.

Exner, J. 1978. *My Story as Told to Ovil Demaris*. New York: Grove Press.

Ford, W. C., J. Randolph, and J. Vadrill. 2012. *The Spurious Letters Attributed to Washington*. New York: Ulan Press.

Frank, J. 2007. *Bush on the Couch: Inside the Mind of the President*, rev. ed. New York: Harper.

Fraser, S. 1993. *Labor Will Rule: Sidney Hillman and the Rise of American Labor*. Ithaca, NY: Cornell University Press.

Giglio, J. 2001. *Truman in Cartoon and Caricature*. Kirksville, MO: Truman State University Press.

Gizzi, J. 2013. "Obama's Dog Flight Reminiscent of FDR's Fala Saga." *News Max*. http://www.newsmax.com/John-Gizzi/obama-dog-flight-bo/2013/08/12/id/520007 (accessed November 26, 2013).

Global Research. 2013. "George W. Bush and Bin Laden Family, Meeting at Ritz Carlton Hotel, NYC, One Day before 9/11." http://bit.ly/ItNP9B (accessed April 28, 2013).

Green, R. 2013. "George Bush's Drug Addictions." *Canadian Mind Products*. http://mindprod.com/politics/bush911drugs.html (accessed November 26, 2013).

Guelzo, A. 1999. *Abraham Lincoln: Redeemer President*. Grand Rapids, MI: Eermands.

History Channel. "Union General McClellan Snubs President Lincoln." http://www.history.com/this-day-in-history/mcclellan-snubs-lincoln (accessed November 26, 2013).

Lengel, E., 2011. "Inventing George Washington." http://www.nytimes.com/2011/03/21/books/inventing-george-washington.html?pagewanted=all&_r=0 (accessed April 9, 2014)

Iaspace. 2008. "Gerald 'Jerry' Ford." https://iaspace.pbworks.com/w/page/10288238/B4%20Gerald%20Ford (accessed November 26, 2013).

James, F. 2010. "Obama Gets 'Royal' Treatment from Opponents." NPR. http://www.npr.org/blogs/itsallpolitics/2010/11/22/131511740/obama-gets-royal-treatment-from-opponents (accessed November 26, 2013).

Knoll, B. 2013. "Did Anti-Mormonism Cost Romney the 2012 Elections?" Huffington Post. http://www.huffingtonpost.com/benjamin-knoll/mitt-romney-mormon_b_4121217.html (accessed November 26, 2013).

Kurtz, H. 2004. "Dan Rather to Step Down at CBS." *Washington Post.* http://www.washingtonpost.com/wp-dyn/articles/A7313-2004Nov23.html (accessed November 26, 2013).

Lengel, E. 2011. "Inventing George Washington." *The New York Times.* http://nyti.ms/ItOQ1v (accessed March 21, 2013).

Liberals Like Christ. 2008. "Why Are Republican Leaders Almost All 'Chickenhawks'?" http://liberalslikechrist.org/about/chickenhawks.html (accessed November 26, 2013).

Luskin, D. 2004. "Life of the Limousine Liberals: What Is John Kerry's Wife (Teresa Heinz Kerry) Hiding?" *Capitalism Magazine.* http://bit.ly/IASA1s (accessed November 26, 2013).

Miller Center. 2013. "American President: A Reference Resource." http://millercenter.org/president/jefferson/essays/biography/3 (accessed November 26, 2013).

Minot, P. 2007. "A Psychiatrist's Perspective on George Bush—Yes, He Is Sick." *DLM Web.* http://www.dlmweb.com/news98.html (accessed November 26, 2013).

Mitchell, F. 1998. *Harry S. Truman and the News Media: Contentious Relations, Belated Respect.* Columbia: University of Missouri Press.

Monticello. "James Callender." http://www.monticello.org/site/research-and-collections/james-callender (accessed November 26, 2013).

Monticello. 2013. "Thomas Jefferson and Sally Hemings: A Brief Account." http://www.monticello.org/site/plantation-and-slavery/thomas-jefferson-and-sally-hemings-brief-account (accessed November 26, 2013).

Moore, D. 2000. "Major Turning Points in 2000 Election: Primary Season, Party Conventions, and Debates." *Gallup News* http://bit.ly/1esBuxp (accessed November 26, 2013).

Moore, J. 2003. "Presidential Draft Dodger George W. Bush." *Buzzflash.* http://www.buzzflash.com/contributors/03/06/05_moore.html (accessed November 26, 2013).

Moore, M. 2004. *Fahrenheit 9/11* (online image). http://www.michaelmoore.com/books-films/fahrenheit-911 (accessed November 26, 2013).

New York Times Editorial Board. 1987. "Gary Hart's Judgment." http://www.nytimes.com/1987/05/05/opinion/gary-hart-s-judgment.html (accessed November 26, 2013).

Newsguy. 2012. "Were Russians about to Catch Hillary in Lesbian Honey Trap?" *The Right Perspective.* http://www.therightperspective.org/2012/04/03/were-russians-about-to-catch-hillary-in-lesbian-honey-trap/#sthash.Xm8QHG3Y.dpbs (accessed November 26, 2013).

Novak, R. 2008. *The Prince of Darkness: 50 Years Reporting in Washington.* New York: Random House.

Nowtheendbegins. 2013. "13 Similarities between Obama and Hitler." http://www.nowtheendbegins.com/pages/obama/obama-and-hitler-similarities.htm (accessed November 26, 2013).

NPR. 2012. "The Thomas Eagleton Affair Haunts Candidates Today." http://www.npr.org/2012/08/04/157670201/the-thomas-eagleton-affair-haunts-candidates-today (accessed November 26, 2013).

Online image. http://on.fb.me/1dCrt4v (accessed April 9, 2014)

Online image. http://politicalhumor.about.com/library/blclintonsexoffender.htm (accessed April 9, 2014)

Online image. http://www.loc.gov/rr/print/swann/herblock/images/s03469u.jpg (accessed November 26, 2013)

Online image. http://bit.ly/1dCtdKU (accessed April 9, 2014)

Online image. http://bit.ly/IlgDRQ (accessed April 9, 2014)

Online image http://bit.ly/18J9Rjm (accessed November 26, 2013)

Online image. http://cnn.it/196YwWQ (accessed April 9, 2014)

Online image. http://eurokulture.missouri.edu/wp-content/uploads/2012/09/obama-nazi.jpg (accessed April 9, 2014)

Online image. http://pegitboard.com/pin/36947d6dcbccc03ad591deab138dbb0c (accessed April 9, 2014)

Online image. http://www.iuptown.com/YaleProtest/bushs_yale_transcript.htm (accessed April 9, 2014)

Online image. http://www.loc.gov/rr/print/swann/herblock/images/s03474u.jpg (accessed November 26, 2013)

Online image. http://www.loc.gov/rr/print/swann/herblock/images/s03536u.jpg (accessed November 26, 2013)

Online image. http://www.loc.gov/rr/print/swann/herblock/images/s03284u.jpg (accessed November 26, 2013)

Online image. http://www.loc.gov/rr/print/swann/herblock/images/s03459u.jpg (accessed November 26, 2013)

Online image. http://www.loc.gov/rr/print/swann/herblock/images/s03502u.jpg (accessed November 26, 2013)

Online image. http://bit.ly/18J33lP (accessed April 9, 2014)

Online video. http://www.youtube.com/watch?v=_RMSb-tS_OM (accessed April 9, 2014)

Online video. http://www.youtube.com/watch?v=pbdzMLk9wHQ (accessed April 9, 2014)

Parker, J. 2008. "McCain Apologizes Profusely for 'Hussein Obama.'" ABC News (blog). http://abcnews.go.com/blogs/politics/2008/02/mccain-apologiz/ (accessed November 26, 2013).

PBS. 2008 "Boogieman: The Lee Atwater Story." http://www.pbs.org/wgbh/pages/frontline/atwater/etc/script.html (accessed November 26, 2013).

Petersen, A. 1949. *Reviling of the Great.* New York: New York Labor News Corporation.

Political Night Train. 2007. "Do the Bloggers Have Hillary's Number? Lesbian Affair with Huma Abedin?" http://politicalnighttrain.wordpress.com/2007/11/25/do-the-bloggers-have-hillarys-number-lesbian-affair-with-huma-abedin/ (accessed November 26, 2013).

Reagan Foundation. 1980. "Debate between the President and Former Vice President Walter F. Mondale, Kansas City, Missouri." http://www.reaganfoundation.org/reagan-quotes-detail.aspx?tx=2238 (accessed November 26, 2013).

Reeves, R. 1975. "Why American Politicians Are So Bad: The Case History of Gerald Ford." *New York Magazine*, October 13, 40.

Reeves, R. 2002. *President Nixon: Alone in the White House.* New York: Simon & Schuster.

Remer, L. 2010. "'Going Negative' Is in the DNA of Our Democracy." *UT San Diego.* http://bit.ly/1gkkOtc (accessed November 26, 2013).

Rosenthal, A. 1992. "Bush Encounters the Supermarket, Amazed." *The New York Times.* http://www.nytimes.com/1992/02/05/us/bush-encounters-the-supermarket-amazed.html (accessed November 26, 2013).

Sack, S. 2013. "GOP Is the Party of the Rich." *Star Tribune*. http://thebestmusi-cyouhaveneverheard.files.wordpress.com/2013/02/republicans-and-the-rich.jpg (accessed November 26, 2013).

Scher, B. 2013. "On Syria, Obama Is More Like Woodrow Wilson Than George W. Bush." *The Week*. http://theweek.com/article/index/248805/on-syria-obama-is-more-like-woodrow-wilson-than-george-w-bush (accessed November 26, 2013).

Shiraev, E., and A. Hooper. July 22, 2011. "Character Attacks against Female Politicians in the United States." A presentation at the First Colloquium on Character Attacks and Defamation, Heidelberg, Germany.

Shorttimer. 2012. "Plus ca change, plus c'est la meme chose, Part IV." The Patriot Perspective. http://thepatriotperspective.wordpress.com/2012/03/10/plus-ca-change-plus-cest-la-meme-chose-part-iv/ (accessed November 26, 2013).

Simonton, D. 2006. "Presidential IQ Openness, Intellectual Brilliance, and Leadership: Estimates and Correlations for 42 U.S. Chief Executives." *Political Psychology* 27 (4): 511–26.

Smith S. 2008. "The Man Who Knew Too Much? The Truth about the Death of the Clintons' Close Friend Vince Foster." *Daily Mail*. http://www.dailymail.co.uk/news/article-508210/The-man-knew-The-truth-death-Hillary-Clintons-close-friend-Vince-Foster.html (accessed November 26, 2013).

Smith, S. 1998. "The Arkansas Connection." *Prorev*. http://prorev.com/connex.htm (accessed November 26, 2013).

Snopes.com. 2008. "Who Is Barack Obama?" *Snopes*. (http://www.snopes.com/politics/obama/muslim.asp (accessed November 26, 2013).

Stranded Alien. 2013. "Did Somebody Say Colombian Prostitutes?" Stranded Alien (online image). http://strandedalien.files.wordpress.com/2012/04/bill-clinton-prostitutes.jpg (accessed November 26, 2013).

Swint, K. 2008. "Founding Fathers' Dirty Campaign." CNN.com. http://cnn.it/196YwWQ (accessed November 26, 2013).

The Guardian. 2006. "Obituary: Gerald Ford." http://www.guardian.co.uk/world/2006/dec/27/guardianobituaries.usa (accessed November 26, 2013).

The Sun. 2012. "Mitt Romney's Pants." http://www.thesun.co.uk/sol/homepage/news/4631729/Mitt-Romneys-pants.html (accessed November 26, 2013).

Unger, C. 2004. "Did the Saudis Buy a President?" *Salon*. http://www.salon.com/2004/03/12/unger_2/ (accessed November 26, 2013).

Unknown. 2008. "Want Change? Just Wait." Expose Barack Obama (online image). http://www.exposebarackobama.com/image/muslim.jpg (accessed November 26, 2013).

Unknown. 2008. "Barack and bin Laden Friends." Goatmilk (online image). http://goatmilk.files.wordpress.com/2008/10/barack_obama_muslim.jpg (accessed November 26, 2013).

Wadler, J. 1988. "The President's Astrologers." *People Magazine*. http://www.people.com/people/archive/article/0,,20099022,00.html (accessed November 26, 2013).

Wasserman, G. 2008. "The Torch Is Passed." *Boston Globe* (online image). http://indiedesign.typepad.com/inspire_political_discour/obamafamily/ (accessed November 26, 2013).

12

The Gao-Rao Affair: A Case of Character Assassination in Chinese Politics in the 1950s

Eric Shiraev and Zi Yang

Introduction

Gao Gang, a senior figure in the Chinese Communist Party (CCP) and former head of the State Planning Commission of China, spent the evening of August 16, 1954, in a long conversation with his wife, Li Liqun, before she went to bed. This would be the last time she saw her husband alive. The next morning, Gao's daughter found him unmoving in his bed. He had already passed away from an overdose of sleeping pills. He was a few months shy of his fiftieth birthday. The funeral, four days later, was brief and without many wails from his close family members. The tombstone on his grave was devoid of an epitaph, except his birth name, Gao Chongde. He was one of the first members of the political elite to be eliminated in a major political purge initiated by the CCP. He had also fallen victim to an almost classical type of character assassination.

The history of the People's Republic of China (PRC) is closely interwoven with the history of the CCP. The party has been a political force inseparable from the People's Republic. Four generations of leadership came and went during several decades after the party's ascendance to power in 1949. Underneath the apparently calm transitions of power, the CCP was constantly in a state of inner competition and struggle among individuals and groups. The competition for power was fierce and often brutal. The losers gave up their official party post or, sometimes, their freedom and lives. To emerge victorious in these conflicts, one has to possess the "sharpest weapons," including the ability to influence the opinions and decisions of the party leaders. Character assassination was frequently chosen as such a weapon.

The Gao Gang–Rao Shushi affair, officially known as the "Gao Gang–Rao Shushi Incident" or "Gao Gang–Rao Shushi Anti-Party Alliance," was the first major purge within the CCP after the establishment of the People's Republic of China in 1949. The two main protagonists of this incident, Gao Gang and Rao Shushi, were at the time top leaders in the party hierarchy. The two men once had promising and successful careers. Their demise and fall were hard and painful.

This chapter is an attempt at understanding character assassinations in Chinese politics. It will illustrate several intricate mechanisms of character assassination used in political struggles within the CCP. We will first briefly discuss the historic background of this case, before proceeding to the analytical portion of the actual character assassination.

Gao Gang's Road to Power

Gao Gang was born Gao Chongde on October 25, 1905, to an impoverished peasant family in Mizhi county of Shaanxi province's northern region, known as Shaanbei. In 1926, while still a high school student, Gao was introduced to the CCP and joined soon after.[1] Following the orders of a local party cell, Gao spent the remainder of the 1920s in the countryside organizing the peasantry and disseminating revolutionary ideas within the ranks of local warlord troops.[2] After overcoming many battles against warlords, Gao, along with his close comrades-in-arms Liu Zhidan, Xie Zichang, and Xi Zhongxun established the Chinese Red Army's first stronghold in the Shaanbei region.

In 1935, Gao became Mao Ze-dong's close confidant. He also enjoyed great command among the Shaanbei Communists.[3] As a result, Gao was selected by Mao to succeed Liu Zhidan after the latter's death in February 1936. Gao served Mao with exceptional loyalty. He closely followed Mao's political agenda. Gao arrived in the Northeast after the conclusion of the Second Sino-Japanese War. During the subsequent takeover of the entire country by CCP troops, Gao played an even greater role as the competent manager of the Northeast's resources and developing industries. He was recognized for his contribution to the Communist victory in 1949 and stood together with other leading Communists atop the Tiananmen Gate Tower while Mao announced the birth of a New China.[4] During the Korean War, Gao played an important role in handling the logistics of the Chinese military forces fighting on the Korean Peninsula. He also managed the strategic communications between China, the Soviet Union, and North Korea. In short, Gao's ascendency to power was swift and spectacular. As often happens in similar cases, some people regard such a meteoric rise with resentment and jealousy.

Rao Shushi came from a much different background and had a somewhat different experience. Born in 1903, Rao was one of the few early CCP leaders who graduated from a university. A native of Linchuan county, Jiangxi province, Rao joined the CCP in 1925. He worked under Liu Shaoqi from 1941 as a member of the Central China Bureau. After October 1949, Rao's career received a boost. He was elevated to become chairman of the East China Military and Administrative Committee, a high position that oversaw an important region of the new People's Republic.[5]

Gao and His Struggle against Liu Shaoqi

From August 1952 to early 1953, the CCP Central Committee's five regional bureau secretaries—Gao Gang (Northeast), Rao Shushi (Eastern), Deng Zihui (Central-Southern), Deng Xiaoping (Southwest), and Xi Zhongxun (Northwest)—were promoted from their respective regions to high positions in Beijing. Gao became the chairman of the State Planning Commission, in charge of drafting national economic policies. Rao was assigned to be in charge of the Organization Department of the CCP Central Committee, controlling the crucial sector of appointments, promotions, and staff management. Deng Zihui took over the Rural-work Department of the CCP Central Committee. Deng Xiaoping became vice premier of the Government Administration Council of the Central People's Government. Xi Zhongxun was to head the Propaganda Department of the CCP.[6] "Five stallions enter the capitol with one racing well past the others," wrote Dong Biwu, a founding member of the CCP to describe the rousing scene at the time.[7] Out of these five leadership posts, Gao's position was especially important due to the nature of his work. Astounding resplendence marked Gao's debut on the national scene. To many observers, it seemed that Gao was Chairman Mao's new favorite in Beijing.

Mao brought Gao to the capital for an important reason. As a man who demonstrated exceptional loyalty, scant ideological deviation, and acute political sharpness, Gao was to be Mao's new closest comrade-in-arms. The political climate in Beijing in 1952 was rather tense due to the friction between Mao and Liu Shaoqi, another seasoned and respected party leader. Representing two drastically different party lines, Mao wished to hastily advance China toward Socialism, while Liu wanted to move at a steadier pace and even attempted to embrace elements of capitalism. Gao had clashed with Liu thrice over similar ideological disagreements when he was running the Northeast. Gao's repeated demonstration of close ideological proximity with Mao, his vast differences with Liu, in addition to his relative isolation from Beijing's "old guards," made him a perfect candidate for Mao's design to weaken Liu and consolidate power.

Mao's plan was implemented during the summer of 1953 at the National Conference on Financial and Economic Work. The conference was meant to be a forum for discussion on financial and economic issues. On July 11, Mao specifically asked Bo Yibo, a close ally of Liu, to self-criticize his work performance in front of the attendees. It was seemingly a standard practice in the Communist organizations of several countries, but Chinese Communists especially valued self-criticism as a way to maintain party discipline. However, self-criticism could also be used as a form of character assassination. In this case, Mao's demand of Bo for a self-criticism was an indirect character attack, launched against Bo but ultimately meant to harm Liu. Having Mao's backing, Gao soon unleashed a range of character attacks against Bo.

On August 1, using Bo's self-criticism as an excuse, Gao attacked Bo's work in the countryside as violating the line of the Central Committee, and particularly Chairman Mao. Gao denounced Bo's "resistance to the development from individual to the collective" and his "wish to base the expectation of economic development of the rural areas on the economic development of the rich peasant."[8] He also attacked Bo on a personal level, labeling him as having an "uncooperative attitude" and developing an "undemocratic style of work."[9] Ostentatiously attacking Bo in front of a large group of party members, Gao also encouraged others at the meeting to criticize Bo. Gao employed the tactic of attacking Bo's work while subliminally striking the fundamentals of Liu and his policies. While relentlessly excoriating his target, Gao "incited dissatisfaction with [Liu Shaoqi] by cleverly quoting words from previous speeches of Comrade Liu Shaoqi."[10]

As a loyal and close follower of the chairman, Gao, up to this point, had been quite successful in guessing Mao's thoughts and plans. This time around, however, Gao misinterpreted Mao's intentions (to keep some party members in check) and elevated himself politically without Mao's approval.

Rao Shushi Attempts to Assert His Authority

In 1953, Gao's ally Rao Shushi was the head of the Organization Department of the CCP Central Committee. A close follower of Liu Shaoqi since 1929, Rao perceived Liu as falling out of Mao's favor and believed Gao Gang would soon be Mao's successor. Rao's position as the head of the Organization Department was very important in the party's hierarchy. While Gao went on the offensive at the National Conference on Financial and Economic Work, Rao mounted his own operation at the Second National Conference on Organization Work. During a meeting held on July 22, Rao attacked the vice chairman of the Organization Department, An Ziwen, a perceived ally of Liu Shaoqi. Rao accused An's draft regarding the antibureaucracy campaign within the Organization Department as "falsified." He said the Organization Department was "like a pond of stagnant water . . . that must be 'shaken up.'"[11]

Rao's attacks alerted other officials in the Organization Department. But his next move shocked the entire party. During the meeting of August 17 and 18, Rao questioned An regarding the "March Name List," a list of proposed politburo members for the coming 8th National Congress of the CCP, as well as a list of personnel changes in various departments. This list was supposed to be circulated only among certain individuals at the top level (such as Mao and Gao). Other top leaders, like Zhou Enlai and Liu Shaoqi, did not know about this list until Rao publically questioned An at the August conference. The revelation about this list shook the party's leadership core. Mao was especially angry at the leaking of this document and Rao's reckless behavior. He went after Rao, saying: "Don't think you know everything because you've been first [Party] secretary of a large region. You still haven't worked at the Center. Why is it that you carried out a struggle against a "high mandarin of the Ministry of Official Personnel Affairs" (meaning An Ziwen) and didn't even notify the Center!"[12]

Mao Changes Course

Gao's and Rao's actions stirred up the underlying tensions within the party leadership. Witnessing unexpected consequences, Mao chose to remove Gao and Rao from power. Gao's vacation in southern China from October 3 to November 2 further reinforced Mao's suspicion of Gao. Mao was especially concerned about Gao's interactions with high-ranking military men, exemplified by his meeting with his old Northeastern colleague Lin Biao. Lin and Gao worked closely in the Northeast during the Civil War period: Lin as the military commander battling against the Nationalists, Gao as the political and logistical buttress of Lin. Detailed discussions of the meeting are still unclear. At the time, such secretive meetings between a powerful military commander and a top politician inevitably greatly worried Mao. During Gao's Guangzhou meeting with another top CCP official, Tao Zhu, Gao reportedly asked Tao about his opinion on becoming the vice chairman of the party, to which Tao replied, "You are the most experienced in practical work."[13] Gao also made promises to Tao regarding a high position in the government, saying, "If you come to the Center, you may be a vice-premier."[14] Gao also told Tao the names of several persons whom he wanted to appoint to positions in the center.[15] The actions of Gao during his month-long vacation in the South, whether known in detail to Mao or not, aroused much suspicion and concern. Gao's and Rao's individual ambitions probably mattered too. Mao decided to act.

At the CCP Central Committee Politburo Extended Session on December 24, Mao said: "There are two commanding centers in Beijing. One is a commanding center led by me; we blow a positive (*yang*) wind and light a positive fire. The other is a commanding center led by someone else; it blows a sinister (*yin*) wind and lights a sinister fire, it reeks of underground water. After all, should governance come from one source, or should it come from multiple sources?"[16] It was quite clear to most attendees of the meeting at whom the chairman was directing his criticism against. At the same meeting, Mao asked the Party Central Committee to draft a "Resolution on Strengthening Party Unity." Interestingly, Mao assigned the task to Liu Shaoqi. This turning point would allow Liu and the old guards to launch a counterattack against Gao during the coming 4th Plenary Session of the 7th CCP Central Committee.

4th Plenary Session of the 7th CCP Central Committee

From February 6 to 10, 1954, the 4th Plenary Session of the 7th CCP Central Committee was held in Beijing. Mao had taken a southbound train on December 24 of the previous year to spend some time away from the capital and to deliberately draw a distance between himself and the political struggles in Beijing. Yet he was in control of the agenda and discussions at the meeting. Liu Shaoqi was put in charge of running the meeting according to Mao's guidelines.[17] The main subject of the plenary session was party unity and the dangers of decentralism.

After an extended period of deliberations, the session unanimously adopted the "Resolution on Strengthening Party Unity." The resolution was doubtlessly directed at Gao and Rao. The following passage is of special interest:

> One of the most important methods of the imperialists and counterrevolutionaries for sabotaging our cause is, first and foremost, to undermine the unity of the Party and to look for agents within our Party . . . These are momentous historical lessons that show that the enemy not only will always seek agents within our Party but in the past has found them, and it may be in the future, too, he will find vacillating and disloyal elements and those who join the Party with ulterior motives to act as his agents.[18]

In Liu Shaoqi's "Report to the 4th Plenary Session of the 7th CCP Central Committee by the Politburo of the CCP," the show of resolve against Gao and Rao was equally lucid, despite the absence of outright name-calling. Entrusted by Mao and the remaining members of the Central Committee Politburo, Liu's speech was forthright against any attempts at splintering the party from within. In particular, Liu sent out stern warnings against divisions and "imperialist agents" within the party. At the end of his speech, Liu emphasized the importance of magnanimity for misguided comrades and the CCP principle of "maintaining a benevolent attitude toward others." And for comrades who took sincere, corrective actions, Liu promised the party would "cure the sickness and save the patient."[19] These rather gentle phrases and idioms, however, could not obscure the agitated tone dominating the entire session. Gao was isolated as an individual harmful to the unity of the party. He felt Mao's anger. On February 6, apparently wishing to redeem himself in front of his comrades, Gao offered self-criticism. He began with praises of the general party line established in 1950, giving high regards to Mao and the Central Committee's leadership. He supported the "Resolution on Strengthening Party Unity" and argued for the significance of its full implementation. According to his own self-criticism, his four mistakes consisted of:

> First . . . my views of comrade Shaoqi are extremely flawed, in which [I] viewed comrade Shaoqi's individual, momentary and unimportant working shortcomings as systematic problems.
>
>   Second . . . I used to discuss my views of comrade Shaoqi with some other comrades, even with non–Central Committee members. This kind of behavior

is against organizational principles and detrimental to Party unity, this is an expression of factionalism, and must be subjected to Party discipline.

Third, my views of some cadres are biased and lack analysis, [if I think] they are good, then they are very good, [if I think] they are bad, then they are very bad . . . To comrades who had previously made mistakes yet wish to correct themselves, I failed to adopt the attitude outlined by the Central Committee's resolution, "begin from the starting point of unity, through criticism and self-criticism, to achieve the objective of unity." This is wrong as well, and cannot contribute to the goal of party unity.

Fourth . . . I personally lack the self-awareness due for a Communist party member, and the spirit of self-criticism. [I] love when others talk about [my] achievements instead of shortcomings.[20]

Two days later, on February 8, Rao Shushi also offered his self-criticism to the attendees. Rao began with a few quotes from the "Resolution on Strengthening Party Unity" and Liu's speech. He admitted faults in building relationships with his comrades.[21] Rao apologized for his bourgeois individualism, his negligence, and careerism.[22] The worst mistake according to Rao was the fact he "did not regard the sabotage of the Party's unity as helping the enemy in threatening the life of the Party."[23] By affirming that "the Party's only Center is the Party's Central Committee . . . and comrade Liu Shaoqi is one of the Central Committee's leading comrades," Rao asked for stringent criticisms from the attendees and rigid discipline from the Central Committee.[24]

Meeting Concerning the Gao Gang Question

The Meeting Concerning the Gao Gang Question was held from February 15 to 25. A total of 43 people spoke, most of whom were harshly critical of Gao. Gao offered more self-criticisms and discussed his liberalism and sectarianism but refused to accept the charges of antiparty activities, saying his personal opinions toward Liu Shaoqi did not mean that he, Gao, was against the party.[25]

As the session continued, Gao felt the mounting pressure against him. Old comrades with a long history of working relations now berated him with stinging language. He grew desperate. On February 17, he attempted suicide by using his bodyguard's firearm. Already aware of the drastic change in his behavior, the suicide was prevented by his family and aides. The Central Committee was immediately notified. Reportedly, Mao was deeply displeased with Gao's action. Gao was immediately placed under house arrest and subjected to supervised education, where he was to be overseen by his secretary, Zhao Jialiang, in studying the classic works of Marxism-Leninism while reflecting upon his mistakes.[26] He did not attend any new meetings in relation to his "problems," and former comrades decided his fate in his absence.

On the last day of the meeting, the twenty-fifth of February, Zhou Enlai delivered a final speech concluding the Gao Gang question. The speech outlined Gao's "Ten Cardinal Crimes." They included disseminating false outlooks on the party's history and its current state of affairs, engagement in sectarian activities aimed against the leading comrades of the party's Central Committee, sowing intraparty discord through the means of rumormongering, cronyism, treating the area under his leadership as his personal property, plagiarizing the works of others, falsely using the name of the Central Committee to cause damage to the prestige of the Central Committee, causing disunity in Sino-Soviet relations by leaking sensitive party information to Soviet counterparts, conspiring to seize party and state power, and practicing a degenerate lifestyle.[27] After announcing Gao's "Ten Cardinal Crimes," Zhou continued with his denouncement of Gao's previous "two superficial self-examinations" and criticized him severely for his "shameful" attempt at committing suicide as a "flagrant betrayal of the Party."[28] Regarding Gao's fate, Zhou proposed to place him under long-term supervised education until he would repent completely.

Meeting Concerning the Rao Shushi Question

Liu's close associate Deng Xiaoping led the discussion meeting concerning the Rao Shushi question. Deng's mission was to further expose Rao's faults and establish his character as Gao's lackey in the assault on the established members of the Party Central Committee. To accomplish this task, the meeting focused on Rao's role as Gao's collaborator during the National Conference on Financial and Economic Work. Seeking to destroy Rao's character, the participants of the meeting dug up a few facts from his past in order to ready the climate of opinion for his final punishment. A total of seven meetings were held in Beijing on the Rao Shushi question. Party members, led by Deng Xiaoping and Chen Yi, openly denounced Rao's activities. Rao's old colleagues from East China, central departments, and ministries were assembled at the meeting to witness the shameful downfall of their old boss and accept the commanding authority of the center. On March 1, 1954, Deng Xiaoping, Chen Yi, and Tan Zhenlin delivered a report concluding the Rao Shushi question. The report highlighted Rao's mistakes and especially targeted the quality of his character. Rao was labeled as an "extremely individualistic bourgeois careerist" with ambitions "constantly on the ascendant."[29] The report associated Rao with Gao, claiming the existence of a "Gao-Rao Anti-Party Clique." This would serve as the critical example for party members for years to come.

In addition to criticizing Rao's behavior in 1953, the report showed Rao's mistakes as deeply entrenched in his biography. For instance, the report alleged his 1943 attempt at removing Chen Yi from the New Fourth Army headquarters by using lies and slanders. Further shots were taken at Rao's 1949 effort at removing Chen Yi and taking over as the chairman of the East China Military and Administrative Committee.[30] But the most severe charge against Rao was his doubt about Mao and the Central Committee's trust in him during 1952, when he openly expressed his dissatisfaction with the Party Central Committee's modus operandi during a meeting with the chairman.[31]

The report pointed out that Rao's tendency to commit serious mistakes was not something unusual. In fact, it was a permanent feature of his character.[32] The report listed his multifarious personal flaws:

> Comrade Rao Shushi had an unsavory personal style, which can be summed up as follows: (1) Rumormongering, hookwinking [sic] superiors and subordinates alike; (2) making promises of promotion to gain support alternating with attacks against those who would not toe his line, or using a combination of both attacking first then giving favors later; (3) grasping the "pigtails" of comrades—finding others' weaknesses and faults to use as a handle for attack or blackmail; (4) deliberately planting "nails" to be used when necessary to launch sudden attacks against others; (5) when arriving at a new position, employing a series of stratagems to pressure and cow others, to establish "who's boss"; (6) fabricating excuses to attack people he did not like—he admitted that he often used different occasions to launch his own attacks; (7) lying and denying what he had just said; (8) presenting a modest and respectful demeanor while actually boosting his own image.[33]

Rao was under a serious character attack in front of his old colleagues and key members of the decision-making echelon of the CCP. Rao's alleged character flaws were now tied to his plot to usurp the party's supreme leadership. This was also a convenient way to expose the alleged "Gao-Rao Anti-Party Clique." (Since the Yan'an Rectification era, "criminals" tended to come in "cliques" rather than as individuals.) By highlighting Rao's mistakes through character assassination and cornering him to capitulate and turn to self-criticism, the party's top leadership reached their goal of eliminating the alleged opposition and then justifying their actions in the eyes of the party members.

Gao's End and Post-Mortem Character Assassination

After his failed suicide attempt, Gao was placed under supervised education at his residence. With the encouragement and persuasion of old comrades, Gao agreed to take time and reflect upon his mistakes. In an April 3 letter addressed to Mao, Gao admitted he had failed the hopes of the center and the chairman. He promised to comply with any measures required by supervised education, in addition to thorough reflections on his past problems.[34]

During this period, Gao completed his confessional material, titled *My Self-Reflection*. Initially he refused to admit his intention to usurp the supreme power of the party and the state. Gao remained reluctant but eventually gave up after the first draft of *My Self-Reflection* was sent back by the reviewer, his old Shaanbei comrade Xi Zhongxun. Xi candidly told Gao's secretary, Zhao Jialiang, "The review of critical issues is very shallow, the conspiracy to usurp the supreme power of the party and state, a crucial question, was not mentioned at all."[35] Upon hearing Xi's comments, Gao understood quite clearly that the admission of such alleged crimes was equal to signing his own death sentence. Yet he also understood that he had to comply. At last, the admission of "usurpation of the supreme power of the party and state" was added to the confession. Before the final draft was dispatched, Gao crossed off "state" from the sentence, explaining to his secretary, "I am already the Vice Chairman of the state, why would I want to be the Chairman?"[36]

Gao remained psychologically withdrawn and desperate after sending his confessional material to the supervising comrades. He attempted to electrocute himself but failed. On August 16, he committed suicide by an overdose of sleeping pills. Despite his physical demise, Gao's name continued to be ridiculed and his behavior condemned. Seven months after his death, at the 1955 CCP National Party Conference, the issue of the "Gao Gang–Rao Shushi Anti-Party Alliance" was placed as the central topic to educate party cadres all across China. Deng Xiaoping's speech at the conference, titled "Report on the Gao Gang, Rao Shushi Anti-Party Alliance," outlined the party's decision about the fate of Gao Gang and Rao Shushi. Deng repeatedly offered high praises for Mao Ze-dong and the party's central leadership while attacking Gao and Rao. He affirmed that the building of Socialism was inseparable from class struggle and that foreign enemies were constantly searching for potential agents within the party.[37] Deng accused Gao and Rao of conspiring "in a deliberate plot to split the Party and seize the supreme power of the Party and the state to serve the interests of imperialism and the bourgeoisie."[38]

Deng then turned to past events and interpreted them as Gao's and Rao's attempts to usurp political power in the country. Gao's and Rao's activities at the National Conference on Financial and Economic Work, where Gao overstepped set boundaries in his offensive against Liu in support of Mao's line, became "evidence" of their conspiratorial activities.[39] Gao Gang's vacation in the South, where he allegedly conspired with high-ranking cadres to "reorganize" the Central Committee and leading organs of the state, was also presented as incriminating evidence against him.[40] Aiming to paint Gao's character as an intriguer and a liar, Deng stated:

> Gao Gang's activities were well aimed at opposing the Central Committee headed by Comrade Mao Zedong. However, the schemer knew his plots could not stand exposure, and therefore he pretended that he had never opposed Comrade Mao Zedong but only opposed Mao's close comrades-in-arms Liu Shaoqi and Zhou Enlai. He knew if he openly opposed Comrade Mao Zedong too early, it would be disadvantageous to his scheme.
>
> What reason could Gao Gang have in opposing leaders long acknowledged by the entire Party such as comrades Liu Shaoqi and Zhou Enlai? As he had no other ammunition to attack them with, Gao fabricated lies and rumors, such as that comrades Liu Shaoqi, Zhou Enlai, and other leading comrades had committed grave mistakes. He spread such rumors in secret, to damage the prestige of Liu Shaoqi, Zhou Enlai, and other comrades.
>
> Gao Gang deliberately attacked comrades of the central leadership for no other purpose than to seize power. He wanted to sweep aside obstacles on his road to seizing power. To achieve his aim, Gao Gang was unscrupulous. Anyone who stood in his way, whatever his name, became the target of his rumors and attacks.[41]

Following his personal attacks against Gao, Deng then turned against Gao's "circles." He criticized Gao's workings in the Northeast Bureau, specifically his favoritism and sectarianism. Deng criticized Gao in promoting his colleagues from the Northeast Bureau to the center.[42] "In the eyes of Gao Gang and his cronies the Northeast had long become 'Gao Gang's Kingdom,'" said Deng.[43] Gao's men, according to Deng, were far from upstanding Communist revolutionaries; rather they "monopolized the Northeast Bureau . . . [and] ostracized and attacked all dissidents."[44]

Deng also lashed out against Rao. He accused Rao of playing "power politics," "as far back as 1943 in the period of Anti-Japanese war."[45] Rao was also accused of individualism and of being a bourgeois speculator.[46] Concluding his speech, Deng scorned Gao's and Rao's entire legacies as party leaders. They appeared as two plotters attempting to implement "bourgeois" (a typical slander term used by the Communists) programs.[47]

"How was it possible for schemers like Gao Gang and Rao Shushi to emerge in our party?" asked Deng, as if he was schooling the party members.[48] In order to prevent such episodes from recurring in the future, Deng suggested that inner-party disputes must be addressed and resolved within the party.[49] Comrades who were willing to acknowledge their mistakes and who actively pursued self-improvement should be offered help and be forgiven. If there was no self-criticism, then strict disciplinary measures must follow.[50] Gao's and Rao's punishments, from this point of view, were completely justified.

The media controlled by the CCP obviously supported the decision about Gao and Rao concluded at the 1955 National Party Conference. The official voice of the CCP Central Committee, the *People's Daily*, was the most vocal source of support. Its editorial dedicated to this event on April 10, 1955, praised the destruction of the Gao-Rao anti-party alliance as "a major victory in the party's history."[51] Another *People's Daily* publication warned party members to remain vigilant after the Gao-Rao incident.[52] An editorial published in the *People's Daily* on April 14, 1955, was titled "Mobilize the Entire Party and the Entire People to Struggle Against Bad People and Bad Things." The editorial specifically used Gao's and Rao's alleged corruption as negative examples of cronyism.[53] Provinces throughout China also demonstrated unanimous support of the National Party Conference's resolution regarding the "Gao-Rao Anti-Party Alliance."[54]

Conclusion

Like in most political struggles during Mao's years in power, the elimination of one or two party bosses was never enough. An entire "clique" of associates had to be identified, publically denounced, and punished. After expelling Gao and Rao from the party, many of their close allies and benefactors in their Northeast and East Bureaus were sacked.[55]

The case of Gao Gang and Rao Shushi was the first major purge after the establishment of the People's Republic of China in 1949. Two of the CCP's top leaders were driven out of power into destitution. One took his own life, and the other was expelled from the party and imprisoned until his death in 1975. Not only does this case demonstrate the merciless nature of political battles in the 1950s, it also shows certain character assassination techniques in the context of that historical period.

One of the most unique features of character assassination in Chinese politics is self-criticism. The custom of self-reflection, followed by the rectification of personal shortcomings for the betterment of one's virtue, has been an integral part of Chinese culture since ancient times. The Confucian tradition was especially keen on using self-reflection for the intent of one's self-improvement. Self-criticism used in the political context dates back to the very incipient stage of the Chinese imperial tradition. A leading example of self-criticism for political purpose would be an article known as *zuijizhao*, or "Rescript for Penitence," a self-criticizing document issued by Chinese emperors during times of national crisis (or perceived national crisis) with the objective of calming the distressed population.

However, self-criticism did not become a form of character assassination until the rise of the CCP in the early twentieth century. Seeking to build a disciplined vanguard party, it required self-reflection as a key personality feature of a Communist. Public self-criticism as a tool of character assassination, however, differs quite drastically from self-reflection. Self-criticism rose to prominence for character assassination purposes during the Yan'an Rectification Movement of 1942–45, in which Mao defeated his political opponents and consolidated his position as the supreme authority among the CCP cadres. Calling its members to "give your heart to the Party," the Rectification Movement's main goal was to solidify the ideological principles of Maoism ("Mao Ze-dong Thought") in the mind of every CCP member, in order to enhance the degree of hierarchical obedience to the chairman. Party members were encouraged to publically confess their past mistakes in order to gain the trust of their fellow comrades and party leaders. Self-criticism sessions were made public to give party members a channel to dissect one's dogmatism in accordance with the principles laid out in Mao's speeches and writings (thus committing "character suicide" in the process of remaking themselves according to Mao's ideological guidance). The writing of self-critical notes was highly encouraged by the party to let the cadres demonstrate their thorough understanding of Mao Ze-dong Thought, moreover to recognize its superiority as the party's prime ideology.[56]

Self-criticism was also utilized as a tool of character assassination in later purges, as it had been in the Gao-Rao affair. By directing Gao and Rao to seriously criticize themselves, the party leaders could attack their associates without being directly engaged in this "messy" process. The content, the tone, and the choice of words in their confessions could indicate the psychological state of the individuals committing "character suicide." On the other hand, the confessions could serve as a legitimate casus belli for further attacks from those who believed that self-criticism was not severe enough. For example, Gao and Rao were attacked during the 1955 CCP National Party Conference for the alleged insincerity and lack of admission in their initial self-criticism. Lastly, the "self-indicting" self-criticism reports could be preserved as convenient firsthand evidence for future character attacks if required.

Name-calling is another rambunctious instrument of character assassination often used in Chinese internal political battles. In the 1950s, Mao deliberately highlighted the significance of class struggle in his political rhetoric. He saw class struggle as a key challenge for his country at the time. (Stalin in the Soviet Union believed in the inevitability of a fierce and increasing class struggle during the early stages of Socialist transition.) To a Western reader, the labels and names used to attack Gao and Rao may not appear malicious enough. Yet in the context of Chinese politics and the Communist ideology, the accusations of "liberalism" and "bourgeois individualism," or charges about being an agent of imperialism were extremely serious. These labels could destroy careers and ruin lives.

The CCP needed obedient followers. Using the principles of so-called democratic centralism (first established by Lenin in Russia) to eliminate dissent and prohibit the emergence of party factions, the CCP leadership was forcing the party's unity. Not surprisingly, Zhou Enlai, in his speech "Comrade Zhou Enlai's Speech Outline at the Discussion Meeting on the Gao Gang Question," associated Gao's behavior with sectarianism, cliquism, decentralism, localism, and departmentalism.[57] At times, direct name-calling was substituted by "criticizing without naming." This seemingly mild form of character attack was used when the time was not appropriate for all-out name-calling. Liu Shaoqi used this technique during the 4th Plenary Session of the 7th CCP Central Committee in criticizing Gao's and Rao's activities opposing the center.

The CCP, despite its origins as a mass party, has put a strong emphasis on extraordinary personal qualities in party members. Liu Shaoqi, in his exemplary work *How to Be a Good Communist*, wrote: "We know that many revolutionaries in China in the past hundred years, or more recently in the past fifty years, began to show signs of corruption and degeneration the moment they had achieved a certain measure of success and risen to some responsible position."[58] Those features should not be part of a new Communist revolutionary's traits. On paper, the party demanded its leading members to be virtuous and free from selfish, arrogant, and hedonistic tendencies. Thus, the accusation of Gao's preference for a degenerate lifestyle (in contrast to the strict, ascetic standards of a true Communist) provided his attackers with enough ammunition to destroy his name.

Finally, erasing Gao's and Rao's images from the people's collective memory was another form of character assassination. Though Rao's power and status in the party were significant, he did not enjoy the huge popularity that Gao had once in the Northeast and in Beijing. Nonetheless, Gao's and Rao's names were rarely mentioned in public after their downfall (except for the purpose of demeaning their work). Visual images have disappeared too. In the defining oil painting *The Grand Founding Ceremony of the People's Republic of China*, completed in 1953, the artist Dong Xiwen illustrated the birth of the People's Republic of China through capturing the very moment when

Mao Ze-dong announced to the world that the "Chinese people have stood up" from the Tiananmen City Gate. As Mao's close comrade-in-arms at the time, Gao was featured prominently and positioned very close to the chairman. A year after the Gao-Rao incident, Dong Xiwen was ordered to remove Gao from the painting and replace him with a pot of flowers. For more than two decades, Gao was absent from public view in the most renowned painting officially sanctioned by the Chinese government. Yet like many others who were erased from the paintings, Gao eventually made a comeback to his original position in the 1953 version when the helm of the state gradually fell into the lap of the pragmatic Deng Xiaoping in 1979. Ironically, Deng was the man who acted as the shock trooper in Mao's punitive expedition against the "Gao Gang–Rao Shushi Anti-Party Alliance."

Notes

1. Dai and Zhao 2011, 17–18.
2. Dai and Zhao 2011, 21–26.
3. Dai and Zhao 2011, 80.
4. Dai and Zhao 2011, 212–14.
5. Dai and Zhao 2011, 312–13.
6. Dai and Zhao 2011, 286.
7. Zhao and Zhang 2008, 75.
8. Dai and Zhao 2011, 303.
9. Dai and Zhao 2011, 304.
10. Teiwes 1990, 163.
11. Dai and Zhao, 2011, 314.
12. Teiwes 1990, 215.
13. Teiwes 1990, 224.
14. Teiwes 1990, 224–25.
15. Teiwes 1990, 225.
16. Dai and Zhao 2011, 333.
17. Zhao and Zhang 2008, 189–91.
18. Teiwes 1990, 237.
19. Liu 1954.
20. Dai and Zhao, 2011, 342–43.
21. Dai and Zhao, 2011, 343–44.
22. Rao 1954.
23. Rao 1954.
24. Dai and Zhao 2011, 345.
25. Dai and Zhao 2011, 347.
26. Zhao and Zhang 2008, 6, 21–22.
27. Zhou 1954.
28. Teiwes 1990, 243.
29. Teiwes 1990, 246.
30. Teiwes 1990, 248.
31. Teiwes 1990, 249.
32. Teiwes 1990, 250.
33. Teiwes 1990, 250.

34. Dai and Zhao 2011, 360.
35. Zhao and Zhang 2008, 69.
36. Dai and Zhao 2011, 361.
37. Teiwes 1990, 256.
38. Teiwes 1990, 257.
39. Teiwes 1990, 258.
40. Teiwes 1990, 259.
41. Teiwes 1990, 262.
42. Teiwes 1990, 263.
43. Teiwes 1990, 264.
44. Teiwes 1990, 263–64.
45. Teiwes 1990, 265.
46. Teiwes 1990, 265.
47. Teiwes 1990, 267.
48. Teiwes 1990, 271.
49. Teiwes 1990, 273.
50. Teiwes 1990, 272–73.
51. Anonymous 1955a.
52. Anonymous 1955b.
53. Anonymous 1955c.
54. Anonymous 1955d.
55. Lin 2009, 346.
56. Gao 2000, 397–99.
57. Teiwes 1990, 244–45.
58. Liu 1951, 10.

Bibliography

Anonymous. 1955a. "Shelun: dang de lishishang de zhongda shengli [Editorial: major victory in the party's history]." *People's Daily*, April 10. http://58.68.145.22/deta1l?record=856&channelid=195504&searchword=&sortfield= (accessed July 15, 2013).

Anonymous. 1955b. "Zhongguo gongchandang jianru panshi de tuanjie [The monolithic unity of the CCP]." *People's Daily*, April 10. http://58.68.145.22/deta1l?record=885&channelid=195504&searchword=&sortfield= (accessed July 15, 2013).

Anonymous. 1955c. "Shelun: dong yuan quan dang quan min tong huai ren huai shi zuo dou zheng [Editorial: mobilize the entire party and the entire people to struggle against bad people and bad things]." *People's Daily*, April 14. http://58.68.145.22/deta1l?record=692&channelid=195504&searchword=&sortfield=(accessed July 15, 2013).

Anonymous. 1955d. "Sichuan, henan, shaanxi deng sheng juxing dangdaibiao huiyi jueding guanche dang de quanguo daibiaohuiyi jueyi [Party congress held in Sichuan, Henan, Shaanxi and other provinces: the decision to implement the resolutions of the Party's National Congress]." *People's Daily*, June 19. http://58.68.145.22/deta1l?record=502&channelid=195506&searchword=&sortfield=(accessed July 15, 2013).

Dai, M., and X. Zhao. 2011. *Gao Gang zhuan* [The biography of Gao Gang]. Xi'an: Shaanxi ren min chu ban she.

Gao, H. 2000. *Hong tai yang shi zen yang sheng qi de: Yan'an zheng feng yun dong de lai long qu mai* [How did the red sun rise over Yan'an? A history of the Rectification Movement]. Xianggang: Zhong wen da xue chu ban she.

Lin, Y. 2009. *Xiang she hui zhu yi guo du: Zhongguo jing ji yu she hui de zhuan xing 1953–1955* [The transition toward socialism: the transformation of China's economy and society 1953–1955]. Xianggang: Xianggang Zhong wen da xue dang dai Zhongguo wen hua yan jiu zhong xin.

Liu, S. 1951. *How to Be a Good Communist*. Peking: Foreign Languages Press.

Liu, S. 1954. "Zhongyang zhengzhiju xiang diqijie disici zhongyangquanhui de baogao [Report to the 4th Plenary Session of the 7th CCP Central Committee by the Politburo of the CCP]." Peking, China, February 6.

Rao, S. 1954. "'Guanyu wode cuowu de ziwojiantao' rao shushi zai zhonggong zhongyang qijie sizhong quanhui shang de jiantaofayan ["The self-criticism regarding my mistakes": Rao Shushi's self-criticism speech at the 4th Plenary Session of the 7th CCP Central Committee]." Peking, China, February 9.

Zhao, J., and X. Zhang. 2008. *Gao Gang zai Beijing* [Gao Gang in Beijing]. Xianggang: Da feng chu ban she.

Zhou, E. 1954. "Zhou enlai tongzhi zai guanyu gaogang wenti de zuotanhui shang de fayan tigang [The speech outline of comrade Zhou Enlai at the Discussion Meeting on the Gao Gang Question]." Peking, China, February 25.

Teiwes, F. C. 1990. *Politics at Mao's Court: Gao Gang and Party Factionalism in the Early 1950s*. Armonk, NY: M. E. Sharpe.

13

A Character Assassination Attempt: The Case of Václav Havel

Martina Klicperová-Baker

Introduction[1]

This chapter focuses on a case study—an attempt at the character assassination of Václav Havel (1936–2011) by the Communist government of Czechoslovakia. The motive was to destroy the reputation of the leading Czech dissident and to stop his human rights campaign. The character assassination primarily targeted Havel as a prominent member of a banned civic organization called Charter 77, which had documented the trampling of human rights in Czechoslovakia and published its famous statement of January 6, 1977. The campaign against Charter 77 gradually escalated and included the whole so-called cultural front (i.e., artists of various professions, performers, and in particular actors since Czech cultural nationalism has been closely tied to Czech theater). The ideological struggle affected many citizens, most of all the open sympathizers of Charter 77, who were severely prosecuted, and those who were forced to publicly denounce the Charter 77 initiative.

At that point, the regime was committing, if not a nationwide character assassination campaign, then at least a very intensive character mutilation. The process of *character breaking*, a comprehensive process, which destroys the core of the character (not just a superficial smearing of the public image), can be partly explained in terms of a well-known psychological phenomenon called *cognitive dissonance* (described in detail further below). It can be argued that the totalitarian corruption of the citizens' morality affected their post-Communist mentality for years to come. It was not until the 1989 Velvet Revolution that the Czech performing artists fully restored their historical role as the core of national conscience and patriotism. They led the nation to liberation from Communism and to reconciliation of those who morally prevailed with those who had collaborated with the regime. Not only was Havel not destroyed by the Communist character assassination attempts, he became a hero of his nation and was repeatedly elected the president of free Czechoslovakia and later also of the Czech Republic. He became an international symbol of the moral struggle for humanistic ideals.

The Contradiction within the Term *Character Assassination*

When I was doing research for this chapter, organizing my archive, scouting the resources in Václav Havel's library, and talking to friends and colleagues in Prague, I also had a rare opportunity to visit with and interview the brother of Václav Havel, Ivan. Dr. Ivan Havel is a scholar, a founder of the Center for Theoretical Studies, which is affiliated with the Academy of Sciences of the Czech Republic and the Charles University. It was he who pointed out the discrepancy within the term *character assassination*—between the *public attack* and the likely prevailing intactness of the *inner morality* of the person—that is, his or her character. In other words, it is not the integrity of the *person's inner character* that is being assassinated, although the term rather misleadingly suggests so, it is rather the *public image* (reputation, or credibility)[2] that is getting smeared in the process.

While the Communist regime in Czechoslovakia in the 1970s and 1980s made forceful attempts to destroy the public image of Václav Havel, he withstood the attacks, prevailed morally, and managed to keep his integrity, as well as both his private and public life in truth.[3] Moreover, those who knew him were not swayed by the attacks; neither were those able to seek alternative information sources (e.g., by means of foreign radio broadcasts, such as Free Europe and Voice of America, or trusted friends) and those who had an insight into the Communist and Soviet propaganda machine. (This was the case for any interested person after the 1960s and, in particular, after the 1968 Soviet occupation and resulting general disenchantment with Communism.)

This chapter argues that although the character assassination of Havel was unsuccessful, coercive propaganda campaigns seem to have contributed to the political demoralization of many of his compatriots.

Czechoslovakia in the 1970s

The country was only slowly recovering from a shock. Its brief period of restored freedom, the promising Prague Spring of 1968, an early Czech version of "glasnost and perestroika" meant to humanize Soviet-imposed Socialism, was crushed. The sudden robust growth of civil society[4] was suffocated. In August 1968, Czechoslovakia was invaded by members of the Warsaw Pact (the political and military alliance of which Czechoslovakia was a member), including the Soviet Union, East Germany, Poland, Hungary, and Bulgaria. The invasion did not just stop the democratization process; it also brought the country way back under totalitarian Communism and severe repression.

To add insult to injury, this process was, paradoxically, called "normalization." George Orwell could not think of a more fitting name.

Yet, the government pretended that the system was democratic. The Communist regimes typically called themselves not just "democracies" but, rather pleonastically, "people's democracies." Following the Moscow-sponsored policy of "peaceful coexistence" with the West, they also cosigned the Final Act of the 1975 Helsinki Accords, including its chapter related to human rights.

The Dissidents of the Regime and Charter 77

Although Czechoslovakia was a signatory of the Helsinki Accords, it trampled on many human rights, civic rights, political freedoms, and freedom of expression. Czech dissidents (Havel among them) decided to call this political bluff of their government and to openly challenge it. The dissidents formed a civic initiative, factually documented the human rights violations in their country in the Charter 77 statement, collected 242 signatures in support of it, made an attempt to formally present the document to the Czechoslovak political authorities, and at the same time made sure the Charter 77 statement would be available for publication in prestigious foreign newspapers. January 6, 1977, was the public beginning of Charter 77.[5]

The statement of Charter 77 had four pages and was very factual. The initial paragraph asserted: "On October 13, 1976, the Czechoslovak Legal Code (article 120) published *The International Pact on Civil and Political Rights and the International Pact on Economic, Social and Cultural Rights* which had been signed in the name of our republic in 1968, confirmed in Helsinki in 1975, and came into force March 23, 1976. Since that time our citizens have the right and our state the duty to comply with them."[6] Further, the authors explicitly welcomed the fact that the Czechoslovak Socialist Republic had expressed adherence to these pacts, declaring people's freedoms and rights as important aspects of civilization; at the same time, they pointed out that many of the civil rights were guaranteed, unfortunately, on paper only.

The core of the Charter 77 proclamation contained an inventory of rights that were being violated, beginning with the freedom of expression: "Tens of thousands of citizens are not allowed to work in their profession because their opinions clash with the official ideology and they are becoming 'victims of apartheid.'" Charter 77 stated that hundreds of thousands of other citizens were being "denied the right of freedom from fear" of losing their life opportunities if they expressed their views; countless young people were being denied studies because of opinions of theirs or their parents; freedom of religion was being systematically restricted, as well as freedom of workers to freely organize and the freedom to travel abroad. The right to seek, receive, and spread information was being infringed upon, as well as the freedom of public expression, publication, and cultural activities. The authors pointed out that young musicians were being put on trial for their art right at the time when this proclamation had been made.

Regarding character assassination, Charter 77 specifically stressed that "public defense against untrue and insulting accusations by official propaganda is rendered impossible (a legal protection against 'attacks on honor and reputation' unambiguously guaranteed by article 17 of the first pact is practically non-existent)," that false accusations could not be refuted, and that any effort to achieve rectification or amendment by judicial means was futile.

Charter 77 pointed out that the instrument of restriction lay in the fact that all institutions and organizations were subjected to the political directives of the apparatus of the ruling party and to the arbitrary decisions of influential individuals. The Charter 77 manifesto concluded that the responsibility for the observance of civil rights fell in the first place on the "political and state power," but

> each and every one of us has a share of responsibility for the general situation and thus, too, for the observance of the enacted pacts which have been binding not only for the government but also for all citizens. The feeling of this co-responsibility, faith in the meaning of civic involvement and the will to exercise it, and the shared need to seek new and more effective means for its expression led us to the idea of establishing the Charter 77, the formation of which we are publicly announcing today.

Charter 77 was not established as an organization with membership and a political program but as

> a free, informal and open association of people of various convictions, various faiths and various professions, who are joined by the desire, individually or jointly, to struggle for respecting of civil and human rights in our country and throughout the world; of the rights granted to man by the both enacted international pacts, the final act of the Helsinki Conference, numerous international documents against wars, violence, and social and spiritual oppression and which are summarized by the Universal Declaration of Human Rights of the UNO.

The Government Reaction against Charter 77

The reaction was swift. The spokesmen of the group, including Havel, were promptly detained for questioning. The Communist Party, assuming that most people would agree with the Charter 77 statement, kept the manifesto secret. A smear campaign was launched to assassinate the character of Charter 77 activists and Havel in particular.

On January 12, all major dailies reprinted the official statement of the regime. It was an extensive article expressively titled "Losers and Usurpers" (Ztroskotanci a samozvanci). The major Communist daily, *Rudé Právo*,[7] filled a substantial part of its second page with the article. (The first page that day was devoted mainly to the heroic work of coal miners.) To make sure that the negative official attitude was clearly communicated, the Charter 77 manifesto was always referred to by the media as "a so-called Charter 77" and as "a pamphlet" (which in Czech is a rather pejorative term meaning a defamatory article or a lampoon).

"Losers and Usurpers" labeled Charter 77 "a subversive, anti-socialist, anti-people and demagogic pamphlet which grossly and falsely slanders the Czechoslovak Socialist Republic and the revolutionary achievements of its people." The statement of Charter 77 was officially framed into a large bourgeois offensive against the successes of Socialism, into a supposed imperialistic anticommunist crusade.

Importantly, the main theme of defamation was not ideological. It did not discuss the main theme of Charter 77—human rights (as the content of the manifesto was kept secret); instead, it was focused on money—bribery, honoraria, and private possessions. Supposedly, the international reactionaries (who wished to turn the wheels of progress backward) corrupted anyone who could be bought: "emigrants but also various losers living in the Socialist countries who for any reason (of their class, reaction interests, for vanity or delusion of grandeur, renegadism, or notorious lack of character[8]) are willing to lend their name perhaps even to a devil." Supposedly, international forces, attempting to create the impression of the existence of a wide anticommunist front, were dragging into it traitors along with disoriented individuals, renegades and turncoats, and criminal and antisocial elements.

Analysts of the anti–Charter 77 propaganda[9] are finding a substantial difference between it and several previous propagandistic waves, especially those which took place in the 1950s and played on the note of threat and fear. This time, the regime asserted that it was not being threatened; on the contrary, it claimed that any attempt at regime change was futile, and so the dissidents were ridiculed. They were called Don Quixotes and compared to dilapidated mossy stones in a mountain torrent, to Judases who worked for "groschen," dauntless scribblers for U.S. dollars.

It was repeated that this "pamphlet" was produced for profit, supposedly at the order of anticommunist and Zionistic centers. The regime tried to trigger

Table 13.1 Paradigm of the anti–Charter 77 article "Losers and Usurpers"

Us: Our People	Them: So-called Charter 77
Peacefulness and progress; industrious, creative atmosphere of our country; advanced Socialist society; political and social security; Socialist democracy; firm friendship with the Soviet Union and other Socialist countries; peaceful offensive of Socialist countries; historical truth; destination Communism	A few conceited losers and usurpers; bankrupt Czechoslovak reactionary bourgeoisie; failed counter-revolutionaries; demagogic agents of imperialism; forestallers of the Helsinki conference on security and cooperation in Europe; usurpers in contempt of people, their interests, and their elected representatives; not a pinch of honor and conscience; anticommunist and Zionist centers paid honorarium to the scribblers of the pamphlet; refuting Socialism as a social system; cold war and ideological diversion

people's hatred and envy by accusations that the dissidents were well paid for their resistance. To a certain degree, this attempt succeeded, as media (especially the newspaper *Rudé Právo* and the Czechoslovak Television network) informed audiences about a wave of petitions from local Communist groups who were refuting the subversive Chartists.[10] Not that these people believed the lies, but by conforming to the regime and its ideology, they accepted the "illusion of an identity, of dignity, and of morality while making it easier for them to part with them."[11]

The regime alleged that the dissidents were against peace, that they were fierce enemies of Socialism, against the Helsinki conference, and that they were "holding people and their interests in contempt"—all that was totally fabricated.

On January 14, Havel, the *spiritus agens* of the movement, did not return from police questioning. He was detained, which, for that matter, was no surprise to him.[12] Jiří Suk and Jan Vladislav[13] describe the threats of at least ten years in prison and the overall intimidating character of the interrogation. After all, Havel's fellow spokesman, Professor Jan Patočka, died after extended interrogation on March 13, 1977. The regime struggled to fabricate a charge for Václav Havel, which would involve subversion of the republic (article 98 of the penal law) and harm to the Czechoslovak interests abroad (article 112). So early after the signing of the 1975 Helsinki Accord, however, that was not easily attainable,[14] even though the accord did not have a legally binding status.

Within two months, on March 9, 1977, "Losers and Usurpers" was followed by a direct and personal radio broadcast by Tomáš Řezáč; it was titled "Who Is Václav Havel?" Its content was again excerpted by all major dailies. This pseudo-documentary pretended to present an objective analysis of Havel's character along with illustrations from personal meetings with him. Thus, Řezáč recalled encounters with Havel in the literary wine bar Viola in the early 1960s and claimed that Havel came across as "immensely conceited"[15] and "manifestly holding in contempt everyone around him." Řezáč further claimed that Havel absolutely lacked any artistic talent and that his only claim to success abroad was due to his proclaimed anticommunism. Řezáč also accused Havel of being paid by a foreign "American or West German reconnaissance patrol or other intelligence service."[16] This was suddenly more than the usual half-truths, slanders, and made-up character flaws; this sounded like treason.

Although incarcerated, Havel decided to fight back "an uneven war against dictatorship."[17] Without delay, on the thirteenth of March, he officially complained to all dailies and requested the retraction of the false statements and lies. Since the request was ignored, Havel later initiated an official legal action bringing the libel charge against the original author (Řezáč) of the text that had been quoted. Jiří Bašta[18] points out that this act disturbed the seemingly smooth progress of the propagandistic disinformation campaign, as nobody had considered the possibility that Havel would dare to appeal to Socialist civil law.[19]

Meanwhile, the propaganda campaign in the media continued. Czechoslovak Television (a government network) followed with its own *Who Is Václav Havel?* program full of lies and slander in the spring of the same year.[20] The program stressed the wealth of the Havel family before their possessions had been nationalized. The director also used interviews with their former employees, as well as a discussion with the director and actors of the Na Zábradlí Theater, where Václav Havel used to work.

Havel requested a release. The interrogators maneuvered him into negotiations and a written statement on conditions of his release from prison. His discharge (May 20, after four and a half months of incarceration) was accompanied by an article in the major Communist daily, *Rudé Právo*, the very next day, which was written to make the public believe that Havel had entirely given up his role in Charter 77. Havel was devastated by the conditions of his release. He felt as if he had just made a deal with Mephistopheles,[21] perceiving the result as his failure, not victory;[22] he was tortured by doubts about his integrity and honor.[23] As is generally known, he continued his mission and in the years to come was jailed again. His longest stay in prison was from May 1979 to February 1983.

In the meantime, the regime escalated and expanded the anti–Charter 77 campaign into a fierce ideological struggle. The focus was on renowned artists and performers; they were pressed to swear allegiance to the regime. The festive loyalty oath took place January 28, 1977, in the historical National Theater, with a live TV transmission.[24]

Since the national revival movement, the National Theater (financed by public donations) has had a solemn meaning for the nation. After all, Czech patriotism is of a cultural character,[25] very closely linked to language and Czech theater as a special public space.[26] The Czechs (a notoriously agnostic nation[27]) even affectionately nickname the National Theater their "*zlatá kaplička*"—the beloved golden chapel.

When a great power attempted to break the spirit of the nation, the National Theater was used as a stage and well-liked actors, artists, and writers became hostages. In 1942, the Nazis produced a ceremony of swearing loyalty to the German Reich there in the presence of outstanding Czech artists. In 1948, the Communists staged a similar declaration of allegiance of Czech artists to Communism there. The National Theater thus became a logical scene for the Communist propaganda on January 28, 1977, as well.

All significant artists (actors, dancers, singers, visual artists), the cultural elite of the nation, were invited to participate and to festively express their allegiance. The presence before the eye of the TV cameras and signatures on attendance rolls were clear signs of loyalty to the regime. The headline on the sheets seemed rather benign; it read: "FOR NEW CREATIVE ACTS IN THE NAME OF SOCIALISM AND PEACE. I am joining the proclamation of the Czechoslovak committees of artists unions."[28] However, the main speech contained strong words of condemnation of Charter 77, and signatures were not collected at the beginning but at the end of the session.

In an absurd theatrical scene, artists were signing a petition against another petition, which they were never allowed to read. The metalanguage of facial expressions in the audience reveals the tragedy of the moment; one can see various nonverbal manifestations of sadness, shame, and fear.[29]

To reach the younger and less conforming public as well, the convention of accomplished classical artists in the National Theater was complemented by an analogous meeting of performers of pop and country music in the Theater of Music a few days later, which was also aired on national television. Altogether, over 7,000 artists signed the anti-Charter declaration, including 76 decorated national artists.[30] The daily press reported the names of the anti–Charter 77 signatories. (It was only appropriate that somebody added to the list the name of Franz Kafka,[31] a famous Prague writer of the absurd who poignantly depicted the terrifying and vain struggle of the individual against an oppressive and overwhelming regime.)

And yet, it was possible to say "no," either indirectly (e.g., one could seek a doctor that day or could complain of some chronic ailment, as did the popular actor Vladimír Menšík) or by simply and boldly refusing to show up in the National Theater, as did a well-liked pair of actors from the National Theater, husband and wife Luděk Munzar and Jana Hlaváčová. They were not even fired from their posts.[32]

* * *

Daily newspapers and weekly magazines published propagandistic articles and cartoons defaming Charter 77 and Havel. The popular humoristic magazine Dikobraz (Porcupine) included three cartoons by Miloš Kánský to accompany the article "From a Stagehand to a Smart Aleck" (Z kulisáka kulišákem) devoted to Havel and mocking him. Although different in form (cartoons with a commentary) from the "serious" newspaper articles, the contents followed the typical character assassination schema of the 1970s: mockery and the claim that money was the sole inspiration of the dissidents. Thus, the article again stressed Havel's bourgeois class origin, elitist upbringing in his early life, and the wealth of his family that he was supposed to inherit. It also smeared his uncle, who supposedly collaborated with the Nazis during the occupation.

The mockery focuses on the theater of the absurd where "little Václav," puffed up by resources from abroad, confronts reality (a sharp thumbtack) and explodes.* The world of the theater is equaled with nonsense, and Havel is described as a little child: "Melancholic little Václav entered the boards which mean the world in a pioneering manner. He started from the bottom. He became a stagehand. The sets and backstage. Illusions and intrigues . . . Absurd theater! Little Václav became a playwright. He wrote plays. Absurd plays. Absurd means nonsensical." The article then concludes with the expected simplification of Havel's motivation: "Václav Havel never cared about morals. Nor about human rights. He cared only about his property."[33]

---

*Unfortunately, we are unable to reproduce the cartoon here due to copyright restrictions. It can be found at the companion website.

Psychology of Compliant Demoralization

A separate analysis would be needed to study the effects of psychological pressure on a person's compliance as well as on his or her character. Among the most relevant here appears the psychological theory of *cognitive dissonance* by Leon Festinger.[34] This theory claims that people are internally motivated to reduce inconsistencies between their beliefs on the one hand and actions on the other. People tend to alter their cognitions and attitudes if they are in conflict with each other, or if they are inconsistent with their behavior. Thus, not only do people behave according to their attitudes but, importantly, when they commit an act inconsistent with their attitudes, these people may reduce the emerging psychological tension by creating justifications and subsequently altering their attitudes to be consistent with the behavior they have already exhibited.

Experimental research shows interesting findings: pressures to compliance differ in their efficiency in a paradoxical way. Strong incitement (a death threat or a major bribery) tends to force people relatively easily to superficial compliance while they keep their inner convictions. The pressure does not change their values. These people can always easily explain their compliance with reference to clear reasons ("I am not suicidal to oppose such a threat" or "I did it for the money, who would not?"). However, a *mild* pressure to comply, which still causes compliance, may have a much *stronger* effect on the psyche of this person. It would be too embarrassing to comply without proper justification; remorse and pangs of guilt would cause what Festinger called a *dissonance*. Perhaps the only way to ease the conscience after an act of compliance has been already committed is to change one's inner beliefs about matters as well; thus, to comply not just superficially but fully, including one's inner convictions.[35]

Communism with its brutal force and great potential for corruption has forced most citizens to compliance. It has hardly changed the minds of those people who were hit the hardest (political prisoners and dissidents), nor the minds of those who were given the most cushy positions. (After all, many of them easily threw away Communist ideology and rebranded themselves as new rich capitalists as soon as the situation after the regime change of 1989 allowed.) Those who were most vulnerable to indoctrination were those who complied but did not profit from the regime all that much. These were people who *had to convince themselves* that they had good reason to collaborate for no real benefit or profit. This process of rationalization is devastating and demoralizing, particularly when the conforming pressure is long lasting and affects a wide population.

Thus, it can be argued that that the Communist political pressure of the 1970s and 1980s led, if not to a nationwide character assassination campaign, at least to a very intensive *character mutilation*, of the elites as well as of the general population. Not only public image was at stake, but also inner convictions and psyche in general. Based on the cognitive dissonance theory, it can be also assumed that the rather subtle force to comply could have been more detrimental to the morality and character of individuals than the coercions committed by Communism or Nazism. When the Communists urged citizens to comply with their ideology in the 1970s, their pressure was hardly life threatening (as it had been in the 1940s and 1950s, i.e., during the Nazi and then the Communist terror). In 1970s, citizens for the most part worried "only" about their good jobs, careers, possible loss of privileges, and good opportunities for their children. Compliance then could not have been explained by a simple "I had to"; nobody really "had to."[36] Thus, deals with the regime involved a deeper compromise and moral corruption, concession of ideals, integrity, and conscience. Specific postcommunist immorality can be recognized as a symptom within a wider syndrome that we label as "post-totalitarian" or "post-communist" mentality.[37] It involves learned helplessness (a person's realization based on experience that nothing can help him or her), suppressed individuality, and last but not least, a higher willingness to abandon moral principles.

A whole new morally noncorrupt generation was needed to grow up and to initiate a rebellion against the regime; these were the children of the young rebels of the Prague Spring of 1968; they triggered the Velvet Revolution of 1989.

The Final Attacks against Havel

Havel prevailed in his struggle for freedom: the smear campaign did not hurt his ability to write and organize the civil society of dissidents. Those who knew him or who were able to get independent information about him were assured of his character; those who did not know him were, for the most part, apolitical. Havel was at his prime when the Communist regime began to crumble in Czechoslovakia again.

The last two serious waves of character assassination attempts materialized in the late 1980s. At that point, the Communist regime was discredited and lacked the support of its big brother, the Soviet Union, which was already at the phase of glasnost and perestroika.

In 1986, Havel was awarded the Erasmus Prize, named after a famous Dutch humanist and awarded annually to a person who has made an exceptional cultural contribution in Europe and beyond. For fear he would not be allowed to return back home and forced into exile, Havel did not travel to accept the prize in person. Yet he did accept the prize *in absentia* and wrote a brilliant essay for the occasion. He also accepted the prize money, not for himself, but for Charter 77.

Such a distinguished appreciation could not be left without an official reaction of the Communist government. The *Rudé Právo* (November 22, 1986) reacted again with the smear article "A Fat Gift[38] from Holland" (Tučná výslužka z Holandska), trying to appeal to the envy of its readers and attempting to reinforce the traditional image of the dissident as a paid lackey of the West. Little did it matter that Havel did not keep the Erasmus Prize money for himself. The regime tried to frame the event as the prize of the filthy rich to an antisocialist traitor, a political and moral loser:

> The church of St. Lorenz was full of men and women in the most expensive outfits, weighed down with golden bracelets, earrings full of genuine pearls and diamonds. There was no ticket for those who did not have at least a million . . . Except several emigrants . . . Václav Havel received a sum of 200,000 guilders from rich and influential people from the tulip country, from directors of the royal Dutch oil company, bosses of the AMRO bank, ministers, presidents, and vice-presidents.

The article also repeated the fabrications of links of Havel's family to the Nazi regime and Gestapo. Václav Havel only briefly and reluctantly ("I have a feeling that if I would deal with the dirty gossip, I would make my own hands dirty") refuted the accusations in the exile journal *Listy*, pointing out, among other things, that at the age of six he could hardly have been a Gestapo spy himself.[39]

Perhaps the final significant attempts at Havel's character assassination came in early 1989, after the so-called Palach week (a general public unrest inspired by the twentieth anniversary of the sacrifice of student Jan Palach, who immolated himself in protest against the growing Czech complacency with Soviet occupation and "normalization"). At that time, Czechoslovak Communists were losing the totalitarian ideological monopoly, glasnost slowly seeped through society, and people started to communicate more openly.

The smear article in *Rudé Právo* was titled, once again, "Who Is Václav Havel" (February 23, 1989). The contents of its first paragraphs did not differ much from the previous articles: obligatory stress on the wealth of the Havel family and fabrication of pro-Nazi attitudes, even links to the Gestapo, elaboration of the "social dam" between young Václav and the rest of the society. Brief attention was given to his early literary career and political activism; the article then focused on mocking him as a "self-invited 'defender' of human rights." *Defender, speaker, charter*—all these words were written ironically, in quotes. It was stressed that Havel, in this year alone, was supposed to be a recipient of many material "rewards" from the West, including 9,000 Tuzex crowns, and another 9,000 for his wife.[40]

However, there was a difference between this and previous articles. The mockery was more subtle, and, most importantly, the latter article concluded with Havel's genuine thoughts. There were extensive quotes from Havel's texts and his reflections on important points of Czech history, on economy—his views on the mismanagement of agriculture, the protection of nature, and the promotion of pluralism in politics as well as in economics. Substantial space was devoted to Havel's political views and philosophy (including a quote from his essay from that time "The Reasons for Skepticism and Reasons for Hope"). There was even a mention of his values: democracy, freedom, environment, national sovereignty, and hope for the future.

Although the article once again framed Havel into the inevitable context of a child from a capitalist family who desires restitution of his possessions, and although there was strong criticism of his political views and subversive inclinations, perhaps for the first time ever, Havel was also granted a public platform for his views.

If the overall tone of the article was surprising, all the more surprising was its sequel: a fairly extensive space was devoted to the reactions of readers. Most unusually, for the first time, there was a plurality of voices. The whole introduction was made up of letters from readers who did not like the confrontational and critical tone of "Who Is Václav Havel." The first reader was upset that a person "whose human and artistic qualities are recognized all over the cultural world" was smeared; another reader appreciated that the Havel family built film studios and the Lucerna palace, with a great concert hall for the nation, and regretted that the country did not have more outstanding families such as the Havels; the next reader appreciated Havel's character, his courage and purposefulness. Finally, there was a testimony of someone who personally knew Havel and criticized the lies written about him, prophetically threatening that if remedy would not be done, "you will see how we shall have a ball."

Memorably, Havel's friends and coworkers got back at *Rudé Právo* and its defamation of Havel when they published in its "Social Chronicle" a paid announcement of Havel's birthday, his photograph along with praise and thanks "for his hard work" and "wishes of good health and continuing success in his work." Since Havel's face was not generally known, his picture easily passed unrecognized by the newspaper censors, as did "his name," Ferdinand Vaněk (a name that Havel used in all his autobiographical plays). Having changed the name of the village where Havel liked to live from a one-word name (Hrádeček) to two words, Malý Hrádek (both expressions meaning "small castle"), the authors of the ad made sure that what the censors missed other friends and colleagues would clearly recognize. Perhaps the editor, when he realized the omission of his staff, recalled the words of his fellow oppressor, Nazi Reinhard Heydrich, "Czechs are laughing beasts"?

The End of Communist Rule

Indeed, the friends of Havel had soon an opportunity to rejoice. The regime crumbled within nine months of the printed prophecy of the abovementioned *Rudé Právo* reader. In November 1989, the actors and artists more than made up for their anti–Charter 77 conformity. They swiftly joined the initiators of the revolution: the students who instigiated the protest and whose demonstration had been brutally suppressed. The theaters went on strike as well, becoming centers of political enlightenment. The cultural elites became the leaders of the Velvet Revolution, which had a distinctly cultural (intellectual and artistic) character.

The playwright and moral philosopher Václav Havel played the key role in the revolution, in the liberation of his nation, and also in great acts of reconciliation. Revolution brought peace between the brutal oppressive forces and the oppressed masses. The revolution indeed became not just an elitist coup, but a great catch-all movement and moral "revelation,"[41] "a symbolically gentle conclusion to the half-century long era of harrowing violence and totalitarianism."[42]

Not that freedom would put a halt to character attacks against Havel altogether. While in the first years after the Velvet Revolution he was generally adored and almost mythified,[43] in later years, especially after his wife Olga passed away and he remarried, the flame of criticism was ignited again. The main medium of smears and gossips was no longer *Rudé Právo*, but tabloids. His new wife, Dagmar, often served as a target for displaced attacks against him. Among the motivations behind the attacks were the following:

(a) Curiosity on the part of the readers and profit motive on the part of the publishers: this was the case for tabloids or sensationalistic books that either tried to reveal unfavorable personal details or constructed grandiose conspiracy theories.

(b) The new predatory or, in Havel's words, "mafioso capitalism": its representatives despised morality and law that stood in opposition to their privatization and entrepreneurial schemes.

(c) The old postcommunist mentality: for too many Havel was a reminder of their own failures and embarrassment, while at the same time, he was the most visible lightning rod for grievances of all sorts.

Conclusion

The case of Václav Havel illustrates that there may be a good defense against character assassination attacks. In this case, wise and principled morality was in a duel with totalitarian propaganda, which for the most part stuck rigidly to the lowest and fabricated arguments: it mainly repeated that the dissidents' sole motivation was their greed. Despite the totalitarian context, many citizens had access to alternative information sources (trusted friends, illegal literature, and foreign broadcasts). They also possessed knowledge and intellectual sophistication, which allowed them to comprehend the true state of affairs.

Thus, even systematic and intensive attacks could not destroy Havel's public image, nor his inner moral character. Moreover, the defamation did not prevent Havel from being recognized as a trustworthy leader at the critical time of the Velvet Revolution. Václav Havel became a loved and respected president and, until the end of his life and beyond, remained a symbol of moral struggle for humanist ideals.

Another matter is how the whole nation coped with the sustained pressure. The reaction of the Czechs to the 1968 invasion and occupation, their passive and creative resistance, was both heroic and resourceful. Even long after that, the Czechs were generally able to withstand the ideological pressure, see through the propaganda, and metacommunicate with each other. The situation changed for the majority after the Czechoslovak top politicians yielded to the pressure of Moscow and opened the way to the 1970s "normalization."[44] Overall helplessness set in; so did a survivalist psychology. Then, dissidence became exceptional. Many citizens seem to have complied more than was necessary. Some justified their conformity by their mere desire to live a normal life; others, by concern for their children. All in all, a substantial part of the populace gave up public resistance and yielded to the totalitarian pressures. For many, such compliance probably also had a significant secondary impact on their everyday psychology.

The mottos of the Velvet Revolution ("The truth and love have to win over lies and hatred," "We are not as they were," and, subsequently, "A thick line behind the past"), coined or voiced by Havel, had a decisive social impact. Although they interfered with the population's coming to terms with the past later, they undoubtedly helped those who were violated by the regime to heal, find their lost pride, and also to generally appease society in the decisive revolutionary times of 1989.

The Czechoslovak experience confirms that the key for defense against character attacks lies primarily in the solid moral profile of the target, in the good education of the populace, which includes good training in political sophistication, and finally, in diverse and pluralistic information resources.

Notes

1. This study was supported by RVO 68081740. The author is also grateful to Dr. Ivan Havel for kind consultation and inspiration and to Dr. Martin Vidlák and the Documentation Center of the Václav Havel Library for advice and help. Special thanks also to Dr. Jindřiška Kotrlová, the librarian at the Institute of Psychology, Academy of Sciences of the Czech Republic, for her great help.
2. After all, *character assassination* is typically understood and defined as "a deliberate and sustained process that aims to destroy the credibility and reputation" (Rojas et al. 2012, 246), not the character itself.
3. "The life within truth," inspired by the philosophy of Patočka, was a dangerous but morally healthy dissident alternative to the conforming life in an oppressive regime. As Havel pointed out in the *Power of the Powerless*, Czechoslovakia was then a society "thoroughly permeated with hypocrisy and lies" (Havel 1991, 135), and "living within the lie can constitute the system only if it is universal" (Havel 1991, 147). Thus, Havel, the dissident, attempted to chip away at that universal system by the life within truth and committing such brave acts as writing an open letter to the president ("Dear Dr. Husák") or drafting a complex analysis of life in an oppressive society (*Power of the Powerless*). He encouraged his fellow citizens to step out of line and threaten the entirety of the regime. By "living the truth," Havel did not mean just his conceptual thought: "It can be any means by which a person or a group revolts against manipulation: anything from a letter by intellectuals to a workers' strike, from a rock concert to a student demonstration" (Havel 1991, 150–51).

4. Krákora 2008.
5. A facsimile of the original declarations in Czech and English can be accessed at the website of Libri Prohibiti at http://libpro.cts.cuni.cz/charta/.
6. This and the following Charter 77 excerpts are quoted and translated from the original Czech text of Charter 77, available at the Libri Prohibiti website, http://libpro.cts.cuni.cz/charta/docs/prohlaseni_charty_77.pdf.
7. http://archiv.ucl.cas.cz/index.php?path=RudePravo/1977/1/12/2.png.
8. Literally "character-less."
9. For example, analyses provided by the study texts of the Institute for Study of the Totalitarian Regimes, http://www.ustrcr.cz/data/pdf/projekty/antologie/tema6.pdf.
10. Růžička 2013.
11. Havel 1992, 133. This is reminiscent of the case of the greengrocer putting the Communist propaganda sign in his shop window.
12. Kriseová 1991.
13. Suk 2013 and Vladislav 2012.
14. Suk 2013, 84.
15. Radio program "Who is Václav Havel," http://mluveny.panacek.com/historie-rozhlasu/2347-rozhlasove-pasmo-kdo-je-vaclav-havel.html.
16. Ibid.
17. Suk 2013, 93. Suk provides a detailed description of the events and a cogent analysis of the subsequent negotiations with the interrogators, including legal file identification numbers.
18. Bašta 2001.
19. Bašta in 2001 further documented that Řezáč was able to back out from the responsibility for the newspaper formulations: he argued that the Czech Press Agency (ČTK) and/or individual editors altered the original broadcast text when they deleted the qualifiers *if, apparently,* and *obviously.* Havel withdrew the legal action on November 20, 1978. The case was finally closed when the court decided Havel would be returned sixty crowns ($2) of his legal fee.
20. http://www.totalita.cz/norm/norm_06.php.
21. Suk 2013, 99.
22. Kriseová 1991, 86.
23. Suk 2013, 101.
24. http://www.totalita.cz/norm/norm_06.php.
25. This is confirmed also by our empirical studies, which illustrate that the core of Czechness tends to be the Czech language (in contrast with the core values of the American nation, that tend to be of a civic character, such as freedom and democracy). Our studies show the two primary values for a representative sample of the Czech Republic were Czech language and culture (rated at 7.75 and 7.13 on a 9-point scale), whereas the least significant value for Czechness turned out to be religion (rated as low as 3.58); see Klicperová-Baker et al. 2007.
26. The Czech theater played a major role in the National Renaissance movement of the nineteenth century; a part of a play, *Fidlovačka,* became a national anthem; theaters played a key role during the Velvet Revolution as scenes of public dialogue; the headquarters of the revolution were in the Magic Lantern Theater; Václav Havel was a playwright. Interestingly, a Czech theater character, Jára Cimrman, also received the most votes in the popular contest for "the Greatest Czech," a competition inspired by the BBC *Greatest Briton* show.
27. The Eurobarometer survey (2010, 204) shows the citizens of the Czech Republic to be the most agnostic within the European region. With only 16 percent of Czech

respondents agreeing that there is a God, the country appears even less religious than Estonians and Swedes (with 18 percent affirmative responses).

28. *Anticharta—Protest umělců proti Chartě* [Anticharter—the protest of artists against the charter]: http://www.ceskatelevize.cz/ct24/domaci/3935-anticharta-protest-umelcu-proti-charte-77/.

29. See YouTube 2013a for brief documentary shots from the historical events of 1942, 1948, and 1977, and YouTube 2013b for brief footage from the National Theater and the Theater of Music.

30. http://www.ustrcr.cz/data/pdf/projekty/antologie/tema6.pdf. The theme: anticharter.

31. Franz Kafka (1883–1924): German-speaking Jewish author of *The Trial*, *The Castle*, and *The Metamorphosis*, among others.

32. However, that was not the case earlier, in the beginning of the 1970s, when people were forced to approve the Soviet ("brotherly") invasion. Then, those who refused were not only laid off but also blacklisted.

33. Pernes 2010, 184.

34. Festinger 1957.

35. Festinger and Carlsmith (1959) conducted a classic experiment that involved participants in an extremely boring task. After they finished, they were asked to lie to the subject who was scheduled after them, saying that the task was interesting. These "liars" received a reward of either $1 or $20. When they were later asked how interesting they really thought the experiment was, Festinger found an interesting relationship: those who were paid *high* mostly preserved their conviction that the task was boring ("I did it for the money" was a sufficient and logical explanation). However, those who were bribed *low* and who lied for a mere $1, without a proper external justification, had to convince themselves they had not lied for a pittance. They made up, after the fact, an alternative, inner justification—convincing themselves they did not lie because they enjoyed the experiment. In fact, they were even willing to volunteer for another experiment. Too low a bribe caused a significant mental change.

36. These moral challenges did not necessarily appear just once in the lifetime during the anti–Charter 77 campaign. Over a decade earlier, in 1969, in the beginning of the so-called normalization, the elites in particular (especially managers and teachers) had to formally declare that they agreed with the Soviet occupation of 1968 as "a brotherly help of friendly armies against counterrevolution."

37. Klicperová et al. 1997.

38. The title of the article, once again, was rather more expressive: *výslužka*, meaning "a gift of food which a guest would take home from a pig slaughter or a wedding": etymologically, something one would earn by a good service.

39. Havel 1987, 48.

40. While many commodities were scarce or impossible to buy with the regular Czech currency, Tuzex crowns enabled buyers to purchase goods of export quality or goods imported from abroad (jeans, electronics, cars), which were available in special Tuzex stores. Tuzex crowns were particularly desirable since they were not freely available, and their mention could have triggered envy in the readers. The sum of 18,000 Tuzex crowns would have been enough for the purchase of a fancy Czech Škoda sports car: http://www.auto.cz/tuzex-1988-co-mohli-koupit-auta-64518.

41. Janát 1997.

42. Shore 1996, 164.

43. Putna 2011.

44. According to some witnesses, the situation seemed worse than the era after the Munich dictate of 1938, as there did not seem to be any prospective change in the political situation in the near future.

Bibliography

Bašta, J. 2001. "Agent REPO—spisovatel (Tomáš Řezáč) ve službách komunistické propagandy" [Agent REPO—a writer (Tomáš Řezáč) in the services of the Communist propaganda]. Sysno 000654476. *Securitas imperii* 8: 6–69.

Císařovská, B., and V. Prečan. 2007. *Charta 77: Dokumenty* [Charter 77: documents]. Prague: Ústav pro soudobé dějiny AV ČR.

Eurobarometer. 2010. *Biotechnology report.* Special Eurobarometer 341 / Wave 73.1. European Commission http://ec.europa.eu/public_opinion/archives/ebs/ebs_341_en.pdf.

Festinger, L. 1957. *A Theory of Cognitive Dissonance.* Stanford, CA: Stanford University Press.

Festinger, L., and J. M. Carlsmith. 1959. "Cognitive Consequences of Forced Compliance." *Journal of Abnormal and Social Psychology* 58: 203–11.

Havel, V. 1987. "Odpověď Václava Havla" [Response of Václav Havel]. *Listy* 2: 48.

Havel, V. 1992. "Power of the Powerless." In *Open Letters. Selected Writings 1965–1990,* 125–214. Selected and edited by Paul Wilson. Vintage Books: New York.

Klicperová, M., I. K. Feierabend, and C. R. Hofstetter. 1997. "In the Search for a Post-Communist Syndrome. A Theoretical Framework and Empirical Assessment." *Journal of Community and Applied Social Psychology* 7: 39–52.

Klicperová-Baker, M., I. K. Feierabend, S. Kovacheva, L. Titarenko, J. Košťál, and C. R. Hofstetter. 2007. *Demokratická kultura v České republice: Občanská kultura, éthos a vlastenectví ze srovnávacího pohledu* [Democratic culture in the Czech Republic: civic culture, ethos and patriotism from a comparative perspective]. Prague: Academia.

Krákora, P. 2008. *Pražské jaro 1968. Pokus o obnovu občanské společnosti* [Prague Spring 1968: an attempt at the restoration of civil society]. Prague: Epocha.

Kriseová, E. 1991. *Václav Havel: Životopis* [Václav Havel: biography]. Brno: Atlantis.

Pernes, J. 2010. *Dějiny Československa očima* Dikobrazu *1945–1990* [The history of Czechoslovakia through the eyes of *Dikobraz* 1945–1990] Prague: Barrister & Principal.

Rojas, R. de Aragon, J. A. U. Blanco, A. J. Faya, C. A. Montaner, and G. Lupi. 2012. *Ready, Aim, Fire! Character Assassination in Cuba.* Miami: Eriginal Books.

Růžička, D. 2013. *Období normalizace—Čs. Televize proti Chartě 77* [Normalization period: Czechoslovak Television against Charter 77]. http://www.totalita.cz/norm/norm_06.php (accessed December 1, 2013).

Shore, M. 1996. "The Sacred and the Myth: Havel's Greengrocer and the Transformation of Ideology in Communist Czechoslovakia." *Contagion: Journal of Violence, Mimesis, and Culture* 3: 163–81.

Suk, J. 2013. *Politika jako absurdní drama: Václav Havel v letech 1975–1989* [Politics as an absurd drama: Václav Havel in 1975–1989]. Prague: Paseka.

Vladislav, J. 2012. *Otevřený deník 1977/1981* [Open diary 1977/1981]. Prague: Torst.

Wikipedia. 2013. "Největší Čech" [The greatest Czech]. http://en.wikipedia.org/wiki/Nejv%C4%9Bt%C5%A1%C3%AD_%C4%8Cech (accessed November 10, 2013).

YouTube. 2013a. http://www.youtube.com/watch?v=LWXIcwCnYyo

YouTube. 2013b. http://www.youtube.com/watch?v=alVS_MvekJo

Editorial Reflections: Modern Cases

Martijn Icks and Eric Shiraev

The three chapters in this section refer mostly to developments in the twentieth century—although one of them also discusses a few events that took place centuries ago—and even more recent times. Several significant and interconnected developments have emerged during this period, all of which are relevant to the subject of this book. The first one refers to the massive technological changes that have forever changed human communications. We have witnessed the dawn of the mass media era. The electricity-powered printing press, radio, television, and, more recently, the Internet can reach millions over the shortest period. New and constantly updated information about people's private lives and their individual personalities have become a daily consumer product. Social roles have changed too: previously "well-known" people grew into a new class of media "celebrities." The line between unfounded rumor about a famous figure and a proven biographical fact has gradually blurred. Character assassins are thus presented with a nearly perfect venue for new character attacks.

The second notable development is associated with the way the power of the emerging mass media has been utilized in different countries. Democracies and authoritarian regimes differ dramatically and in many ways. In democratic societies, private newspapers, magazines, radio, and television networks contribute to the competitive political process and transparent elections in particular. At the same time, free mass media provide an unprecedented opportunity for competing political parties, groups, and private individuals to launch character attacks against their opponents or anyone else they choose. Furthermore, legal rules in democracies guarantee freedom of speech, thus safeguarding the words and images conveyed through print and broadcast media in character attacks. The chapter on presidential campaigns in the United States provides a few examples of such attacks by presidential candidates and their "teams" against other candidates and incumbent presidents. Regardless of how inappropriate, nasty, or distasteful some of the mentioned attacks may appear, contemporary research shows that character attacks have so far been an effective weapon in the modern competitive political process. We believe they will likely retain this role in the future.

Character assassination as a policy tool was also successfully utilized in authoritarian political systems. In the twentieth century, Fascist, Nazi, or Communist governments used the advancements of communication technologies as a unique opportunity to control information in their countries by means of ideological censorship. The cases involving China in the 1950s and Czechoslovakia in the 1970s and 1980s show how political authorities sanctioned and organized smear campaigns against several targeted individuals. Although these two cases are separated by a quarter of a century and concern very different cultures, the authoritarian methods used in both of them appear very similar. A character assassination attempt begins "from above": someone gives a go for an attack. Such a trigger can be an official speech or a newspaper publication. Next, some designated party leaders—chief character assassins—launch more significant attacks. They fabricate facts, exaggerate, falsify, and smear their victims according to a plan. Then the attacks emerge in the obedient, politically controlled press: typically, in newspaper editorials. Then the entire country is mobilized to support the publications and to condemn the "villain." Unfortunately, those who found themselves under attack had little or no opportunity to defend and respond: they no longer had access to the media.

In Communist China, the character assassination campaign against Gao Gang and Rao Shushi went relatively smoothly. The two alleged foes were accused of various awful activities, and their reputations were destroyed. Their former comrades apparently had little choice but to join the smear campaign: had they dared to disagree or protest, the authorities would have easily eliminated them. However, recent history also shows that a changing political climate can eventually undermine censorship and become a serious threat to authoritarian political regimes. If authorities lose their grip on information, if they lose the trust of most people, they subsequently lose their ability to launch successful character attacks against their political enemies. The case of Václav Havel illustrates this development well. This case also shows that many individuals could become complacent with the ongoing character assassination of a prominent individual so long as a legitimate authority sanctions this action and as far as they, by not condemning the attack, achieve certain individual gains, including job security or peer approval.

Twenty-first-century technological developments are inevitably changing the nature of character attacks. One important aspect of the ongoing change is the scope and speed of attacks. One cheap shot or nasty comment against a political candidate posted on the web can become viral (and essentially global) in hours. A second changing feature is an attack's longevity. In the past, newspapers could be destroyed and videotapes erased. These days, any text or image can be stored almost indefinitely. Getting rid of unpleasant material has become all but impossible in this digital age. Therefore, character attacks on the web are essentially timeless because they remain easily accessible; they can also be downloaded, copied, and forwarded at any time.

Have today's web-based attacks become nastier, more vicious, than those launched in the 1950s or some centuries ago? Are we all becoming emotionally overwhelmed with online negativity? We do not think so. On the contrary, we believe that one's constant exposure to a constant stream of character attacks, a barrage of blames against and denigrations of other people, may in the future cause individuals to experience emotional and cognitive "desensitization" toward such character attacks: the condition under which one stops paying serious attention to the ubiquitous negative words and images flying around. Do we have a reliable method, besides a crystal ball, to test this forecast? The question remains open.

Epilogue

Martijn Icks and Eric Shiraev

Now that the authors have presented their cases, it is time for us, the editors, to offer a few parting comments. What do we know about character attacks? What did we learn from all these chapters covering different epochs, events, and personalities? As we suggested on the first pages, there are several common or, as we call them, "central" features in character attacks. They tend to appear in most historic settings, and they probably reflect most significant, consistent, and maybe universal qualities of the human mind and behavior. There are also "peripheral" features of character attacks that are rooted in specific historic contexts and individual circumstances. Technology, culture, and politics play a vital role in determining the form, the contents, the complexity, and the swiftness with which character attacks are delivered.

Nature of Character Assassination

Attackers target other people's moral and social "selves." Their victims are usually public persons who have taken care to build up their positive images, emphasizing their good intentions and deeds, high morality, and trustworthiness. To damage these images, perpetrators have to convince their audiences that they are false. The attackers want to publically reveal the ugly "truth" underneath. Many character attacks, in short, center on implicit or explicit accusations of someone's hypocrisy, depravities, and transgressions. Time and time again, emperors, kings, popes, presidential candidates, political dissidents, and Communist officials turn out to lack the virtuous traits they or their supporters claim. The pope might state to be God's spokesperson on earth, but Luther and his sympathizers reveal that he is really the Antichrist. In the Batavian Republic, the scandalous private life of President Schimmelpenninck goes on display to undermine the image of the wholesome family man. A top Communist official in China is exposed as a greedy agent of capitalism. In all these cases, attacks are geared specifically to undermine the "good" side of an individual's public identity. Values and historical perspectives, of course, define what is "good" in a particular city or country and under specific circumstances.

Following a different strategy, character assassins may also target their victims' competence. Christian authors portrayed the Prophet Muhammad as a misguided person who had unwittingly founded a false religion. Medieval young kings were attacked for being juvenile, inept, and unable to govern. In the twentieth century, attacks on Presidents Nixon and Reagan focused on their alleged mental incapacities. Even if the moral integrity of these victims is not necessarily questioned, their alleged incompetence still disqualifies them—as attackers assert—for the status and position they enjoy or aspire to.

Purpose of Character Assassination

"No man, no problem." Attributed to a dictator, this infamous phrase has become a powerful reminder about politics' lethal edges. Character assassination does not require direct physical destruction. One devastates or demolishes someone's reputation instead. Yet by destroying a person's reputation, another goal is achieved. "Kill one's reputation, kill one's cause." This cause can simply be a political office that the perpetrator covets for himself or his associates— hence, for instance, the Burgundian slanders against Louis of Orléans in medieval France—but can also be embedded in a wider ideological struggle. In this book, we have seen examples of character attacks that were ultimately aimed against Islam, Catholicism, Western capitalism, and other worldviews. The victims of these attacks are invariably portrayed as symbols or agents of these ideologies. Thus the defamation of a person also has ideological implications. In other cases, perpetrators aim to delegitimize a certain regime or dynasty, as was the case with the hostile accounts against Roman emperors. When the motives of character attacks transcend direct competition for political office, even the dead are not spared. Their legacy can be discredited by means of slander and allegation, or—in the case of totalitarian regimes—a sustained effort can be made to erase their existence from public memory altogether. In Communist China as well as in the Soviet Union, governments regularly "doctored" official paintings and photographs to remove the images of fallen politicians. "Erase one's image, delete the memory about this person."

Directions of Character Assassination

Character attacks do not necessarily involve the powerful attacking the weak. Attacks go in every direction within social hierarchies. Equals attack their kin. Cicero was callously attacked by his peers. Medieval nobles attacked their fellow aristocrats. French revolutionary politicians launched endless attacks against one another, as do politicians in modern democracies, especially during electoral campaigns. In other cases, the rival parties are on distinctly different levels of power and influence. Luther was a German monk of no particular prominence when he started to criticize the practices of Catholicism and attacked the character of the pope, prompting the Church to go after the alleger. An oppressive Communist regime used the obedient media to slander the dissident Havel. Remarkably, the more powerful party is not always the winner in such hierarchical struggles, even if it controls the media and has much larger financial and political resources. Both Luther and Havel prove that much depends on the public appeal of the message; when it strikes a chord with people, it becomes impossible to stop.

Audience of Character Assassination

Character attacks take place because people witness, listen to, and read their content. In fact, every attack requires a perceiving and reflecting audience. In the world of politics, fellow power players become such an audience. Yet in many other cases, the audience is larger. Cicero's attacks often occurred during exclusive meetings with his fellow senators, but ultimately, the Roman people chose individuals for political office. With the rise of printing, newspapers, radio, TV, and the Internet, potential audiences have become ever wider. As a result, character attacks have become more professional, often following well-developed strategies. At the same time, small mistakes can have catastrophic consequences. When Cicero misspoke in the Senate, he was only heard by the select company of those present. When a twenty-first-century U.S. presidential candidate misspeaks, the information of his or her failure immediately goes global and is repeated ad nauseam, providing attackers with almost endless fuel reserves.

Effectiveness of Character Attacks

What are the specific criteria of an effective character attack? Obviously, an ultimate goal is achieved when a competing candidate loses a campaign or a rival politician resigns from office. Such outcomes are easy to detect. However, it is much more difficult to measure support for a political ideology or religion as a result of character attacks. In democracies, we can look at the dynamics of public opinion. The key challenge here is not to confuse correlation with causation. If one event took place after the other, it does not necessarily mean that the first has definitely caused the second. The fact that Sarah Palin, the second female presidential candidate in the United States' history, was viciously attacked in 2008 by the media does not mean that she lost the elections because of that. She was probably an incredibly weak candidate to begin with.

We also should consider the attacks' side effects. Character assassins can misfire. Moreover, their actions may in fact cause the opposite effect: the victim's recognizability and the public's approval may even grow. Havel was under attack by the official media of a much-hated regime. This brought him name recognition, admiration, and the support of millions around the world, who would not have even recognized his name before the attacks had taken place. Celebrities and their publicists are aware of this phenomenon of "negative publicity": anything notable that is told about you is good.

Defense against Character Attacks

Defenses should be different in open and in authoritarian political systems. In open systems, most individuals have a range of opportunities to respond to the attacks against them. Historically, this was not always the case: as many French politicians found out during the Terror and the Restoration, false allegations conveyed in character attacks could end careers and often became death sentences. In more advanced democracies, people are likely to use political and legal means to react and defend their reputation. It is true that free speech may encourage character attacks: one may, in principle, say anything against another person. Yet at the same time, free speech has legal limits. Slander, for example, has boundaries. Litigation is a powerful defensive weapon against character attacks. In authoritarian systems, on the other hand, such limits against character attacks are for the most part arbitrary, severely limited, or nonexistent.

What else have we learned? Obviously we were trying to understand only a small slice of this incredibly rich, diverse, and intriguing phenomenon. It has dawned on us that character assassination is a bigger pie than we dared to expect when we were starting this project a few years ago—and we knew it was big to begin with. But we are not ending our work anytime soon. Let us share online what we have learned and what we and others will be learning in the future. We invite you to join our discussion on our site and on Facebook. You are welcome to discuss, contribute, and enlighten! It should be an interesting journey.

Index

Printed and bound in the United States of America